IDEAS IN

THE PROVINCE OF LEGISLATION
DETERMINED

IDEAS IN CONTEXT

Edited by Wolf Lepenies, Richard Rorty, J. B. Schneewind
and Quentin Skinner

The books in this series will discuss the emergence of intellectual traditions and of related new disciplines. The procedures, aims and vocabularies that were generated will be set in the context of the alternatives available within the contemporary frameworks of ideas and institutions. Through detailed studies of the evolution of such traditions, and their modification by different audiences, it is hoped that a new picture will form of the development of ideas in their concrete contexts. By this means, artificial distinctions between the history of philosophy, of the various sciences, of society and politics, and of literature may be seen to dissolve.

This series is published with the support of the Exxon Education Foundation

THE PROVINCE OF
LEGISLATION DETERMINED

Legal theory in eighteenth-century Britain

DAVID LIEBERMAN

Professor, School of Law
University of California, Berkeley

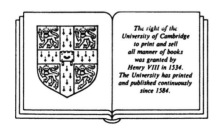

The right of the
University of Cambridge
to print and sell
all manner of books
was granted by
Henry VIII in 1534.
The University has printed
and published continuously
since 1584.

CAMBRIDGE UNIVERSITY PRESS

CAMBRIDGE

NEW YORK   NEW ROCHELLE   MELBOURNE   SYDNEY

PUBLISHED BY THE PRESS SYNDICATE OF THE UNIVERSITY OF CAMBRIDGE
The Pitt Building, Trumpington Street, Cambridge, United Kingdom

CAMBRIDGE UNIVERSITY PRESS
The Edinburgh Building, Cambridge CB2 2RU, UK
40 West 20th Street, New York NY 10011–4211, USA
477 Williamstown Road, Port Melbourne, VIC 3207, Australia
Ruiz de Alarcón 13, 28014 Madrid, Spain
Dock House, The Waterfront, Cape Town 8001, South Africa

http://www.cambridge.org

First published 1989
First paperback edition 2002

A catalogue record for this book is available from the British Library

Library of Congress Cataloguing in Publication data
Lieberman, David.
The province of legislation determined: legal theory in
eighteenth-century Britain / David Lieberman.
p.   cm. – (Ideas in context)
Bibliography.
Includes index.
ISBN 0 521 24592 3
1. Law – Great Britain – History and criticism.   2. Statutes – Great
Britain – History.   I. Title.   II. Series.
KD612.L54   1989
349.41–dc19   88-27435   CIP
[344.1]

ISBN 0 521 24592 3 hardback
ISBN 0 521 52854 2 paperback

*To my mother
and the memory of my father*

CONTENTS

PREFACE

The objectives and subject-matter of this book are set out in my introduction. The book itself began in research I originally undertook as a graduate student at University College London. I was only able to embark on this project, to pursue it and to bring it to a conclusion by accumulating a great number of substantial intellectual debts. I am delighted and relieved to have the chance to acknowledge the most important of these in a public manner.

I first thank the several friends and scholars who have offered detailed comments on the entire draft of this book. I am richly indebted to them all: to Jimmy Burns, John Burrow, Stefan Collini, Martin Krygier, Quentin Skinner, Peter Stein, John Thompson and Jan Vetter. Each has supplied me with valuable criticism and advice, and all of their many suggestions have guided me throughout the process of preparing the final version. For some of these friends, my indebtedness is long-standing. Stefan Collini, on whom I have often imposed before, showed great kindness and care in scrutinizing the book's final draft, eliminating numerous errors and introducing many improvements. I owe a profound debt to John Thompson, who started advising me in my years as an undergraduate, and who has ever since remained a much-needed source of counsel and encouragement. Quentin Skinner, another of my undergraduate teachers, introduced me to the historical study of political thought, generously supported my studies after I ceased to be his student, and in his own teaching and scholarship provided inspiration and the model for my less successful attempts to practice this discipline. I also make special mention of Jimmy Burns to whom I owe the most. Like others of his graduate students, I have depended on his patient criticism and unselfish instruction. And like other scholars of Bentham and eighteenth-century political ideas, I have relied on his masterful studies and unrivaled command of the source materials for this period. In my own case, however, my indebtedness extends well beyond the usual conventions of studentship and scholarship; my only regret in completing this book is that I have failed to produce a better work to testify to his guidance and friendship.

I acknowledge with equal pleasure my indebtedness to those who helped with particular sections of this work. Larry Klein's advice and many insights served to clarify for me the historiographic issues considered in the introduction. John Baker examined with greater care than it deserved a preliminary version of part II, when he rescued me from numerous errors and solecisms, and helped me better to understand the legal materials I was seeking to use. Istvan Hont and Michael Ignatieff supplied detailed comment on my interpretation of Lord Kames and the Scottish Enlightenment, as later did David Cohen, Nicholas Phillipson, and Donald Winch. I have learned most about eighteenth-century English society from the writings and ever instructive conversation of John Brewer and Joanna Innes. Their characteristically shrewd comments and telling questions have had a deep impact on my discussion, particularly in the introduction and part III.

My research on Jeremy Bentham involved many impositions on the scholars associated with the Bentham Project at University College London, who greeted my excessive requests with exceptional kindness. I thank John Dinwiddy, Fred Rosen and William Twining for being such tolerant critics and generous scholarly hosts. I somehow managed to avoid exhausting the great patience of Claire Gobbi and Stephen Conway, who facilitated my examination of the Bentham papers and always shared their expertise. I was particularly fortunate to pursue this research at a time when Jerry Postema and Ross Harrison were engaged in their own, now-published volumes on Bentham. What I owe to their fine scholarship and stimulating company is far more extensive than the specific points of indebtedness identified in the notes to part IV.

Material contained in chapters 1 and 2 appeared earlier in an article on "Blackstone's Science of Legislation," in the April, 1988, issue of *Journal of British Studies*; material in chapters 7 and 8 appeared in my contribution to *Wealth and Virtue. The Shaping of Political Economy in the Scottish Enlightenment*, edited by Istvan Hont and Michael Ignatieff (Cambridge, 1983); and material in chapter 12 appeared as "Bentham's Digest" in the 1985 volume of *The Bentham Newsletter*. I thank my former editors and publishers for permitting me to reproduce this material here. I am also grateful to Dr C. E. Croft for allowing me to quote his unpublished Cambridge University dissertation on Lord Chancellor Hardwicke. Robert Willman showed me particular generosity in sharing the products of his unpublished research on Blackstone.

For the past ten years I have benefited from the generosity of several institutions. My graduate studies were supported by research fellowships awarded by the Institute of Historical Research (London University), and by the American Bar Foundation's Legal History Program. I am especially grateful to the Master and Fellows of

St Catharine's College, Cambridge, for electing me to a four-year research fellowship, during which time I completed much of my work on this book. I am indebted to my former colleagues at St Catharine's for their encouragement and fellowship, as well as for their fine material support. For their many acts of friendly assistance, I thank the staffs of the British Library, the D.M.S. Watson Library of University College London, the Cambridge University Library and the Squire Law Library, and the Law Library of the University of California, Berkeley.

The final version of my manuscript was completed with the encouragement and many kindnesses of colleagues at the Jurisprudence and Social Policy Program and the School of Law of the University of California, Berkeley. I thank Margo Martinez and Celia Ronis for their expert and graciously discharged help on my typescript. I also gratefully acknowledge the diligent research assistance given by Martha-Elin Blomquist, Rosann Greenspan and especially Roger Rabb.

I last record with special joy my great gratitude to Carol Brownstein for her patient counsel and unfailing encouragement.

ABBREVIATIONS

Bowring   *The Works of Jeremy Bentham, published under the supervision of his Executor, John Bowring*, 11 vols. (Edinburgh, 1838–43)

Comm   Blackstone, William, *Commentaries on the Laws of England*, ed. Joseph Chitty, 4 vols. (London, 1826) ["1 *Comm* 26" indicates *Commentaries*, vol. 1, p. 26]

Comment   Bentham, Jeremy, *A Comment on the Commentaries*, ed. J. H. Burns and H. L. A. Hart (with *A Fragment on Government*) (London, 1977)

Corr.   *The Correspondence of Jeremy Bentham*, volume I: 1752–76 and volume II: 1777–80, ed. Timothy L. S. Sprigge (London, 1968); volume III: 1781–88, ed. Ian R. Christie (London, 1971)

Fragment   Bentham, Jeremy, *A Fragment on Government*, ed. J. H. Burns and H. L. A. Hart (with *A Comment on the Commentaries*) (London, 1977)

Morals and Legislation   Bentham, Jeremy, *An Introduction to the Principles of Morals and Legislation*, ed. J. H. Burns and H. L. A. Hart (London, 1970)

Laws in General   Bentham, Jeremy, *Of Laws in General*, ed. H. L. A. Hart (London, 1970)

UC   The Manuscripts of Jeremy Bentham in University College London (Roman numerals indicate box number; Arabic numerals indicate page number)

ENGLISH LAW REPORTS

Ambler   Ambler, Charles, *Reports of Cases argued and determined in the High Court of Chancery* (1790), 2nd edn by John Elijah Blunt, 2 vols. (London, 1828)

Atkyns   Atkyns, John Tracy, *Reports of Cases argued and determined in the High Court of Chancery* (1765–68), 3rd edn by Francis William Sanders, 3 vols. (London, 1794)

Burrow   Burrow, James, *Reports of Cases adjudged in the Court of King's Bench* (1766–80), 3rd edn, 5 vols. (London, 1777–90)

Cowper   Cowper, Henry, *Reports of Cases adjudged in the Court of King's Bench* (London, 1783)

Douglas   Douglas, Sylvester (Baron Glenbervie), *Reports of Cases argued and determined in the Court of King's Bench* (1783), 4th edn by William Frere, 4 vols. (London, 1813)

LCE   White, Frederick Thomas and Owen Davies Tudor, *A Selection of Leading Cases in Equity* (1849–50), 2nd edn, 2 vols. (London, 1858)

Lofft   Lofft, Capel, *Reports of Cases adjudged in the Court of King's Bench* (London, 1776)

P Williams   Williams, William Peere, *Reports of Cases argued and adjudged in the High Court of Chancery* (1740–49), 4th edn by Samuel Compton Cox, 3 vols. (London, 1787)

Ridgeway   Ridgeway, William, *Reports of Cases argued and determined in the King's Bench and Chancery* (London, 1794)

Strange   Strange, John, *Reports of adjudged cases in the Courts of Chancery, King's Bench, Common Pleas and Exchequer* (1755), 3rd edn by Michael Nolan, 2 vols. (London, 1795)

Term Rpts   Dunford, Charles and Edward Hyde East, *Reports of Cases argued and determined in the Court of King's Bench*, 8 vols. (London, 1817)

Vesey Sr.   Vesey, Francis (Senior), *Cases argued and determined in the High Court of Chancery* (1771), 3rd edn, 2 vols. (London, 1788)

W Blackstone   Blackstone, William, *Reports of Cases determined in the Several Courts of Westminster Hall* (1780), 2nd edn by Charles Henage Elsley, 2 vols. (London, 1828)

West   West, Martin, *Reports of Cases argued and determined in the High Court of Chancery* (London, 1827)

Introduction

The eighteenth century, according to the judgment of its current
historians, was England's century of law. As E. P. Thompson has put
it, "'The Law' [was] elevated during this century to a role more
prominent than at any period" of English history.[1] The culture of law,
it is increasingly observed, extended throughout the social fabric,
conditioning popular protest as much as formal public debate. "From
the hue-and-cry to the macabre carnival of the public hanging," notes
Roy Porter, "the law and its execution were not just Government fiats
or ruling-class weapons but an intimate part of community life."[2] Law
and legal process were equally fundamental to the political dynamic of
this community. "Most Englishmen experienced government and
understood politics through their dealings with the law," John Brewer
has argued. In this society, "all parties – government, radical and
spectators... recognized the potency of [the law's] symbols and rituals,
knew how significant a platform its institutions provided and what a
powerful legitimizing force its endorsement could be."[3] Even Sir
Lewis Namier was forced to conclude that, "in the eighteenth century,
Parliamentary politics were transacted, to a disastrous extent, in terms
of jurisprudence."[4]

These remarks echo those of contemporary observers who were also
struck by the distinctiveness of England's fabric of legality. Montesquieu, in a celebrated and much repeated judgment, reported that
England boasted the only constitutional order which had political
"liberty" for its "direct end."[5] Adam Smith maintained that in no

---

[1] E. P. Thompson, "Eighteenth-century English Society: Class Struggle Without Class?"
Social History, III (1978), 144.

[2] Roy Porter, *English Society in the Eighteenth Century* (Harmondsworth, 1982), p. 150.

[3] John Brewer, "The Wilkites and the Law, 1763–74," in John Brewer and John Styles (eds.),
An Ungovernable People. The English and Their Law in the Seventeenth and Eighteenth Centuries
(London, 1980), pp. 133, 135.

[4] L. B. Namier, *The Structure of Politics at the Accession of George III*, 2 vols. (London, 1929), I,
54.

[5] Charles Louis de Secondat, Baron de Montesquieu, *The Spirit of the Laws* (1748), trans.
Thomas Nugent and introduction by Franz Neumann (New York, 1949), p. 151.

1

other nation had the rules of law achieved such "great exactness" in their execution.[6] "'Tis the great advantage and happiness of us of this Nation," explained Lord Chancellor Hardwicke, "to live under a Government...secured to us by the best body of Laws that human wisdom can frame."[7]

This book is concerned with that part of the legal experience of eighteenth-century England represented in the more formal and systematic contemporary reflection on the nature of law in general and the character of the English system of law in particular. In so considering legal theory, we address a subject that enjoyed a prestige nearly equal to that of the law itself. "The science of jurisprudence," observed Burke "[is] the pride of human intellect...the collected reason of ages, combining the principles of original justice with the infinite variety of human concerns."[8] My first objective in examining this eminent eighteenth-century science is to recover an important contemporary discussion of the rival claims of common law and legislation within the English legal system, to suggest how this discussion illuminates more general and familiar themes in the political thought of the period, and especially to indicate the way in which questions regarding legal change and law reform came to be framed in terms of this discussion. To do so, I explore the legal literature in which the issue was explicitly raised as well as the contemporary developments in the law and society which were thought relevant to its consideration. The result is a study of eighteenth-century intellectual history which draws upon an unusually wide range of legal materials.

In many cases, such as the discussion of Blackstone's *Commentaries on the Laws of England* in part I, I am dealing, of course, with major and celebrated landmarks, as familiar to the historians of political and constitutional ideas as to historians of law. But, as I seek to show in highlighting the overlooked programmatic features of the *Commentaries*, Blackstone's famous production needs to be placed alongside the much less familiar work of legal antiquarians, such as Daines Barrington and Francis Hargrave, and of the authors of practical manuals of law, such as Richard Burn. The historical researches of Barrington, Hargrave and Burn (considered in part III) contain weighty statements of the common law approach to legal improvement, and this material is

---

[6] Adam Smith, *Lectures on Jurisprudence*, ed. R. L. Meek, D. D. Raphael, and P. G. Stein (Oxford, 1978), p. 275.

[7] British Library Additional Manuscript 36, 115. ff. 103 (a); cited in Clyde Elliott Croft, "Philip Yorke, First Earl of Hardwicke – An Assessment of his Legal Career," unpublished Ph.D. thesis, Cambridge University, 1982 p. 148 n346.

[8] *Reflections on the Revolution in France* (1790), in *The Works of the Right Honorable Edmund Burke* (1865–7), 8th edn, 12 vols. (Boston, 1884), III, 357.

especially important for the recovery and elucidation of the neglected Baconian tradition of English legislative theory, which dominated Hanoverian discussion of statute reform. Indeed, as I suggest in treating the penal doctrines of William Eden and Samuel Romilly, this Baconian tradition also set the basic structure for the legislative programs of the eighteenth-century criminal law reformers, whose proposals are often incorrectly assessed in terms of later law reform conventions.

Although this book is not designed as a traditional work of legal history, part II draws heavily on eighteenth-century case law and discusses the judicial career of Lord Chief Justice Mansfield. The decisions of Mansfield's court greatly enrich our understanding of common law orthodoxy, particularly in regard to the place of natural jurisprudence in common law theory. The eighteenth-century perception of Mansfield's court as the instrument of dramatic legal improvement and as a recent exemplification of "the wisdom of the common law" serves to clarify the confidence with which common lawyers associated the challenge of legal modernization with the historic institutions of customary law. And in turning to the legal ideas of Lord Kames, I explore how the model of legal development identified in the recent and past achievements of the English courts furnished an important bridge between the legal speculation of Hanoverian England and the prestigious styles of historical jurisprudence and social philosophy developed during the same period in Scotland.

This broad survey of eighteenth-century legal development and legal thought, in turn, provides the background for another of this study's major objectives, which is to advance a new account of Jeremy Bentham's earliest explorations in jurisprudence. The examination (in part IV) of what Bentham's first legislative program owed to his engagement with the English discussion of common law and legislation is designed to supplement earlier scholarship which has properly directed attention to Bentham's debts to continental sources.[9] However, in considering Bentham's relationship to contemporary developments in English legal thought, I also wish to establish a general historical theme: that Bentham's legislative science should be regarded not as the definitive ideology of law reform produced in eighteenth-century England, but rather as one among several approaches to legislation and legal improvement elaborated at this time. The recovery of these rival reform traditions would, I believe, revise our understanding of

[9] See, as leading examples, Elie Halévy, *La Formation du Radicalisme Philosophique*, 3 vols. (Paris, 1901–4), and, more recently, L. J. Hume, *Bentham and Bureaucracy* (Cambridge, 1981).

Bentham's legacy and of the intellectual orientation of the Victorian law reform movement, though these implications are not pursued in this book. All I hope to show here is just how much history was lost in the nineteenth-century conviction, as voiced by Lord Brougham, that "the age of Law Reform and the age of Jeremy Bentham are one and the same... No one before him had ever seriously thought of exposing the defects in our English system of Jurisprudence."[10]

The central place of law and legal ideas in English political and social thought is scarcely a novel claim, and in the detailed interpretation of such figures as Blackstone and Bentham there is little danger of scholars neglecting the specifically legal dimensions of their thought. The importance of law and jurisprudence is in this way well established. But there has been no recent survey of the general development of legal theory in the age of Blackstone and Bentham.[11] Consequently, it is useful to begin this discussion by briefly relating its concerns to the available intellectual histories of eighteenth-century England.

For this purpose it is convenient to invoke two particularly powerful and influential interpretative syntheses. The first of these received classic exposition over a century ago in Leslie Stephen's twin-volume *History of English Thought in the Eighteenth Century*. This study set out historical background for the long-influential Victorian surveys (including Stephen's own later monument, the three-volume *The English Utilitarians*) which provided the first thorough assessments of the rise and influence of Benthamism.[12] For Stephen and his generation, English political thought in the eighteenth century revolved around the polar star of Locke's *Second Treatise of Government*. Locke's was "the formal apology of Whiggism" and "his writings became the political bible of the following century."[13] The historical trajectory from Lockean Whiggism to reforming Benthamism was an uncomplicated, natural progression. Locke's contractarian political doctrines were themselves "almost identical with the utilitarian formula," and his ethical theory furnished the "primary impulse" for "the moralists

[10] "Speech on the Present State of the Law" (1828), in *Speeches of Henry Lord Brougham ... with Historical Introductions*, 4 vols. (Edinburgh, 1838), II, 287.

[11] There is, for example, nothing for the eighteenth-century comparable to the general accounts of seventeenth-century legal theory presented in J. G. A. Pocock's *The Ancient Constitution and the Feudal Law* (Cambridge, 1957) or Richard Tuck's *Natural Rights Theories. Their Origin and Development* (Cambridge, 1979).

[12] See Stephen's *The English Utilitarians*, 3 vols. (London, 1900); Halévy, *La Formation du Radicalisme Philosophique*; and A. V. Dicey, *Lectures on the Relation between Law and Public Opinion in the Nineteenth Century* (London, 1905).

[13] Leslie Stephen, *History of English Thought in the Eighteenth Century* (1876), 2 vols. (London, 1962), II, 114.

who, in later phraseology, have been called utilitarians."[14] At mid-century Hume "stated" the "essential doctrines of utilitarianism" with unique "clearness and consistency," and "from Hume to John Stuart Mill, the doctrine received no substantial alteration."[15] The "dominant school of the century" comprised the theological utilitarianism of William Paley and his fellow Anglican divines.[16] Bentham's own utilitarian theory merely constituted "Paley *minus* the belief in hell-fire." His distinctive intellectual achievement was to transfer "the doctrine of utility from the sphere of speculation to that of immediate legislation."[17]

To sustain the primacy in eighteenth-century speculation of "the purely English or utilitarian school of which Bentham became in later years the accepted prophet,"[18] Stephen introduced a variety of interpretative devices. Certain major intellectual developments were fully acknowledged but accommodated outside this central theme. Adam Smith, whose *Wealth of Nations* was outranked in importance by no other book "published in Great Britain during the last half of the eighteenth century," was placed in a separate chapter on "political economy," equipped with its own historical origins and development.[19] Edmund Burke – "incomparably the greatest man who has ever given the whole force of his intellect to the investigation of political philosophy in England" – was granted an exalted but isolated achievement in proclaiming a doctrine antithetic to "all the contemporary political speculation," namely "the conception of a nation as a living organism of complex structure and historical continuity."[20] Other, non-utilitarian political speculation was dismissed for not being theoretical enough. Accordingly, the "mass of pamphlets and speeches" which recorded the Augustan preoccupation with "liberty, corruption and luxury," the Whig obsession with "the Pretender," and the endless parliamentary distraction with "the Excise and the Hanoverian subsidies" was judged to lack "even a show of political philosophy."'Notwithstanding the incessant "jargon about standing armies and annual parliaments," the "first half of the eighteenth century had...produced no English book upon the theory of politics capable of communicating any great impulse to speculation."[21]

If the central trajectory of English eighteenth-century social thought thus connected the Lockean exposition of "the principles of the Revolution of 1688" to the Benthamic legislative science "to reform

[14] *Ibid.*, II, 115, 68.   [15] *Ibid.*, II, 73.   [16] *Ibid.*, II, 89, 103.
[17] *Ibid.*, II, 106. See also Stephen, *English Utilitarians*, I, 235–6, 288–9.
[18] Stephen, *English Thought in the Eighteenth Century*, II, 174.
[19] *Ibid.*, II, 269.   [20] *Ibid.*, II, 195.   [21] *Ibid.*, II, 111, 157–8.

society anew,"[22] the resulting historical question for Stephen was the
century-long hiatus before utilitarianism emerged as a programmatic,
reforming ethic. This delay was readily explained in terms of the
prolonged "period of political stagnation" which followed the
"accession of George I," a time when the "governing classes enjoyed
the power they had acquired by the Revolution," when "not one
constitutional question of the least importance arose," when "the
nation indolently drifted towards an unknown future," and when in
result "Englishmen rather played with political theories than seriously
discussed them."[23]

Stephen's image of social thought in eighteenth-century England
thus contained one serious theory, utilitarianism, which slumbered
through the long period of political conservatism, stagnation and
empty political rhetoric until it was awakened in service of a
comprehensive reform program by Bentham.[24] This was a picture
much favored by Bentham himself, and the accompanying emphasis on
what Ernest Barker described as the "complacent development of the
eighteenth century" became a standard theme of such histories,
particularly those attending to law and legal theory.[25] Maitland wrote
that "a time of self-complacency came for the law, which knew itself
to be the perfection of reason."[26] James Bryce likewise remarked on the
"genial optimism" of the age which "took the law as it stood to be the
best possible," an attitude that received authoritative expression in the
writings of Bentham's great adversary, William Blackstone, who found
"little to criticize and nothing to require amendment in rules and a
procedure which half a century later few ventured to justify."[27]

The limitations of Stephen's reading of eighteenth-century
intellectual history easily appear when confronted by a second
influential interpretative framework of more recent coinage. This
second reading can be termed (as has been done in a related context) the
"republican synthesis."[28] Although this synthesis is the product of
many separate and substantial contributions, for our purposes here it
can be best explored through the work of J. G. A. Pocock who has

---

[22] *Ibid.*, II, 114, 215.   [23] *Ibid.*, II, 141, 111.   [24] *Ibid.*, II, 106.

[25] Ernest Baker, *Traditions of Civility* (Cambridge, 1948), p. 284.

[26] F. W. Maitland, "History of English Law" (1902), *Selected Historical Essays*, ed. Helen M.
Cam (Cambridge, 1957), p. 113.

[27] James Bryce, *Studies in History and Jurisprudence*, 2 vols. (Oxford, 1901), II, 615. In more recent
scholarship, something like this image of the period survives in the work of Namier and his
school. For characteristic statements, see Namier, *Structure of Politics*, I, 21, and Richard Pares,
King George III and the Politicians (Oxford, 1953), pp. 2–3.

[28] So termed by Robert E. Shalhope in his "Toward a Republican Synthesis: The Emergence
of an Understanding of Republicanism in American Historiography," *William and Mary
Quarterly*, XXIX (1972), 49–80.

done most to chart and elaborate the classical republican (or, in his preferred usage, "civic humanist") themes of early-modern social thought.[29]

On Pocock's reading, early-modern republican ideology centered on a deeply moralized ideal of citizenship, conceived as the active exercise of civic virtue and participation in the common good which alone enabled the individual to achieve his full moral capacity and the community to maintain republican self-government. Civic virtue and republican association were ever vulnerable to the mortal diseases of corruption and self-interest, and the inevitable conflict between virtue and corruption featured as the organizing category of the republican perception of political life. In eighteenth-century England, following upon the seventeenth-century constitutional struggles and the Harringtonian tendency to identify the patriotic citizen with propertied independence, republicanism involved an intense preoccupation with the preservation of constitutional balance and parliamentary independence along with a no less intense disquiet over the perceived corrupting impact of commercial prosperity. In the polemics of the Walpolean era and in the arguments against imperial policy in the American colonies, for example, such concerns informed and structured the standard criticisms of Whig leadership and the mechanisms of Whig political management: its parliamentary system of an enlarged Executive, placemen and the Septennial Act; its financial system of public credit, excise and National Debt; and its military system of standing armies and swollen navies. "From 1688 to 1776 (or after)," Pocock observes, "the central question in Anglophone political theory was not whether a ruler might be resisted for misconduct, but whether a regime founded on patronage, public debt, and professionalization of the armed forces did not corrupt both governors and governed; and corruption was a problem in virtue."[30]

Pocock has been especially articulate in disclosing the ways in which the recovery of this "civic humanist mode of discoursing about politics"[31] has transformed our general understanding of English

---

[29] The first version of Pocock's interpretation is contained in chapters 3 and 4 of J. G. A. Pocock, *Politics, Language and Time. Essays on Political Thought and History* (London, 1972), though the thesis received fullest elaboration in *The Machiavellian Moment: Florentine Political Thought and the Atlantic Republican Tradition* (Princeton, 1975). Many of his most recent contributions are collected in *Virtue, Commerce, and History. Essays on Political Thought and History, Chiefly in the Eighteenth Century* (Cambridge, 1985). For the larger body of scholarship of which Pocock's work forms a part, see the bibliographic surveys supplied by Shalhope in "Toward a Republican Synthesis" and "Republicanism and Early American Historiography," *William and Mary Quarterly*, XXXIX (1982), 334–56, and by Pocock in "The Varieties of Whiggism from Exclusion to Reform," in *Virtue, Commerce, and History*, pp. 215–310.

[30] "Virtues, Rights and Manners. A Model for Historians of Political Thought," *Virtue, Commerce, and History*, p. 48.   [31] *Ibid.*, p. 39.

thought in the eighteenth century. Among the most spectacular victims
of the interpretation is "the myth of Locke" and the attendant
"obsession with liberalism."[32] Instead of Locke serving, as in
Stephen's account, as the period's scriptural authority, he becomes
conspicuous for his "indifference to the paradigm of virtue"and plays
"no predominant role" in the formulation of the "Whig canon" of
republican authorities.[33] Equally, the periodization of political debate
is revised. The familiar landmark of the Revolution of 1688 slips from
prominence, and the so-called Financial Revolution – "the development of the Bank of England and the National Debt" – emerges as
"the turning-point in the history of English and Scottish political
ideology."[34] Finally, what Stephen confidently dismissed as those
"most transparent of artifices" – the commonplace "generalities about
liberty, corruption and luxury" and the standard "jargon about
standing armies and annual parliaments"[35] – are revealed to be the
hallmarks of a coherent and well-entrenched theory of politics constructed upon "the civic ideal in its expressly republican form."[36]

The republican synthesis has not served simply to recover large areas
of eighteenth-century political debate discounted by earlier generations.
The renaissance and seventeenth-century routes to eighteenth-century
orthodoxies have been illuminated, and in Pocock's most recent
studies, the themes of Anglophone republicanism have been projected
suggestively into the first decades of the nineteenth century.[37] Nor has
the interpretation been confined to the exposition of "Anglophone
political theory" narrowly conceived. The same civic ideal and the
widely ramifying contemporary reflection upon it furnish "a major
key to eighteenth-century social thought," supply the "most fundamental problem" of the period's "moral philosophy," and inform
"nearly all eighteenth-century philosophy of history."[38] Yet, at the

[32] J. G. A. Pocock, "The Myth of Locke and the Obsession with Liberalism," in J. G. A.
Pocock and Richard Ashcraft, *John Locke: Papers Read at the Clark Library Seminar* (Los
Angeles, 1980), and "Authority and Property: The Question of Liberal Origins," in *Virtue,
Commerce, and History*, pp. 51-71.

[33] Pocock, "The Myth of Locke," p. 18, and "Authority and Property," p. 66.

[34] J. G. A. Pocock, "The Machiavellian Moment Revisited: A Study in History and Ideology,"
Journal of Modern History, LIII (1981), 64-5.

[35] Stephen, *English Thought in the Eighteenth Century*, II, 157-8, 111.

[36] J. G. A. Pocock, "Cambridge Paradigms and Scotch Philosophers," in Istvan Hont and
Michael Ignatieff (eds.), *Wealth and Virtue. The Shaping of Political Economy in the Scottish
Enlightenment* (Cambridge, 1983), p. 245.

[37] "The Varieties of Whiggism from Exclusion to Reform," in *Virtue, Commerce, and History*,
pp. 215-310.

[38] "The Mobility of Property and the Rise of Eighteenth-Century Sociology," p. 115, "1776:
The Revolution against Parliament," p. 78, "Varieties of Whiggism," p. 231, *Virtue,
Commerce, and History* (and see generally chapters 10 and 11).

same time that the recovery of "the paradigm of virtue and corruption"[39] has accommodated and clarified such a range of speculation, the republican synthesis falls silent in the face of what to earlier scholars seemed among the eighteenth century's most significant and characteristic intellectual episodes. "Bentham concealed his origins if he had any," Pocock reports, and the "parameters within which occurred the mutation of discourse that produced him and his mind are hard to establish and seem not to belong to the history of English public debate."[40]

This study seeks to establish just such a context within the history of English public debate for Bentham and Benthamic legislative science, and to the extent that this aim presumes the importance of the historical development it scrutinizes, the treatment recalls the concerns of Stephen's history. Where it departs decisively from his account is in rejecting Stephen's picture of the historical background to Bentham as a period of ideological consensus and untroubled political complacency. Here the discussion shows its major debt to Pocock's scholarship, and to those social and political historians who have so qualified and revised previous characterizations of Hanoverian England as a nation, in Namier's words, "at one in all fundamental matters."[41] Yet even though the "republican synthesis" informs much of the initial orientation of the investigation, it makes only a limited impact on its detailed findings. This too deserves comment.

The failure of "the paradigm of virtue and corruption" to accommodate the emergence of Benthamic legislative science need not be taken as a direct challenge to the republican synthesis itself. As Pocock always has been careful to stress, his chronicle of civic humanism "was a 'tunnel history'" which "pursued a single theme, that of the *vivere civile* and its virtue, to the partial exclusion of parallel phenomena."[42] Among the "parallel phenomena" avowedly excluded was the "philosophic and juristic" mode of "discoursing about politics," termed by Pocock the "law-centered paradigm" and associated, in turn, with scholasticism, civil and natural jurisprudence,

---

[39] "Virtues, Rights and Manners," p. 48.
[40] "Varieties of Whiggism," p. 277. See also "The Mobility of Property and the Rise of Eighteenth-Century Sociology," p. 123, and *Machiavellian Moment*, p. 547.
[41] Namier, *Structure of Politics*, I, 21. The critics are numerous, but I have learned especially from E. P. Thompson, "Patrician Society, Plebeian Culture," *Journal of Social History*, VII (1974), 382–405, and "Eighteenth-century English Society: Class Struggle Without Class?," and from John Brewer, *Party Ideology and Popular Politics at the Accession of George III* (Cambridge, 1976).
[42] Pocock, "Machiavellian Moment Revisited," p. 53. See also "Cambridge Paradigms," pp. 245–6.

possessive individualism and liberalism.[43] The two traditions, while contemporaneous, "are markedly discontinuous with one another because they premise different values, encounter different problems, and employ different strategies of speech and argument."[44] Any study, such as this one, addressed to the specifically legal theory of eighteenth-century Britain would naturally fall on the juristic side of the division. Should this chosen concentration on "styles of thought based on jurisprudence" be taken to imply an argument "for neglecting, or reducing the importance of, styles based upon republican rhetoric"?[45]

That this question needs investigating at all is a consequence of current debate over two major arenas of eighteenth-century intellectual history – the Enlightenment in Scotland and republicanism in America. In both cases, an impressive body of interpretation emphasizing classical republican strains has now been challenged by studies stressing the centrality of alternative intellectual frameworks: in the case of Scotland, the natural jurisprudence tradition of Grotius and his successors; in the case of America, the liberal rights theory of Locke and his successors.[46] Given the juristic foundations of these rival frameworks, Pocock has described the challenge (in the context of Scotland) as "an attempt to restore the history of political thought in general to the high road so long marked out by philosophy and jurisprudence."[47] The result has been a contest over what Donald Winch has termed "alternative interpretative routes" which seems likely to dominate the next phase of research, notwithstanding the several contributors who have urged "a reconciling of the two positions."[48]

As all the contributors to this debate have recognized, the recovery of the historical context for any text must include reference to the work's intellectual context, and this in turn has prompted the effort to situate the text in its appropriate framework of method, orientation,

---

[43] See "Machiavellian Moment Revisited," "Cambridge Paradigms," and especially "Virtues, Rights and Manners," *Virtue, Commerce, and History*, pp. 37–48.

[44] "Virtues, Rights and Manners," p. 39.

[45] "Machiavellian Moment Revisited," pp. 53–4.

[46] For the relevant literature concerning Scotland, see the material cited by Pocock in "Cambridge Paradigms," p. 248 n31; the essays by Hont and Ignatieff, by Moore and Silverthorne, and by Winch in *Wealth and Virtue*; and the essays by Forbes and by Haakonssen in R. H. Campbell and Andrew S. Skinner (eds.), *The Origins and Nature of the Scottish Enlightenment* (Edinburgh, 1982). For the literature on America, see Shalhope's articles, "Toward a Republican Synthesis" and "Republicanism and Early American Historiography," and the contributions discussed in the exchange between Banning and Appleby, in *William and Mary Quarterly*, XLIII (1986), 3–34.

[47] "Cambridge Paradigms," p. 248 (on Scotland). For the American material, see his discussion in "Varieties of Whiggism," pp. 253–74.

[48] Donald Winch, "Adam Smith's 'enduring particular end'," *Wealth and Virtue*, p. 263. See also Pocock, "Cambridge Paradigms," p. 248, and Banning, "Jefferson Ideology Revisited: Liberal and Classical Ideas in the New American Republic," *William and Mary Quarterly*, XLIII (1986), 3–19.

style of argument and doctrinal presuppositions. (For our purposes here, we need not delay over the important issue of whether such frameworks should be construed as intellectual traditions, languages, modes of discourse or paradigms.) At the same time, though, certain dangers are already made apparent in concentrating eighteenth-century intellectual history on the essentially classificatory exercise of determining whether a particular work, or doctrine or theorist is discoursing in "the vocabulary or language of civic humanism" or "that of civil jurisprudence."[49] The enterprise tends to depict the "languages" in question as remarkably autonomous and isolated, a characterization which seems dubious given the very absence of agreement over which language best accommodates particular texts or figures.[50] Here distinctions and classifications which perhaps best serve purely heuristic purposes seem to be distorted on account of their being called upon to do simply too much service. Moreover, by focusing in this fashion on the rivalry between "alternative interpretative routes," opportunities for synthesis and advance seem to be lost in the attempt to maintain the hegemony of any single favored approach. Isaac Kramnick, for example, in his writings on late eighteenth-century political thought has sought to combat the republican thesis by identifying the presence of other, largely Lockean ideological sources. Yet, having so displaced republicanism, in his characterization of the Lockean alternative he seems content to ignore the insights achieved by the scholarship on republicanism and instead to return unrepentantly to earlier mappings of the intellectual terrain.[51] Perhaps most damaging overall, our agreement to differ over the choice between "alternative interpretative routes" fails to raise fundamental questions as to whether the alternative traditions and vocabularies have been properly identified in the first place, whether, in fact, they have constituted "outstandingly discontinuous" styles of political theory, whether the relationship between the traditions has remained constant across periods and polities, and whether these materials are best excavated by way of "tunnel histories."[52] The outcome is to make the study of the eighteenth

[49] Pocock, "Cambridge Paradigms," p. 248.
[50] See Winch's characteristically telling observations in "Adam Smith's 'enduring particular end'," pp. 263–4.
[51] See Isaac Kramnick, "Religion and Radicalism: English Political Theory in the Age of Revolution," *Political Theory*, V (1977), 505–34, and "Republican Revisionism Revisited," *American Historical Review*, LXXXVII (1982), 629–66. In the second article in particular Kramnick's argument for a break in English political argument at 1760 seems simply to disregard the intervening work on the Tory, Dissenter and Wilkite traditions of protest by Linda Colley, *In Defiance of Oligarchy: The Tory Party, 1714–60* (Cambridge, 1982), and "Eighteenth-Century English Radicalism before Wilkes," *Transactions of the Royal Historical Society*, 5th series, XXXI (1981), 1–19, and by John Brewer in "English Radicalism in the Age of George III," in J. G. A. Pocock (ed.), *The British Revolutions: 1641, 1688, 1776* (Princeton, 1980).
[52] I here utilize Pocock's terminology, (see the discussion above at n42 and n44).

century unhelpfully dependent on the discussion of earlier periods. For while it is abundantly clear that our present understanding of eighteenth-century ideologies has been enormously advanced by the recovery of what was received from the seventeenth century and before, it hardly follows that we must confine our analysis of eighteenth-century thought to those anyway contentious categories which have proved useful for the study of earlier periods. The stage has been reached when it makes sense to look for an alternative to the present alternatives.

The option pursued here is to examine legal ideas not with the aim of establishing the primacy of jurisprudence as an approach to eighteenth-century social thought, but in order dramatically to enlarge the issues and sources through which this thought is considered and characterized. The nature and potential advantages of this shift can be disclosed by returning to a judgment by Pocock cited above. In maintaining the centrality of republican ideology through the period "from 1688 to 1776 (or after)," Pocock notes that "the central question in Anglophone political theory" did not concern the grounds of resistance but "whether a regime founded on patronage, public debt, and professionalization of the armed forces did not corrupt both governors and governed," and that this ensured that "political thought" moved "out of the law-centered paradigm" of rights theory and into the republican "paradigm of virtue and corruption."[53] This may well be an entirely correct evaluation of the relative unimportance of resistance theory compared with republicanism in these years. Still, however this specific question should be settled, its solution ought not to prevent us from considering the wisdom of surveying the period's political thought in terms of these two rhetorically juxtaposed issues. The formula inevitably excludes from view the variety of contemporary concerns and responses to eighteenth-century parliamentary government which centered *neither* on questions of legitimate resistance *nor* on the corrupting impact of Whig political management.

It is precisely with one such range of response to eighteenth-century political life that this study is concerned: the reaction to the emergence of parliament as an active law-making institution. From the standpoint of either the "law-centered paradigm" or the "paradigm of virtue and corruption," the issues raised by parliament's legislative practice may appear as second-order questions. Nonetheless, it was these issues which provided the stimulus for more general reflection on the nature of England's legal inheritance, the challenges to the nation's institutions

---

[53] *Virtue, Commerce, and History*, p. 48. This claim has in turn been challenged by the counter-demonstration of the importance of Lockean resistance theory in the period after 1760; see Kramnick, "Republican Revisionism Revisited."

posed by social and economic growth, and the appropriate avenues in England to legal reform and improvement. By the first decades of the nineteenth century such law-related reform issues regularly occupied the center of national political debate. Earlier historians of English thought, such as Leslie Stephen, naturally turned their attention to the ideas and movements which seemed to shape this reformism, so much so that their interpretations of the eighteenth century became seriously distorted by the preoccupation with this single development. In contrast, our recent neglect of the juristic setting in which the debate on legal change and law reform first developed has greatly impoverished our notion of the "central questions of Anglophone political theory," and generated intellectual histories in which distinctive voices of English reform have been rendered unnecessarily mysterious.

The background to the body of theory to be examined here lies in a surprisingly neglected consequence of the consolidation of parliamentary government in the years following the 1688 Revolution. Accompanying the establishment of a regular, annual parliamentary session was the dramatic increase of the King-in-Parliament's exercise of its constitutional powers to make law.[54] According to the statistics assembled by P. D. G. Thomas, the parliaments of George III legislated at over four times the rate of the parliaments of William III. In the period 1760–1820, parliament enacted on average 254 statutes per session; in William's reign, the period 1689–1702, the figure stood at 58.[55] Such statistical summaries of legislative output are extremely

[54] On the development of parliamentary government during William's reign, see Jennifer Carter, "The Revolution and the Constitution," in Geoffrey Holmes (ed.), *Britain after the Glorious Revolution* (London, 1969), pp. 39–58. For the resulting increase in legislation, see Henry Horwitz, *Policy and Politics in the Reign of William III* (Manchester, 1977), p. 325, and Joanna Innes and John Styles, "The Crime Wave: Recent Writing on Crime and Criminal Justice in Eighteenth-Century England," *Journal of British Studies*, XXV (1986), 380–435. This theme receives fuller analysis by Innes and Styles in "The Bloody Code in Context: Eighteenth-Century Criminal Legislation Reconsidered. A Report of Work in Progress" (unpublished paper, December, 1984). I am much indebted to both authors for permission to examine this unpublished study.

[55] P. D. G. Thomas, *The House of Commons in the Eighteenth Century* (Oxford, 1971), p. 61:

Number of Acts of Parliament, 1689–1820

		Public	Private	Average per session
William III	1689–1702	343	466	58
Anne	1702–1714	338	605	78
George I	1714–1727	377	381	58
George II	1727–1760	1447	1244	81
George III	1760–1820	9980	5257	254

crude, ignoring differences in scope and legal consequence among acts and hiding the irregularities in the pattern of law-making. For present purposes, however, what commands attention is the ample contemporary awareness of the development marked by these rough figures.

"Within these last two hundred and fifty years," Francis Stoughton Sullivan instructed the university students of Dublin in the 1760s, "the inhabitants of Europe...seem to have been seized with an epidemic madness of making new laws." In no place was the epidemic so severe "as Britain."[56] In 1756 Lord Hardwicke complained that "our statute books have of late years increased to such an enormous size, that no lawyer, not even one of the longest and most extensive practice, can pretend to be master of all the statutes that relate to any one case that comes before him."[57] At mid-century, Blackstone noted that the English statute law had "swelled to ten times a larger bulk" since the time of Sir Edward Coke; at the end of the century, John Huntingford reported that the statute book had "nearly doubled in bulk" since the time of Blackstone.[58]

Nowhere was the growth of legislation more striking than in the area of penal policy. Parliament's capital statutes had extended the penalty of death on such a scale that by 1771 William Eden conjectured whether "the extirpation of mankind" would "be supposed" the "chief object of legislation in England."[59] Blackstone earlier had likewise observed "the vast increase of capital punishment," and estimated that English law contained 160 capital crimes without benefit of clergy.[60] In 1819, Thomas Fowell Buxton put the number at 223, claiming further that of these 150 had been "made capital during the last century," and that there were men still "living at whose birth our code contained less than seventy capital offences, and we have seen that number more than trebled."[61]

Scarcely less powerful evidence of legislative activism was provided in the variety of statutes through which parliament expanded the responsibilities and authority of the justices of the peace. Between 1663 and 1776, Norma Landau relates, the number of offences parliament placed under the summary jurisdiction of the justices increased

---

[56] Francis Stoughton Sullivan, *An Historical Treatise on the Feudal Law, and the Constitution and Laws of England* (London, 1772), p. 7.

[57] Hardwicke's speech to the House of Lords, cited in William Holdsworth, *A History of English Law*, 16 vols. (London, 1922–66), XI, 374.

[58] 1 *Comm* 11; John Huntingford, *The State of the Statute Laws Considered* (London, 1796), p. 7.

[59] William Eden, *Principles of Penal Law* (1771), 2nd edn (London, 1771), p. 306.

[60] 4 *Comm* 441 and 4 *Comm* 18.

[61] Buxton's speech to the House of Commons, cited in Leon Radzinowicz, *A History of English Criminal Law and its Administration from 1750*, 5 vols. (London 1948–86), I, 4–5.

threefold, from 70 to over 200.[62] The new acts, Henry Zouch claimed in 1786, had rendered the English magistrate "one of the most powerful Ministers of Justice in the known world."[63] The more general growth of justices' duties was graphically recorded in the steady enlarging of Richard Burn's famous justices' handbook, each edition after the 1755 original requiring new additions to accommodate recent parliamentary statutes and the subsequent case law. The two-volume manual reached four volumes in its tenth edition of 1766, and by its eighteenth edition in 1797 stood at nearly three times its first dimensions. When in the 1750s Henry Fielding campaigned for stronger local administration of the law, he was at pains to distinguish the justices' new duties from any substantial change in their effectiveness. He readily acknowledged the "common and popular complaint" that the magistrate enjoyed "already too much power," but insisted that this was to mistake "business for power." The justice's business was "indeed multiplied by a great number of statutes," but these had nonetheless not "enlarged his power."[64]

So obvious was the radical increase in the number of acts of parliament that contemporary attention naturally turned to explaining the development. Lord Hardwicke (himself responsible for two major instances of Hanoverian legislation, the 1747 Highland Acts and the 1753 Marriage Act) claimed that "the degeneracy of the present times, fruitful in the inventions of wickedness, hath produced many new laws...to suppress mischiefs, which were growing frequent amongst us."[65] It was more conventional, however, to cite less disturbing reasons why, in Sullivan's words, England "necessarily require[d] a great number of laws."[66] One important convention linked what Blackstone termed the kingdom's singular "multiplicity of law" to the special requirements of civil liberty.[67] "It has been frequently remarked with great propriety," Alexander Hamilton explained in 1788, "that a voluminous code of laws is one of the inconveniences necessarily connected with the advantages of free government."[68] The same

---

[62] Norma Landau, *The Justices of the Peace, 1679–1760* (Berkeley, 1984), p. 246.

[63] Henry Zouch, *Hints respecting the Public Police* (London, 1786), p. 1. I am indebted to Joanna Innes for this reference.

[64] Henry Fielding, *An Enquiry into the Late Increase of Robbers, with some Proposals for Remedying this Growing Evil* (1751), in *The Complete Works of Henry Fielding*, 16 vols. (New York, 1967), XIII, 16.

[65] Cited in Philip C. Yorke, *The Life and Correspondence of Philip Yorke, Earl of Hardwicke*, 3 vols. (Cambridge 1913), I, 135.

[66] Sullivan, *Constitution and Laws of England*, p. 8.

[67] See 3 *Comm* 325–27, and the discussion below, chapter 1 at nn81–2.

[68] Alexander Hamilton, "Federalist 78," in Alexander Hamilton, James Madison and John Jay, *The Federalist Papers* (1787–88), ed. Clinton Rossiter (New York, 1961), p. 471.

multiplicity of law, it was further explained, resulted inevitably from the nation's commercial prosperity and social advance. By the end of the century, this argument too had become commonplace:

> The laws of a nation circumstanced like England, in its vast influx of wealth and extension of commerce, must increase to such a number, and consist in so great a variety of particulars, as to render it impossible for the generality of subjects to be masters of them...such is the natural and necessary course of things.[69]

If eighteenth-century parliaments were thus recognizably making law at an unprecedented rate, the development in itself might well be presumed not to have provided any special stimulus for legal theory. Parliamentary statute was already a principal source of English law, and legal commentators could point to past occasions, like the statutes of Edward I, when the legal system had received extensive legislative addition. Few of the figures under discussion here believed there to be any formal improprieties in the eighteenth-century parliament's exercise of its legislative will. It is indeed during this period that constitutional lawyers have traditionally fixed the point at which parliamentary sovereignty came to be unambiguously identified with legislative omnipotence.[70] Notwithstanding the much-remarked upon "swelling of the statute book," legal historians have long concluded that this was still an era when "legislation played a tiny part in the development of private law."[71] In Maitland's stylish formulation, "in this 'age of reason'...the British parliament seems rarely to rise to the dignity of a general proposition, and in our own day the legal practitioner is likely to know less about the statutes of the eighteenth century than he knows about the statutes of Edward I, Henry VIII and Elizabeth."[72]

It is, of course, only hindsight which makes possible these historical judgments, and for contemporary observers neither the frequently marginal impact of parliament's legislative productions nor the acknowledged constitutional legitimacy of its actions supplied reassurance. The swollen statute book increasingly preoccupied legal commentators, and by mid-century appeared as a major issue in legal

[69] Huntingford, *Statute Laws Considered*, p. 17. For similar contemporary accounts of the relationship between legal complexity and social development, see Adam Smith, *Lectures on Jurisprudence*, ed. R. L. Meek, D. D. Raphael, and P. G. Stein (Oxford, 1978), p. 16, and Sullivan, *Constitution and Laws of England*, pp. 5–7. Blackstone's treatment is discussed below, chapter 1 at n80.

[70] See, for example, A. V. Dicey, *Introduction to the Study of the Law of the Constitution*, 9th edn (London, 1939), pp. 41–8.

[71] S. F. C. Milsom, "Reason in the Development of the Common Law," *Law Quarterly Review*, LXXXI (1965), 497.

[72] Maitland, "History of English Law," p. 114.

speculation. The sheer volume of the legislation – at a scale, according to the tendentious estimate of the Lord Chancellor, beyond the mastery of even the most experienced lawyer[73] – raised awkward implications for the standard "maxim of laws of England, that the want of knowledge thereof shall not excuse a man..."[74] The extreme particularity and limited provenance of so much of this law-making seemed to reduce the legislature, in Horace Walpole's words, to "a mere quarter sessions, where nothing is transacted but turnpikes and poor rates."[75] But what attracted the gravest concern was the perceived qualitative failures of this legislation and the damage thereby inflicted on the legal system overall. As it was put in 1796, "To the perplexed state of the statute code may be imputed, the reproach and ridicule which has been frequently thrown on the laws of England."[76]

In many cases the eighteenth-century lawyers' dissatisfaction with the statute book no doubt reflected little more than an increasingly secure and prosperous profession's impatience with interference from outside.[77] Early in his legal career the future parliamentary law reformer, Samuel Romilly, encountered a splendid instance of this attitude in the person of Serjeant Hill, whose own comprehensive plan of legal improvement comprised the repeal of "all the statutes" and the burning of "all the reports" of a date later "than the Revolution."[78] For the most part, however, legal writers proved more cautious and more considered in their anxieties over parliamentary law-making. In 1786, one such legal critic, John Rayner, buttressed his own attack on parliament's legislative practice by assembling a formidable canon of authority against the statute book. The distinguished legal antiquary, Daines Barrington, had charged "the legislature with ignorance and falsehood." Richard Burn, an author "of some authority," maintained that a statute of Queen Anne's reign was "neither grammar nor common sense" and "a disgrace to the statute book." He also described "one of the parliamentary penalties" as "ridiculous," while Sir William Blackstone judged "the statutes for preserving game" as "not a little obscure and intricate, and the grammatical mistakes glaring and numerous." Lord Mansfield, Chief Justice of the Court of King's Bench, claimed "from the bench" that "the bankrupt laws have

---

[73] See Hardwicke's comments cited above at n57.
[74] Huntingford, *Statute Laws Considered*, pp. 17–18.
[75] Cited in Pares, *George III and the Politicians*, p. 4.
[76] Huntingford, *Statute Laws Considered*, p. 26.
[77] On the social and professional success of bar and bench in the period, see Geoffrey Holmes, *Augustan England. Professions, State and Society, 1680–1730* (London, 1982), especially pp. 120–42.
[78] Samuel Romilly, *Memoirs of the Life of Sir Samuel Romilly, written by himself, with a selection of his Correspondence*, 2nd edn, 3 vols. (London, 1840), I, 72.

done more harm than good." Mansfield's fellow justice, Edward Willes, "observed that nothing could be more oppressive than the present system of game laws." And Sir William Ashhurst termed the Qualification Act "a blundering statute."[79]

The strictures against acts of parliament, such as those which Rayner calculatedly paraded, clearly operated at a variety of levels. In some cases, as in Blackstone's disparagement of the game laws, it was the policy of the legislation that was being attacked.[80] In other cases, parliament was criticized for using improper means to achieve proper ends. Thus, many eighteenth-century penal law reformers recognized that the legislature had unsystematically though extensively increased the number of capital statutes in order to prevent criminal acts, but insisted that this tactic actually undermined effective criminal deterrence.[81] But the most frequent complaint, and one which directly exposed to question parliament's institutional capacity to produce successful legislation, concerned the poor formulation, careless drafting, glaring inaccuracies and disturbing inconsistencies to be found in the statute book. Lord Mansfield claimed that the provisions of the Carolinian Statute of Frauds and Perjuries relating to wills had probably overturned "many more fair wills... than fraudulent" simply because parliament had carelessly "slipped in" the inappropriate term "credible" in describing the witnesses required for a valid will.[82] In the case of a Hanoverian bankruptcy act, he observed that "the English language does not afford more general words than those used in the enacting part of this statute."[83] In the 1770s Bentham pointed to the same problem in more scathing tones:

> In no book that ever saw the light of day will the reader find examples of nonsense so unfathomable as what is frequently to be met with in our Statute book. Because there is no Style so repugnant to every purpose of language as that which distinguishes and disgraces the work of our Legislature.[84]

Such stylistic disgraces forced the courts to employ a complex set of guidelines for the construction of statutes, and their formulation and use likewise testified to the defects of parliamentary legislation.

---

[79] John Rayner, *Observations of the Statutes relating to the Stamp Duties* (London, 1786), Prefatory Discourse, pp. iii–xxvii.

[80] This and other examples are discussed below, in chapter 2.

[81] See the discussion below, in chapter 10.

[82] *Windham* v *Chetwynd*, (1757) 1 Burrow 414, 417–20.

[83] *Janson* v *Willson*, (1779) 1 Douglas 257, 259.

[84] UC cxl. 90. See also UC xcv. 1: "It is difficult enough to determine what in matters of detail the intention of the Legislator *ought* to be: but it is often still more difficult to determine what they were."

Blackstone, for example, presented ten such rules for construing acts of parliament. Some of these referred to matters of legal policy, such as the rule that penal acts were to be construed strictly. But many merely reflected the frequent difficulties of determining what parliament had meant, such as the rule that "one part of the statute must be so construed by another, that the whole may (if possible) stand," or the rule that "a saving, totally repugnant to the body of the act, is void."[85] Even relatively straightforward guidelines could be undermined by the realities of parliament's legislative practice. Legal writers often maintained that the preamble of an act was to be used to interpret the statute, as it furnished "a key to open the meaning of the act."[86] However, once scholars began rigorously to study the statute book, it became evident that the rule generated as many problems as it sought to solve. As Daines Barrington revealed in his authoritative *Observations on the More Ancient Statutes*, most preambles dwelt "upon a pretence, which was not the real occasion of the law, when, perhaps the proposer had very different views in contemplation." Hence, any attempt to interpret the law by this means was likely to mistake the legislature's intention, as well as the true state of the law when the act was passed.[87] As was often the case, it was Bentham who believed he had got to the bottom of these intricacies through a simple piece of reduction:

> It is the incapacity and inattention of Legislators only that can give currency to such loose expressions, and give occasion to call in any such rules as [Blackstone] has given.[88]

The "incapacity and inattention" of England's legislators presented a major challenge to eighteenth-century legal commentators, and in what follows we shall pursue their diagnoses of the problem and their favored strategies for resolving it. Of less direct concern for this purpose are the origins and nature of the problem itself: the reasons for parliament's increased legislative activity, the changes in its lawmaking, or the accuracy of the contemporary evaluation of its

---

[85] 1 *Comm* 87–92.

[86] Ballow, H. [?], *A Treatise of Equity [1737], with the additions of Marginal References and Notes*, by John Fonblanque, 2 vols. (London, 1793–4), I, 428–9. Blackstone did not include the rule and Bacon explicitly rejected it in *De Augmentis Scientiarum*. See *The Works of Francis Bacon*, ed. James Spedding, Robert Leslie Ellis and Douglas Denon Heath, 14 vols. (London, 1857–74), V, 102–3. For a more conventional treatment, see Edward Wynne, *Eunomus: Or, Dialogues concerning the Law and Constitution of England*, 4 vols. (London, 1774), III, 145–6.

[87] Daines Barrington, *Observations on the More Ancient Statutes ... with an Appendix being a proposal for new modelling the Statutes* (1766), 3rd edn (London, 1769), p. 353, and see also the discussion at p. 403 of "the title of a statute." Barrington's *Ancient Statutes* are discussed below, in chapter 9.   [88] *Comment*, p. 160.

legislative handiwork. Nonetheless, something deserves to be said of this aspect of the matter, if only to emphasize how far we presently are from pronouncing confidently on the subject.

The absence of detailed knowledge about eighteenth-century statute is not without its ironies. Of all eighteenth-century institutions, none has received such detailed and lavish collective scrutiny as has parliament under Namierite gaze. Nonetheless, Namier's agenda for parliamentary history effectively ignored the "peculiar club's" constitutional function to make law, since the "idea that Parliament should enact a legislative programme each session was completely unknown."[89] In the absence of more careful examination, historians have tended to adopt the arguments of the nineteenth-century reformers who portrayed the Hanoverian parliaments as scenes of complacency and irresponsibility, if not outright corruption. The Commons' committees of the 1820s and 1830s discovered ample evidence to assemble a picture of eighteenth-century legislative practice distinguished by exorbitant costs, procedural iniquities and an abiding lack of concern on the part of most legislators for their legislative responsibilities.[90] These committees were of course convened to find abuses, but it is unnecessary to dismiss their findings as mere special-pleading. Many of their criticisms of parliamentary procedure were already being voiced in the eighteenth century. Still, what the nineteenth-century reformers lacked was any incentive to make sense of the manner in which their predecessors legislated, and their litany of abuses was never designed to provide a full account of how the swollen statute book came to be fashioned.

Information on how parliament made law was available throughout the eighteenth century in a variety of legal treatises and collections of precedents concerned with the legislature's constitutional powers and the formalities of parliamentary procedure as a whole. Many of these dated from the seventeenth century, and unlike the early nineteenth-century legislative handbooks, they were not composed as practical manuals for use in the procurement of private acts. In addition to these

[89] L. B. Namier and John Brooke, *The History of Parliament. The House of Commons 1754–1790*, 3 vols. (History of Parliament Trust, H.M.S.O., 1964), I, 183. In the volume-long "introductory survey" to these three volumes, Namier and Brooke devote three pages to legislation. Namier's description of the House of Commons as the "peculiar club" first appeared in *Structure of Politics*, I, 3.

[90] For the investigations and recommendations of the nineteenth-century committees on private bill procedure, see Orlo Cyprian Williams, *The Clerical Organization of the House of Commons 1661–1850* (Oxford, 1954), pp. 234–5, 240–61 and his *The Historical Development of Private Bill Procedure and Standing Orders in the House of Commons*, 2 vols. (H.M.S.O., 1948–49), I, 46–55, 77–8. The Committees' findings are criticized in Sheila Lambert, *Bills and Acts: Legislative Procedure in Eighteenth-Century England* (Cambridge, 1971), pp. 101–2.

works, further information was contained in the separate sets of
Standing Orders promulgated by the Commons and Lords. From these
sources it is possible to construct a reasonably full outline of the
intricate and time-consuming process by which an ever-escalating
number of submitted bills secured parliamentary enactment.[91]

That part of the process which later attracted greatest criticism was
the stage at which bills came before committees in the Commons for
detailed examination and amendment. Aside from those government
measures which appeared before the standing Committees of Supply
and of Ways and Means, these committees were normally appointed on
an individual basis for each bill after it had received a second reading,
major bills being sent to a Committee of the Whole House, and private
or more specialized bills going before select committees. Excepting the
massive class of estate bills which were first presented in the Lords, the
majority of bills were initiated in the Commons. Thus, frequently, the
most concentrated parliamentary evaluation of any proposal occurred
at this stage in a bill's progress towards the statute book.

As later critics emphasized, the normal conditions in the Commons'
committees could easily frustrate systematic or judicious review of a
legislative proposal. Select committees regularly faced considerable
difficulties in attracting members to their meetings. Individual members
were left to their own initiative to secure attendance on bills they
supported, and the quorum rule often had to be disregarded.[92] As these
committees were usually chaired by the member who first sponsored
the bill and was therefore often interested in securing its passage as
introduced, a low attendance could prevent serious criticism from
occurring at the committee stage.[93] In the case of more important bills
before Committees of the Whole House, criticism was perhaps more
forthcoming, but similar problems obtained. Attendance again proved
a major obstacle. Though the tactic was infrequently used, opponents
of a bill could often block its passage simply by withdrawing and
thereby deny the Commons its required quorum of forty members.[94]

---

[91] The literature is reviewed by Catherine Strateman [Sims] in the introduction to her edition of
The Liverpool Tractate, an Eighteenth-Century Manual on the Procedure of the House of Commons
(New York, 1937). See also Lambert, *Bills and Acts*, chapters 2–4; Thomas, *The House of
Commons*, chapter 3. The most informative contemporary treatment, the *Liverpool Tractate*,
remained in manuscript throughout the period. In his 1781 preface to the second volume of
Precedents of Proceedings in the House of Commons, 4 vols. (London, 1776–96), John Hastell
announced his intention to continue the work with an account of "Proceedings of passing
Bills," but this never appeared.

[92] See Thomas, *The House of Commons*, pp. 119–20 and *Liverpool Tractate*, pp. 25–6.

[93] For a characteristic rehearsal of this charge, see the 1772 criticisms of Sir William Meredith,
cited in Holdsworth, *History of English Law*, XI, 560.

[94] See Thomas, *The House of Commons*, p. 167.

When attendance improved, conditions in the House could hinder a careful, collective examination of a legislative proposal. As James Boswell discovered following his first visit to the House of Commons in 1763, "my respect for it greatly abated by seeing it was such a tumultuous scene."[95] Many of the more notorious scenes of tumult and confusion took place when the Commons assembled as a Committee of the Whole House, where the Speaker's formal authority was absent.[96] Even if these occasions were less frequent and engagingly anarchic than the parliamentary diarists of the period at times suggest, the lack of control over members' attention easily hampered legislative practice. The author of *The Liverpool Tractate*, a contemporary tract on legislative procedure, explained that whatever the formal rules guiding "proceedings at committees," when "this fine theory comes to be reduced into practice," much "inconveniency" and "woeful experience" ensued. Most members had "some favourite point in view which ingrosses their whole attention," so that when these members "meet and jumble their several conceits together," "great care and attention" was required "to prevent one part of your act contradicting another, or even one clause" from "contradicting itself." There was "likewise great danger" that a clause might "creep in late in the day which shall absolutely annul and make void all that went before it." "It must be observed by those who usually attend committees that prudence and patience" were "sometimes not so happily blended in the same person as might be wished."[97]

So little study has been devoted to the legislation created by this process that we still lack any very sophisticated way of categorizing eighteenth-century statute law. The basic contemporary classification of statutes into "private" and "public" acts was a technical distinction referring to the different formulae by which royal assent was given to the acts and the different rules for their promulgation. Although some contemporary commentators sought to identify substantive differences in the technical categories, firm lines of distinction prove impossible to sustain.[98] As private bills were liable to higher parliamentary fees, this consideration naturally distorted the categories, and the categories themselves tended to collapse under the normal processes of parliamentary law-making. For example, those local acts establishing the various municipal agencies and improvement commissions which have attracted the notice of historians of local government, underwent private bill procedure, but were classified as public acts.[99] Other types

---

[95] *Boswell's London Journal 1702–1703*, edited by Frederick A. Pottle (London, 1950), p. 213.
[96] Thomas, *The House of Commons*, pp. 277–81.   [97] *Liverpool Tractate*, pp. 9–10.
[98] See, for example, Blackstone's discussion at 1 *Comm* 85–6.

of privately promoted bills which also followed private bill procedure would be supplied with a public clause and receive assent as public acts. However, at various intervals in the century, the royal printer classified these acts as private statutes.[100] Again, enclosure acts followed private bill procedure and received enactment as private acts. But after 1750, when their numbers soared, parliament began giving them public clauses as well.[101] The courts dispensed with the legislature's own categories and instead distinguished between "general" and "special" acts. This classification, though, had its own ambiguities. Special acts, for example, included statutes concerning "any particular Place or Town," or "one or divers particular counties," or "acts relating to the Bishops only," or even "Acts for the Toleration of Dissenters."[102]

Political historians have often ignored the complications, and instead distinguished roughly between the regular handful of statutes involving clear matters of state, such as the mutiny acts or the annual financial legislation appearing before the standing Commons Committees of Supply and of Ways and Means, and the great mass of statutes which were "private, local and facultative ... [and] only entered by accident into national politics."[103] The distinction conveniently frees political history of the overwhelming bulk of parliamentary law-making, but at the cost of establishing a bizarrely narrow and formalist category of "national" legislation.[104] Standard legislative process regularly blurred the distinction between government and private measures, and even the clearest cases of private statutes should perhaps not be excluded from "national legislation" simply on account of what type of interest promoted them. A sovereign legislature which annually enacts a steadily growing number of private enclosure bills is making public policy as much as if it enacted a general law establishing a separate administrative procedure for the purpose. The eighteenth-century parliament, if not its historians, at least appears to have recognized this. The Duke of Bridgewater's first canal bill of 1762, for example, was introduced, sponsored and adopted as a private act. But the debate on the proposal indicates the House of Commons' appreciation that the implications of its legislative action extended well beyond the locality immediately affected by its decision.[105]

---

[99] Lambert, *Bills and Acts*, pp. 85, 150.   [100] *Ibid.*, pp. 172–8.

[101] *Ibid.*, pp. 176n, 1 / n. For a contemporary assessment on the misleading distinction between private and public acts, see Bentham's remarks in *Comment*, pp. 126–32.

[102] Lambert, *Bills and Acts*, pp. 179–80.   [103] Pares, *George III and the Politicians*, p. 3.

[104] Pares, for example, treated the statutes "imposing customs duties or regulating overseas trade" as only "ostensibly national" since the legislation "often had local implications and M.P.'s handled it as agents of local interests," *ibid.*, p. 3.

[105] See Williams, *Private Bill Procedure*, I, 35–7, and Lambert, *Bills and Acts*, pp. 150–1, 175.

Legal historians have naturally shown greater care over the contents of the statute book. Sir William Holdsworth, two volumes of whose *History of English Law* contains what is still the fullest survey of the eighteenth-century legislation, distinguished among local and private acts, and developed a topical classification of local statutes. The bulk of eighteenth-century acts he surveyed under the headings of "public law" and "commerce and industry." Under the latter class, he treated the "legislative regulation of all branches of commerce and industry," a rather unwieldy grouping of statutes which sought to regulate trades and manufactures, protect military materials and production, secure army and naval recruitment, develop and modify the navigation acts and corn laws, grant monopolies and patents, direct colonial agriculture and control colonial trade, permit enclosure, and structure relations between masters and workmen.[106] Under public law (a category of law less exclusively composed of statutes), he discussed such local legislation as the statutes obtained by vestries, towns, boroughs, and county justices to adjust the administration of laws governing the poor and vagrants, or to levy rates or to secure improvements for highways and streets. "Local government" also accommodated the often similarly purposed acts establishing *ad hoc* bodies such as commissioners of sewers, turnpike trusts, or corporations to administer the poor laws, along with the mass of modifications to the poor laws, settlements laws, highway laws and the statutory additions to the responsibilities of the justices of the peace.[107] Notwithstanding the breadth and untidyness of Holdsworth's main categories, they still had to be supplemented by a more explicitly miscellaneous class of statutes concerning "various branches of the law."[108]

Holdsworth joined previous legal historians in stressing the limited impact of these statutes on legal development. "Eighteenth-century legislation upon various branches of the law and legal doctrine," he confirmed, "though not negligible in bulk, cover[ed] very little ground."[109] His account of how this legislation secured enactment drew explicitly upon the criticisms of nineteenth-century reformers, so that the emphasis remained on the inefficiencies and amateurishness of parliamentary law-making, and the disorder and inconsistencies of its handiwork.[110] Generally absent from his survey were those legislative efforts or procedural innovations which did not conform to the reformers' catalog of past abuses. There was no appreciation of the

---

[106] Holdsworth, *History of English Law*, XI, 388–518.
[107] *Ibid.*, X, 158–236, 256–332.
[108] *Ibid.*, XI, 527–613.
[109] *Ibid.*, XI, 519.   [110] *Ibid.*, XI, 321–87.

elements of professionalization in eighteenth-century legislating, scant mention of parliament's own efforts to take charge of the statute book, and no category for private law reform initiatives of a less than local character.[111]

Our knowledge of such developments is largely owing to the recent researches of Sheila Lambert and to those social historians of crime who have stimulated new interest in the Hanoverian parliaments' legislative sensibilities. It is Lambert's work, above all, that has made possible a serious investigation of the eighteenth-century parliament specifically as a law-making institution.[112] Particularly suggestive are her findings regarding those lawyers whose professional activities included legislative agency. The very presence in London of a group of private lawyers who served as legislative draftsmen and who monitored the progress of bills through the legislature in itself suggests that parliamentary legislation was a more professional and less haphazard enterprise than conventionally allowed. Lambert's discovery of the practice of the most successful legislative agent in the years 1732–62, a Bencher of Lincoln's Inn named Robert Harper, and her account of the literally hundreds of bills he drew and their remarkable rate of enactment indicates considerable predictability and stability in the law-making process.[113] Not only was Harper engaged by private parties seeking estate or enclosure bills, but he also drafted more public bills concerning copyright and poor laws, and even government initiated legislation.[114] The range conforms to a system of legislating which readily mixed private and government involvement, and in which parliament as a body most often was responding to discrete legislative initiatives.[115] The institutional and professional procedures through which this occurred would offer no necessary limit to the amount of legislation produced, nor ensure consistency and co-ordination among particular enactments. Yet even here, Lambert has insisted on the seriousness of parliament's consideration of specific legislative proposals. Nor, it appears, was the legislature immune to the arguments of those urging a more systematic effort to review and order its legislative creation. In 1751, for example, the Commons appointed four select

---

[111] Holdsworth generally confined his discussion of eighteenth-century reform to the 1705–06 Act for the Amendment of Law, and otherwise emphasized the experimental value for future reform of various local acts. See *History of English Law*, X, 332–9 and XI, 519–27, 372n.

[112] This includes her editorship of the *House of Commons Sessional Papers of the Eighteenth Century* [facsimile edn], 147 vols. (Wilmington, Del., 1975–7), as well as her monograph, *Bills and Acts*.

[113] *Bills and Acts*, pp. 7–8, 11.   [114] *Ibid.*, pp. 65, 76–7, 198–225.

[115] *Ibid.*, pp. 51, 71–7. See also Williams, *Clerical Organization*, pp. 159–79, for further details on the conduct of government legislation in the Commons.

committees charged with the task of inspecting the great numbers of acts on trade, highways, felonies and the poor, as well as the fee structure on private bills. During the same period, the Expiring Laws Committee was particularly active and promoted legislation which, in effect, turned all the temporary penal acts into permanent law. The committee on the trade laws eventually reported that·the subject was too voluminous for any proposals to be made, and none of the other committees fared much better in generating statutes.[116] Still, the neglected episode reveals a fairly ambitious project of reform, and later in the century less sweeping efforts proved more fruitful.[117]

Further insights into the nature of eighteenth-century statute have followed from the exploration of what has always appeared the most dramatic and important manifestation of parliament's legislative activism: its creation of "one of the bloodiest criminal codes in Europe."[118] Some of the most creative and influential of recent writing on eighteenth-century society has highlighted the importance of "the bloody code" to understanding the peculiar structure and operation of authority and social power in Hanoverian England.[119] Of greatest interest for our discussion, however, are those contributions to the study of eighteenth-century crime and penal law which have forced us to reconsider just what sort of "great fact" confronts us in the form of this "flood of legislation."[120] Ambiguities immediately arise over quite what is meant by the familiar charge that the legal system underwent, in Blackstone's phrase, a "vast increase of capital punishment." As John Langbein has noted, "the multiplication of capital statutes" did not leave England with "two hundred separate crimes in the modern sense that could be punished with death." Rather, in the absence of "general definitions" for categories of crimes, parliament was

---

[116] *Commons Sessional Papers*, I, 39–41 (Lambert's introduction). For the committee on the penal laws, see also J. M. Beattie, *Crime and the Courts in England 1660–1800* (Princeton, 1986), pp. 520–30.

[117] See the examples of statute consolidation cited by Holdsworth, *History of English Law*, XI, 372n.

[118] Hay, "Property, Authority and the Criminal Law," in Douglas Hay *et al.*, *Albion's Fatal Tree: Crime and Society in Eighteenth-Century England* (London, 1975), p. 19.

[119] See Hay, "Property, Authority and the Criminal Law," pp. 17–26, and E. P. Thompson, *Whigs and Hunters. The Origin of the Black Act* (London, 1975). For important criticisms of the account of law developed in these works, see Peter King, "Decision-Makers and Decision-Making in the English Criminal Law, 1750–1800," *Historical Journal*, XXVII (1984), 25–58; John H. Langbein, "*Albion's* Fatal Flaws," *Past and Present*, XCVII (1983), 96–120; and the series of articles by John Styles: "Criminal Records," *The Historical Journal*, XX (1967), 977–81; "Our Traitorous Money Lenders," in Brewer and Styles, *An Ungovernable People*; and "Embezzlement, Industry and the Law in England, 1500–1800," in Maxime Berg, Pat Hudson, and Michael Sonenscher (eds.), *Manufacture in Town and Country before the Factory* (Cambridge, 1983), pp. 173–210.

[120] Hay, "Property, Authority and the Criminal Law," p. 18.

"constantly having to add particulars in order to compensate for the want of generality."[121] A second ambiguity appears over the presumed change in legislative attitudes prompting the unprecedented increase in the number of capital acts. It was in the sixteenth century that the legislative expedient was introduced of removing the privilege of benefit of clergy from certain felonies and thereby making capital such major crimes as murder, robbery, burglary, horse-theft and some forms of house-breaking. In the 1690s the device was again adopted when parliament, as part of a more general review and adjustment of the criminal justice system, enacted several statutes extending capital punishment to a variety of property offences by removing benefit of clergy. Much of the later mass of eighteenth-century capital acts followed this established practice, removing clergy from particular offences – such as sheep-stealing, thefts on rivers, stealing black lead from mines – in response to specific outbreaks of crime. However, when the death sentence was actually inflicted in these years, it was still the sixteenth-century statutes which were usually being applied.[122]

A third, crucial ambiguity emerges over the sort of penal policy these capital statutes sustained. "The history of punishment over the century and a half after 1660," John Beattie explains, "is most notably the story not of the enlargement of the capital code that is so frequently emphasized (important as that is) but of the remarkable broadening of secondary punishments."[123] In the terms of Beattie's challenging interpretation, the "bloody code" unevenly extended the punishment of last resort in a penal system which was being transformed by the introduction of, and increasing reliance upon the new secondary punishments of transportation and imprisonment. This account, as Beattie has shown, is an extensive revision of the usual narrative of England's penal history and, thus, of the potential explanations for the "bloody code."[124] Indeed, on the basis of this study we would do well to abandon "the eighteenth century" as a useful unit for discussing these legal developments. But, the same interpretation also issues an important challenge to conventional treatments of parliament's law-making. The crucial legislative episodes in the transformation of England's penal system in Beattie's presentation, such as the 1718 Transportation Act, the 1752 Murder Act or the 1779 Penitentiary Act, did not occur in the form of random, local initiatives entering the statute book through customary fits of parliamentary absent-minded-ness. Instead, these represented clear public measures, enacted amidst

---

[121] Langbein, "*Albion's* Fatal Flaws," p. 118.
[122] See Beattie, *Crime and the Courts*, pp. 141–7, 451–6, 495–500, 513–9.
[123] *Ibid.*, pp. 450–1. [124] *Ibid.*, pp. 620–1.

extended debate, often as part of a more general assessment of criminal law and penal policy.[125] These acts were scarcely typical eighteenth-century enactments, but their example is perhaps sufficient to caution against taking too widely the familiar and still-repeated charges of parliament's "extraordinarily incompetent" efforts "to use its legislative powers," and the "mood of unrivaled assurance and complacency" in which it discharged its law-making responsibilities.[126]

This recent scholarship instructs us of the important ways in which eighteenth-century parliamentary law-making was not simply a matter of "incapacity and inattention." It, however, leaves untouched the brute fact of a statute book "swelled to ten times a larger bulk" since the time of Sir Edward Coke and the profound contemporary disquiet over the implications of this development. "We have it from the highest authority, that, in the multitude of counsellors there is safety," Lord Hardwicke observed in his final year on the Woolsack, "but we in this nation may from experience say, that in the multitude of legislators there is confusion; for our statute books are increased to such an enormous size, that they confound every man who is obliged to look into them."[127] And this disturbing consequence of stable parliamentary government featured critically in contemporary perceptions of the law. On the one hand was parliament's emergence as an active legislative institution. As the *London Magazine* put it in a 1770 article on "Forms of Parliament," "the chief business of Parliament is to make new laws, revive or abrogate old ones."[128] On the other hand were the perceived failures of parliament in the discharge of its "chief business." The author of *The Liverpool Tractate* found he could not "help setting out of the way" to comment on the harsher realities of legislating in eighteenth-century Britain. "The truth of this," he reported, "will be evident to any one who looks into the House when in a Committee about nine o'clock at night, and I believe it is a surprise to every one who knows how Laws are made to find things no worse than they are."[129]

Even those in the eighteenth century who boasted much less intimate knowledge of "how Laws are made" could still be confident that things were already quite bad enough. What is next to be explored is the range and the character of the legal speculation that attended to the perceived failures of the statute law.

---

[125] *Ibid.*, pp. 470–83, 500–13, 520–30, 573–82.

[126] P. S. Atiyah, *The Rise and Fall of Freedom of Contract* (Oxford, 1979), p. 92, and Hay, "Property, Authority and the Criminal Law," p. 19.

[127] Hardwicke's speech to the House of Lords, cited in Holdsworth, *History of English Law*, XI, 374.

[128] Cited in Thomas, *House of Commons*, p. 45.   [129] *Liverpool Tractate*, pp. 9–10.

I

Blackstone and the *Commentaries*

1

◁ ═══════════════════════════════════ ▷

The laws of England

England in the eighteenth century witnessed the composition of a single great classic of law which overshadowed all other contemporary legal writing, Sir William Blackstone's *Commentaries on the Laws of England*. "It has been said," one of Blackstone's nineteenth-century editors reported, "that this work...is the most valuable which has ever been furnished to the public by the labour of any individual."[1] According to Maitland, within a period of five hundred years only two lawyers proved capable of producing a full synthetic statement of the law in England: Bracton and Sir William Blackstone.[2] So overwhelming was the achievement of the *Commentaries* that the literary creation nearly consumed the identity of its author. Thus Blackstone received notice in numerous law tracts and at Westminster Hall simply as "the learned Commentator on the Laws of England."

The remarkable success of the *Commentaries* is quickly revealed in its record of publication.[3] The work was based on a course of lectures which Blackstone began delivering at Oxford in 1753. This was the first occasion on which English law was taught at an English university, and Blackstone designed a set of lectures that would provide "a general map of the law." Between 1765 and 1769 this map was published as the four-volume *Commentaries on the Laws of England*. Eight editions quickly followed before Blackstone's death in 1780. Between 1783 and 1849 the *Commentaries*, by then acknowledged "an essential part of every Gentleman's library," went through another fifteen editions.[4] At mid nineteenth century, the work received extensive revision at the hands

---

[1] 1 *Comm* vii (editorial preface).
[2] F. W. Maitland (ed.), *Bracton's Note Book*, 3 vols. (London, 1887), I, 8 (editorial introduction).
[3] For details on the first eight editions of the *Commentaries*, see William Hammond (ed.), *Blackstone's Commentaries on the Laws of England*, 4 vols. (San Francisco, 1890) and for the nineteenth-century editions, see A. V. Dicey, "Blackstone's *Commentaries*," *Cambridge Law Journal*, IV (1932), 286–307.
[4] Blackstone, *Commentaries on the Laws of England*, 4 vols., ed. Edward Christian (London, 1803), I, x (editorial advertisement).

of H. J. Stephen, and in this form continued to be republished through to the twentieth century.

The *Commentaries* was of course more than an eighteenth-century best-seller, more indeed than a reliable introduction to law in England. The primary and lasting value of the work rested upon Blackstone's consummate success in presenting English law as a rational and coherent system. In a characteristic expression of eighteenth-century Enlightenment, Blackstone achieved for the laws of England what others had secured for the secrets of revealed religion or the mysteries of the natural world: a technical and arcane body of knowledge, previously the exclusive domain of a professional caste, had been reduced to first principles, elegantly displayed and rendered comprehensible for a polite audience.

Few have supposed the mantle of the Enlightenment *philosophe* an appropriate garb for Sir William Blackstone. Yet he himself, in his 1758 inaugural lecture as Vinerian professor which subsequently served to introduce the *Commentaries*, chose to present his enterprise by invoking that self-conscious daring of the intellect which distinguished the age, in the words of his most famous critic, "in which knowledge is rapidly advancing towards perfection."[5] If the study of English law had previously been excluded from university education, this was the legacy of "monastic prejudice" which only "a deplorable narrowness of mind" could wish to see perpetuated. "To the praise of this age," Blackstone rejoiced, "a more open and generous way of thinking begins now universally to prevail," and he could therefore "safely affirm" that no subject "how *unusual* soever" was "improper to be *taught* in this place, which is proper for a gentleman to *learn*." Moreover, since law was "a science" that distinguished "the criterions of right and wrong," that employed the "noblest faculties of the soul," and that exerted the "cardinal virtues of the heart," it proved a "matter of astonishment and concern" that it was ever "deemed unnecessary to be studied in a university." Indeed, "if it were not before an object of academical knowledge, it was high time to make it one."[6]

Blackstone's efforts to bring the study of English law to Oxford formed part of a broader concern, which he shared with other legal writers, to establish the law's credentials as a subject of general learning. As S. F. C. Milsom has stressed, the *Commentaries* was without precedent in the canon of English legal letters, and many of the most remarkable and admired features of the work can be seen to reflect the special demands of Blackstone's situation in "addressing laymen" and

---

[5] *Fragment*, p. 393.   [6] 1 *Comm* 26–7.

seeking to give them "an overall view" of the legal system "from the outside."[7] There was first the sheer literary grace and accomplishment of the work. Blackstone, in the terms of Bentham's famous concession, was the "first of all institutional writers" to teach "Jurisprudence to speak the language of the Scholar and the Gentleman."[8] "The *Commentaries*," as Dicey later put it, "live by their style."[9] Equally dramatic was Blackstone's unrivaled achievement in presenting the law as an ordered and rational body of knowledge. Whereas the legal texts of "our ancient writers," Blackstone observed, revealed a "very immethodical arrangement," his special "endeavour" in the *Commentaries* was "to examine" the law's "solid foundations, to mark out its extensive plan, to explain the use and distribution of its parts, and from the harmonious concurrence of those several parts to demonstrate the elegant proportion of the whole."[10] This endeavour likewise recalls Blackstone's concern to reach a non-professional audience, for as Bentham emphasized in this context, "among the most difficult and most important of the functions of the *demonstrator* is the business of *arrangement*."[11]

In fact, for Blackstone, this business of arrangement constituted a more imposing and central challenge than simply that of finding a suitable structure for the exposition of the law. For those outside the legal profession, few aspects of English law were so conspicuous as its repellent technicalities and unfathomable intricacies – "the gloomy labyrinth," in the young Gibbon's frustrated judgment.[12] On this basis, English law was compared unfavourably with Roman jurisprudence, the study of which Blackstone enviously noted, "has ever been deservedly considered as no small accomplishment of a gentleman," while the English "system of laws" had been "neglected and even unknown."[13] The reasons for the neglect were not difficult to discern. "It has been thought impracticable to bring the Laws of England into a *Method*," explained an earlier eighteenth-century commentator, "and therefore a Prejudice has been taken up Against the Study of our Laws, even by Men of Parts and Learning."[14] Moreover, legal writers were equally clear that unless English law did indeed display what in this context Matthew Hale described as "method, order and apt distri-

---

[7] S. F. C. Milsom, "The Nature of Blackstone's Achievement," *Oxford Journal of Legal Studies*, I (1981), 3.   [8] *Fragment*, p. 413.

[9] Dicey, "Blackstone's *Commentaries*," p. 294.

[10] 3 *Comm* 265–6; 4 *Comm* 443.   [11] *Fragment*, p. 414.

[12] *Edward Gibbon's Autobiography* (1827), ed. M. M. Reese (London, 1971), p. 59.

[13] 1 *Comm* 5.

[14] Thomas Wood, *An Institute of the Laws of England, or The Laws of England in their Natural Order, according to Common Use* (1720), 4th edn, corrected (Dublin, 1724), p. i.

butions,"[15] then it could not be ranked among the authentic objects of rational comprehension. According to the case set out by Sir William Jones in 1781, if the law was "merely an unconnected series of decrees and ordinances" it would remain a useful subject, "though its dignity be lessened." But if "Law *be* a *Science*" and so "claim an exalted rank in the empire of *reason*," then "it must be founded on principle," which further meant that "the great system of jurisprudence, like that of the Universe," had to consist "of many subordinate systems," all "connected by nice links and beautiful dependencies" and each "reducible to a few plain *elements*."[16]

Blackstone has rarely earned notice for his methodological novelty or sophistication. He "was not a rigorous thinker," Daniel J. Boorstin concluded; and when his legal methods are now examined, the discussion can confidently proceed in the presumption that as a theorist "Blackstone is supremely unconvincing."[17] Nonetheless, Blackstone showed an unusual degree of self-consciousness and confidence over his conceptualization of the English legal system, and in the *Commentaries* especially drew attention to the importance of the classificatory features of his work. As a law student, he boasted that he had made himself "pretty well master" of the law in but "two years," a feat due to his success in having "reduced [the law] to a system."[18] In the *Commentaries*, he defended his decision to include much "obsolete and abstruse learning" – such as "prosecuting any real action for land by writ of *entry*, *assise*, *formedon*, writ of *right*, or otherwise" – for the sake of exhibiting "the whole fabric together," without which it was "impossible to form any clear idea of the meaning and connection of those disjointed parts, which still form a considerable branch of the modern law."[19]

Most revealing of Blackstone's preoccupation with method and arrangement were his prefatory remarks to his outline preview of the *Commentaries*, the *Analysis of the Laws of England*. There he critically considered the previous attempts at "reducing our Laws to a System," starting with an appreciative notice of "Glanvil and Bracton, Britton

---

[15] Matthew Hale, Preface to *Un Abridgment des plusieurs Cases et Resolutions del Common Ley...per Henry Rolle* (London, 1668), p. 6.

[16] William Jones, *An Essay on the Law of Bailments* (London, 1781), p. 123. See also Wynne, *Eunomus*, I, 6–7 and II, 52–7.

[17] Daniel J. Boorstin, *The Mysterious Science of Law (An Essay on Blackstone's "Commentaries")* (Cambridge, Mass., 1941), p. 189; Duncan Kennedy, "The Structure of Blackstone's *Commentaries*," *Buffalo Law Review*, V (1979), 211.

[18] The anecdote comes from "a close college friend" and is presented in I. G. Doolittle, "Sir William Blackstone and his *Commentaries on the Laws of England* (1765–69): A Biographical Approach," *Oxford Journal of Legal Studies*, III (1983), 110.

[19] 3 *Comm* 196.

and the author of Fleta," and then moving on to rebuke the efforts of Fitzherbert and Brooke "and the subsequent Authors of *Abridgments*," criticize the approaches of Bacon, Coke and Cowel, praise the example of Finch, and finally to identify Matthew Hale's own *Analysis* as "the most natural and scientifical" of "all the Schemes hitherto made public for digesting the Laws of England" and Blackstone's chosen model. The brief survey not only recorded the first of Blackstone's several profound debts to Hale's jurisprudence, but also made plain his sensitivity to the past failings of the profession to construct a rational arrangement of English law. This was one of the special areas of legal learning in which Blackstone took pains to present himself as the author of "a Method in many respects totally new."[20]

For his contemporary readers, moreover, Blackstone's organization and conceptualization of the system of law in England proved a revelation, as the *Commentaries* was found to have furnished reason and erudition where confusion and technicality hitherto obtained. Lord Chief Justice Mansfield, when asked to recommend reading for a future lawyer, confidently cited "Mr. Blackstone's *Commentaries*" – "*There* [he] will find analytical reasoning diffused in a pleasing and perspicuous style. *There* he may imbibe imperceptibly the first principles on which our excellent laws are founded, and THERE he may become acquainted with an uncouth crabbed author, Coke upon Littleton, who has disappointed many a Tyro, but who cannot fail to please in modern dress."[21] In similar spirit, Sir William Meredith mobilized the familiar rhetoric of the Enlightenment to characterize and extol Blackstone's achievement – "Proud am I to repeat my Admiration of your *Commentaries*... which have introduced to our acquaintance a system that was most important for every man to know; yet, till you brought

---

[20] William Blackstone, *An Analysis of the Laws of England* (London, 1756), pp. v–viii. On the general problem of rational arrangement in English legal writing, see A. W. B. Simpson, "The Rise and Fall of the Legal Treatise: Legal Principles and the Forms of Legal Literature," *University of Chicago Law Review*, XLVIII (1981), especially 636–41, 655, and Milsom, "Blackstone's Achievement." The seventeenth-century models are reviewed in Barbara J. Shapiro, "Law and Science in Seventeenth-Century England," *Stanford Law Review*, XXI (1969), 727–66, and Wilfrid Prest provides an exemplary discussion of one important effort in "The Dialectical Origins of Finch's *Law*," *Cambridge Law Journal*, XXXVI (1977), 326–52. Some of the most challenging of current treatments of Blackstone's methods have linked the *Commentaries* to the tradition of civilian Institutional treatises. See O. F. Robinson, T. D. Fergus, W. M. Gordon, *An Introduction to European Legal History* (Abingdon, Oxon., 1985), pp. 374–6, 385, and especially Michael Lobban, "Blackstone and the Science of Law," *Historical Journal*, XXX (1987), 311–35, and John W. Cairns, "Blackstone, An English Institutist: Legal Literature and the Rise of the Nation State," *Oxford Journal of Legal Studies*, IV (1984), 318–60, which details the differences between Hale and Blackstone at pp. 347–50.

[21] Cited in John Holliday, *The Life of William late Earl of Mansfield* (London, 1797), pp. 89–90.

it from Darkness into Light, had been as carefully secreted from common understanding, as the Mysteries of Religion ever were."[22]

Blackstone's prestigious "map" of the English legal system divided the law into four parts, each comprising one volume of the *Commentaries*. Book One, "Of the Rights of Persons," discussed civil rights and constitutional matters. Book Two, "Of the Rights of Things," dealt with property law. Book Three, "Of Private Wrongs," summarized the law of civil offences. Book Four, "Of Public Wrongs," treated penal law. Although the substance of the *Commentaries* was devoted to the laws of England, Blackstone only embarked on this discussion following an account "Of the Nature of Laws in general." This section set out the formal legal theory upon which the detailed treatment of English law was based.

Blackstone defined all law as a "rule of action, which is prescribed by some superior, and which the inferior is bound to obey."[23] The law of nature was identified with God's will: "when He created man, and endued him with free will," God "laid down certain immutable laws of human nature" which "regulated and restrained" that free will, and "gave [man] also the faculty of reason to discover the purport of those laws."[24] "This law of nature, being coeval with mankind and dictated by God himself," in turn, provided the ethical foundation for all other law.

> It is binding over all the globe, in all countries, and at all times: no human laws are of any validity, if contrary to this; and such of them as are valid derive all their force, and all their authority, mediately or immediately, from this original.[25]

Hence, in the hypothetical case of a human law commanding individuals to commit murder, Blackstone concluded that "we are bound to transgress that human law, or else we must offend both the natural and the divine."[26] Blackstone then completed this presentation by formally defining "municipal laws" – the law established in a particular civil community – as "a rule of civil conduct prescribed by the supreme power in a state, commanding what is right and prohibiting what is wrong."[27]

---

[22] William Meredith, *Letter to Dr. Blackstone by the Author of the Question Stated, to which is prefixed, Dr. Blackstone's Letter to Sir William Meredith* (London, 1770), p. 2. For other, like-minded, contemporary evaluations, see Thomas Bever, *A Discourse on the Study of Jurisprudence and the Civil Law* (Oxford, 1766), pp. 35–36, and Robert Joseph Pothier, *A Treatise on the Law of Obligations or Contracts*, translation, introduction and notes by William David Evans, 2 vols. (London, 1806), I, 75 (editorial introduction).

[23] 1 *Comm* 38.   [24] 1 *Comm* 39–40.   [25] 1 *Comm* 41.

[26] 1 *Comm* 42–3.   [27] 1 *Comm* 44.

Although most of Blackstone's remarks on natural law were concentrated in this initial discussion, he returned to these doctrines frequently in treating English law. He explained the origins of civil society through a contractarian transfer of natural rights, these rights, like the law of nature, being held incapable of complete abridgement by the municipal law. He invoked the law of nature when presenting the rights of foreign ambassadors and the royal prerogative in declaring war. His account of the duties of parents to their children involved further reference to the laws of nature, as did his analysis of the civil offences against religion. He began his statement of English property law with a discussion of property rights in the state of nature, and his account of civil injuries recalled his earlier catalogue of natural rights. The fourth volume of the *Commentaries* introduced penal law with an explanation of society's right to punish, which Blackstone derived from a natural right to punish offences against the law of nature.[28]

All this confirms the rather obvious point that Blackstone did not presume to comment on English law without first equipping the commentary with the appropriate philosophical introduction, which here entailed a discussion of "what we call ethics or natural law."[29] Its inclusion, once more, reflected the special demands created by his audience and the specific type of legal literature he designed for it. As Blackstone explained at the outset of a chapter-length exploration of the rights of nature to property, such "enquiries, it must be owned, would be useless and even troublesome in common life" and might be omitted altogether "when law is to be considered" solely as "a matter of practice." However, when law was treated "as a rational science," then it was never "improper or useless to examine more deeply the rudiments and grounds" of "positive constitutions," and this meant an investigation of how positive rules had their "foundation in nature or in natural law."[30]

For the content of his natural law doctrines Blackstone cited such standard authorities as Grotius, Pufendorf, Locke, Barbeyrac and Montesquieu, and through these references he ensured that the science of English law would not be found insularly ignorant of the prestigious and influential body of Grotian natural law theory. Edward Christian, one of Blackstone's eighteenth-century editors, treated these sections of the *Commentaries* as a conventional borrowing of the established seventeenth- and eighteenth-century natural jurists, and later writers, in turn, cited Blackstone as an authority of the natural law foundations of

[28] See: 1 *Comm* 47–48, 123–6, 1 *Comm* 253–4, 257–8, 1 *Comm* 446–7, 4 *Comm* 41, 2 *Comm* 1–15, 3 *Comm* 119, 4 *Comm* 7–8.
[29] 1 *Comm* 41.   [30] 2 *Comm* 2.

English law.[31] Virtually every other eighteenth-century legal author who, like Blackstone, aimed his work beyond a purely professional audience likewise invoked natural law arguments. Thomas Wood, for example, presented the "law of Nature" as the first of six "principal foundations" of the law in England, citing the testimony of St. German and invoking a version of Coke's dictum that "nothing that is contrary to Reason is consonant to Law."[32] Edward Wynne maintained further that "the Law of Nature" had "ever been considered as part of the Common Law."[33] Richard Wooddeson insisted not only that natural law was the ultimate ethical foundation of law in England, but that "civil legislators have no rightful authority to forbid what the law of nature injoins, or to injoin what that forbids."[34] Through these claims, legal writers joined Blackstone in sustaining both a conventional understanding of the ethical sources of English law and the more general orthodoxy that law itself, in the words of a practical manual of the period, had always to be recognized as "a moral science, since the end of all law is justice; and justice, in the most extensive sense of the word, differs little from virtue itself."[35]

None of these contemporary commonplaces would warrant retailing at such length were it not for the amount of past interpretative energy that has been devoted to showing that what Blackstone wrote about the law of nature was unnecessary or inconsistent or even unintended. In these accounts, Blackstone often appears as a muddled or irresponsibly casual thinker who would have avoided embarrassment simply by jettisoning the law of nature. These interpretations cannot be sustained, but they still deserve careful examination as they raise quite basic issues about the character of English legal theory during this period.

Ernest Barker produced the most sweeping case against natural law theory in maintaining that "the English thinkers and lawyers of the eighteenth century have little regard for natural law and natural rights," as was only fitting since "natural law is generally repugnant to the genius of English legal thought." It was, admittedly, therefore rather "curious and even paradoxical" to find such concepts "in the

---

[31] Blackstone's use of continental authorities is discussed in Paul Lucas, "*Ex parte* Sir William Blackstone, 'Plagiarist'; A Note on Blackstone and Natural Law," *American Journal of Legal History*, VII (1963), 142–58; F. T. H. Fletcher, *Montesquieu and English Politics, 1750–1800* (London, 1939), p. 121, and Ernest Barker, *Essays on Government*, 2nd edn (Oxford, 1951), pp. 129ff. For a later use of Blackstone's natural law doctrine, see Ballow[?], *Treatise of Equity*, I, 9 (Fonblanque's note).

[32] Wood, *Institute of the Laws of England*, p. 4. [33] Wynne, *Eunomus*, III, 112.

[34] Richard Wooddeson, *Elements of Jurisprudence* (London, 1783), p. 32. See also Robert Chambers, *A Course of Lectures on the English Law* (1767–73), ed. Thomas M. Curley, 2 vols. (Madison, Wis., 1986), I, 83–94, 116.

[35] Ballow[?], *Treatise of Equity*, I, 1.

pages of the sober Blackstone," but these were examples of "the ghost of the idea of natural law" which "occasionally" in the period "haunt[ed] English thought."[36] Enough perhaps has been already presented to indicate that in natural law theory eighteenth-century lawyers were dealing with a more substantial earthly presence than Barker's judgments allow. At Blackstone's Oxford, Grotius and Pufendorf were the acknowledged "ornaments of the last century" and the established "fathers of modern jurisprudence,"[37] and thanks to several important recent studies, we are well placed to recognize the extensive impact of Grotian natural jurisprudence on the social thought of seventeenth- and eighteenth-century Britain and Europe.[38]

In the case of the *Commentaries*, one of the oddest consequences of dismissing natural law theory is that the rejection eliminates the ethical support for what Blackstone celebrated as the single most important attribute that distinguished and glorified the system of law in England. "The idea and practice of this political or civil liberty," Blackstone claimed, "flourish in their highest vigour in these kingdoms, where it falls little short of perfection."[39] The manner in which "this inestimable blessing" of civil liberty was secured and perfected formed a connective theme of the *Commentaries*, the repeated point of homage in Blackstone's treatment of customary law, constitutional arrangements, legal process, and English legal history. There was of course no novelty in Blackstone's praise of English liberty, or in his finding such matters operating "very differently" among "the modern constitutions of other states."[40] What needs emphasis, though, is the relationship between the celebration of civil freedom and the general ethical theory of the *Commentaries*. Civil liberty, such as that which England so uniquely enjoyed, was "no other than natural liberty so far restrained by human laws (and no farther) as is necessary and expedient for the general advantage of the public." The core of natural liberty was constituted by the "absolute rights of man" which, like the law of nature

---

[36] Barker, *Traditions of Civility*, pp. 309, 311, 318–19.

[37] See Bever, *Discourse on the Study of Jurisprudence*, pp. 35–6n.

[38] In addition to the material cited above in the Introduction at n46, see Duncan Forbes, *Hume's Philosophical Politics* (Cambridge, 1975), chapters 1–2; Knud Haakonssen, *The Science of a Legislator: The Natural Jurisprudence of David Hume and Adam Smith* (Cambridge, 1981). For seventeenth-century English legal and political thought, see Tuck, *Natural Rights Theories*, chapters 3–6, and James Tully, *A Discourse on Property. John Locke and his Adversaries* (Cambridge, 1980). Knud Haakonssen's "Hugo Grotius and the History of Political Thought," *Political Theory*, XIII (1985), 239–65, surveys the implications of Grotius' theory for broader developments in eighteenth-century moral and social thought. For a valuable late-eighteenth century appraisal see, James Mackintosh, *A Discourse on the Study of the Law of Nature and Nations* (1799), in *Miscellaneous Works of... James Mackintosh*, 3 vols. (London, 1846), I, 339–87.

[39] 1 *Comm* 126–7.   [40] 1 *Comm* 127.

itself, represented "one of the gifts of God to man at his creation, when he endued him with the faculty of free will." When man entered into society, he gave up the "power of acting as one thinks fit" subject solely to "the law of nature," and obtained thereby civil security and the "advantages of mutual commerce." But whatever the diverse and manifest benefits of organized social life, the divinely orchestrated condition of natural liberty established that "the principal aim of society" remained "to protect individuals in the enjoyment of those absolute rights, which were vested in them by the immutable laws of nature."[41] These ethical doctrines in turn meant that when Blackstone proudly invoked Montesquieu's conclusion "that the English is the only nation in the world where political or civil liberty is the direct end of its constitution,"[42] he celebrated the English system in a particularly ambitious and momentous fashion. For by the "immutable laws of nature" the political peculiarity of the English system was elevated to nothing less than the realization of the "principal aim" of all organized civil association.

While these considerations point to the cost of eliminating the law of nature from the *Commentaries*, they still leave open the separate question of how consistent Blackstone's natural law teaching was with the rest of his legal doctrines. It is in respect of his specific theory of English law that critics have found his natural law precepts so unsatisfactory, perceiving them to be compromised by his historical conception of common law and contradicted by his conception of parliamentary sovereignty.

According to one group of scholars, Blackstone viewed law as an essentially historical and cultural phenomenon, and his notion of legal legitimacy centered on his appreciation of the law's status as an historically refined body of rules peculiarly adapted to English society. Although Blackstone discussed "eternal, immutable laws of good and evil,"[43] he had scant interest in rigorous metaphysical theories of law. Holdsworth, for example, maintained that Blackstone "preferred to build upon the stable foundation of the concrete facts of life" and not "upon the shifting sands of the conflicting theories of ingenious philosophers." Like Edmund Burke, he "was essentially historically minded" and showed "an intense reverence for the constitution and the law which had gradually been evolved through the centuries."[44]

---

[41] 1 *Comm* 123–6.   [42] 1 *Comm* 145.   [43] 1 *Comm* 40.

[44] Holdsworth, *History of English Law*, XIII, 127, and "Gibbon, Blackstone and Bentham," *Law Quarterly Review*, LII (1936), 53. For similar evaluations, see Barker, *Traditions of Civility*, pp. 311–12, and Daniel J. Boorstin, *The Mysterious Science of Law* (Cambridge, Mass., 1941), pp. 72–4.

In emphasizing this concern with law and history, Holdsworth highlighted a prominent feature of the *Commentaries* and one of the established preoccupations of English legal thought. This was the common lawyers' traditional understanding of the fundamentals of English law in terms of a body of legal practices which had originated in the Saxon era and which had been preserved without break through the vicissitudes of the kingdom's history. As Pocock demonstrated in his classic discussion of the seventeenth-century career of "the ancient constitution," this approach to English law carried potent political implications. Just as English lawyers interpreted their civil liberties as an ancient body of historic rights, so their attitude to constitutional norms and political authority turned on their reading of the past.[45] Hence, there were special incentives for an English lawyer to consider the law in an historical fashion, and Blackstone responded fully to them, recognizing both the legal and political importance of treating English law as an historical entity. He concluded the *Commentaries* with a separate chapter on "the Rise, Progress and Gradual Improvements of the Laws of England" and committed himself to a full litany of what Duncan Forbes has styled the tenets of "vulgar whiggism." Thus, as examples, he described trial by jury as an immemorial common law right, insisted that the Norman conquest had not violated constitutional continuity, and viewed Magna Carta as a straightforward confirmation of Anglo-Saxon liberties.[46]

In presenting his legal history, Blackstone enjoyed distinct advantages over his predecessors. In the seventeenth century the actual historical identity of English law remained in fierce dispute, but Blackstone was quick to invoke the legacy of 1688 to avoid such difficulties. When discussing the historical character of England's original contract between king and subject, he pragmatically observed that "whatever doubts" were hitherto brought to the subject "by weak and scrupulous minds," these "must now entirely cease, especially with regard to every prince who hath reigned since the year 1688."[47] In his treatment of Magna Carta he confidently, and rather inaccurately alleged that "it is agreed by all our historians" that the charter reaffirmed "the ancient customs of the realm," meaning "the old

---

[45] Pocock, *Ancient Constitution and the Feudal Law.*
[46] See Forbes, *Hume's Philosophical Politics*, pp. 251–3. The creativity and sophistication of Blackstone's legal history has been canvassed recently in a valuable study by Robert Willman, "Blackstone and the 'Theoretical Perfection' of English Law in the Reign of Charles II," *Historical Journal*, XXVI (1983), 39–70, though since challenged by John W. Cairns, "Blackstone, the Ancient Constitution and the Feudal Law," *Historical Journal*, XXVIII (1985), 711–17.
[47] 1 *Comm* 233.

common law which was established under the Saxon princes."[48] In addition to the valuable security furnished by the Glorious Revolution, Blackstone drew further advantage and stimulus from the increasingly sophisticated models of legal history produced by his contemporaries, and exemplified in the works of Montesquieu, Daines Barrington and Lord Kames. As Kames in particular instructed, all legal systems demanded historical examination, for law only became "a rational study" when it was "traced historically."[49]

In addition to these ideologically charged concerns, Blackstone's interest in history in the *Commentaries* also reflected a more mundane matter. This was, quite simply, the difficulty of providing an effective explanation of the system of law in eighteenth-century England without recourse to "the antiquities of our English jurisprudence." "The obsolete doctrines of our laws," Blackstone explained, "are frequently the foundation upon which what remains is erected," so that it was altogether "impracticable to comprehend many rules of the modern law, in a scholarlike scientifical manner, without having recourse to the ancient."[50] Some of these "antiquities" were of profound import, as in the case of the origins of the parliament. Many were relatively trivial. But even the less dramatic examples revealed the unavoidable need for an historical exposition of the law. Thus, when Blackstone covered the rule of property inheritance that estates "shall lineally descend" but "never lineally ascend" – a rule peculiar to English law and often criticized for violating "maxims of equity and natural justice" – he stressed that it was necessary to consider "the occasion of introducing" the rule "into our laws" in order to show its being "founded upon very good reason." And such reason, "drawn from the history of the rule itself," was plainly "more satisfactory than that quaint one of Bracton, adopted by Sir Edward Coke, which regulates the descent of lands according to the laws of gravitation."[51]

The *Commentaries* accordingly discloses Blackstone's ready commitment to an extensively historical treatment of English law. Indeed, for Dicey, Blackstone's skill and judgment were nowhere more elegantly displayed than in "his unrivaled success at blending the history with the exposition of English law."[52] However, our primary concern here is to relate this legal history to Blackstone's legal theory, and this

---

[48] William Blackstone, *Law Tracts in Two Volumes* (Oxford, 1762), II, xii, and see 4 *Comm* 416–17. For an opposing contemporary treatment, see Barrington, *Ancient Statutes*, p. 3.

[49] Henry Home (Lord Kames), Historical Law Tracts, 2 vols. (Edinburgh, 1758), I, v, and see the discussion below, chapter 7 at nn23–6.

[50] 2 *Comm* 44. See also the dictum of Edward Wynne, that "an infinite number of questions receive the only light they are capable of from the reflection of history," *Eunomus*, I, 59.

[51] 2 *Comm* 208, 210–12.   [52] Dicey, "Blackstone's *Commentaries*," 296.

requires a more detailed investigation of his formal account of common law.

Blackstone defined common law in historical terms. The *lex non scripta* was principally composed of the ancient customs of the realm "used time out of mind, or in the solemnity of our legal phrase, time whereof the memory of man runneth not to the contrary."[53] He further equipped common law with a fairly precise historical identity, associating it with the Saxon laws collected by Alfred and later consolidated by Edgar and Edward the Confessor.[54] Bentham thought this line of explanation simply absurd. It was obvious that much of common law was of more recent vintage, and the general attempt to depict any individual custom as "immemorial" was straightforwardly implausible in that it was always available to regress to some earlier epoch when that particular custom simply could ñot have existed – "At worst the deluge if all others fail."[55]

But Bentham was purposefully misleading on this point. Blackstone did not think his formal definition of common law required that this law was entirely constituted by a permanent and unchanged set of ancient rules.[56] He explicitly warned against excessive confidence in the identification of the origins of any specific legal practice. "Nothing," he reported, was "more difficult than to ascertain the precise beginning and first spring of an ancient and long established custom," and nothing more easy than to "mistake for nature what we find established by long and inveterate custom."[57] Like Bentham, Blackstone perceived that many parts of the common law were fairly modern, and that the law had undergone a process of continual change and amendment.[58] "Traditional laws in general," like England's *lex non scripta*, "suffer by degrees insensible variations in practice," and although it was "impossible to define the precise period in which that alteration accrued," nevertheless "we plainly discern the alteration of the law from what it was five hundred years ago."[59] And precisely because common law had been changed and altered through time by various hands, it was "now fraught with the accumulated wisdom of ages" and thereby attained a level of excellence unavailable in less historically informed systems of law-making.[60] Common law was thus a matter of change and correction as well as continuity, a process in which "the

---

[53] 1 *Comm* 67.
[54] 1 *Comm* 64–7, and see 4 *Comm* 408–14.
[55] *Comment*, p. 178, and see pp. 164–70, 178–80, 234–8.
[56] 1 *Comm* 64.
[57] 1 *Comm* 67, 2 *Comm* 11.
[58] See, for example, his discussion of copyholds, 2 *Comm* 147–50.
[59] 4 *Comm* 409.   [60] 4 *Comm* 442.

fundamental maxims and rules of the law … have been and are every day improving."[61]

In adopting this conception of common law development, Blackstone displayed another major intellectual debt to Matthew Hale and to Hale's mentor, John Selden.[62] As we shall see, a crucial element in eighteenth-century attitudes to legal change and law reform drew upon Hale's influential statement of the special strengths of the common law, which on account of its "long experience and use," had successfully "wrought out" the "errors, distempers or iniquities of men or times" and become incorporated into the "very temperament" of "the English nation."[63] But, in so acknowledging and elucidating the critical importance of common law history to Blackstone and his generation, we have still not exhausted the theory of common law set out in the *Commentaries*, much less witnessed an abandonment of natural law commitments.[64]

Blackstone never suggested that common law was ethically legitimate simply because it was historical, nor did he maintain that this law itself comprised only an historically formed bundle of legal rules. England's *leges non scriptae* contained customs which received "the force of laws, by long and immemorial usage, and by their universal reception throughout the kingdom."[65] This formula in part indicated that the issue of whether a particular practice was an authentic custom could be stated as a question of whether it had been "used time out of mind." But not every immemorial custom was by reason of its antiquity a part of the common law, and the issue of which customs enjoyed "the force of law" also turned on the question of legal legitimacy in general. This was made clearest when Blackstone turned to the process by which it became revealed which customs had in fact been received as common law in England. This occurred through the practice of the courts, where the common law judges served as the "living oracles of the law," and where their decisions furnished "the principal and most authoritative evidence" of which customs formed "a part of the common law." The "*opinion of the judge*," however, was not "the same

---

[61] 4 *Comm* 442.

[62] On the contribution of Selden and Hale to this historical understanding of common law, see Tuck, *Natural Rights Theories*, pp. 83–4, 133–39, which revises in part Pocock's earlier treatment in *Ancient Constitution*. Blackstone cites Hale's *History of the Common Law of England* throughout his chapter summary of English legal development, 4 *Comm* 407–43, and acknowledges Selden at 1 *Comm* 64.

[63] Matthew Hale, *The History of the Common Law of England* (1713), ed. Charles M. Gray (Chicago, 1971), p. 30.

[64] In what follows, I am much indebted to A. W. B. Simpson, "The Common Law and Legal Theory," in A. W. B. Simpson (ed.), *Oxford Essays in Jurisprudence*, 2nd series (Oxford, 1973).   [65] 1 *Comm* 64.

thing" as "*the law*" itself, and history was not the sole criterion by which judges ruled on the composition of common law. Thus, when the judges discovered a previous judicial opinion of the law to be "contrary to reason, much more if it be contrary to the divine law," they declared "not that such a sentence was *bad law*, but that it was *not law*, that is, that it is not the established custom of the realm." And since a determination "contrary to reason" was "not law," "our lawyers are with justice so copious in their encomiums on the reason of the common law; that they tell us that the law is the perfection of reason, that it always intends to conform thereto, and that what is not reason is not law."[66]

Blackstone's natural law doctrines, in other words, did not operate in the sense that common law could be treated as a series of deductions from principles of reason or nature. The content of law – the custom received as law in England – was an historical artifact. But historical pedigree did not alone determine which customs were received as common law, and the more general ethical bases of human law ensured that nothing "contrary to reason" would be allowed as law. Because Blackstone conceived of the legal validity of custom in this manner he was able to collapse the traditional distinction between the "established customs" and the "established rules and maxims" of common law. The latter referred to such general principles of justice or legal policy as the rule, "that no man shall be found to accuse himself." Like customs, they were revealed to be part of the common law only "by showing it hath been always the custom to observe" them. And again, like customs, they were only lawful in that they contained nothing "contrary to reason."[67]

One substantial implication of this formulation of common law theory, central to the practice of the eighteenth-century common law courts, was that it further explained how the courts were competent to decide new cases for which there existed no settled pattern of judicial decisions. As Wooddeson explained, "where the positive laws are silent, all courts must determine on maxims of natural justice dictated by reason; that is, according to the law of nature."[68] Thus, when Blackstone discussed the law of personal property, he found no difficulty in the fact that this area of law went unmentioned in "our ancient law-books" and had emerged only "since the introduction and

---

[66] 1 *Comm* 69–71, and see Blackstone's corresponding discussion of "particular customs" at 1 *Comm* 76–77. For other contemporary versions of this understanding of precedents, see Hale, *History of the Common Law*, pp. 45–6; Wynne, *Eunomus*, III, 174–5; Capel Lofft, *Reports of Cases adjudged in the Court of King's Bench* (London, 1776), p. v.

[67] 1 *Comm* 68.

[68] Wooddeson, *Elements of Jurisprudence*, p. 80.

extension of trade and commerce." The courts had been able to develop this body of law by determining cases according to the dictates of "reason and convenience, adapted to the circumstances of the times."[69]

Although Blackstone was convinced that the practice of common law could not be explained simply by appeal to historical rules and cases, he rarely utilized his natural law precepts in order directly to assess or criticize the substance of the common law. It is no doubt the absence of this sort of criticism which had made him appear so much more "historically minded" than philosophically informed. In this sense, Blackstone certainly did restrict the impact of natural law theory, and it is appropriate to notice the main devices through which this occurred. Of most importance was the distinction he drew between the "*absolute* rights of individuals" which were created by the law of nature, and their "*relative*" rights which were the creations of "states and societies."[70] This distinction, when translated into duties and obligations, generated two principal categories of offences, offences "*mala in se*" and offences "*mala prohibita*." The former referred to "natural duties" prescribed by the law of nature which no human law could "abridge or destroy." The latter category comprised "things in themselves indifferent," which only became "right or wrong" on the basis of positive rules.[71] He then defined the range of absolute rights and offences "*mala in se*" so restrictively that it became clear that most law operated outside the sphere of natural rights and duties.[72] The conservative implications of the distinction were neatly drawn in the discussion of property law. Blackstone acknowledged a natural right to property, basing his discussion on the authority of Grotius, Pufendorf, Barbeyrac and Mr Locke.[73] But he went on to insist that although the original right to property was natural, the transmission of property was a purely civil matter. Accordingly, the rules applying to wills, testaments, rights of inheritance and successions were "all of them creatures of the civil and municipal laws," and "this one consideration" would "help to remove the scruples of many well-meaning persons, who set up a mistaken conscience in opposition to the rules of law."[74] Thus, when Blackstone treated the complex and seemingly arbitrary rules governing the lineal descent of estates, he did not fail to remind the reader that this area of law did not directly relate to any natural

---

[69] 2 *Comm* 385, where Blackstone also alleges the influence of Roman law principles in these cases.

[70] 1 *Comm* 123-4.   [71] 1 *Comm* 54-5, 57-8.

[72] See 1 *Comm* 123-6, and the discussion by H. L. A. Hart, "Blackstone's Use of the Law of Nature," *Butterworths South African Law Review*, (1956), 169-74.

[73] 2 *Comm* 6-8.   [74] 2 *Comm* 12-13.

rights or duties, and "there is certainly therefore no injustice done to individuals, whatever be the path of descent marked out by the municipal law."[75]

The second technique Blackstone employed to insulate the law from "well-meaning" criticisms concerns his treatment of legal fictions. This was a standard device used by the courts to adapt the historic forms of common law to altered social circumstances. As Blackstone appreciated, fictions rendered the law burdensomely complex, left the mechanics of litigation incomprehensible to the layman, and were a frequent object of popular complaint. He viewed legal fictions, however, as an unavoidable feature of England's law and insisted that they actually furthered the capacity of the courts to achieve justice.[76] These arguments figured in one of the most elegant passages of the *Commentaries*, where Blackstone concluded his presentation of the system of civil remedies, an extremely technical body of law which demanded nearly three hundred pages to summarize. He conceded that this law was "apt at our first acquaintance to breed a confusion of ideas."[77] But the "intricacy of our legal process" which produced the appearance of confusion was "one of those troublesome, but not dangerous evils, which have their root in the frame of our constitution." When the "influence of foreign trade and domestic tranquillity" led to the decay of England's "military tenures," the common law judges "quickly perceived" that the "old feudal actions" were "ill suited" to the succeeding "commercial mode of property" which "required a more speedy decision of right, to facilitate exchange and alienation." But instead of "soliciting any great legislative revolution in the old established forms," they "endeavoured by a series of minute contrivances" to adapt the existing legal actions "to all the most useful purposes of remedial justice." These contrivances became "known and understood," and the "only difficulty" which remained "[arose] from their fictions and circuities." But once the necessary historical exposition was supplied, "that labyrinth [was] easily pervaded":

> Our system of remedial law resembles an old Gothic castle, erected in the days of chivalry, but fitted up for a modern inhabitant. The moated ramparts, the embattled towers, and the trophied halls, are magnificent and venerable, but useless, and therefore neglected. The inferior

---

[75] 2 *Comm* 211. For a more detailed account of this feature of the *Commentaries*, see the discussion by Robert P. Burns, "Blackstone's Theory of the 'Absolute' Rights of Property," *University of Cincinnati Law Review*, LIV (1985), 67–86.

[76] See his discussion of ejectments at 3 *Comm* 205–6.   [77] 3 *Comm* 265.

apartments, now accommodated to daily use, are cheerful and commodious, though their approaches may be winding and difficult.[78]

Once it became plain that there was nothing in this historical process and mass of "fictions and circuities" which violated the dictates of reason or natural law, it became possible to advance a further set of arguments to defend the notorious complexity and alleged uncertainty of England's law.[79] If England had more law than other nations, this did not represent "confusion" but the necessary consequences of peculiar social conditions. The examples of legal simplicity found in the laws "of arbitrary governments," or "of wild and uncultivated nations," or "of narrow domestic republics" were scarcely relevant to the conditions in England. It was misguided to "require the same paucity of laws, the same conciseness of practice, in a nation of freemen, a polite and commercial people, and a populous extent of empire."[80] These same matters were even more effectively explained by invoking the distinctive glory of English law: civil liberty. If England had a singular "multiplicity of law," this was due to each civil injury being provided with a particular legal remedy for the better security of property. This particularity of law further meant that less discretion was "left in the breast of the judges," as was "essential to a free people."[81] If the complexity and intricacy of the law created delays in the judicial process, this again was "the genuine offspring of that spirit of equal liberty which is the singular felicity of Englishmen." Quick judicial deliberations, as Montesquieu demonstrated, characterized the legal systems of despotic states, whereas "in free states, the trouble, expense and delays of judicial proceedings are the price that every subject pays for his liberty." And "from these principles" it naturally followed that justice in England ought to be slower than anywhere else, since the courts "set a greater value on life, on liberty, and on property."[82]

Of course, as Bentham readily perceived, once Blackstone embarked on this line of explanation, the *Commentaries* easily shifted into crude apologetics, in which it became difficult to conceive of any existing practice which might not escape censure.[83] Blackstone, as we have seen, did not seek to justify English law solely by appeal to its status as historic usage. Nonetheless, the manner in which he conducted his

---

[78] 3 *Comm* 267–8. See also 2 *Comm* 288–9 and 3 *Comm* 329, where Blackstone again emphasizes the need for law to accommodate swift property exchange in a commercial society.

[79] See 3 *Comm* 325 and 423, where Blackstone acknowledges popular complaints on this head.

[80] 3 *Comm* 325–6. For similar contemporary arguments linking legal complexity and social development, see the discussion above, Introduction at n66.

[81] 3 *Comm* 266, 327.   [82] 3 *Comm* 423–4.   [83] See *Fragment*, pp. 404–13.

exposition of the law enabled him to avoid any careful distinction between an historical explanation and a moral justification. A cogent example of this useful ambiguity emerged in result of Blackstone's account of the Toleration Act, and his apparent defense of the laws punishing religious dissent. This was subjected to several attacks, the first mounted by Joseph Priestley in 1769. Blackstone responded in the same year, and in subsequent editions altered the offending passages in the *Commentaries*. But his main argument in his *Reply to Dr. Priestley's Remarks* was that Priestley had altogether mistaken the nature of his explanation of the laws enforcing religious uniformity:

> I have indeed illustrated this doctrine with a few historical remarks to show the motives of originally enacting these penal laws... But Dr. Priestley hath attributed to me the adoption of those principles, which I only meant to mention historically, as the causes of the laws I condemn.[84]

Blackstone, in developing his historical analysis of common law, did not believe he had abandoned his natural law doctrines. However, other scholars have found an incompatibility between his natural law theory and his account of parliamentary sovereignty. Frederick Pollock, in this context, referred to Blackstone's "lip-service to natural law." C. K. Allen maintained that natural law was "indeed inconsistent with the whole tenor of Blackstone's precepts concerning legislation, and seems to be added as a kind of pious after-thought."[85] Barker noted the same confusion, and Dicey found he could make no sense of Blackstone's conception of the moral foundations of positive law.[86] The most extreme version of this thesis has been advanced by Paul Lucas, who has argued that Blackstone on parliamentary sovereignty could not contradict Blackstone on natural law because Blackstone had never advanced an authentic natural law theory in the first place. Instead, his definition of law displayed a "Hobbesian character," and Blackstone "must be regarded as a forerunner of Austinian jurisprudence."[87]

---

[84] William Blackstone, *A Reply to Dr Priestley's Remarks on the Fourth Volume of the Commentaries on the Laws of England* (1769), reprinted in *An Interesting Appendix to Sir William Blackstone's Commentaries on the Laws of England* (Philadelphia, 1773), p. 39, and see 4 *Comm* 52–6.

[85] Frederick Pollock, "A Plea for Historical Interpretation," *Law Quarterly Review*, XXXIX (1923), 165; C. K. Allen, *Law in the Making*, 5th edn (London, 1951), pp. 427–8.

[86] Ernest Barker, *Essays on Government*, 2nd edn (Oxford, 1951), p. 129; Dicey, *Law of the Constitution*, pp. 41–2, 64.

[87] Paul Lucas, "*Ex parte* Blackstone," 149, 156. In what follows, I am much indebted to two important earlier discussions: John N. Finnis, "Blackstone's Theoretical Intentions," *Natural Law Forum*, XII (1967), 163–83, and Gerald Stourzh, *Alexander Hamilton and the Idea of Republican Government* (Stanford, Ca., 1970), pp. 9–22. See also the valuable recent re-examination of these issues in Michael Lobban, "Blackstone and the Science of Law."

According to Blackstone, the "supreme power" in every state was occupied by the legislature, "sovereignty and legislature" being "convertible terms."[88] In England, this sovereign authority was exercised by the British parliament, an "aggregate body" composed of the king, the lords spiritual and temporal, and the House of Commons. "All the parts" of this legislature "form a mutual check upon each other," and "like three distinct powers in mechanics, they jointly impel the machine of government."[89] Because this complex piece of joinery uniquely combined the blessings of monarchic, aristocratic and democratic government, while eliminating the defects found in their pure forms, the government of England was able to pursue "the true line of the liberty and happiness of the community."[90]

Having identified the composition of parliament, Blackstone next turned to the nature of its constitutional authority, and here presented an unambiguous affirmation of the sovereign power of the British legislature.

> It hath sovereign and uncontrollable authority in the making, confirming, enlarging, restraining, abrogating, repealing, reviving, and expounding of laws, concerning matters of all possible denominations, ecclesiastical, or temporal, civil, military, maritime, or criminal; this being the place where that absolute despotic power, which must in all governments reside somewhere, is entrusted by the constitution of these kingdoms.[91]

As Bentham observed, the "vehemence ... of this passage is remarkable. He ransacks the language: he piles up ... the most tremendous epithets he can find."[92] And as other critics have charged, it is not obvious how we are to reconcile parliament's "absolute despotic power" for law-making with Blackstone's earlier pronouncements on the laws and rights of nature which no human laws could contradict.

At the outset, though, it is important to notice that the apparent difficulty relates to Blackstone's general conception of sovereignty, rather than to his treatment of the British parliament. For Blackstone, all sovereign power is legislative, all governments must contain a sovereign power, and that sovereign power must be "absolute despotic power." Given this understanding of sovereignty, it was obvious that if the authority existed in Britain, as it had to, then it was held by parliament. Blackstone, moreover, believed this conception easily vindicated by the legislative record of the recent past. Parliament had demonstrated its supreme power by changing the succession to the

---

[88] 1 *Comm* 46.
[90] 1 *Comm* 155.
[92] *Fragment*, p. 480.

[89] 1 *Comm* 50–2, 154–5.
[91] 1 *Comm* 160.

throne, by altering the established religion of the realm, and even by changing the constitution itself, "as was done by the act of union, and the several statutes for triennial and septennial elections." "In short," parliament could "do every thing that is not naturally impossible, and therefore some have not scrupled to call its power... the omnipotence of parliament," though Blackstone acknowledged finding the phrase "rather too bold."[93]

Some of Blackstone's contemporaries recognized that the perceived difficulty rested on his confusions regarding the nature of sovereignty itself. Bentham was probably clearest on this. Bentham accepted that any act of parliament, no matter how misguided or ethically unacceptable, was nonetheless good law, and he believed Blackstone, in virtue of his natural law doctrine, to have equivocated on this point.[94] Bentham further argued that unless there was an express convention in a state to this purpose, it was impossible to identify any clear criterion by which sovereign power in a specific instance could be said to exceed its authority. In this sense, sovereignty was "unavoidably *indefinite*." Blackstone erred by supposing that because in most states the limits of sovereign power were "*indefinite*," sovereignty was therefore "*infinite*." In fact, Bentham insisted, ample examples were available to show that the conclusion simply did not follow.[95] James Sedgwick in his *Remarks Critical and Miscellaneous on the Commentaries* developed much the same criticism. Blackstone, he observed, simply meant to assert that "the extremest reach of the power of parliament is not ascertained by any known and visible limits." Parliament's authority was in this sense unlimited because it was often called upon "to act on sudden and unexpected exigencies," when its actions could only be circumscribed "by those general principles of justice and sound policy which ought ever to give bounds to the extent of undefined dominion." Blackstone's mistake, again, was to treat the inevitably undefined limits of parliamentary authority as an "absolute despotic power" to do every thing "not naturally impossible."[96]

Other critics, however, concentrated on the question of where Blackstone had located sovereignty. James Wilson, for example, accepted "that in every state there must be somewhere a power supreme, arbitrary, absolute, uncontrollable." His principal objection to Blackstone was that he had disregarded the authority which remained with the people who had first established government

---

[93] 1 *Comm* 161.　　　[94] *Comment*, pp. 54–5.

[95] *Fragment*, pp. 484–5, 488–9.

[96] James Sedgwick, *Remarks Critical and Miscellaneous on the Commentaries of Sir William Blackstone* (London 1800), p. 126.

through their original contract.[97] The fact that this charge was launched in a work published in the newly created American republic reflects a danger Blackstone was eager to repel in his own treatment of parliamentary sovereignty. By the mid eighteenth century, natural law arguments and original contracts were increasingly invoked by radical theorists opposed to Whig hegemony, leaving conservative thinkers, like Blackstone, to resist the radical implications of these doctrines.[98] Throughout the *Commentaries*, he was at pains to demonstrate that his own discussion of natural rights and the contractarian origins of political authority did not entail any revolutionary conclusions.[99] "Mr. Locke," he noted, "perhaps carries his theory too far," and the proposition advanced by Locke and "other theoretical writers" that the people enjoyed "a supreme power to remove or alter the legislative" when it violated "the trust reposed in them" could never be directly translated into constitutional law. To suppose a law for this purpose was to suppose a law for the "dissolution of the whole form of government," and no sovereign power, being supreme, could sanction a law for its own annihilation, a law "which at once must destroy all law." Therefore, so long as the English constitution survived, "we may venture to affirm, that the power of parliament is absolute and without control."[100]

The parliament's absolute authority could thus only be "controlled" by a situation involving the dissolution of the constitution as a whole, and although Blackstone clearly acknowledged the possibility, he insisted that it had to occur outside the sphere of constitutional law and the proper operation of sovereignty. "Whenever necessity and the safety of the whole shall require it," he explained, "future generations" might be forced to exercise "those inherent (though latent) powers of society, which no climate, no time, no constitution, no contract, can ever destroy or diminish."[101] But, such "*extraordinary* recourses to first

---

[97] James Wilson, "Lectures on Law" (1791), cited in Morton J. Horwitz, *The Transformation of American Law 1780–1860* (Cambridge, Mass., 1977), p. 19. And see the discussion by John V. Jezierski, "Parliament or People: James Wilson and Blackstone on the Nature and Location of Sovereignty," *Journal of the History of Ideas*, XXXII (1971), 95–106.

[98] For the radical use of natural law theory, see especially John Dunn, "The Politics of Locke in England and America in the Eighteenth Century," in J. W. Yelton (ed.), *John Locke: Problems and Perspectives* (Cambridge, 1969), pp. 45–80; H. T. Dickinson, *Liberty and Property. Political Ideology in Eighteenth-Century Britain* (London, 1977), and Kramnick, "Republican Revisionism Revisited," 629–66.

[99] Blackstone's concern to combat political radicalism has been suggested as the central intention of the *Commentaries* in two recent accounts: Robert Willman, "Blackstone and the 'Theoretical Perfection' of English Law in the Reign of Charles II," *Historical Journal*, XXVI (1983), 39–70, and Stanley N. Katz, in William Blackstone, *Commentaries on the Laws of England: A Facsimile of the first edition of 1765–1769*, 4 vols. (Chicago, 1979), I, x (editorial introduction).

[100] 1 *Comm* 52, 161–2.   [101] 1 *Comm* 245.

principles" could never be incorporated "in the *ordinary* course of law."[102] The "supposition of *law*" was therefore "that neither the king nor either house of parliament (collectively taken)" was "capable of doing any wrong" in the specific constitutional sense that "any adequate remedy" to the "oppressions which may happen to spring from any branch of the sovereign power must necessarily be out of the reach of any *stated rule*, or *express legal* provision."[103]

If Blackstone understood parliamentary power as a "sovereign and uncontrollable authority" to make law, this did not merely involve his making explicit the nature of sovereignty itself. It also required clarification of a controversial common law doctrine which suggested that acts of parliament "contrary to reason" were void in themselves and, as such, could be rejected by the common law judges. The doctrine received its most famous airing in Coke's decision in Bonham's case, where the oracle of law declared that "in many cases the common law will control acts of parliament...sometimes it will judge them completely void." It remains unclear precisely what Coke intended by this, particularly with regard to the extent of the judiciary's power.[104] But despite these difficulties, it was possible to take the statement at face value. In a case of 1710, Chief Justice Holt described Coke's claim in Bonham's case as "a very reasonable and true saying," and then utilized it to counter a statute.[105] Moreover, though these episodes did not concern Coke's dictum, eighteenth-century lawyers were well aware that prominent portions of their law had developed through judicial evasion of acts of parliament. When Barrington, for example, discussed the common law fiction of common recovery used to break an entail, he immediately observed that among the "glaring improprieties" of the device was "that it is directly in opposition to the express and clear words of a subsisting law."[106] In a similar fashion, Charles Butler noted that the courts' preservation of uses under "the application of trusts" was "both against the words and the spirit of the statute of uses," and hence questioned whether this "was not a subject more proper for legislative than judicial provision."[107]

Eighteenth-century lawyers were thus furnished with historic examples of the courts acting against statutes and with a doctrine which justified the common law's "control" of acts of parliament in certain instances. But while the application of Coke's doctrine ensured that no

---

[102] 1 *Comm* 250–1.   [103] 1 *Comm* 244–5.

[104] For a full discussion, see Samuel E. Thorne's introduction to his edition of *A Discourse upon the Exposition and Understanding of Statutes* (San Marino, Cal., 1942).

[105] Cited, with other examples, in Allen, *Law in the Making*, pp. 421–7.

[106] Barrington, *Ancient Statutes*, p. 116, where other examples are given.

[107] *The Reminiscences of Charles Butler, Esq. of Lincoln's Inn* (London, 1822), pp. 42–3.

part of English law was "contrary to reason," it appeared to achieve this result only by threatening parliament's legislative sovereignty. When viewed from this standpoint, legal orthodoxy stood firmly against the constitutional implications of Bonham's case. As Barrington maintained in this context, "let the inconveniences of a statute be what they may, no judge or bench of judges can constitutionally dispose with them; their office is *jus dicere* and not *jus dare*."[108] Barrington's Latin maxim had been favored by Bacon and was regularly cited throughout the Hanoverian period to characterize the English judge's constitutional powers. Even the most zealous and effective defenders of the judiciary's proper powers to adapt and refine the common law as demanded by new social circumstances were careful to dissociate this capacity from an unconstitutional authority to challenge directly parliament's legislative will. Accordingly, in a decision of 1776 which concerned the legislative sanctions against Roman Catholics, Chief Justice Mansfield asserted that "the statutes against Papists were thought, when they passed, necessary to the safety of the state," and "upon no other ground" could "they be defended." Still, regardless of whether "the policy be sound or not," these statutes had to be applied "according to their true intent and meaning," for "the legislature only can vary or alter the law."[109] Even the author of *A Treatise of Equity*, who insisted upon the court of equity's necessary responsibility to exempt cases from the positive rules of law in order to preserve "natural justice" additionally stressed that "equity cannot intermeddle" when "the law has determined a matter with all its circumstances" – "for the Chancellor to relieve against the express provision of an act of parliament would be the same as to repeal it."[110]

Blackstone dealt with the question as part of a general account of the rules adopted by the courts for the construction of statutes. He observed that "if there arise out of [acts of parliament] collaterally any absurd consequences, manifestly contradictory to common reason, they are, with regard to those collateral consequences, void." By emphasizing that the rule concerned such "collateral consequences," Blackstone simply introduced a traditional notion of the courts' equitable interpretation of statutes. In the case of an unreasonable collateral consequence, the judges properly concluded "that this consequence was not foreseen by the parliament, and therefore they are at liberty to expound the statute by equity, and only *quoad hoc* disregard it."[111] But,

108 Barrington, *Ancient Statutes*, p. 116.
109 *Foone v Blount* (1776), Cowper 464, 466.
110 *Treatise of Equity*, I, 17–19.   111 1 *Comm* 91.

he carefully distinguished this rule from the alternative version "generally laid down" that "acts of parliament contrary to reason are void." This latter, more common formulation Blackstone interpreted as a constitutional claim, and on the basis of his own theory of legislative supremacy he promptly rejected it:

> If the parliament will positively enact a thing to be done which is unreasonable, I know of no power in the ordinary forms of the constitution that is vested with authority to control it: and the examples usually alleged in support of this sense of the rule do none of them prove that where the main object of a statute is unreasonable, the judges are at liberty to reject it; for that were to set the judicial power above that of the legislature, which would be subversive of all government.[112]

Blackstone, then, when faced with the challenge of an unreasonable act of parliament, reverted to his concept of sovereignty rather than his natural law precepts. As a result the *Commentaries* offered no direct, programmatic guidance on the question of the validity of an act of parliament which violated the laws of nature. Clearly, for Blackstone, there could be no constitutional solution to the question, and in regard to the broader ethical dimensions of the question he preferred to speak generally of those possible monstrous instances of sovereign folly which might legitimately destroy the entire fabric of government in England. Yet, while recognizing the consequent equivocation and even evasiveness of his position, there remains no reason for following earlier commentators in dismissing Blackstone's natural law precepts as "lip-service" or "a pious after-thought." Such a dismissal, as we have seen, would seriously undermine his account of common law legitimacy. More significantly, the suggested rejection of natural law from the *Commentaries* by historians concerned to chart the rise of parliamentary sovereignty severely perverts the whole tenor of Blackstone's understanding of the state of the law in contemporary England. The interpretative mistake is to presume that Blackstone's attitude to parliamentary law-making was fully disclosed in his formal doctrines of constitutional sovereignty.

[112] 1 *Comm* 91.

◁ ══════════════════════════════════ ▷

2

Blackstone's science of legislation

Few features of the *Commentaries* have suffered such unfortunate neglect as Blackstone's stated aim that his work should furnish guidance to "such as are, or may hereafter become, legislators."[1] Legislative instruction figured as a major programmatic objective for Blackstone's celebrated law book, and his concerns in this area illuminate some of the most distinctive elements of his novel career in legal science and legal education.

Parliamentary legislation was first mentioned on page ten of volume one of the *Commentaries*, and the judgment there presented initiated a theme sustained and embellished over four large volumes:

> The mischiefs that have arisen to the public from the inconsiderate alterations in our laws are too obvious to be called in question... For, to say the truth, almost all the perplexed questions, almost all the niceties, intricacies, and delays (which have sometimes disgraced the English, as well as other courts of justice) owe their original not to the common law itself, but to innovations that have been made in it by acts of parliament.[2]

The mischiefs of statute received ample illustration at Blackstone's hands. The Hanoverian Mutiny Act, for example, which failed fully to specify the crimes and punishments it authorized stood accused of compromising the fundamental genius of the legal system. Among "the greatest advantages of our English law," Blackstone observed, was that "not only the crimes themselves which it punishes, but also the penalties which it inflicts, are ascertained and notorious." As a result, "nothing" was left to "arbitrary discretion" and the security of the subject was accordingly protected. By violating such principles, the Mutiny Act took that group of men "whose bravery has so often preserved the liberties of their country" and reduced them "to a state

---

[1] 4 *Comm* 11.   [2] 1 *Comm* 10.

of servitude," for, as Coke had explained, "it is one of the genuine marks of servitude to have the law which is our rule of action, either concealed or precarious." Montesquieu more recently had warned against the special danger to a free state of "introducing slavery in any particular order or profession," to which Blackstone could only add, "much less ought the soldiery to be exception to the people in general, and the only state of servitude in the nation."[3]

The statutes on the poor earned similar treatment, likewise being represented as misguided deviations from the principles of common law. The poor laws, Blackstone felt forced to acknowledge, "remain very imperfect and inadequate to the purposes they are designed for." In former times, "when the shires, the hundreds, and the tithings were kept in the same admirable order in which they were disposed by the great Alfred," no one remained idle and "consequently none but the impotent...needed relief." The Elizabethan Poor Law appeared "entirely founded on the same principle." However, once this system was "neglected and departed from," the legislature was forced to embrace "miserable shifts and lame expedients...in order to patch up the flaws occasioned by this neglect." This was the "fate," Blackstone concluded, "that has generally attended most of our statute laws, where they have not the foundation of the common law to build on."[4]

In his preliminary discussion of penal law, Blackstone adopted a tone more strident than elsewhere in the *Commentaries*, observing at the outset that even in England "we shall occasionally find room to remark some particulars, that seem to want revision and amendment."[5] The need for revision was again chiefly due to damaging legislative initiatives, not least those relating to the Hanoverian parliaments' seemingly uncontainable enthusiasm for the death penalty. Blackstone condemned outright several of the more infamous capital statutes and mounted an eloquent case for penal reform.[6]

Such instances of specific charges against specific acts of parliament could be multiplied. But doubtless the most telling example of Blackstone's preoccupation with the "mischiefs" of the statute law is provided in his discussion of trials by jury. Blackstone's reverence for the institution was scarcely unexpected. As Jean Louis DeLolme reported later in the century, "the trial by jury is that point of their liberty to which the people of England are most thoroughly and

[3] 1 *Comm* 416–17.
[4] 1 *Comm* 365. See also 2 *Comm* 342–43, where Blackstone again advances the argument with regard to the failed legislative attempts to regulate "alienation by deed" since "the disuse of the old Saxon custom of transacting all conveyances at the county court."
[5] 4 *Comm* 3.
[6] See the discussion below, chapter 10 at nn51–7.

universally wedded."[7] Blackstone, himself, sought to exploit this consensus, explaining that he would "not mispend the reader's time in fruitless encomiums on this method of trial," but instead directly proceed to its detailed analysis, "from whence indeed its highest encomium will arise; since the more it is searched into and understood, the more it is sure to be valued." By the completion of these researches, trial by jury had been championed as nothing less than "the glory of the English law" and "the most transcendent privilege which any subject can enjoy or wish for."[8] To celebrate the jury fully and properly, as in the case of so much else the *Commentaries* identified for celebration, was to understand its pivotal place in the scheme of English liberty. Historically, jury trials, by preserving "in the hands of the people that share which they ought to have in the administration of public justice," had prevented feudal England from degenerating into a military oligarchy.[9] Currently, juries checked the abuse of judicial power, and thereby assisted in that balancing of judicial independence which was required for the maintenance of constitutional freedom.[10] Like England's mixed constitution, the jury system uniquely counter-poised and blended popular and aristocratic social elements into a wholesome institutional balance.[11] So powerful indeed was the jury that Blackstone boldly enlisted this ancient Saxon monument to combat the more sober conjectures of Montesquieu regarding the ultimate durability of English freedom:

> And therefore, a celebrated French writer who concludes that because Rome, Sparta, and Carthage have lost their liberties, therefore those of England in time must perish, should have recollected that Rome, Sparta, and Carthage at the time their liberties were lost, were strangers to the trial by jury.[12]

This was, of course, classic Blackstonean whiggery. His conclusions and even more the insular self-congratulation of the account all seem to epitomize that unreflective and complacent attitude which Bentham lampooned as "every thing is as it should be" Blackstone.[13] However, this is arguably to perceive the situation precisely in reverse. For Blackstone's panegyrics additionally served as the groundwork for an extensively rehearsed attack on the present threats to juries introduced by parliamentary statute. What began in the *Commentaries* as a characteristically adulatory retailing of conventional claims on behalf of

---

[7] Jean Louis DeLolme, *The Constitution of England, or an Account of the English Government* (1771) (London, 1775), p. 161.

[8] 3 *Comm* 350, 379.

[9] 3 *Comm* 380.

[10] 3 *Comm* 379–80 and 1 *Comm* 269–70.

[11] 3 *Comm* 379–81.

[12] 3 *Comm* 379.

[13] *Fragment*, p. 407.

a distinctive legal practice moved on to a critique of recent parliamentary interventions.

"Every new tribunal, erected for the decision of facts, without the intervention of a jury," the *Commentaries* ominously explained, "is a step towards establishing aristocracy, the most oppressive of absolute governments."[14] The reasons for the warning were revealed first in Blackstone's discussion of the Court of Requests, a Tudor court for the recovery of small debts that had been strengthened by Hanoverian statute. Proceedings at the court were swifter than at common law, in part because of the absence of juries. The omission of juries, Blackstone emphasized, was "entirely in derogation of the common law" and represented a "remedy" to the "inconvenience" of common law process which "may itself be attended in time with very ill consequences." Not only did the court's discretionary powers "create a petty tyranny in a set of standing commissioners," this example of "the disuse of the trial by jury may tend to estrange the minds of the people from that valuable prerogative of Englishmen, which has already been more than sufficiently excluded in many instances."[15]

Blackstone rehearsed the same theme at greater length in his treatment of summary convictions. This was the judicial process empowering magistrates or commissioners to receive accusations and try offenders without the assistance of juries. Here Blackstone's protests had greater weight, since summary convictions constituted an increasingly important device in the administrative machinery of Hanoverian government. The Commissioners of Excise and Revenue proceeded by this method, and the steady extension of the powers of the justices of the peace to determine cases by summary conviction furnished contemporaries with a major instance of parliament's legislative activism.[16] The institution, Blackstone sharply noted, was "designed professedly for the greater ease of the subject," by providing "speedy justice" and sparing the freeholders from "frequent and troublesome attendances to try every minute offence." But "the common law" was "a stranger to it," and the expedient had "of late been so far extended" as now "to threaten the disuse of our admirable and truly English trial by jury, unless only in capital cases." By so augmenting the justice's duties, summary convictions further meant that "many gentlemen of rank and character" were positively discouraged "from acting in the commission." "And from these ill consequences we may collect the prudent foresight of our ancient lawgivers," who would never allow such matters "to be determined by

[14] 3 *Comm* 380.   [15] 3 *Comm* 82.
[16] See the discussion above, Introduction at nn62–4.

the opinion of any one or two men; and we may also observe the necessity of not deviating any further from our ancient constitution."[17]

The third and most urgent rendering of the plea appeared as part of Blackstone's concluding remarks on the English criminal trial in the final volume. Again he appealed to the "excellent forecast" of the "founders" of England's law, who "contrived that no man" could be convicted in the king's court unless "by the unanimous suffrage of twelve of his equals and neighbours." Again he insisted "that the liberties of England cannot but subsist, so long as this *palladium* remains sacred and inviolate." The danger, however, did not come from "open attacks," but rather from "secret machinations" and "new and arbitrary methods of trial," and regardless of how "*convenient*" such devices might seem, "let it be again remembered that delays and little inconveniences" were "the price that all free nations must pay for their liberty," that such "inroads upon this sacred bulwark of the nation" violated "the spirit of our constitution," and that "though begun in trifles, the precedent may gradually increase and spread to the utter disuse of juries in questions of the most momentous concern."[18]

In these instances of legal change, Blackstone regarded parliament's actions as shortsighted and dangerous deviations from the principles of common law. In his comments on the poor laws, he further maintained that "most of our statute laws" proved ineffectual "where they have not had the foundation of the common law to build on."[19] These claims were extended powerfully when he shifted to the broader question of parliament's impact on the legal system as a whole. There was, of course, much to extol in parliament's constitutional achievements. As regularly occurred in the *Commentaries*, Blackstone followed Hale, whose *History of the Common Law* had praised parliament for "the great regard" it had often demonstrated "to preserve and maintain" the common law.[20] In the inspiring struggle of English liberty, parliament had participated critically in the "step by step" restoration of "that ancient constitution" of Saxon freedom which had been nearly obliterated by the Norman monarchy's "scheme of servility."[21] Yet, for Blackstone, this central process of England's history – "the complete restitution of English liberty … since its total abolition at the conquest" – had been completed in law over half a century earlier, in the reign of Charles II. Parliament's legislation of the period, especially the statute abolishing military tenures and the *habeas corpus* act,

---

[17] 4 *Comm* 280–2. The issues raised by Blackstone's protest are examined in Landau, *Justices of the Peace*, especially Part 4.

[18] 4 *Comm* 349–50.

[19] 1 *Comm* 365.

[20] Hale, *History of the Common Law*, pp. 35–6.

[21] 4 *Comm* 420.

constituted "a second *magna carta*, as beneficial and effectual as that of Runing-Mead." Accordingly, Blackstone chose this as the era when "to fix this *theoretical* perfection of our public law," since this was the historical moment at which "the constitution of England had arrived to its full vigour, and the true balance between liberty and prerogative was happily established by *law*."[22]

Yet, at the same time that Blackstone granted parliament its contributions to the historical development of "our public law," he presented far less generous judgments when considering such matters as "the administration of common justice between party and party."[23] Relatively early in his career as a student of English law, as is recorded in a letter of 1745, Blackstone reached the conclusion that the common law, as "it stood in Littleton's days," composed a "regular edifice" with each apartment "properly disposed" and "all uniting in one beautiful symmetry." Since then, however, this structure had been "swollen, shrunk, curtailed, enlarged, altered and mangled by various and contradictory statutes," which had substituted "many of its most useful parts" with "preposterous additions... of different materials and coarse workmanship," designed according "to the whim, or prejudice, or private convenience of the builders." As a result, the law now formed "a huge irregular pile" with its "harmony quite annihilated," so that it became impossible to penetrate "this new labyrinth" unless "the model of the old house" was perceived.[24] Creating such a "model of the old house," as we have seen, became a leading objective for Blackstone in the *Commentaries*, where the same critical reading of England's legal development was retained. "The common law of England," Blackstone reported in his introductory chapter to the four volumes, had fared "like other venerable edifices of antiquity, which rash and unexperienced workmen [had] ventured to new-dress and refine, with all the rage of modern improvement." In consequence, "its symmetry [had] been destroyed, its proportions distorted, and its majestic simplicity exchanged for specious embellishments and fantastic novelties."[25]

Blackstone's comments on parliament's destructive legislative energies, and even his architectural metaphor, contrast powerfully with

---

[22] 4 *Comm* 438–40 and 439n. This was the time of only the "*theoretical* perfection" of the law on account of the "great practical oppression" during Charles II's reign. For a fuller treatment, see Willman, "Blackstone and the 'Theoretical Perfection' of English Law."

[23] 4 *Comm* 427, where the phrase is used, after Hale, in reference to the consolidation of "the distributive justice of the kingdom" secured in the reign of Edward I; see 4 *Comm* 425 and Hale, *History of the Common Law*, pp. 101–2.

[24] See "Blackstone's Letter... whilst a student at the Middle Temple," *Harvard Law Review*, XXXII (1918–19), 975–6 (spelling modernized).   [25] 1 *Comm* 10.

his later pronouncements in the *Commentaries* on the altogether triumphal manner in which the common law judges had transformed England's Gothic castle "to all the most useful purposes of remedial justice."[26] In drawing this latter assessment, moreover, Blackstone specifically praised the judges for having "wisely avoided soliciting any great legislative revolution in the old established forms."[27] The judiciary's success, by implication, was a measure of parliament's failure. Nor was this a lesson Blackstone was prepared to leave merely implicit, for he had preceded his celebration of the judicial modernization of common law by stressing that

> when laws are to be framed by popular assemblies, even of the representative kind, it is too Herculean a task to begin the work of legislation afresh, and extract a new system from the discordant opinions of more than five hundred counsellors... who, that is acquainted with the difficulty of new-modelling any branch of our statute laws (though relating but to roads or to parish-settlements) will conceive it ever feasible to alter any fundamental point of the common law, with all its appendages and consequents, and set up another rule in its stead?[28]

Unfortunately, the past achievements of the common law judges could offer no immediate solution to the more recent "specious embellishments and fantastic novelties" supplied by acts of parliament. Indeed, given Blackstone's constitutional doctrines, no institutional mechanism could exist to regulate parliament's sovereign law-making. But the constitutional situation still allowed for other, less direct remedies to the problem of statute. As Blackstone explained in his 1758 inaugural lecture as Oxford's first Vinerian professor of English law (which he later used for the introduction to the *Commentaries*), "the science thus committed to his charge" formed "a species of knowledge, in which the gentlemen of England have been more remarkably deficient than those of all Europe besides." In England, the study of law had been "neglected, and even unknown, by all but one practical profession," although every subject had reason to be informed of at least that part of the law "with which he is immediately concerned."[29] In the case of those of "landed property," however, this need for legal knowledge was profound and extensive. Such gentlemen would be called upon to act as jurors and justices of the peace, and most important, such men as parliamentary representatives would also serve as "the guardians of the English constitution, the makers, repealers,

---

[26] 3 *Comm* 268, and see the discussion above, chapter 1 at n78.
[27] 3 *Comm* 268.   [28] 3 *Comm* 267.   [29] 1 *Comm* 4–6.

and interpreters of the English laws." "And how unbecoming must it appear," Blackstone observed, for "a member of the legislature" to be "utterly ignorant" of the law:

> Indeed it is perfectly amazing that there should be no other state of life, no other occupation, art or science, in which some method of instruction is not looked upon as requisite, except only the science of legislation, the noblest and most difficult of any... but every man of superior fortune thinks himself *born* a legislator.[30]

Having so introduced the claims for "the science of legislation," Blackstone went on to invoke the "too obvious to be called in question" mischiefs that had resulted from ill-conceived "alterations in our laws," promptly noting that "how far they have been owing to the defective education of our senators [was] a point well worthy the public attention." He continued by citing the testimony of Coke who had also "warmly" lamented the "confusion introduced by ill-judging and unlearned legislators," and then concluded:

> And if this inconvenience was so heavily felt in the reign of Queen Elizabeth, you may judge how the evil is increased in later times, when the statute book is swelled to ten times a larger bulk, *unless it should be found that the penners of our modern statutes have proportionably better informed themselves in the knowledge of the common law.*[31]

Enabling English legislators to better inform themselves of the common law was thus made explicit as a central objective for legislative science in England. That the primary content of this modern jurisprudential science should be the traditional wisdom of an elegantly displayed common law followed naturally from Blackstone's diagnosis that statute generally failed whenever it departed from common law structures, and from his broader assessment of the relative merits of the main components of England's legal system. Once this central point of Blackstone's legislative instruction is recovered, many of the most innovative features of his career and corpus come together as a unified whole. There was, first, the great emphasis and declared novelty concerning the proper method for "reducing our Laws to a System."[32] This classification and synthesis required such novel treatment not merely as a result of the attempt to instruct non-professionals, but also on account of the substance of the instruction to be received. It was vital to exhibit England's historic system of law as a genuinely rational and coherently organized system in order further to reveal the past

---

[30] 1 *Comm* 9.   [31] 1 *Comm* 10–11 (emphasis added).
[32] See the discussion above, chapter 1 at n32.

damage which resulted from uninformed legislative modifications and in order to disclose the legal structure upon which responsible law-making might in future occur. And, second, it was of course no less vital to get the instruction to those "gentlemen of considerable property" who were "ambitious of representing their country in parliament."[33] Hence, once more, the novelty and practical significance of Blackstone's position as the first teacher of English law at an English university (an Oxford innovation soon after followed at Dublin and Cambridge), and of his fashioning a legislative primer which spoke, as Bentham conceded, "the language of the Scholar and the Gentleman."[34]

The eventual use of the *Commentaries* in the nineteenth century as the standard introductory text for the beginning professional law student has done much to obscure the work's initial and more ambitious pedagogic purposes.[35] Nonetheless, something of the original situation can be restored by considering those of Blackstone's contemporaries who shared his concern to introduce English legal studies to the universities. Blackstone's own position was in many ways dependent on the enterprises of Charles Viner, the author of a twenty-three volume *Abridgment* of English law. It was Viner who established the study of English law at Oxford on a permanent basis through his benefaction of the Vinerian professorship and several law fellow-ships.[36] Blackstone was appointed the first Vinerian professor in 1758, and evidence suggests it was his advance knowledge of Viner's bequest which led him five years before, following an unsuccessful candidacy for the chair of civil law, to take the unprecedented step of offering English law lectures at the university.[37] Viner's aim in his endowment was to improve the professional education of lawyers by enabling them to receive instruction before proceeding to attendance at the courts of Westminster. Blackstone fully shared this proposal, designing his lectures and his *Commentaries* both for the starting law student and for

[33] 1 *Comm* 9.

[34] *Fragment*, p. 413. For the attempts in the eighteenth century to use the universities to revive legal education, see Holdsworth, *History of English Law*, XII, 77–101, and H. G. Hanbury, *The Vinerian Chair and Legal Education* (Oxford, 1958). For the continental parallels, see Cairns, "Blackstone, An English Institutist," pp. 321–37.

[35] This perhaps best accounts for the unfortunate error still made by legal scholars that "Blackstone was writing primarily a textbook for law students"; see Richard A. Posner, "Blackstone and Bentham," *Journal of Law and Economics*, XIX (1976), 605.

[36] For Viner's career and endowment, see Holdsworth, *History of English Law*, XII, 162–71, 739–41, and J. L. Barton, "Legal Studies," in L. S. Sutherland and L. G. Mitchell (eds.), *The History of the University of Oxford: The Eighteenth Century* (Oxford, 1986), pp. 600–5.

[37] See Lucy Sutherland, "William Blackstone and the Legal Chairs at Oxford," in René Wellek and Alvaro Ribeiro (eds.), *Evidence in Literary Scholarship: Essays in Memory of James Marshall Osborn* (Oxford, 1979), pp. 229–40.

the non-professional. Indeed, he went even further than Viner in proposing that university education might be made a requirement for members of the profession.[38]

Nor was Blackstone alone in appreciating the advantages of utilizing the universities for introducing law studies to those not destined for a professional career. Nearly thirty years before he began lecturing, his case had been argued for him by Thomas Wood in *Some Thoughts concerning the Study of the Laws of England in the Two Universities*. Like Blackstone, Wood protested against Roman law's continued monopoly of legal education at the universities and the attendant neglect of English law, which "sets the understanding of an English-man on a wrong bias and makes him less capable of serving at home in many public stations." He particularly despaired of the aristocratic prejudice against legal study, the "inbred Contempt," as he put it, "of the Laws of his own Country."[39] Again like Blackstone, Wood sought to advance these educational reforms by composing a comprehensive synthesis of English law, his 1720 *An Institute of the Laws of England, or The Laws of England in their Natural Order, according to Common Use*. As explained in the preface, Wood's aim was not only "to help the students in the Inns of Court and Chancery, but moreover to recommend the Study of the English Laws to our young nobility and gentry, and to the youth of our universities."[40] The *Institute* went through several editions in the first half of the century before being totally eclipsed by the *Commentaries*.[41] Like Blackstone once more, Wood in his legal survey pointed to the dangerous state of the statute law. For Wood, however, the main advantages of teaching law to "our young nobility and gentry" referred to the improved status the law would enjoy once it became established as an authentic academic subject. Blackstone transformed this attitude into a specific program by supplying the connection unnoticed by Wood, which was to see the governing classes' ignorance of the law as the cause of parliament's legislative failures. Once the problem had been perceived in this way, its solution became obvious.

This contemporary situation displays the *Commentaries* to be a far more engaged and programmatic exercise than has conventionally been

---

[38] The implications of the proposal for the social composition of the profession are stressed by Paul Lucas in "Blackstone and the Reform of the Legal Profession," *English Historical Review*, LXXVII (1962), 456–89. On the accuracy of Blackstone's fears regarding the social decline of the profession, see Holmes, *Augustan England*, pp. 135–50.

[39] Thomas Wood, *Some Thoughts Concerning the Study of the Laws of England in the Two Universities* (1708) reprinted in Wood, *Institute of the Laws of England*, pp. 1–3.

[40] Wood, *Institute of the Laws of England*, p. v.

[41] See the remarks of Chief Justice Mansfield cited in *Reminiscences of Charles Butler*, p. 131.

allowed. From this perspective, for example, Blackstone's generally neglected warning that English liberties "can only be lost or destroyed by the folly or demerits of its owner: the legislature" would appear to deserve as much attention as his much-quoted preceding judgment that "political or civil liberty flourish in their highest vigour in these kingdoms, where it falls little short of perfection."[42] Of course, the lessons the *Commentaries* gave England's future legislators were most often deeply conservative in nature. Blackstone claimed that parliament could build only upon "the foundation of the common law," and there was no place in his legislative science for "any great legislative revolution."

To sustain this teaching of legislative restraint, he not only insisted upon the common law's continued capacity to accommodate the nation's legal requirements, but vigilantly minimized and defended its faults and limitations. Edward Gibbon probably offered the most gentle version of this typical view of the *Commentaries* when he noted that Blackstone approached the law's defects, "with the becoming tenderness of a pious son who would wish to conceal the infirmities of his parent."[43] However, given the circumstances which prompted this service as the common law's eloquent apologist, it seems scarcely appropriate to reduce Blackstone's legal conservatism to the familiar invocations of the *Commentaries'* "spirit of nationalistic self-satisfaction," or the "influence of general social complacency on Blackstone's thought."[44] If, as Dicey suggested, the *Commentaries* supplied an early and authoritative account of parliament's legislative omnipotence, then what demands equal emphasis is the profound uneasiness with which Blackstone perceived the practical implications of this constitutional doctrine.[45] And if, as Maine alleged, Blackstone's views were "always a faithful index of the average opinions of his day," then we are dealing with a body of average opinion peculiarly preoccupied with issues of law reform and legal development.[46]

Fortunately, the more constructive aspects of Blackstone's career and legal masterpiece were not lost on his contemporary audience. Even within the circle of Bentham's early intimates, there were those who were unprepared to follow the young critic in finding little more

---

[42] 1 *Comm* 126–7.
[43] Cited in Holdsworth, *History of English Law*, XII, 727.
[44] Simpson, "The Rise and Fall of the Legal Treatise," 658, and Kennedy, "The Structure of Blackstone's *Commentaries*," 371.
[45] See the discussion above, chapter 1 at nn85–6.
[46] Henry Maine, *Ancient Law. Its Connection with the Early History of Society and its Relation to Modern Ideas* (1861), reprint of the Beacon Paperback edition, intro. Raymond Firth (Gloucester, Mass., 1970), p. 244.

in the *Commentaries* than the doctrines of a "tranquil copyist and indiscriminate apologist" crippled by an unrelenting "hydrophobia of innovation."[47] As Bentham's friend and advisor of the 1770s and 1780s, George Wilson, put it to the author of *A Fragment on Government*:

> Bentham...don't you feel now and then some compunction at the thought of the treatment your Fragment gives to Blackstone? Of all the men that ever sat on a Westminster Hall Bench, he is perhaps the only one that ever attempted any thing that had the good of the people or the improvement of the law for its object, independently of professional interest or party politics.[48]

Bentham, it is clear, felt no remorse over the treatment the *Commentaries* received at his hands. But, as George Wilson shrewdly perceived, not the least of Bentham's polemical triumphs in *A Fragment on Government* was to bury so effectively Blackstone's positive strategy for legislative science and legal improvement.[49]

---

[47] *Comment*, pp. 180, 202.
[48] *Fragment*, p. 543. Bentham claimed that it was Wilson's influence which led to the 1789 decision finally to publish *An Introduction to the Principles of Morals and Legislation*; see *Fragment*, p. 534.
[49] Bentham's attack on Blackstone is treated at length below, in chapter 11.

II

The judiciary

3

◁ ══════════════════════════════════════ ▷

Equity, principle and precedent

The second part of this study provides a more detailed, albeit selective, exploration of that part of the English legal process for which Blackstone reserved his highest commendations: the common law system developed and administered by the judiciary. It focuses on the capacity of this system to respond to new social and legal needs, and on the theory of the judicial office which sanctioned such legal creativity. The story is pursued chiefly through a survey of the career of Lord Mansfield, Chief Justice of King's Bench from 1756 to 1788, and through an analysis of the legal ideas of the Scottish judge, Lord Kames.

In turning to the judiciary, we are still attending to that body of legal doctrine concerned with the proper relationship between common law and statute. Indeed, the practice of the courts both reflected and lent crucial support to those who construed the relationship in such a way so as to restrict the scope of parliamentary action. Thus the emphasis remains the Blackstonean one of placing the claims of common law somehow *against* the statute book. Nevertheless, our primary concern is not with instances of the courts acting against statutory interference. Instead, interest centers on the courts' handling of its own common law rules, often in areas of law where legislation had had little impact. One basic reason for this has already been revealed in our discussion of the *Commentaries*: the controversial doctrine that the courts might "control" unreasonable acts of parliament by declaring them void had become by the mid eighteenth century (whatever it may have been in Coke's day) a distinct constitutional liability. The reported judgments of the courts provide frequent instances of fulsome judicial attacks on ill-drafted and misconceived acts of parliament, and judges like Mansfield and Kames insisted upon the inherent superiority of the courts over parliament as vehicles for developing legal rules. Still, none of the most dedicated defenders of judicial creativity was prepared, any more than Blackstone, to claim that the courts might control parliament's legislative will.

This certain constitutional restraint, however, was less important than might initially appear. It is unnecessary and even misleading to think of the courts' declaring statutes void as a principal common law tactic for "controlling" acts of parliament. In the long view of English legal history, the manner by which common law controlled legislation was to render it superfluous. The remarkable durability and adaptability of the common law system was what secured its primacy within the legal system. Throughout the century, despite the huge and often disturbing growth of statute law, it was still accurate for law writers to invoke the judicial dictum that "the judgments of Westminster Hall are the only authority that we have for by far the greatest part of the law of England."[1] The truth of this statement did not rest on the failure of the legislator so much as upon the courts' success in developing remedies for new legal problems without the help of legislation.

Probably the most cogent example of this in English legal history was the one artfully exploited by Blackstone – the common law transformation of the law of real property. The law of entails, the creation of uses, the formula of a collusive common recovery, the re-emergence of uses in the form of trusts, the standard eighteenth-century strict family settlement were all the creations of the courts. No doubt, it would caricature poorly the historical process to explain the emergence of such devices as the fictional common recovery to break an entail as a common law tactic deployed to prevent parliament from enacting legislation to the same purpose. Rather, the sixteenth-century conveyancers and judges who adopted this formula sought to resolve through the machinery of the courts a practical problem in land holding. As Maitland observed of an earlier episode in this process, "Men are but living from hand to mouth, arguing from one case to the next case, and they do not see what is going to happen."[2] Nonetheless, what is significant for the eighteenth century is that such practical problem-solving could appear as a preemptive strike against legislative action. When Blackstone treated the law of civil injuries he ascribed to the judges precisely such intentions. Not only had the judges succeeded in remodeling their "Gothic castle," they had furthermore "wisely avoided soliciting any great legislative revolution in the old established forms." Barrington and Butler, with more embarrassment, likewise

---

[1] For a late example, see James Ram, *The Science of Legal Judgment* (London, 1834), title page.

[2] Maitland, "English Law, 1307–1600" (1894), in *Selected Historical Essays*, p. 132. On this general theme, see also the valuable discussion in S. F. C. Milsom, "Reason in the Development of the Common Law," 496–517.

viewed many of the same episodes in the development of the law of real property – a series of judicial innovations which had forestalled legislative reform.[3] It is this supposed preemptive capacity of the common law system which makes the story of eighteenth-century judicial innovation so crucial to the discussion here.

To begin with, however, it might seem that the common law, even in the terms of Blackstone's effusive celebration, was poorly equipped to accommodate effectively such change and innovation. This suspicion, for example, informed much of Bentham's hostility to common law and his belief that the system could never properly differentiate between the requirements for legal stability and a blind adherence to the legacy of the past.[4] There was doubtless much in the *Commentaries* to encourage this sort of interpretation. As in the example of his account of the Toleration Act, Blackstone did not always distinguish his ability to provide an historical explanation for the law from a justification of it.[5] Moreover, Blackstone was hardly at his most convincing in attributing so much of the complexity of English law exclusively to the effects of uninformed statutory interference, rather than acknowledging this to be the not altogether advantageous legacy of its more general historical development. At this level, Blackstone's conservative confidence in the enduring wisdom of the common law reflected a failure to face squarely the problem of how suitable this law was for a society remarkably unlike the one in which it had originated. In turning to Mansfield and to Kames, we address jurists for whom this problem clearly had more meaning and who viewed the substance of the unwritten law with far more critical candor than Blackstone. Yet while they distance themselves from him over the degree to which the historic common law deserved alteration, they relied on a theory of the common law similar in essentials to that set out in the *Commentaries*. The law remained a set of customary practices ultimately founded on rational precepts. This understanding of common law, as we shall next find, did not necessarily lead to conservative conclusions. It also could be mobilized on behalf of programs of reform.

In spare outline, the defense of judicially orchestrated legal improvement rested on two claims. There was, first, a reading of the historical character of common law which was especially sensitive to the problem of legal obsolescence. And second, there was the aggressive invocation of the law's foundations in principles of nature and reason which might operate in the absence of case law and even at the expense

---

[3] See the discussion above, chapter one at n78 and nn106–7.
[4] Bentham's critique of common law is the subject of chapter 11.
[5] See above, chapter 1 at n84.

of historic precedents. The sort of legal change these arguments were deployed to encourage naturally demanded a fair degree of flexibility on the part of the judiciary. Judges were to develop new legal remedies, or more commonly, to adapt established legal forms to new purposes. In either case the judge was engaged in an activity recognizably more complex than applying an established rule of law to a particular case. Such instances of judicial creativity are a notorious problem in legal theory, and in the eighteenth century treatment of the question almost invariably involved discussion of the classical doctrine of equity in law. Blackstone, for instance, followed a traditional approach by citing Grotius'Aristotelian definition of equity as "the correction of that, wherein the law (by reason of its universality) is deficient." Since in law "all cases cannot be foreseen or expressed," the legal system required "somewhere a power" for defining "those circumstances, which (had they been foreseen) the legislator himself would have expressed and these are cases, which according to Grotius, '*lex non exacte definit, sed arbitrio boni viri permittit*'."[6]

This classical conception of equity was adopted and expanded in the more systematic works on equity jurisprudence which first appeared in England during this period. These accounts always introduced the subject as Blackstone had done, by insisting upon the impossibility of constructing a system of legal rules which might achieve the ends of justice in all possible cases.[7] Richard Francis, in his 1727 *Maxims of Equity*, formulated the point in theological terms by stressing that "human Providence is too weak to make Laws which shall prove just in all cases."[8] John Mitford, in his influential treatise on Chancery pleadings which first appeared in 1780, gave the position a more empirical foundation. "The wisdom of legislators in framing positive laws to answer all the purposes of justice," he reported, "has ever been found unequal to the subject."[9] Given this, John Fonblanque, in his 1793–94 edition of *A Treatise of Equity*, maintained that it was necessary "in every well-constituted government" to provide a power for

[6] 1 *Comm* 61–2.

[7] Few tenets of legal theory enjoyed such an axiomatic status. For other versions, not treated in the text, see Francis Bacon, *De Augmentis Scientiarum* (English trans.), Book 8, chapter 3, Aphorisms 10 and 32, *Works of Bacon*, V, 90, 94; Matthew Hale, *Considerations Touching the Amendment or Alteration of Laws*, in Francis Hargrave (ed.), *A Collection of Tracts, Relative to the Law of England* (London, 1787), p. 257; Richard Wooddeson, *A Systematical View of the Laws of England*, 3 vols. (London, 1792–3), I, 192–4; Sylvester Douglas (Baron Glenbervie), *Reports of Cases argued and Determined in the Court of King's Bench*, 4th edn by William Frere, 4 vols. (London, 1813), I, iii.

[8] Richard Francis, *Maxims of Equity, Collected from and Proved by Cases* (London, 1727), "To the Reader," p. 2 (pagination added).

[9] John Mitford (Lord Redesdale), *A Treatise on the Pleadings in suits in the Court of Chancery by English Bill* (1780), 5th edn (London, 1847), p. 3.

"supplying that which is defective, and controlling that which is unintentionally harsh, in the application of any general rule to a particular case."[10] In these harsh cases, a judge ruled directly according to those principles of justice which supported the positive legal edifice. Mitford accordingly described equity as a "resort to natural principles," while the author of *A Treatise of Equity* identified it with "the whole of natural justice" and "the law of God and nature."[11] Late in the century, the distinguished Scottish historian and professor of law, John Millar, neatly summarized this conventional understanding of equity: "it is necessary ... to forego in many cases the benefit of that uniformity and certainty derived from the strict observance of a general rule, and by introducing an exception from the consideration of what is equitable in particular circumstances, to avoid the hardship which would otherwise fall upon individuals."[12]

Several conclusions followed from equity's operating in terms of the special circumstances of individual cases. For Fonblanque this meant that such judicial discretion "must not be considered as a power to make a new law or to dispense with any established law."[13] Blackstone further argued that this precluded equity from being construed as a system of rules. "Equity thus depending, essentially, upon the particular circumstances of each individual case," he explained, "there can be no established rules and fixed precepts of equity laid down, without destroying its very essence, and reducing it to a positive law."[14] This also implied that the equitable authority of a judge could not be circumscribed even in those cases where a general pattern of equitable practice pertained. According to Francis, this represented "the great Difference between a Court of Law and a Court of Equity," since the former "rigidly adheres to its own established Rules, be the Injustice arising from thence ever so apparent," whereas "the Court of Equity will not adhere to its own most established Rules, if the least Injustice arises from thence."[15]

According to the classical account, equity represented an essential though distinguishable feature of any judge's authority. In England, however, equity was the province of specific courts, an institutional arrangement unique to English law. This separation of law and equity had profound consequences, for eventually English equity emerged as a separate system of general rules which could only be described as

---

[10] Ballow [?], *Treatise of Equity*, I, 6 (Fonblanque's note).
[11] Mitford, *Pleadings in Chancery*, p. 3; *Treatise of Equity*, I, 9.
[12] John Millar, *An Historical View of English Government* (1803), 4 vols. (London, 1812) IV, 278.
[13] *Treatise of Equity*, I, 6 (Fonblanque's note).   [14] 1 *Comm* 62.
[15] Francis, *Maxims of Equity*, "To the Reader," p. 3.

"equitable" in the sense that they were administered in certain courts
known as "courts of equity."[16] This development was already apparent
by the eighteenth century, and remarked by most law writers. As
Blackstone shrewdly noted, "Grotius or Pufendorf" would scarcely be
able "to discover by their own light, the system of a court of equity in
England."[17] However, hardly any writer chose to understand the
whole of English equity simply in terms of the customary practices of
the equity courts, and this complicated the jurisprudential picture
enormously. Indeed, there are few legal topics of the period quite so
nebulous as the equitable character of English law, and the status of
"general rules" in English equity jurisprudence.

Notwithstanding the English institutional peculiarity, it was still
possible for lawyers to conceive of at least the origins of English equity
in terms of the classical definition. Even this required a substantial
misreading of the legal past. The medieval doctrine of the Chancellor
adjudicating disputes according to "Conscience" had to be conflated
with the classical notion of any judge making equitable exceptions to
general rules, and the common law forms which equity had historically
modified had to be reduced to a body of positive rules.[18] Lord
Chancellor Hardwicke, for example, accounted for the rise of England's
most important equity court by reference to the Chancellor's historic
function of issuing original writs under the Great Seal to suitors at
common law. Cases arose where "the common law afforded no
remedy" and the Chancellors, "most commonly churchmen, men of
conscience," would seek to provide a remedy by summoning the
litigants and laying "it upon the conscience of the wrongdoer to do
right."[19] It was not difficult to present this sort of judicial activism in
more classical terms. Thus, Mitford observed more generally that
"early... in the history of our jurisprudence the administration of
justice by the ordinary courts appears to have been incomplete, and to
supply the defect the courts of equity have exerted their jurisdiction."[20] Much of the standard Chancery practice could be seen to follow
from this rubric. Chancery adjudicated upon cases regarding trusts

---

[16] This is a truncated version of Maitland's famous definition in *Equity: A Course of Lectures*, ed.
A. H. Chaytor and M. J. Whittaker (Cambridge, 1932), p. 1.

[17] 3 *Comm* 433. See also Mitford's more prosaic formulation, "It is not a very easy task accurately
to describe the jurisdiction of our courts of equity," Mitford, *Pleadings in Chancery*, p. 5n.

[18] For general accounts of Chancery's development, see J. H. Baker, *An Introduction to English
Legal History*, 2nd edn (London, 1979), pp. 83–95, and S. F. C. Milsom, *Historical Foundations
of the Common Law*, (London, 1969), pp. 74–87. The meaning of "conscience" in early modern
English law has now been helpfully examined by Louis A. Knafla in "Conscience in the
English Common Law Tradition," *University of Toronto Law Journal*, XXVI (1976), 1–16.

[19] Hardwicke (then Philip Yorke) gave this explanation in his arguments in R v *Hare and Mann*,
(1719) 1 Strange 146, 151.   [20] Mitford, *Pleadings in Chancery*, p. 4.

(which common law could not recognize), cases concerning mortgages (which common law could not treat as mere securities for debt), and commanded the specific performances of contracts (where common law damages proved inadequate). Correspondingly, equity would not interfere in cases where suitable remedies existed at common law.[21] Moreover, throughout the century cases still appeared in which the chancellor granted exceptions to legal rules or decreed by invoking the "conscience of the court."[22] Something of the continued particularity of Chancery practice, which Blackstone held to be the "essence of equity," was demonstrated almost by default in the many areas of adjudication which John Fonblanque found impossible to resolve "into system" in his edition of *A Treatise of Equity*.[23]

Perhaps the most sustained attempt to treat English equity in entirely orthodox terms was Francis' *Maxims of Equity*. Francis began his didactic text by drawing a sharp distinction between common law which was bound by "strict Rules of Law" and equity which was "bound not to suffer an Act of Injustice to prevail, though it be warranted by the Forms and Proceedings of Law."[24] He then discussed English equity under fourteen maxims or formal principles of natural justice, such as "he that will have equity done to him, must do it to the same person," "he that hath committed Iniquity shall have not Equity," and "Equity suffers not a Right to be without a remedy." When actual Chancery cases were cited, these served merely to illustrate such equitable principles. Although Francis acknowledged that one could find established "Rules of Equity" consolidated in Chancery case law, he insisted that such rules had been "preserved inviolable" only because "they have never been found to be unjust," and thereby ensured that these formal maxims, and not the rules, remained the essence of equity in England.[25]

England's equity courts, as Francis explained, preserved the just application of legal rules in all cases. But this orthodox solution to the

---

[21] For the general background concerning trusts and mortgages, see A. W. B. Simpson, *An Introduction to the History of Land Law* (Oxford, 1962), pp. 182–94, 225–8, and on the performance of contracts, see A. W. B. Simpson, *A History of the Common Law of Contract*; Volume 1: *The Rise of the Action of Assumpsit* (Oxford, 1975), pp. 595–8. For contemporary discussions, on mortgages, see Hardwicke's decree at *Casbourne v Inglis and Scarfe*, (1737) West 221; on the performance of contracts, see Hardwicke's decrees at *Buxton v Lister and Cooper*, (1746) 3 Atkyns 383, *Penn v Lord Baltimore*, (1750) 1 Vesey Sr. 444, and see also *Treatise of Equity*, I, 24–33, Jeffrey Gilbert, *The History and Practice of the High Court of Chancery* (London, 1758), pp. 219–21, and John Joseph Powell, *Essay upon the Law of Contracts and Agreements*, 2 vols. (London, 1790), II, 1–4.

[22] See the examples cited below at n43.

[23] See *Treatise of Equity*, I, 245–52 (on marriage bonds); I, 363–4 (on failure of consideration); II, 447–8 (on evidence); II, 493–4 (on bills of discovery).

[24] Francis, *Maxims of Equity*, "To the Reader," p. 3.   [25] *Ibid.*

problems believed inherent in the operation of any legal system generated its own difficulties. Equity might appear to sanction a degree of judicial discretion which could undermine the system of rules of law altogether. As Blackstone observed, "the liberty of considering all cases in an equitable light must not be indulged too far, lest thereby we destroy all law, and leave the decision of every question entirely in the breast of the judge."[26] It was here that the peculiarity of the English institutional arrangement impinged most strongly on the treatment of equity jurisprudence. The normal need to balance the claims of equity against the stability of legal rules was transformed into a constitutional issue regarding the extent to which Chancery might interfere with and overrule the common law.

This issue centered in the famous seventeenth-century dispute between Coke and Ellesmere, the political dimension of which was evidenced in James I's keen interest in the outcome.[27] The jurisdictional struggle was largely resolved in that period, but even in the eighteenth century Chancery judges were still extremely cautious in asserting the nature of their discretionary powers, lest this appear as a claim on behalf of prerogative courts. Hardwicke, for instance, took care to dissociate his equitable power from an authority to invade the jurisdictions of other courts, and the maxim *aequitas sequitur legem* became a favored doctrine in Chancery.[28] Something of the earlier constitutional struggle certainly echoed in Chief Baron Gilbert's presentation of Chancery as a court of "very small and inconsiderable beginning" with procedures "totally before unheard of," and which "though it was very much impugned even towards its first original creation...is now grown to that degree, that it has swallowed up most of the other business of the common law courts."[29]

At a more theoretical level, equity could appear not merely as an institutional jurisdiction distinct from common law, but as a system of adjudication essentially antithetic to the genius of English jurisprudence. This critical view of equity turned on the relationship commonly drawn between the operation of strictly defined legal rules and the maintenance of English liberty. Blackstone instructed that it

---

[26] 1 *Comm* 62.

[27] The events are summarized in Baker, *Introduction to English Legal History*, pp. 92–3.

[28] Hardwicke discussed the maxim *aequitas sequitur legem* in *Hervey* v *Aston*, (1738) West 350, 425. For examples of his refusing to extend Chancery jurisdiction where remedies existed elsewhere, see *Anon.*, (1746) 3 Atkyns 350, *Jesus College* v *Bloom*, (1745) 1 Ambler 54, *Lord Montague* v *Dudman*, (1751) 2 Vesey Sr. 396. Hardwicke's circumspection in this regard is emphasized by Croft in his dissertation, "Philip Yorke, First Earl of Hardwicke – An Assessment of his Legal Career," pp. 226–32.

[29] Jeffrey Gilbert, *The History of Chancery*, p. 14.

was "essential to a free people" for judicial determinations to "be published and adhered to." Thus, while "in many other countries every thing is left in the breast of the judge to determine," in England the judge "is only to *declare* and *pronounce*, not to *make* or *new-model*, the law."[30] In a more polemical manner, Lord Camden crisply explained in 1765, "the discretion of a judge is the law of tyrants."[31] It was by this standard, moreover, that English law was frequently defended against the reproach of excessive complexity and disorder. As Matthew Hale maintained, though the common law was "more particular than other Laws" and therefore "more numerous and less methodical," this still "recompenceth with greater advantages: namely, it prevents arbitrariness in the Judge, and makes the Law more certain."[32]

This belief in the relationship between English liberty and the distinctive certainty of English justice was also endorsed by more detached observers. Montesquieu, in the famous examination of the English constitution which had "political liberty" as its "direct end," stressed that the judgments of the courts were fixed "to such a degree as to be ever conformable to the letter of the law."[33] Adam Smith concurred that "an other thing which greatly confirms the liberty of the subjects in England" was "the little power of the judges in explaining, altering, or extending or correcting the meaning of the laws." Smith went on to contrast the circumspection of the common law judges with the judicial discretion enjoyed in Chancery, and concluded that "the Chancellor is certainly as arbitrary a judge as most."[34]

The discretionary powers of the equity judge seemed contrary to the objectives and character of English law from another standpoint. This was in terms of the more general concern to preserve legal "certainty" against possible judicial disruption. As Bacon claimed, "Certainty is so essential to law that law cannot even be just without it... It is well said also, 'That that is the best law which leaves least to the discretion of the judge'; and this comes from the certainty of it."[35] Increasingly in the eighteenth century, this position was taken up by utilitarian moralists to develop an understanding of precedent close to the modern doctrine of *stare decisis*. William Paley, for example, insisted that precedents "should not be overthrown" so that "the discretion of judges may be bound down by positive rules." Such "deference to

---

[30] 3 *Comm* 327.
[31] Cited, with other examples, in Joseph Parkes, *A History of the Court of Chancery* (London, 1828), pp. 461-2. [32] Hale, *Rolle's Abridgment*, preface p. 3.
[33] Montesquieu, *Spirit of the Laws*, p. 153.
[34] Smith, *Lectures on Jurisprudence*, pp. 275, 282.
[35] Bacon, *De Augmentis Scientiarum*, Book 8, chapter 3, Aphorism 8, *Works of Bacon*, V, 90, and see Aphorism 46, *Works of Bacon*, V, 96.

prior decisions" not only served the liberty of the individual, but also ensured that "upon every occasion in which his legal interest is concerned," the subject knew "how to act and what to expect."[36] By this standard, equity again appeared as something suspect. "It is a common objection against our Courts of Equity," Francis acknowledged, "that their Power being Absolute and extraordinary, their Determinations must consequently be uncertain and precarious ... [and] the unhappy suitor must enter into a Court of Equity with Doubts and Fears."[37]

English equity did not lack for defenses against such charges, and law writers were eager to explain how England's equity courts threatened neither the certainty of the law nor the liberty of the subject. But although these defenses were easily assembled and amply documented, they could only be deployed at the cost of turning equity into a legal entity scarce resembling the classical model upon the basis of which most accounts of English equity were introduced.

One such response involved a more careful formulation of the nature of Chancery's status as a "court of conscience" so as to preclude the Chancellor's conscience from operating as an instrument of arbitrary justice. Lord Nottingham adopted this tactic in the late seventeenth century when he described the Chancellor's conscience as "merely *civilis et politica.*"[38] The implications of this were neatly illustrated in a Chancery decree of 1734 in a case on a trust estate executed as part of a marriage settlement. The Master of the Rolls, Sir Joseph Jekyll, determined for the plaintiff, and of chief interest here is the care Jekyll took in explaining the nature of his discretionary authority under "conscience." He introduced his decision by noting that were he to determine the issue according to "*honour, gratitude, private conscience &c.,*" he would have to conclude that the plaintiff's "claim should never have been made." But once made, the title had to be recognized since the law was clear:

> though proceedings in equity are said to be *secundum discretionem boni viri,* yet when it is asked, *vir bonus est quis?* the answer is *qui consulta patrum qui leges juraque servat*; and as it is said in *Rook's* case that discretion is a science, not to act arbitrarily according to men's wills and private affections, so the discretion which is exercised here is to be governed by the rules of law and equity...[39]

By so viewing equitable discretion, Jekyll made certain that Chancery

---

[36] William Paley, *The Principles of Moral and Political Philosophy* (London, 1785), p. 508.
[37] Francis, *Maxims of Equity,* "To the Reader," p. 1.
[38] Cited in Baker, *English Legal History,* p. 94.
[39] *Cowper v Cowper,* (1734) 2 P Williams 720, 734, 753.

would not "over-turn the grounds or principles" of law, even in such cases where the judge acknowledged the resulting hardship.[40] Yet, while thus insulating Chancery from the stigma of arbitrary justice, Jekyll had also fashioned an image of equity in England remarkably unlike that of Francis, according to whom the court of equity would ignore even the "most established Rules" when "the least Injustice arises from thence."

In addition to this argument, probably the most powerful tactic for defending equity against the charge of arbitrary proceedings was found in the actual practice of Chancery. In the vast majority of cases, Chancellors did not decide issues by appeals to conscience or natural justice, but in accordance with the settled pattern of Chancery precedents. As Blackstone insisted, "the system of our courts of equity is a laboured connected system governed by established rules"; or as Mitford maintained, "principles of decision...adopted by the courts of equity, when fully established...are considered by those courts as rules to be observed with as much strictness as positive law."[41]

In making this claim English lawyers were quick to draw upon the recent experience of Lord Hardwicke's twenty-year career in Chancery from 1736 to 1756 when considerable advances were made in settling equity as a system of case law.[42] Hardwicke, in fact, frequently exercised his authority in a more conventional equitable fashion to supply defects in established legal remedies, to grant exceptions in particular harsh cases, and to pronounce decrees according to the conscience of the court.[43] In correspondence with Lord Kames he maintained that unless some discretionary power was preserved in Chancery it "might lay a foundation for an equitable relief even against decrees in equity."[44] However, for his contemporaries, as for later historians, the more striking feature of his judgeship was what he achieved towards consolidating Chancery practice into a system of general rules. Barrington in 1766 offered one of the earliest of such evaluations when he defended English equity from the charge of "uncertainty" by observing that, "near twenty years of well-considered

---

[40] *Ibid.*, 754.

[41] 3 *Comm* 432, and Mitford, *Pleadings in Chancery*, p. 4n.

[42] Croft's unpublished dissertation, "Philip Yorke, First Earl of Hardwicke – An Assessment of his Legal Career," provides the most recent and the most comprehensive survey of his accomplishments at Chancery. Reed Browning attempts a synthetic account of Hardwicke's legal and constitutional ideas in *Political and Constitutional Ideas of the Court Whigs* (Baton Rouge, 1982), chapter 6.

[43] For leading examples, see: *Garth v Cotton*, (1750) 1 LCE 559; *Newcoman v Bethlem Hospital*, (1741) 1 Ambler 8, 2 Ambler 785; *Scroggs v Scroggs*, (1755) 1 Ambler 272, 2 Ambler 812; *Stace v Mabbott*, (1754) 2 Vesey Sr. 552.

[44] Cited in Philip C. Yorke, *Life of Hardwicke*, II, 554.

decrees, made by the same most consummate lawyer without reversal, have now established so clear, consistent, and beneficial a system of equity, that ignorance only can reproach it with being *jus vagum aut incognitum.*"[45]

Hardwicke's concern to settle Chancery practice was displayed in the careful formulation of his decrees and in his eagerness to deduce general rules out of the relevant, often apparently contradictory, Chancery precedents. Hence, his judgments frequently included an elaborate review of earlier decisions, as well as a more precise presentation of the loosely stated general rules of equity advanced in the pleadings.[46] Even in those situations depending "on the latitude of discretion of a court of equity," he urged Chancery to "go by some rule" lest its deliberations "be attended with inconvenience and uncertainty."[47] His cautious respect for established precedents was revealed in those instances where he refused to grant equitable relief in order not to "break in on an established rule, and make a precedent of bad consequence."[48] Similar again were the few cases where Hardwicke corrected his own first thoughts or previous decrees upon the discovery of contrary precedents.[49] As he frankly confessed in a ruling in 1755, "I am under some difficulty for the sake of the precedent."[50]

Contemporaries may well have over-estimated Hardwicke's success at operating equity as a settled system of general rules, particularly those who made tendentious use of his example in criticism of the less circumspect judicial style of Lord Mansfield.[51] But there can be no real doubt of the influence Hardwicke commanded during his Chancellorship, nor of his impact on those who sought to characterize English equity as a system of fixed rules. Legal writers could often rely on his decrees for complete statements of the law applied in Chancery. Fonblanque made use of this expedient in his edition of *A Treatise of Equity*, as did Francis Hargrave in his discussion of the Hanoverian statute of mortmain.[52] Hargrave, moreover, was able to describe

[45] Barrington, *Ancient Statutes*, p. 498. See also Croft's similar conclusions in "Philip Yorke, First Earl of Hardwicke," pp. 215–16, 474–8.
[46] For examples, see: *Bishop of Cloyne* v *Young*, (1750) 2 Vesey Sr. 91; *Lord Dudley* v *Lord Warde*, (1751) 1 Ambler 113; *Ex parte Dumas*, (1754) 2 Vesey Sr. 582; *Jewson* v *Moulson*, (1742) 2 Atkyns 417; *Hopkins* v *Hopkins*, (1738) West 606.
[47] *Aston* v *Aston*, (1749) 1 Vesey Sr. 264.
[48] *Arnold* v *Chapman*, (1748) 1 Vesey Sr. 108, 109.
[49] *Hume* v *Edwards*, (1749) 3 Atkyns 693; *Casbourne* v *Scarfe and Inglis*, (1737) 1 Atkyns 603.
[50] *Ex parte Macklin*, (1755) 2 Vesey Sr. 675.
[51] See, for example, Andrew Stuart, *Letters to the Right Honorable Lord Mansfield* (Dublin, 1773), p. 5.
[52] See *Treatise of Equity*, I, 87–92 (on contract rights of a *feme covert*), I, 114–15 (on fraud) and Francis Hargrave (ed.), *Collectanea Juridica, Consisting of Tracts Relative to the Law and Constitution of England*, 2 vols. (London, 1787), I, 433–57.

equity in historical terms as a "power for dispensing with positive rules of law" which had now become "generally confined" to "those cases in which length of time has almost sanctified the practice."[53] From this, it might appear that English equity had simply conformed to the general processes of customary law. "Particular decisions," as John Millar observed, "become the foundation for general rules, which are afterwards limited by particular exceptions, and these exceptions being also generalized and reduced into different classes, are again subjected to future limitations."[54] The development and routine operation of these general rules in Chancery naturally prevented equity from functioning in the arbitrary manner feared by common lawyers. However, this again meant that equity ceased to resemble that process of natural justice depicted during the same period by Francis. Rules of equity, it seemed, were not to be found in formal maxims and principles, but in such technical and artificial rules of practice as, "the distinguishing between a mortgage at *five per cent*, with a clause of reduction to *four*, if the interest be regularly paid, and a mortgage at *four per cent*, with a clause of enlargement to *five*, if the payment of the interest is deferred; so that the former shall be deemed a conscientious, the latter an unrighteous, bargain."[55]

In the face of this exceptional complexity of theory and institutional practice, Blackstone offered in the *Commentaries* what he considered the first systematic presentation of equity jurisprudence in English law.[56] The account is not always clear, in part because of his failure to distinguish sharply enough his initial discussion of equity in terms of Grotius' definition from his later treatment of equity as the practice of the English equity courts. His guiding argument, however, was reasonably plain. This was to insist that no theoretical construction could adequately explain the separation of law and equity in English jurisprudence:

> The very terms of a court of *equity* and a court of *law*, as contrasted to each other, are apt to confound and mislead us: as if the one judged without equity, and the other was not bound by any law...the system of jurisprudence in our courts both of law and equity are now equally artificial systems, founded on the same principles of justice and positive

---

[53] Cited in Yorke, *Life of Hardwicke*, II, 422–3.
[54] Millar, *Historical View of English Government*, IV, 280.
[55] Cited by Blackstone, with other examples, at 3 *Comm* 432–3.
[56] See 3 *Comm* 429, "nothing is hitherto extant that can give a stranger a tolerable idea of the courts of equity subsisting in England." Holdsworth, however, maintained that Blackstone underestimated the existing literature on equity, in "Blackstone's Treatment of Equity," *Harvard Law Review*, XLIII (1929), 1–3.

law; but varied by different usages in the forms and mode of their
proceedings.[57]

Blackstone then developed this position through a critique of what he
took to be the principal claims made for equity jurisprudence: (1) "it
is the business of a court of equity in England to abate the rigour of the
common law"; (2) "a court of equity determines according to the spirit
of the rule and not according to the strictness of the letter"; (3) "*Fraud,
accident* and *trust* are the proper and peculiar objects of a court of
equity"; (4) "a court of equity is not bound by rules or precedents, but
acts from the opinion of the judge, founded on the circumstances of
every particular case."[58]

For part of his critique Blackstone employed the tactic used by other
legal writers and appealed to equity's developed status as a restricted
and settled system of general rules. To counter the claim that equity
abated "the rigour of the common law," he pointed to the many
instances in which equity failed to interfere with common law practice.
With regard to the matters of "fraud, accident, and trusts," he
indicated that equity in fact shared this jurisdiction with the courts of
law. To overturn the notion that equity was not "bound by rules or
precedents," he again pointed to the practice of English equity:

> The system of our courts of equity is a laboured connected system,
> governed by established rules, and bound down by precedents, from
> which they do not depart, although the reason of some of them may
> perhaps be liable to objection.[59]

For the rest of his critique Blackstone again appealed to the practice
of the courts. But here his argument ran in a different direction. Instead
of pointing to the manner in which equity had come to operate as
settled law, he asserted that *all* the English courts enjoyed an equitable
authority. He therefore dismissed the notion that equity was distinctive
in adjudicating "according to the spirit of the rule" by stressing that
"so also does a court of law... Here by *equity* we mean nothing but the
sound interpretation of the law."[60] The same argument reappeared in
an unambiguous denial that the equity courts enjoyed any special
relation to natural justice:

> Equity then, in its true and genuine meaning, is the soul and spirit of all
> law: *positive* law is construed, and *rational* law is made by it. In this, equity
> is synonymous to justice; in that, to the true sense and sound
> interpretation of the rule.[61]

---

[57] 3 *Comm* 429, 434. Maitland took this to be analogous to his own treatment, see Maitland,
Equity, pp. 12–14.   [58] 3 *Comm* 430–3.

[59] 3 *Comm* 432.   [60] 3 *Comm* 430–1.   [61] 3 *Comm* 429.

To demonstrate the artificial nature of the separation of law and equity Blackstone thus supplied two arguments. Equity was like law because both systems were bound by rules and precedents, and equity was also like law because both systems allowed an equitable interpretation of their rules. Both the accuracy and the compatibility of these doctrines have been challenged, and the most recent editor of this section of the *Commentaries*, John Langbein, has joined earlier scholars in finding the discussion "baffling."[62] The account is perhaps more complicated than confused, and the complication has less to do with Blackstone's understanding of equity than with his theory of common law. For in his second argument, Blackstone returned to his natural law precepts, and drew upon the conception of precedent these precepts entailed. In this sense, the elusive identity of English equity was simply a reflection of the ambiguous status of precedents in common law.

Blackstone, as we have seen, included in his account of common law the established principle that "what is not reason is not law." When the common law judges encountered a previous judicial sentence that was "contrary to reason" or "to the divine law," they rejected the decision as being "*not law*" rather than as "*bad law*." This view of precedent reversal was linked to the more general doctrine that distinguished the common law itself from particular precedents. The "decisions of courts" furnished "the evidence of what is common law," Blackstone reported, but "*the law* and the *opinion of the judge*" were not "one and the same thing."[63] This insistence that precedents and rulings served merely as "evidence" of the common law testified to the unwillingness of common lawyers to construe England's *lex non scripta* solely as a body of positive rules. The relevant distinction between authentic positive law and the common law was carefully delineated by James Sedgwick in his *Remarks on the Commentaries*. Sedgwick observed that "in the administration of statutory law" the magistrate "has only to apply that law to the affair under trial." "In common litigations," however, "those general principles which are the essence of justice itself are to be resorted to, and the adjudged cases consulted, with a view to their application, so far as they are accordant with the spirit of equity, and not for the mere *dictatum* of the adjudged case itself."[64] It was this view of precedents which Hardwicke adopted in observing that "law or equity does not depend on the particular cases, but on the

---

[62] Blackstone, *Commentaries: Facsimile of the first edition*, III, viii (editorial introduction). For earlier criticisms, see Holdsworth, "Blackstone's Treatment of Equity," pp. 3–6, and the objections of Alexander Fraser Tytler discussed below, chapter 8 at nn53–4.

[63] 1 *Comm* 71, and see above, chapter 1 at n66.

[64] Sedgwick, *Remarks on the Commentaries*, pp. 69–70.

general reason running through them," and which Mansfield invoked in maintaining that the law was founded not in cases, but "in equity, reason and good sense."[65]

This attitude to precedents, moreover, afforded the common law judges a good measure of flexibility for applying and refining common law rules, particularly in those areas of litigation where the existing case law appeared undeveloped. "In omitted cases," wrote Bacon, "let reason be esteemed prolific and custom barren." Such judicial authority also implied that the courts could adjudicate novel cases on the basis of reason and principles of natural justice, and without recourse to legislation. As Bacon further noted, "the power of supplying, extending, and moderating laws, differs little from that of making them."[66] And, of course, if common law was viewed in this light, as Blackstone insisted, it looked at the theoretical level remarkably like equity. Both were artificial systems of judicial practice ultimately grounded in rational principles which particular cases served to illustrate.

Yet while distinguishing the common law from precedents, Blackstone still granted these precedents considerable weight, lest the law be threatened by that uncertainty and arbitrariness usually associated with equity jurisprudence. He therefore strongly affirmed the "established rule" that judges were "to abide by former precedents where the same points come again in litigation," for the judge was sworn to determine "not according to his own private judgement, but according to the known laws and customs of the land."[67] According to Blackstone, then, common law could not be equated with precedents, but precedents were to be followed in order "to keep the scale of justice even and steady, and not liable to waver with every new judge's opinion."[68] The overall harmony of this labored conception of precedents was affirmed in his summary formula, "that precedents and rules must be followed, unless flatly absurd or unjust."[69] Nevertheless, the fact that precedents could be viewed in two lights meant that eighteenth-century lawyers could appeal to the genius of common law and refer to two rather different things. There were those, like Mansfield, who took precedents to be illustrations of those rational principles which were the essence of common law; while others, including especially the critics of Mansfield, viewed common law as a fixed body of precedents which constituted those positive rules that

---

[65] *Aston* v *Aston*, (1749) 1 Vesey Sr. 264, 266; *James* v *Price*, (1773) Lofft 219, 221.
[66] Bacon, *De Augmentis Scientiarum*, Book 8, chapter 3, Aphorisms 11 and 37, in *Works of Bacon*, V, 90, 95.
[67] 1 *Comm* 69.   [68] 1 *Comm* 69.   [69] 1 *Comm* 70.

were the substance of common law. These rival understandings of principles and precedents in turn affected what lawyers made of the place of equity in English law. If common law was principle, then the law resembled equity, and the common law judge enjoyed considerable flexibility in applying and modifying the rules of law. If common law was precedent, then law was opposed to equity, and the equitable authority of the judge needed to be contained to prevent its undermining the law itself.

For Blackstone the common law was both principle and precedent. However, in the presence of judges like Kames and Mansfield whose reforming enterprises involved a rigorous appeal to principles of natural justice and equity, it became difficult to see how one part of the Blackstonean structure could be upheld except at the expense of the other. The problem at least was not lost on the leading protagonist:

> PRECEDENT and PRINCIPLE often had a hard struggle which should lay hold of Lord Mansfield; and he used to say that he ought to be drawn placed between them, like Garrick between TRAGEDY and COMEDY.[70]

[70] John Lord Campbell, *The Lives of the Chief Justices of England* (1849), 2 vols. (Boston, 1850), II, 417.

4

◁ ═══ ▷

Legal principles and law reform

Even before the completion in 1788 of his thirty-two-year career as
Chief Justice of the Court of King's Bench, Mansfield's contemporaries
came to view his judgeship as a unique episode in legal creativity and
innovation. Admirers hailed "the founder of the commercial law" of
England, while critics protested that "no period of English law of
whatever length" might be produced "wherein so many of its settled
rules have been reversed as during the time of this judge."[1] His most
fulsome eulogist, Lord Campbell, celebrated the jurist who had
achieved "more for the jurisprudence of this country than any
legislator or judge or author who has ever made the improvement of
it his object."[2] His most shrill detractor, Junius, condemned the figure
who had "made it the study and practice of his life to undermine and
alter the whole system of jurisprudence in the Court of King's
Bench."[3]

The published evidence of Mansfield's judicial achievement is
contained in a dozen-odd volumes of eighteenth-century law reports.[4]
These are an important source which deserve greater attention from
historians of eighteenth-century social and political ideas. But they also
present special problems which warrant no less careful consideration.

---

[1] The contrasting comments of Sir Francis Buller in *Lickbarrow* v *Mason*, (1787) 2 Term Rpts
63, 73 (cited in full below, chapter 5 at n80), and of Thomas Jefferson in 1785, *The Writings
of Thomas Jefferson*, ed. Paul Leister Ford, 10 vols. (New York, 1892–99), VII, 451 (cited in
Horwitz, *The Transformation of American Law*, p. 18).

[2] Campbell, *Chief Justices*, II, 566.

[3] "Letter to the Public Advertiser" (1771), in *The Letters of Junius*, ed. C. W. Everett (London,
1927), p. 254.

[4] Mansfield's personal papers were destroyed in the fire caused by the Gordon Riots. However,
a collection of his judicial notebooks has recently come to light which will greatly improve
our understanding of his career on the Bench. On these, see Edmund Heward, *Lord Mansfield*
(Chichester, 1979), pp. 45–64, and James C. Oldham, "Eighteenth-century Judges' Notes:
How They Explain, Correct and Enhance the Reports," *American Journal of Legal History*,
XXXI (1987), 9–42. Mansfield's biography and professional career are detailed in Campbell,
Chief Justices, II, 302–584, and in Holliday, *Life of Mansfield*. The most helpful general account
of his judicial career remains C. H. S. Fifoot, *Lord Mansfield* (Oxford, 1936).

Throughout the period England still lacked any official system of standard law reporting. Mansfield, as his contemporaries fully recognized, was singularly blessed in the private reporters he attracted, and it is easy to mistake the novelty and distinctiveness of his judicial leadership simply on account of the unmatched quality of the law reports covering his tenure at King's Bench.[5] Moreover, a series of even the most accurately reported judicial edicts, produced over a span of thirty-two years in response to discrete legal disputes, is inevitably a cumbersome and disjointed source which can be rendered into a synthetic body of legal ideas only through some brisk and often ruthless editing. Even then, exceptions will exist and a great number of mundane cases will be ignored. Given the nature of this material, it is useful to begin a discussion of the eighteenth-century judiciary by examining at length two particularly illuminating cases: *Omychund* v *Barker* and *Millar* v *Taylor*. Mansfield was a leading participant in each case, and each case provided the occasion for expansive judicial reasoning and rhetoric which serves to introduce many of the leading issues attending judicial activism in this period.

Omychund v *Barker* appeared before the court of Chancery in 1744 where it was determined by Lord Hardwicke in consultation with the common law Chief Justices Willes and Lee, and Chief Baron Parker.[6] The bill was brought by Omychund against the heirs of the defendant for a debt of £7,600 which Barker had contracted in Calcutta while employed by the East India Company. The determination of the dispute turned on the rules of evidence. The case is illustrative not only of the ways in which the courts appealed to legal principles and natural jurisprudence in the effort to reshape legal practice, but also of the manner in which Britain's new commercial and imperial circumstances put strain on its inherited forms of justice.

Barker's defense argued that the debt alleged by Omychund could not be proved in an English court because Omychund could not swear to a Christian oath. Abundant authority existed to support the claim. The testimony of Fleta, Bracton, Britton, Fortescue and especially Coke were cited to prove the common law rule that "an infidel" could not be a witness in an English court. Omychund, being a "Gentoo," was accordingly disqualified. No firm precedents could be cited against the rule, enabling Barker's defense to insist that Omychund's

---

[5] See, for example, the contemporary praise of Mansfield's first reporter, Sir James Burrow, in Richard Burn, *Observations on the Bill...for the Better Relief and Employment of the Poor* (London, 1776), p. 25, and Bentham, *Comment*, p. 214n. Also see the discussion by Holdsworth, *History of English Law*, XII, 110–18.

[6] *Omychund* v *Barker*, (1744) 1 Atkyns 21.

testimony could not be introduced "without overturning the law entirely."[7]

But, as Blackstone was later to emphasize, the law was also the perfection of reason; and reason, according to the arguments advanced on Omychund's side, plainly demanded that non-Christians be allowed as witnesses lest the courts render themselves incapable of adjudicating the increasing numbers of extra-European disputes involving British merchants and agents. This position was developed by the future Lord Chief Justice Mansfield, then Solicitor General William Murray, who acted as one of Omychund's counsel. Murray maintained that the absence of established precedents for an "infidel's" testifying in an English court could not be taken as an authoritative statement of the law, since the omission merely reflected prior historical circumstances:

> 'Tis said there is no one precedent or case of a heathen sworn according to the ceremonies of his own religion, ever existed before in England in courts of justice, proceeding according to the common law ... No wonder that it has not existed before, because all our commerce is carried on by our going to them, instead of their coming here ... The arguments of the other side therefore prove nothing; for does it follow from hence that no witnesses can be examined in a case that never specifically existed before, or that an action cannot be brought in a case that never happened before?[8]

The absence of prior cases in no way impugned the capacity of the court to adjudicate an issue that "never specifically happened before," since the law itself was not solely constituted by historic cases and precedents:

> Reason, stated to be the first ground of all laws, by the author of the book called *Doctor and Student*, and general principles must determine the case; therefore the only question is, whether upon principles of reason, justice and convenience, this witness ought to be admitted.[9]

Murray went on to stress the distinctive strengths of those historically refined rules of common law whose first ground was found in "principles of reason, justice and convenience." In so doing he invoked the influential conception, associated with Hale and later adopted by Blackstone, of the special strengths of customary law; and as Blackstone was to do, Murray immediately contrasted the achievement of common law with the less wholesome process of legal development available through statute:

---

[7] *Ibid.*, 27; the references to Coke are to 2 Inst 479, 719; 3 Inst 165; 4 Inst 279.
[8] 1 Atkyns 21, 31.   [9] *Ibid.*, 32.

All occasions do not arise at once; now a particular species of *Indians* appears; hereafter another species of *Indians* may arise. A statute very seldom can take in all cases, therefore the common law, *that works itself pure* by rules drawn from the fountain of justice, is for this reason superior to an act of parliament.[10]

Omychund's other counsel, the Attorney General Dudley Ryder, adopted a similar attitude over the rules of evidence. He conceded Coke's rule "that an infidel cannot be a witness," only to argue that if exceptions "were not allowed" to such rules, "it would be better to demolish" them. The sole "general rule" of evidence taken "without exception" was the principle of law "that the best evidence shall be admitted which the nature of the case will afford." And the circumstances in *Omychund* v *Barker* clearly dictated that Coke's rule was to be sacrificed to this fundamental principle.[11]

The judicial determination of the issue followed these claims. Chief Justice Lee advanced a particularly forceful statement of the law's natural foundations which enabled the courts to overcome Coke's rule. "The rules of evidence," he maintained, "are to be considered as artificial rules framed by men for convenience." These he contrasted to the "one rule [that] can never vary, *viz.* the eternal rule of natural justice." This was a case which had to be judged in terms of the commands of "natural justice," and "considering evidence in this way is agreeable to the genius of the law of England."[12]

Hardwicke, in stating the ruling of the court, reasoned similarly. He invoked the "one general rule of evidence, *the best that the nature of the case will admit*" to overcome the settled common law prohibition against the testimony of infidels.[13] He further argued that Coke in any case had mistaken the reason of the law regarding oaths. The purpose of such oaths, as had been amply argued by the leading natural law authorities, was to prove the conscience of the witness and not, as Coke implied, to protect the Christian faith:

> This falls in exactly with what Lord Stair, Puffendorf [*sic*], &c., say, that it has been the wisdom of all nations to administer such oaths as are agreeable to the notion of the person taking, and does not at all affect the conscience of the person administering, nor does it in any respect adopt such religion.[14]

Through these appeals to the reason of the law and the dictates of natural justice, Hardwicke's court effected a much-needed modification of the rules of evidence in response to new social developments. The

---

[10] *Ibid.*, 33. [11] *Ibid.*, 28, 29. [12] *Ibid.*, 46.
[13] *Ibid.*, 49. [14] *Ibid.*, 50.

court had not merely granted an exception to the rule found in Coke's *Institutes*, it had moved against the rule itself. Furthermore, the flexibility with which the court had handled the "artificial" rules of evidence was not nearly so straightforward as their natural law arguments implied. Throughout this period, for example, Quakers were barred as witnesses in criminal cases by a Hanoverian statute. The court's granting such a right to "gentoos," even in civil actions, was thus an even more striking departure. Indeed, after the decision in *Omychund* v *Barker*, the legislative restrictions against Quakers appeared rather anomalous to some contemporary observers.[15]

In addition, the law of evidence was frequently treated in terms of the general "practice of the courts," and when so viewed it appeared as one of the least easily altered types of legal rules. The stability of judicial forms is a crucial priority in any legal system, particularly one eschewing arbitrary proceedings, since it is vital for suitors to know what evidence they can produce, when they are to produce it, and what importance the courts will grant it. Hence, there was some cogency to the defense's argument in *Omychund* v *Barker* that such evidence had simply not been allowed in a court before. Mansfield, who was not particularly well known for his devotion to the settled procedure at King's Bench, still appreciated the danger to the legal system of "break[ing] the established Rules and Methods of Proceeding."[16] Hardwicke, of course, shared the same concerns. Thus in a case of 1737 he refused to permit evidence being given "*viva voce*" in his court, as this would disrupt the settled practice of Chancery:

> The constant and established proceedings of this court are upon written evidence... This is the course of the court, and the course of the court is the law of the court... There never was a case, where witnesses have been allowed to be examined at large at the hearing; and though it might be desirable to allow this, yet the fixed and settled proceedings of the court cannot be broke through for it.[17]

Hardwicke's adherence to the "fixed and settled proceedings of the court" in this and numerous other cases enhances the importance of the ruling in *Omychund* v *Barker*. Hardwicke, as we have seen, was eager to prevent his equitable authority from serving as an instrument for legal

---

[15] The act disqualifying Quakers is 2 Geo II c 24. Mansfield discussed the anomaly between the act and Hardwicke's ruling in 1775; see *Atcheson* v *Everitt*, Cowper 382.

[16] *Hewson* v *Brown*, (1760) 2 Burrow 1034.

[17] *Graves* v *Budgel*, (1737) 1 Atkyns 444. Hardwicke's view of the relation between the "course of the court" and the "law of the court" was set out at length in an early tract on the judicial authority of the Master of the Rolls; see Philip Yorke (Lord Hardwicke), *A Discourse of the Judicial Authority Belonging to the Office of Master of Rolls in the High Court of Chancery* (London, 1727).

disruption.[18] His decision to admit the evidence of a "Gentoo" reflected the position of any law reformer: the law needed to be stable and settled, but this claim had at times to be sacrificed to other legal principles in order to achieve material justice. In the English legal system, this sacrifice could be effected by the courts, because England's law accommodated both precedents and principles.

A final reason for introducing *Omychund* v *Barker* as an illustrative case is that the importance and broader implications of Hardwicke's decision were well recognized by his contemporaries. No contemporary used the decision more forcefully than Edmund Burke. During the trial of Warren Hastings, the House of Lords refused to admit a large body of evidence from Indian courts which Burke sought to introduce. Burke argued that this strict adherence to the rules of evidence was not only unjust, but that it ran contrary to the eighteenth-century legal experience. The judicial record demonstrated that the courts had viewed the historic rules of evidence as inappropriate for Britain's altered social conditions, and had modified these rules according to the dictates of natural justice.

> As commerce, with its advantages and necessities opened a communica-
> tion more largely with other countries; as the law of nature and nations
> (always a part of the law of England) came to be cultivated...as new
> views and combinations of things were opened, this antique rigour and
> overdone severity [of the common law] gave way to the accommodation
> of human concerns, for which the rules were made, and not human
> concerns to bend to them.

Accordingly, Lord Hardwicke, "in a case the most solemnly argued of any within memory of man," declared there to be "but ONE rule of evidence – the best that the nature of the case will admit." It was on the basis of this "master rule," rather than the historic practice of the court, that the Lords were to determine the admissibility of the evidence in the trial of Hastings.[19]

Burke went on to consider the arguments pleaded by Murray, whose "ideas go to the growing melioration of the law, by making its liberality keep pace with the demands of justice and the actual concerns of the world." Throughout his career at the bar and on the bench, he refused to restrict "the infinitely diversified occasions of men and the rules of natural justice within artificial circumscriptions," and instead

---

[18] See the discussion above, chapter 3 at nn48–50.
[19] Burke, "Report from the Committee of the House of Commons appointed to inspect the Lords' Journals in relation to their Proceedings on the Trial of Warren Hastings, Esq." (1794), in *The Works of the Right Honorable Edmund Burke* (1865–67), 8th edn, 12 vols. (Boston, 1884), XI, 77.

sought to adapt the law "to the growth of our commerce and of our empire." Burke then concluded by presenting recent legal history as an unqualified vindication of Mansfield's conception of the common law:

> From the period of this great judgment to the trial of Warren Hastings, Esq., the law has gone on continually working itself pure (to use Lord Mansfield's expression) by rules drawn from the fountain of justice.[20]

In the event Burke's claims failed to persuade the House of Lords. Nonetheless, his forceful reasoning offers an important commentary on these judicial innovations, as well as a useful insight into his own political ideas. It is perhaps common to think that when Burke drew attention to the need for political institutions to provide for both conservation and change, the emphasis remained decidedly on conservation. But it was doubtless the case for Burke, as for Blackstone, that his optimistic confidence in the capacity of England's historic institutions to endure was buttressed by the recognition of recent instances like this when such institutions proved themselves fully competent in adapting "to the growth of our commerce and our empire."

Other law writers, moreover, who lacked Burke's powers of rhetoric and his political purposes, concurred with his analysis of the judicial response to this body of legal rules. John Fonblanque, for example, writing in the 1790s, acknowledged that it was impossible to resolve the rules of evidence "into system" or "give to them that comprehension which is necessary to system." This, however, did not reflect legal uncertainty so much as the need for the law to keep pace with social developments. "The evidence to be allowed by law," he observed, "should be suited to the habits, opinions and the state of society," and therefore, "we cannot but expect its rules to vary with the varying exigences of the subjects to which it is to accommodate itself." Hence, in this legal area the courts were always prepared to sacrifice rules to prevent "a failure of justice," and precedents remained firmly subservient to principles:

> General rules of evidence may therefore be considered as afforded by the decisions of certain cases and entitled to govern all cases similar... But, if other circumstances enter into the case,... and, if the principle does not reach such additional circumstances, it should seem that the rule ought not to be applied, if a failure of justice may be apprehended from its application.[21]

[20] *Ibid.*, XI, 84.
[21] Ballow [?], *Treatise of Equity*, II, 447–8 (Fonblanque's note).

The second illustration of judicial law reform is found in a case determined by Mansfield's court of King's Bench in 1769. *Millar* v *Taylor* was popularly known as the case of Literary Property. As in *Omychund* v *Barker*, the litigation reflected new commercial conditions – here the court moved to define and settle property relations of those engaged in London's expanding book trade. In so doing, the court once more displayed its readiness to consider the place of the law of nature and legal principle in English legal practice. "The judges," according to one recent assessment, "were forced to examine the very foundations of property law in the eighteenth century."[22]

At issue in *Millar* v *Taylor* was the nature of an author's right to his "copy" after he had sold his work to a bookseller. Copyright, as defined by Mansfield, was "an incorporeal Right to the sole printing and publishing of somewhat [something?] intellectual, communicated by Letters."[23] Millar, a London bookseller, had bought the copyright to James Thomson's poem, *The Seasons*. He brought this action against another bookseller, Taylor, who had published *The Seasons* without Millar's consent.

The only settled law on the subject was the act of 8 Anne c 19, which protected the author's copyright for a period of 14 years after the initial sale of his work to a bookseller. In this case, Taylor had republished the work after the expiration of this fourteen-year period. Thus, if the statute alone had been consulted, Millar would have had no remedy against Taylor's republication. But the court did not proceed on this basis. Their decision turned on whether an author enjoyed a perpetual right to his copy according to the laws of nature. If natural law sanctioned this property right, then the right existed in common law as well. The law of nature was an acknowledged source of law in England, where law was praised as the perfection of reason.

The rulings in *Millar* v *Taylor* provide some of the most powerful instances of the use of natural law theory in Mansfield's court. The judgment given by Sir Richard Aston demonstrates particularly well the extent to which English law and ethics were identified through appeals to principles of natural justice. Aston maintained that the case could only be resolved by considering "certain great Truths and sound propositions which we, as rational beings; we, to whom Reason is the great law of our nature, are laid under the obligation of being governed by." These considerations he admitted might seem "abstract," but fortunately they had been "most ably illustrated by the learned author of *The Religion of Nature Delineated*."[24] He then proceeded to cite large

---

[22] *Millar* v *Taylor*, (1769) 4 Burrow 2303. The circumstances of the case are summarized at 2309.   [23] *Ibid.*, at 2396.   [24] *Ibid.*, at 2337.

extracts verbatim from William Wollaston's moral philosophy, which next he corroborated with passages from Locke, Grotius, Pufendorf, Barbeyrac and Bynkershoek. All these natural law authorities were interpreted to support an author's perpetual property right to his literary productions. These authors, in turn, were taken as authorities for the English courts:

> If the above principles and reasoning are just, why should the common law be deemed so narrow and illiberal, as not to recognize and receive under its protection a Property so circumstanced as the present? The Common Law, now so called, is founded on the Law of Nature and Reason. Its grounds, maxims and principles are derived from many different fountains...from natural and moral Philosophy, from the Civil and Canon law, from logic, from the use, custom and conversation among men, collected out of the general disposition, nature and condition of Human Kind.[25]

Aston's position was confirmed by Edward Willes, and followed by Mansfield. As Willes and Aston had explored the relevant natural law authorities at length, the Chief Justice did not enter into great detail. But his decision forcefully summarized the same point. This was a case in which common law drew directly from the fountain of justice:

> The common law, as to the copy before publication, can not be found in custom...From what source, then, is the common law drawn...From this argument: because it is just that an author should reap the pecuniary profits of his own ingenuity and labour. It is just that another should not use his name, without his consent...I allow then sufficient to shew "it is agreeable to the principles of Right and Wrong, the fitness of things, convenience, and policy, and therefore to the Common Law, to protect the copy[right]..."[26]

The natural law right for copy to be perpetual thus established, it was then confirmed by the common law court. This of course necessitated a somewhat labored reading of the statute which had protected an author's copyright only for a term of 14 years. This was in fact swiftly accomplished. The court interpreted the act merely to have established certain additional penalties for the violation of a right to copy during the fourteen year period. It did not revoke or alter the writer's common-

---

[25] *Ibid.*, at 2343.
[26] *Ibid.*, at 2397–8. The looseness with which the Bench utilized its moral terminology seems to contrast with the original legal reception of these terms; see Louis A. Knafla, "Conscience in the English Common Law Tradition," 1–16.

law right founded in the law of nature. Therefore, Millar had his remedy under the usual common law of personal property.[27]

The King's Bench ruling had not been unanimously endorsed, and the issue went before the House of Lords in the following year. There it was determined that an author did not enjoy a perpetual copyright to his published writings.[28] But even this reversal is instructive. The Lords ruled that no such right existed at common law because the right was *not* sanctioned by the law of nature. The reversal thus did not reflect a rejection of the premises upon which Mansfield's court had ruled. The Lords only differed with regard to the substance of the relevant natural law doctrines. In their ruling, the Lords followed the arguments presented by Taylor's counsel in the hearing of the dispute at King's Bench. As Aston observed in his introductory remarks, "all the objections to this Property or Right being allowed or protected by the common law, rest entirely upon arguments...'that such allowance or protection is contrary to right reason and natural principles.'"[29] The whole issue of literary property, then, centered on the natural law foundations of common law. Both King's Bench and the House of Lords adopted this approach, and both considered the statute law to operate on this occasion as a gloss on the law of nature.[30]

One important argument presented to the House of Lords, however, departed from these premises. This was advanced by Mansfield's great judicial rival, the former Chief Justice of Common Pleas and Chancellor, Charles Pratt, Lord Camden, who invoked a constitutional doctrine in rejection of the King's Bench ruling. The decision of the issue at King's Bench was wrong, not because the judges had mistaken the law of nature, but because Mansfield had legislated from the bench:

> ... it is said that it would be contrary to the ideas of private justice, moral fitness, and public convenience, not to adopt this new system. But who has a right to decide these new cases, if there is no other rule to measure

---

[27] Blackstone, incidentally, acted as counsel in two cases concerning copyright: *Millar v Taylor* (above) and *Tonson v Collins*, 1 W Blackstone 301 and 1 W Blackstone 321. In both cases he argued that the law of nature sanctioned an author's perpetual copyright.

[28] See William Cobbett, *Parliamentary History of England*, 36 vols. (London, 1806–20), XVII, 953–1003.   [29] 4 Burrow 2303, 2337.

[30] For another contemporary discussion of the issue, see the 1774 Court of Session ruling in James Boswell (ed.), *The Decision of the Court of Session, Upon the Question of Literary Property* (Edinburgh, 1774). The Scottish judges ruled against a perpetual copyright, as it was not sanctioned by the law of nature. Lord Kennet provided the standard argument: "I am of opinion that Literary Property is not in the law of Scotland. It is not in the law of nature which is one of the great fountains of our law." Only Lord Monboddo dissented, adopting an argument analogous to Mansfield's ruling.

by but moral fitness and equitable right? Not the judges of the common law, I am sure. Their business is to tell the suitor how the law stands, not how it ought to be... That excellent judge, Lord Chief Justice Lee, used always to ask counsel..."Have you any case?" I hope judges will always copy the example, and never pretend to decide upon a claim of property without attending to the old black letter of our law, without founding their judgment upon some solid written authority, preserved in their books or in judicial records.[31]

To support this claim Camden drew upon a strikingly different understanding of common law from that which supported Hardwicke's decree in *Omychund* v *Barker* and Mansfield's ruling in *Millar* v *Taylor*, and this alternative conception cut away the grounds for judicial innovation. The absence of precedents, Camden implied, represented the absence of law, while the requirements for legal certainty confined the judges to "attending the old black letter" of the law. This approach further suggested that the judges were constitutionally barred from allowing the "antique rigour" of the law to give way "to the accommodation of human concerns" or "to keep pace with the demands of justice," in the manner insisted upon by Burke before the House of Lords.

According to legal orthodoxy the office of the judge was *jus dicere* and not *jus dare*. Camden's argument forcefully highlighted the restrictive implications of this formula for the judiciary. But Camden's arguments obtained only if the *jus* in question was identified entirely with precedents, judicial records, and the "old black letter of our law." Once the courts returned to the principles of common law, as regularly occurred under Mansfield's leadership, the restrictive implications seemed to vanish. And the traditional distinction between *jus dicere* and *jus dare* appeared to have left many issues unresolved.

[31] Cobbett, *Parliamentary History*, XVII, 998–9. For more sympathetic comments on Mansfield's tendency to blur the distinction between the office of judge and legislator, see Campbell, *Chief Justices*, II, 439, and Fifoot, *Lord Mansfield*, p. 227.

5

◁ ═══════════════════════════════════════ ▷

Mansfield and the commercial code

Lord Campbell introduced his mid-nineteenth-century account of the judicial achievement of Lord Mansfield with an effusive version of an assessment first elaborated some seventy years earlier in the closing phase of Mansfield's public career. "In the reign of George II," Campbell explained, "England had grown into the greatest manufacturing and commercial country in the world, while her jurisprudence had by no means been expanded or developed in the same proportion." Parliament "had literally done nothing" to adjust English law to "the concerns of a trading population," and "the common law judges" had likewise most often proved "too unenlightened and too timorous" in the cause of legal improvement. Elevated to the Bench in 1756, following two decades of triumphal professional and parliamentary advancement, Lord Chief Justice Mansfield "saw the noble field that lay before him, and he resolved to reap the rich harvest of glory which it presented to him."[1]

In current work on English legal history, Mansfield still often survives as "the towering figure" who "dominated the legal scene" and whose legal ideas served as "the harbinger of the new age."[2] Nevertheless, the burden of recent scholarship has been to qualify the common picture of Mansfield's court as an aggressive instrument for legal change and historical discontinuity. A. W. B. Simpson, writing in the context of one of Mansfield's most controversial rulings, insists that "Mansfield was no innovator in legal matters" and that "his ideas commonly involved no more than a bold and striking affirmation of views expressed by others."[3] Even in the field of commercial law, where the personal nature of Mansfield's achievement seemed least open to challenge, it is clear that his accomplishments rested on foundations laid by others. His predecessor at the Court of King's

---

[1] Campbell, *Chief Justices*, II, 402–3.
[2] Atiyah, *Freedom of Contract*, pp. 120, 180.
[3] Simpson, *Common Law of Contract*, p. 618.

Bench at the opening of the century, Sir John Holt, supplied the
statement conventionally taken as the *locus classicus* on the common
law's insularity and incompetence in dealing with mercantile affairs
prior to Mansfield. Yet, notwithstanding Holt's declaration that
"Lombard Street" would not "give laws to Westminster Hall," it was
under his chief justiceship that much of the law covering negotiable
paper was first systematized in the English courts – an accomplishment
thought sufficient to secure Holt's rival claim to Mansfield's mantle as
"the founder" of England's commercial law.[4]

This scholarly revision has made it possible to view Mansfield's
judicial leadership as essentially a performance in legal consolidation
and refinement, and as the culmination of an extended period of uneven
but not insubstantial legal development. Indeed, given the strong
pressure for continuity within the common law system it is unlikely
that Mansfield could have accomplished so much had he been operating
in as much of a legal vacuum as his admirers supposed. Still, if his
contemporaries tended to misread the situation by over-estimating the
personal character of Mansfield's contribution, this too is significant,
particularly for our purposes here. In their magnification of the Chief
Justice's achievement, they were provided with an especially vivid
example of what could be achieved by that part of the English legal
system which, as Burke reminded the House of Lords, continued to
draw from the fountain of justice. Thus, one contemporary legal writer
commenting on Mansfield's career may have assumed the proper note
of caution in observing that "a complete system of jurisprudence
cannot be suddenly erected." But he raised the point not simply to
acknowledge the Chief Justice's debts, but rather "to excite our
wonder that so much has been done in this respect within the last thirty
years."[5]

As with so many other features of English legal development, the
peculiar history of the commercial law was largely the result of the
resilience and durability of the common law system.[6] On the continent,
the substantive rules of commercial law were formalized within

---

[4] J. Milnes Holden, *The History of Negotiable Instruments in English Law* (London, 1955), pp.
76–84, 112–13, 113n.

[5] James Allen Park, *A System of the Law of Marine Insurances* (London, 1787), p. xliv.

[6] I have drawn heavily on the interpretation suggested by J. H. Baker, "The Law Merchant and
the Common Law before 1700," *Cambridge Law Journal*, XXXVIII (1979), 295–322, as well
as the more traditional treatment in L. Stuart Sutherland, "The Law Merchant in England in
the Seventeenth and Eighteenth Centuries," *Transactions of the Royal Historical Society*, 4th
series, XVII (1934), 149–76. The first development in England of a published literature on the
law merchant is treated by Daniel R. Coquillette, "Legal Ideology and Incorporation II: Sir
Thomas Ridley, Charles Molloy and the Literary Battle for the Law Merchant, 1607–1676,"
Boston University Law Review, LXI (1981), 315–71.

independent merchant courts. This process did not occur in England, where by the Tudor period common law had established its hegemony in the adjudication of mercantile disputes. The problems of accommodating merchant litigation within the framework of common law justice was regularly stressed by seventeenth- and eighteenth-century merchant polemicists who urged the erection of separate merchant courts on the continental model. They first emphasized the inadequacy of the substantive rules of common law for adjudicating mercantile causes. Malachy Postlethwayt, writing in 1755, noted that "the municipal laws of England" were "not sufficient for ordering and determining the affairs of traffic and matters relating to commerce."[7] The broader dangers of this situation were bluntly drawn by Josiah Child in 1693: "it is well if we can make our counsel, being common lawyers, understand one half of our case, we being amongst them as in a Foreign Country, our language strange to them, and theirs as strange to us."[8]

Equally marked was the anxiety that the technical methods of procedure at law would seriously hamper the resolution of commercial disputes. John Cary, writing two years after Child, warned against forcing merchants into Westminster Hall, "where all things are tried by Nice Rules of Law."[9] Child himself provided a tellingly extravagant illustration of how institutional rivalries and inappropriate rules of evidence created legal torture for the English merchant forced to rely on native courts of justice. Disputes relating to "martain affairs" were initiated in "the Admiralty court," where "after tedious Attendance and vast Expenses" the cause was removed by "writ of Prohibition" to King's Bench. There, after "great expenses of Time and Money," resolution would prove impossible, since most of the commercial documents were not recognized as good "evidence of Law." Accordingly, the suit was moved to Chancery, "where after many years tedious travel to Westminster, with black boxes and green bags, when the Plaintiff and Defendant have tired their Bodies, distracted their minds, and consumed their Estates, the Cause if ever it be ended, is commonly by order of that Court referred to Merchants, ending miserably where it might have had at first a happy issue if it had begun right."[10]

In the half century which separated Child from Mansfield's

---

[7] Malachy Postlethwayt, *The Universal Dictionary of Trade and Commerce, translated from the French of the Celebrated Monsieur Savary, with Large Additions and Improvements*, 2 vols. (London, 1751–5), II, 22.

[8] Josiah Child, *A New Discourse of Trade* (London, 1693), pp. 113–14.

[9] John Cary, *An Essay on the State of England, in Relation to its Trade* (Bristol, 1695), p. 27.

[10] Child, *New Discourse of Trade*, pp. 113–15.

appearance in King's Bench, the common law had doubtless improved its record in handling commercial disputes. The "law-merchant" was increasingly adopted in judicial rulings, and judges more regularly appealed to professional testimony to guide the courts' interpretation of technical instruments and documents. Child, for example, had looked to parliament to redress the legal needs of the mercantile community through statute. Writing in 1757 on bills of exchange, Postlethwayt argued the opposite case. "In matters of law," he observed, "*Westminster Hall* should...control *St Stephen's Chapel.*" His reasoning, moreover, indicated that the common lawyers were not the only group to have grown suspicious of the prospect of reform through legislative enactment. "The statutes," he explained, "which do not always quadrate with the sense and spirit of the law, would subvert a great part of it, and render all the reported cases useless to posterity...whereby we should have no law certain at all."[11] Thus, the merchant community could expect more legal uncertainty from parliamentary acts than from the increasingly settled pattern of common law decisions.

Despite such evidence of improvement, it would be wrong to suppose that the problems raised by Child and Cary had become irrelevant by 1756 when Mansfield was appointed to the Bench. Postlethwayt, whatever his confidence in Westminster Hall over Parliament, was still advocating the creation of independent merchant courts in 1755, enlisting the testimony of Cary, Child and Defoe, and drawing upon the desirable "experience" of "other nations."[12] Even in those areas like the law regulating bills of exchange, where the greatest consolidation had occurred, there was little to constitute a "system of jurisprudence" such as law writers eagerly discerned in Mansfield's later judgments. The common law courts, despite the increased availability in England of systematic treatises on the "law-merchant," still frequently determined mercantile causes by directing a common jury to decide the issue according to the individual circumstance of each case.[13] This procedure, later repudiated by Mansfield, had serious limitations. By leaving so much of the determination to turn on the particular details of each case, it produced much irregularity of decision on the same points of law. Thus Hardwicke, in a 1734 suit concerning the parole acceptance of a bill of exchange, was forced to remark that "it was much to be wished the

---

[11] Postlethwayt, *Dictionary of Trade*, I, 277.

[12] *Ibid.*, II, 236–9. See also Wynne, *Eunomus*, I, 12–13.

[13] For examples of this procedure, see *E. India Co.* v *Chitty*, (1743) 2 Strange 1175, and *Hankey* v *Trotman*, (1746) 1 W Blackstone 1, 1–2.

courts of Westminster Hall were more uniform in their resolutions; especially in cases which occur so often, and which are of such universal concern."[14]

Not only did this technique fail to serve the purposes of legal certainty, it could also produce decisions at odds with established mercantile usage. Another Hardwicke decree is illustrative. In 1753 the Chancellor granted relief against a common law determination in a case concerning the negotiability of a navy bill. Though he did not send the issue back to common law, he clearly recognized the decision as unfortunate because it had violated general commercial practice. Hence, in his decree he placed particular stress on "the evidence of the custom among merchants to explain the letter of attorney...which could not be otherwise understood." He then concluded, in the spirit of Cary's warning, that "nice and critical construction is not to be put on these powers either at law or in equity, but the usage is to be regarded."[15]

In addition to the experience of the courts, the legal literature of the period affords further indication of the continued awkwardness of common lawyers in treating commercial topics. And here, as in so much else, the learned Commentator on the laws of England deserves a place of special prominence. "Blackstone's whole account of personal property," in Simpson's phrase, "smells of the countryside," and in contrast to the remarkable clarity and comprehension he achieved in his account of real property, the Commentator's treatment of commercial and mercantile matters was abrupt and sketchy.[16] The apparent clumsiness generally followed from his attempt to accommodate these topics within the not always helpful classifications and technical categories of the common law. He devoted a mere thirty pages to contract, in a chapter also treating grants and gifts. He discussed contracts of employment as part of the law of "masters and servants," essentially as a branch of feudal status. In his account of the law covering insurances, he frankly confessed his inability to reduce the leading court decisions "to any general heads."[17]

The next generation of legal writers were quick to note Blackstone's general failure in these areas of law. Sir William Jones, for example, introduced his 1781 treatise on the law of bailments by emphasizing the

---

[14] *Lumley* v *Palmer*, (1734) Ridgway 72.
[15] *Ekins* v *Macklish*, (1753) 1 Ambler 184, 186, 188. See also *Kruger* v *Wilcox*, (1755) 1 Ambler 252, and *Baker* v *Paine*, (1750) 1 Vesey Sr. 456.
[16] Blackstone, *Commentaries: Facsimile of the first edition*, II, xii (editorial introduction).
[17] 2 *Comm* 442–70, 1 *Comm* 422–32, 2 *Comm* 460. Milsom supplies an important rejoinder to the usual criticisms of Blackstone's handling of these topics in "The Nature of Blackstone's Achievement," pp. 7–8.

importance of this body of law to the common affairs of a commercial nation: "there is hardly a man of any age or station, who does not every week and almost every day contract the obligations or acquire the rights" contained in this area of law. But it was not the importance of the subject matter alone which moved Jones to produce his "short and perspicuous discussion of this title." Such a discussion was "especially" necessary since "our excellent Blackstone, who of all men was best able to throw the clearest light on this, as on every other subject, has comprised the whole doctrine in three paragraphs, which, without affecting the merit of his incomparable work, we may safely pronounce the least satisfactory part of it."[18]

The writings of Richard Wooddeson, one of Blackstone's earliest successors to the Vinerian Chair, furnish further evidence to the same effect. As Vinerian professor, Wooddeson of course had to lecture on English law. But in order to avoid a mere repetition of the *Commentaries*, he devoted attention to those areas which Blackstone omitted or described briefly. As a result, much of his *A Systematical View of the Laws of England* concentrated on equity and commercial law. Still, as Wooddeson frankly confessed elsewhere, in contrast to Blackstone when he first composed the *Commentaries*, he had the advantage of writing after Mansfield. The "law of merchants," he explained, had "of late years been wonderfully elucidated, and reduced to rational and firm principles, in a series of litigations before a judge, long celebrated for his great talents, and extensive learning in general jurisprudence, and still more venerable for his animated love of justice."[19]

In turning now to Mansfield's actual contributions to the development of the commercial law, it is useful to distinguish two objectives which underline his many judicial determinations. First was his firm insistence that commercial matters, as on the continent, had to be decided under the separate system of legal rules known as the "law-merchant." Here he relied not on the substance of the historic common law, but rather on the heterogeneity of the common law system. Secondly, he was equally clear that the common law courts needed to adjudicate upon merchant cases in such a way as to establish a settled system of general legal rules, rather than a collection of individual precedents. His achievement in this regard rested on his consummate utilization of several procedural devices which enabled him to transform particular

---

[18] Jones, *Law of Bailments*, pp. 2–3.
[19] Wooddeson, *Elements of Jurisprudence*, p. 92. See also Hanbury, *Vinerian Chair*, pp. 64–78.

cases into a system of "easily learned and easily retained" rules of commercial law.[20]

The first part of this strategy, the claim that the rules governing commercial transactions were to be drawn from the law-merchant, was scarcely novel. As Postlethwayt casually reported in 1755, "there is another law called the law-merchant, which is a special law, differing from the common law of England, proper to merchants, and is become a part of the law of the realm." This "special law," moreover, was founded on "customs and usages immemorial."[21] Legal writers tended to treat the same matter more formally, identifying the law-merchant with the law of nations and the general equitable principles contained in that system of jurisprudence. Thus, Chitty described the law-merchant as "a system of equity founded on the rules of equity," and John Joseph Powell maintained that the law was "founded upon the law of nature and nations."[22] This orthodoxy was set out at length by George Joseph Bell in his monumental treatise on "mercantile jurisprudence":

> The law-merchant is universal: It is part of the law of nations, grounded upon the principles of natural equity, as regulating the relations of men who reside in different countries, and carry on the intercourse of nations, independently of the local customs and municipal laws of particular states.[23]

This law of nations, moreover, was readily acknowledged to be part of English law. Just as the common law courts adopted parts of the civil and canon law, so they recognized the law of nations and with it the law-merchant.[24] The convention that the law of nations was relevant to the practice of the English courts was a point Mansfield himself stressed in a ruling of 1764 concerning the immunity of diplomats and their servants from legal prosecution. The "privilege," he declared, "depends upon the law of nations," and its presence in

---

[20] "The daily negotiations and property of Merchants ought not to depend upon Subtleties and Niceties, but upon Rules, easily learned and easily retained, because they are the Dictates of Common Sense, drawn from the Truth of the Case," *Hamilton* v *Mendes*, (1761) 2 Burrow 1198, 1214.

[21] Postlethwayt, *Dictionary of Trade*, II, 22.

[22] Joseph Chitty, *A Treatise on the Laws of Bills of Exchange, Checks on Bankers, Promissory Notes, Bankers Cash Notes and Bank Notes* (London, 1799), p. 7, and Powell, *Law of Contracts and Agreements*, I, 341.

[23] George Joseph Bell, *Commentaries on the Laws of Scotland and the Principles of Mercantile Jurisprudence* (1804), 2nd edn (Edinburgh, 1810), p. ix.

[24] See Blackstone's account at 1 *Comm* 43 and 4 *Comm* 66 (law of nations), and at 1 *Comm* 75 (*lex mercatoria*).

English law was demonstrated in good common law fashion by appeal to earlier precedents. Thus, the Chief Justice recalled the case of *Buvot v Barbot* where "Lord Talbot declared a clear opinion – 'That the Law of Nations in its full extent was part of the law of England... That the Law of Nations was to be collected from the practice of different nations, and the authority of writers.' Accordingly, he argued and determined from such instances, and the authority of Grotius, Barbeyrac, Bynkershoek, Wiquefort, &c, there being no English writer of eminence upon the subject."[25]

The corollary to this in commercial matters was found in the many cases which Mansfield determined according to foreign legal authorities who, again, had been received by the English courts. Characteristic, then, were his comments in a ruling in the second year of his chief justiceship involving a disputed policy of marine insurance:

> Nor indeed can any Determination be made, on the principles of our Municipal laws: for the question concerns foreigners as well as natives; and is a question of general law, not of any particular and local law... "Whether this was a total loss or not" must be determined by the Law of War, and by the Law of Nature, that is, of right Reason.[26]

In many such cases, Mansfield's adherence to foreign legal authorities represented continuation of common law practice, and the formal distinction between "our municipal law" and this "general law" proved reasonably clear. Nonetheless in many of the most common areas of commercial law this distinction was considerably blurred in English practice by the frequent introduction of legal analogies and categories derived from the common law itself. It was in these situations that Mansfield's insistence on adhering to the law-merchant was most crucial.

The law of negotiable paper provides a leading example of the difficulty, which can be illustrated by comparing the approaches of Mansfield and Blackstone.[27] Blackstone apparently sought to accommodate the law regulating negotiable instruments within the general structure of the common law of contract:

[25] *Triquet* v *Bath*, (1764) 3 Burrow 1478, 1480–81.
[26] *Goss* v *Withers*, (1758) 2 Burrow 683, 689; for a similar ruling see *Anthon* v *Fisher*, (1782) 3 Douglas 166.
[27] For the historical background on commercial credit during the period, see: T. S. Ashton, *An Economic History of England: The Eighteenth Century* (London, 1955), pp. 167–73, 185ff; B. L. Anderson, "Money and the Structure of Credit," *Business History*, XII (1970), 85–101; and B. L. Anderson, "Provincial Aspects of the Financial Revolution of the Eighteenth Century," *Business History*, XI (1969), 11–22.

The payee... either of a bill of exchange or promissory note has clearly a property vested in him (not indeed in possession but in action) by the *express* contract of the drawer in the case of a promissory note, and, in the case of a bill of exchange, by his *implied* contract, *viz.* that, provided the drawee does not pay the bill, the drawer will...[28]

By adopting this position, Blackstone immediately encountered difficulties. By viewing the payee as vested with a "property in action" he attributed to him what the common law recognized as a "*chose* in action." This was a species of property "where a man hath not the occupation, but merely a bare right to occupy the thing in question."[29] The difficulty was that according to common law this species of property could not be transferred: "no *chose* in action could be assigned or granted over, because it was thought to be a great encouragement to litigiousness if a man were allowed to make over to a stranger his right of going to law."[30] An application of this rule, then, would directly defeat the purposes of negotiable instruments as a fluid form of commercial credit. Blackstone, of course, recognized this and acknowledged that "assignation is the life of paper credit." He was hence forced to exempt this type of *chose* in action from the general common law rule. "This property," he explained, "may be transferred and assigned from the payee to any other man, contrary to the general rule of the common law, that no *chose* in action is assignable."[31]

Blackstone, at the cost of the explanatory gymnastics, had achieved the proper conclusion and ensured that such instruments enjoyed the necessary transferability in law. But the general approach was misleading, in that what he specifically had not done was to view negotiable instruments as a distinct form of property governed by a separate system of legal rules. The potential confusions were exploited in the courts by counsel who fashioned their pleadings in terms of legal analogies drawn from the common law of property. Thus, many of Mansfield's rulings turned on the point that this approach would undermine the system of commercial credit:

The holder of a bill of exchange or promissory note is not to be considered in the light of an assignee of the payee. An assignee must take the thing assigned, subject to all the equity to which the original party was subject. If this rule applied to bills and promissory notes, it would stop their currency.[32]

---

[28] 2 *Comm* 468.   [29] 2 *Comm* 396–7.
[30] 2 *Comm* 442.   [31] 2 *Comm* 468.
[32] *Peacock* v *Rhodes*, (1781) 2 Douglas 633, 636.

A Mansfield ruling in 1758 proceeded on the same lines. The defendant sought to avoid payment of a bank note by treating it as mere evidence of a debt which the defendant did not owe the eventual holder of the note, and produced a Holt decision in support of this interpretation. Mansfield again responded by emphasizing the need to recognize such notes as a distinct form of property governed by their usage in commerce:

> It has been very ingeniously argued...but the whole fallacy of the argument turns upon comparing Bank Notes to what they do not resemble, and what they ought not to be compared to...They are not Goods, nor Securities, nor Documents for debts, nor are so esteemed: But are treated as Money, as Cash, in the ordinary course and transaction of Business, by the general Consent of Mankind.[33]

Correctly identifying such creditory instruments as a form of property did not finish the battle. Further difficulties emerged in viewing the parties to a negotiable instrument, as Blackstone suggested, in contractual terms. Here negotiable instruments ran up against the doctrine of consideration. According to common law, contracts were only valid provided they were founded on a sufficient consideration. As set out in the *Commentaries*:

> A Consideration of some sort or other is so absolutely necessary to the forming of a contract, that a *nudum pactum*, or agreement to do or pay any thing on one side, without any compensation on the other, is totally void in law.[34]

If, then, negotiable instruments were contracts for debts, they required such consideration for their legal enforcement. But, of course, there was no such contractual consideration linking the merchant from whom a bill was drawn to the party who eventually held the bill. Again, any strict application of the common law doctrine would undermine the function of such instruments, and again, Blackstone appreciated the difficulty. His solution in this instance was to produce something of a legal fiction. "Every note from the subscription of the drawer," he claimed, "carries with it an internal evidence of a good consideration."[35] Accordingly, the absence of consideration could not be averred

---

[33] *Miller* v *Race*, (1758) 1 Burrow 452, 457. Also see *Goss* v *Nelson*, (1757) 1 Burrow 226, *Grant* v *Vaughan*, (1756) 3 Burrow 1516.

[34] 2 *Comm* 445. For an account of the doctrine of consideration, see Baker's discussion in *Introduction to English Legal History*, pp. 279–82, 291–3, and in "Origins of the 'Doctrine' of Consideration, 1535–1585," in M. S. Arnold, T. A. Green, S. A. Scully and S. D. White (eds.), *On the Laws and Customs of England: Essays in Honor of S. E. Thorne* (Chapel Hill, 1981).   [35] 2 *Comm* 446.

to avoid liability on a note since the instrument itself carried proof of such consideration, and as a result such negotiable notes could be absorbed within the more general common law doctrines concerning contractual relations.

Mansfield's contrasting approach was illustrated in 1765 in the case of *Pillans* v *Van Mierop*. The suit arose over a bill of exchange which had been drawn for the plaintiffs by a Rotterdam merchant house. Van Mierop, a London merchant, agreed to accept the bill. In the interim, the Rotterdam house failed, enabling the defendant to seek to avoid the bill by claiming the absence of consideration:

> They argued, and principally insisted, that for one man to undertake "to pay another man's debt," was a void Undertaking; unless there was some consideration for such undertaking; and that a mere general promise... was a *nudum pactum*.[36]

Mansfield's ruling did not proceed along the lines of Blackstone's account. He did not maintain that the bill itself necessarily contained sufficient proof of the required consideration, but instead insisted that the law which was to govern such matters, the law-merchant, simply contained no doctrine of consideration at all:

> This is a matter of great consequence to Trade and Commerce in every light... If there be no fraud, it is a mere question of Law. The Law of Merchants, and the Law of the Land, is the same... A *nudum pactum* does not exist in the Usage and Law of Merchants... In commercial cases amongst merchants, the want of consideration is *not* an objection.[37]

In the same ruling the Chief Justice went on to advance a more controversial position, that "the ancient Notion about the want of Consideration" was developed for "the sake of Evidence only." He thereby suggested that English law recognized two broad categories of contracts, written agreements and parole agreements, and that the rule of consideration applied only to the latter group. He further proposed (somewhat belatedly in the light of the intervening case law) that the 1677 Statute of Frauds "proceeded upon the same principle."[38] This account entailed a rather drastic reformulation of the doctrine of consideration in general terms and was rejected by later judges.[39] Most of the subsequent discussion of the case has focused on this part of

---

[36] *Pillans* v *Van Mierop*, (1765) 3 Burrow 1663, 1664–5.
[37] *Ibid.*, at 1669.   [38] *Ibid.*, at 1669.
[39] See Dunford and East's notations of *Rann* v *Hughes*, (1778) 7 Term Rpts 350n. Simpson argues that this attempt to view consideration as a point about evidence is less historically suspect than generally assumed; see Simpson, *Common Law of Contract*, pp. 617–19, 407.

Mansfield's decision, but this controversy does not impinge on Mansfield's more restricted point, relevant to our purposes here. This was the statement that these matters were to be decided according to the "Law of Merchants," and that therefore the want of consideration was irrelevant because the doctrine did not exist in the relevant body of legal rules.

In subsequent legal literature, Mansfield's position was sustained, sometimes with explicit repudiation of the Blackstonean approach. John Joseph Powell, for example, in his 1790 treatise on contract law, presented an orthodox account of consideration, maintaining that contracts without consideration, even if put in writing, constituted "*nuda pacta*" unenforceable at law. But in treating "voluntary bonds" and "notes of hand," to which the doctrine did not apply, Powell insisted that these were not to be taken as "an exception out of this rule." Instead, these represented a "distinct species" of property "governed by the same law as a bill of exchange, which is the law-merchant." The doctrine of consideration did not apply because "the want of consideration is no *essential* defect in a contract" under that law.[40] The same explanation appeared in Fonblanque's 1793–94 edition of *A Treatise of Equity*. Fonblanque, moreover, noted that Blackstone in "his great and comprehensive work" had "laid himself particularly open to observation" in these matters. The law did not treat negotiable instruments as an "exception to the general rule" of consideration because of their "written proof," rather the law altogether ignored the matter of consideration "in order to strengthen and facilitate that commercial intercourse which is carried on through the medium of such securities."[41]

Other legal writers, observing more broadly the elaboration of England's commercial law, joined Mansfield in emphasizing how these rules operated to ensure the speed and ease of mercantile exchange. Again, like Mansfield, they carefully distinguished the mercantile law from the "particular laws" of individual nations, and regarded its presence in the English courts as the product of a process of legal incorporation. By the 1780s Sir William Jones could refer to Pothier's treatise on contracts as "law at Westminster as well as at Orleans," and by the end of the century Joseph Chitty could condense the intervening legal development in simple terms:

> Our courts, subservient, as it were, to the necessity and circumstances of the time, have, in favour of commerce, adopted a less technical mode of

---

[40] Powell, *Law of Contracts and Agreements*, I, 340–1.
[41] Ballow [?], *Treatise of Equity*, I, 334–5 (Fonblanque's note).

considering *personalty* than *realty*; and in support of commercial transactions have established the law-merchant.[42]

But despite the ease of Chitty's presentation, the legal development, as seen in the case of negotiable instruments, was not without its complexities and potential conflation of doctrines.

In addition to ensuring that the English courts decided commercial disputes under the proper set of legal rules, Mansfield was concerned to use such cases as a vehicle for establishing commercial law on a clear and public footing. "I desire nothing so much," he announced from the bench in 1777, "as that all questions of mercantile law should be fully settled and ascertained."[43] It was the realization of this objective that so distinguished Mansfield's labors and which furnished the basis for the contemporary celebration of the "founder" of England's "commercial law." Not that his admirers maintained anything so naive as that Mansfield had been the first English judge to adjudicate commercial disputes, nor even that the "commercial law" he "founded" was of his own creation. Rather, what they proposed was that under Mansfield's guidance the commercial law had for the first time been refined and harmonized into a system of "certain general principles" capable of serving "as a guide to the future."[44]

In so seeking to resolve "all questions of mercantile law," Mansfield exploited several institutional devices as well as his more personal abilities. There is ample testimony not only to his legal talents, but also to his effective political skills and imposing intellectual powers.[45] Hearing him direct the judicial opinion of the House of Lords in 1772, James Boswell reckoned that "Lord Mansfield spoke as well as [he] could conceive any man to do. It was really a feast to hear him." Yet on experiencing the Chief Justice's leadership at closer range, Boswell discovered with less comfort that Mansfield's "cold reserve and sharpness, too, were too much... It was like being cut with a very, very cold instrument."[46]

Mansfield in early career had acquired a sound knowledge of mercantile affairs and of the law-merchant. During his practice at the bar he was retained by London merchant groups, and throughout his

---

[42] Jones, *Law of Bailments*, p. 29; Chitty, *Laws of Bills of Exchange*, p. 7.

[43] *Buller* v *Harrison*, (1777) Cowper 565, 567.

[44] The formulation of Sir Francis Buller in *Lickbarrow* v *Mason*, (1787) 2 Term Rpts 63, 73, discussed below at n80.

[45] The highlights of Mansfield's political career and legal practice are conveniently summarized by Fifoot, *Lord Mansfield*, pp. 27–51.

[46] *Boswell for the Defence 1769–1774*, ed. William K. Wimsatt and Frederick A. Pottle (New Haven, 1960), pp. 108, 184.

judgeship he maintained regular social and professional contact with the City's leading figures. In parliamentary debate he displayed a good command of commercial issues and a healthy distrust for the more short-sighted manifestations of mercantilist policy.[47] What was of greatest consequence was his particular mastery of those continental legal sources which contained the most sophisticated learning on the law-merchant and related areas of the law of nations. In 1753 he had been called upon by the Duke of Newcastle to compose a formal reply to a Prussian Memorial protesting English wartime policy for the seizure of neutral ships. The tract, drawn from a full range of leading natural law authorities, received the special commendations of Montesquieu and Vattel, a point to which English lawyers did not fail to draw attention.[48] After his appointment as Chief Justice Mansfield served on, and apparently guided, the Commission of Appeals for prize cases. This earned him the description in the *Commentaries* as "a judge whose masterly acquaintance with the law of nations was known and revered by every state in Europe."[49] Campbell, always eager for his heroes to mix in the right company, recorded that "the learned on the continent of Europe...placed his bust by the side of Grotius and D'Aguesseau."[50] The same reputation and expertise provided the foundation for one of Junius' most scathing gibes: "the Roman code, the law of nations, and the opinion of foreign civilians are your perpetual theme, but who ever heard you mention Magna Charta or the Bill of Rights with approbation or respect?"[51]

In drawing upon foreign legal sources for his commercial law rulings, Mansfield was thus drawing on sources a good deal less foreign to him than to most English lawyers. And this was particularly important because so much of the task of refining this jurisprudence depended on his ability to present comprehensive statements of the law in the context of determining individual cases.

Mansfield also cultivated and exploited the support and co-operation of the merchant community in London. He extended the practice utilized by his predecessors of soliciting professional testimony to prove and clarify merchant usage in the courts.[52] The procedure was especially valuable in the interpretation of technical documents and

---

[47] See Campbell, *Chief Justices*, II, 344–5, and Holliday, *Life of Mansfield*, pp. 129–67.
[48] See 3 *Comm* 70 and Holliday, *Life of Mansfield*, p. 424. Mansfield's tract was published later in the century by Francis Hargrave (ed.), *Collectanea Juridica*, I. 129–67.
[49] 3 *Comm* 70. Also see Ram, *Legal Judgement*, p. 174.
[50] Campbell, *Chief Justices*, II, 397.
[51] "Letter to Lord Mansfield" (1770), *Letters of Junius*, p. 178.
[52] For the practice by Holt and Denison in King's Bench, see Holden, *Negotiable Instruments*, pp. 79n, 101–2n; for Hardwicke in Chancery, see above at n15.

instruments, as was best evidenced in Mansfield's many rulings on the law of marine insurances. Thus, in one case which turned on the proper procedure for assessing damages to a ship's cargo, he directly observed that "the moment the Jury brought in their verdict, I was satisfied that they did right...[as] I thought a good deal of the point, and endeavoured to get what assistance I could by conversing with some gentlemen of experience in adjustments."[53] In another insurance dispute, regarding the technical meaning of the "outward bound" part of a ship's voyage, the Chief Justice ruled "that insurance brokers and others might be examined, as to the general opinion and understanding of the persons concerned in the trade."[54] Again, in a third case, Mansfield noted in his ruling that he prepared his decision "by talking with intelligent persons very conversant in the knowledge and practice of insurances."[55]

Besides enlisting this professional advice and guidance, the Chief Justice took equal pains to ensure that the actions of his court were correctly perceived by the merchants themselves. In one case on negotiable instruments already cited, Mansfield delayed giving judgment in order to review the arguments at the bar and formulate a more comprehensive ruling. In so doing, he was quick to reassure the merchant community that his delay did not reflect any judicial indecision: "Lord Mansfield said he would not wish to have it understood in the City that the Court had any doubt about the point."[56] No less revealing was a case of 1779 where the Chief Justice granted a retrial and actually reversed his own original determination of the suit. In explaining his actions, Mansfield emphasized that at the original hearing he had "laid great stress" on the testimony of "Mr Gorman," who was "an eminent merchant." Still, it was appropriate to review the decision, as he had "heard since that people in the City are dissatisfied with the verdict."[57]

This attention to professional opinion and guidance comprised only part of the means by which Mansfield relied on merchant support to develop the commercial law. More important and more distinctive was his use of special juries composed of merchants for the trial of commercial disputes.[58] As in other areas of common law development,

---

[53] *Lewis* v *Rucker*, (1761) 2 Burrow 1167, 1172.

[54] *Camden* v *Cowley*, (1763) 1 W Blackstone 417.

[55] *Glover* v *Black*, (1763) 3 Burrow 1394, 1401.

[56] *Miller* v *Race*, (1758) 1 Burrow 452, 457.

[57] *Lilly* v *Ewer*, (1779) 1 Douglas 72, 73–74.

[58] On common law special juries, see James C. Oldham, "The Origins of the Special Jury," *University of Chicago Law Review*, L (1983), 137–221; merchant juries are discussed at pp. 173–5.

the refinement of commercial law turned on the ability of the bench to remove certain issues from the consideration of the jury and to subsume them under the operation of authoritatively settled and delineated rules of law.[59] Before Mansfield, common law judges regularly determined mercantile disputes by instructing a common jury to find according to the particular circumstances of each case. This, as we have observed, could lead to irregularity in the determination of similar suits as well as to the production of decisions at odds with established merchant usage. Beyond these weaknesses, the procedure in itself also failed to generate clear legal rules for guidance in future cases. Such cases produced only a "general verdict" based on the jury's findings, and the grounds upon which they reached their decision would not appear on the record.

The difficulties this created drew comment from many legal writers, among them James Allan Park, whose *A System of Law of Marine Insurances* appeared in the penultimate year of Mansfield's chief justiceship. In his introductory remarks, Park noted that although some "sixty cases upon matters of insurance" had come before "common law jurisdiction" prior to Mansfield, these cases went little way towards establishing a system of law. Besides being poorly reported in "loose notes mostly taken at trials *nisi prius*," such cases "very often" contained "no opinion at all, but merely a general verdict." From this it "necessarily" followed that "the principles" guiding the court's determination "could never have been widely diffused nor generally known."[60]

Mansfield himself pointed to the same problem on several occasions. In a decision of 1774 concerning the nature of "barratry" in marine insurance, he stressed that although reported precedents had been cited in the pleadings, none was "strong enough to fix the bounds of what is or is not barratry." Such "general verdicts," he maintained, "are not to be regarded as certainty is never to be had from them, it not appearing on what grounds the jury found."[61] Four years later the Chief Justice raised the same objection in even more explicit terms. The case centered on the question of whether a clergyman, by virtue of

---

[59] For this broad characterization of the nature of common law development, I am especially indebted to J. H. Baker, "English Law and the Renaissance," *Cambridge Law Journal*, XLIV (1985), 46–61 and "The Law Merchant and the Common Law before 1700," and to S. F. C. Milsom, "Law and Fact in Legal Development," *University of Toronto Law Journal*, XVII (1967), 1–19 and "The Past and the Future of Judge-Made Law," *Monash University Law Review*, VIII (1981), 5–18.

[60] Park, *System of the Law of Marine Insurances*, p. xl.

[61] *Vallejo and Echalia* v *Wheeler*, (1774) Lofft 631, 643–4, and Cowper 143; also see *Nutt* v *Bourdieu*, (1786) 1 Term Rpts 323.

having drawn a series of large bills, was entitled to protection under the bankruptcy acts. Mansfield argued that the suit should be determined by settling in law the sphere of the acts, and in the process repudiated the alternative approach adopted by his predecessor at King's Bench:

> With regard to what passed at the trial in *Wilson*'s case, with great respect to Lord Chief Justice Lee's memory, I think the jury asked him a very proper question: whether this drawing and redrawing [of notes] was, in point of *law*, a trading in merchandise within the statutes concerning bankrupts... But the report says "He told them it was a question of *fact* and *not* of *law*." With all deference to his opinion, it was a question of law upon the fact. It may be proper to leave it to the jury whether the person gets a profit or remits other people's money; but the fact being established, the result is a matter of law.[62]

"The great object" in "mercantile law," Mansfield frequently declared, "is certainty," and this required that "the grounds of decision be precisely known."[63] To secure this great object the Chief Justice regularly reserved points of law for the consideration of the full court sitting *in banc* on cases previously determined at *nisi prius*, frequently by Mansfield himself. This was done either by directing a special case or by making a motion for a new trial.[64] The technique had particular advantages for raising and refining points of law. Unlike other common law procedures for examining questions of law, the special case and motion for a new trial allowed for a complete review of all the evidence produced at the original hearing. Since the evidence was presented to the court by the original trial judge, this gave him extensive control over the subsequent proceedings. "The judge's note," as J. H. Baker observes, was made into "the principal vehicle of discussion" of new legal questions.[65] These cases were retried before special juries composed of merchants, and the court was able to take

---

[62] *Hankey* v *Jones*, (1778) Cowper 745, 751–2; Mansfield was counsel in *Wilson*'s case.

[63] *Milles* v *Fletcher*, (1779) 1 Douglas 231, 232. For similar statements, see *Alderson* v *Temple*, (1768) 4 Burrow 2235, *Tyrie* v *Fletcher*, (1777) Cowper 666, *Bond* v *Nutt*, (1777) Cowper 601, *Drinkwater* v *Goodwin*, (1775) Cowper 251.

[64] On these procedures see Baker, *Introduction to English Legal History*, pp. 71–4, 119–21, and M. J. Prichard, "Nonsuit: A Premature Obituary," *Cambridge Law Journal*, XVIII (1960), 88–96.

[65] J. H. Baker, "From Sanctity of Contract to Reasonable Expectation?" *Current Legal Problems* (1979), 20. For a typical example of the procedure see the report of Mansfield's presentation in *Saunderson* v *Rowles* (1767) 4 Burrow 2064, 2067: "He stated very particularly and minutely from his own notes taken down at the trial, (which he read to the audience *verbatim*) the exact state of the facts as they came out upon the evidence: which he chose to do, that the Bar and the students might be fully and exactly apprized of the circumstances whereupon the court grounded their opinion."

advantage of their expertise for authoritatively settling merchant usage as rules of law. By perfecting these procedures Mansfield was able to mold individual cases into a system of commercial jurisprudence.

Much was done to advance the certainty of the law simply by bringing these cases before the more public forum of the Court of King's Bench. Often these motions for retrial were obtained not to reverse the original decision, but specifically "to settle the point more deliberately, solemnly and notoriously."[66] This objective was neatly illustrated in a case in 1760 which the Chief Justice first heard at *nisi prius*, and then brought into King's Bench in order to settle a rule for the calculation of interest on unpaid debts. As he admitted at the second trial, "the difference is very small in the present case, and scarce worth litigating between these parties." None the less, "I am glad of the opportunity which this case offers, of discussing the question and settling the point, to be a Rule for all cases of the same nature that may hereafter arise."[67] Such examples continued late into his judgeship. In a ruling of 1781, the Chief Justice similarly noted, "I am glad this question was saved, not from any difficulty there is in the case, but because it is important that general commercial points should be publicly decided."[68]

In addition to providing better publicity for commercial cases, the new trials offered an opportunity for an expansive and comprehensive discussion of merchant usage and the relevant legal authorities. Because of the professional experience of the jurors as well as Mansfield's particular talent for presenting clear and discrete statements of the law, it became possible to settle large areas of mercantile law in only a few actual cases. Perhaps the greatest success lay in the area of insurances, where, as Park maintained, previous decisions had failed to clarify the law. In the first years of his judgeship, Mansfield brought a series of cases into King's Bench to raise such general matters as capture and recapture, or the methods for assessing damages at sea, or the construction of technical maritime terms. Each case included an elaborate review of the evidence presented at the trial hearing and a full rehearsal of the appropriate legal sources:

> Lord Mansfield observed in general that a large field of argument had been entered into; and that it would be necessary to consider the Law of Nations, our own laws, and acts of Parliament; and also the Law and Customs of merchants, which make a part of our laws.[69]

---

[66] *Luke* v *Lyde*, (1759) 2 Burrow 882, 887.
[67] *Robinson* v *Bland*, (1760) 2 Burrow 1077, 1085.
[68] *Peacock* v *Rhodes*, (1781) 2 Douglas 633, 636.
[69] *Goss* v *Withers*, (1758) 2 Burrow 683, 692.

The purpose of this detail and exactitude, as he regularly reminded the court, was to establish certain rules for future cases:

> Lord Mansfield said it was very necessary that the Determinations upon policies of insurance should be fixed and certain. And therefore they would consider this matter, and look into the cases, and then (within the term) give their Opinion.[70]

By virtue of this technique, Mansfield later on in his judgeship was able to refer back to these early decisions not as particular rulings on individual disputes, but as systematic formulations of "the large principles of the Marine Law":[71]

> The great object in every branch of the law, but especially in mercantile law, is certainty...I took great pains in delivering the opinion of the court in the cases of *Goss* v *Withers* and *Hamilton* v *Mendes*. I read both those cases over last night, and I think that from them the whole law between insurers and insured as to the consequences of capture and recapture may be collected.[72]

The assistance of the special jury of merchants was crucial to the success of this process, and commentators like Campbell properly drew attention to how much of "the improvement of the commercial law" followed from Mansfield's efforts at "rearing a body of special jurymen at Guildhall" who generally served on "all commercial causes." As a law student in the 1800s, Campbell encountered "several of these gentlemen" who still "were designated and honoured as 'Lord Mansfield's jurymen.'" "One in particular," he recalled, "Mr. Edward Vaux, who always wore a cocked hat, and had almost as much authority as the Lord Chief Justice himself."[73]

In some cases the court relied on the jurors' expertise by directing the jury to determine which of the various rules contested for at trial represented the authentic merchant usage. Once the correct rule thus had been identified, the court could then establish it as a rule of law to apply in future litigation. In a case of 1761, the court needed to find the correct method for assessing damages to a ship's cargo. In his ruling Mansfield made plain the court's indebtedness to its jurors in establishing in law the proper "rule of estimation." "The special Jury," he stressed, contained "many knowing and considerable

---

[70] *Pelly* v *Royal Exchange Assurance Company*, (1757) 1 Burrow 341, 347.
[71] *Hamilton* v *Mendes*, (1761) 2 Burrow 1198, 1214. For other early insurance decisions, see *Wilson* v *Ducket*, (1762) 3 Burrow 1361, *Glover* v *Black*, (1763) 3 Burrow 1394, *Salvador* v *Hopkins*, (1765) 3 Burrow 1707.
[72] *Milles* v *Fletcher*, (1779) 1 Douglas 231, 232.
[73] Campbell, *Chief Justices*, II, 407.

merchants" who "understood the question very well, and knew more of the subject of it than any body else present." They had "formed their judgement from their own notions and experience, without much assistance from any thing that passed" in the courtroom.[74]

In these cases the cause of legal certainty was advanced by distinguishing as sharply as possible those aspects of a case which were to be determined by the application of settled legal rules and those which would turn on the case's particular circumstances. The distinction between matters of law and matters of fact served to increase legal certainty by reducing the number of issues previously left to the jury's discretion. Here the co-operation of the special jury was again vital in that it proved impossible to secure the desired distinction between law and fact where the jury opposed it.[75]

The point was demonstrated by way of negative example in a series of cases the Chief Justice heard in the later years of his career. These concerned the standard "reasonable time" provision attached to bills of exchange which limited the time allowed for their encashment. The very term "reasonable time" suggested that the period in question might well vary according to what in fact proved "reasonable" in a particular situation, and accordingly was a proper question for the jury to consider in its deliberation. Prior to Mansfield the courts appear to have proceeded on this basis.[76] But the Chief Justice insisted that "reasonable time" should be established as a point of law, as a fixed period of time settled according to merchant usage, lest the courts fail to provide an effective guide for the future. Thus in a suit in 1782, he instructed the jury to ignore the matter of "reasonable time" in its consideration of the facts of a particular case:

> Nothing is more mischievous than uncertainty in mercantile law. It would be terrible if every question were to make a cause, and to be decided according to the temper of a jury. If a rule is intended to apply to and govern a number of like cases, that rule is a rule of law.[77]

In this case the Chief Justice managed to prevail, but in general the jurors refused to support the attempt to fix "reasonable time" as a "rule of law." In a case of the same year, Mansfield was forced to grant

---

[74] *Lewis* v *Rucker*, (1761) 2 Burrow 1167, 1168.
[75] Given how much of Mansfield's judicial achievement in the field of commercial law depended upon a process of collaboration between bench and jury, it is ironical that what is best known of the Chief Justice's experience of juries are the clashes and opposition he suffered in the 1770s seditious libel prosecutions. As Mansfield explained to Boswell, juries generally took direction "except in political causes"; see *Boswell for the Defence*, pp. 184–5.
[76] See for example *Hankey* v *Trotman*, (1746) 1 W Blackstone 1, 1–2.
[77] *Medcalf* v *Hall*, (1782) 3 Douglas 113, 115.

three separate trials before giving up the point.[78] The issue reappeared in a dispute of 1786, and again Mansfield insisted that "wherever a rule can be laid down with respect to this reasonableness, that should be decided by the Court and adhered to by everyone for the sake of certainty." But once more the jury remained intransigent, and ultimately it proved impossible to settle the meaning of "reasonable time" as a settled rule of law.[79]

More often, however, Mansfield succeeded in securing the "great object" of certainty for large areas of mercantile law. To his contemporaries this achievement represented not only the distinctive feature of his judgeship, but also a decisive break with the past. Probably the earliest version of this assessment was furnished by Sir Francis Buller, Mansfield's disciple at King's Bench. In a ruling of 1787 Buller tendentiously contrasted previous practices with the record of the last "thirty years" when "the commercial law of this country" had "taken a very different turn from what it did before":

> Before that period we find that in courts of law all the evidence in mercantile cases was thrown together; they were left generally to a jury, and they produced no established principle. From that time we all know the great study has been to find some certain general principles, which shall be known to all mankind, not only to rule the particular case then under consideration, but to serve as a guide for the future. Most of us have heard these principles stated, reasoned upon, enlarged, and explained, till we have been lost in admiration at the strength and stretch of the human understanding. And I should be very sorry to find myself under a necessity of differing from any case on this subject which has been decided by Lord Mansfield, who may be truly said to be the founder of the commercial law of this country.[80]

Subsequent legal literature confirmed Buller's evaluation. In the final years of Mansfield's chief justiceship legal texts on major fields of commercial law began to appear. Their very publication affords the most telling evidence of the degree to which the Chief Justice's court had achieved "a guide to the future." Three works were produced between 1789–91 on the law of bills of exchange.[81] Among these, John

---

[78] *Appleton* v *Sweetapple*, (1782) 3 Douglas 137.
[79] *Tindal* v *Brown*, (1786) 1 Term Rpts 167, 168, and see Holden, *Negotiable Instruments*, pp. 129–32. On the distinction between points of law and fact, also see *Edie* v *East India Company*, (1761) 2 Burrow 1216 and *Grant* v *Vaughan*, (1764) 3 Burrow 1516, where Mansfield granted retrials upon discovering that he had mistakenly directed the jury to determine a usage which was already settled in law.
[80] *Lickbarrow* v *Mason*, (1787) 2 Term Rpts 63, 73.
[81] See Holden, *Negotiable Instruments*, pp. 143–4.

Bayley's *Short Treatise* has often been received as the first authoritative textbook on the subject. While Bayley did not explicitly refer to Mansfield, he introduced the work by noticing "the many modern determinations upon the law of Bills and Notes" which afforded "sufficient apology for an attempt to collect and methodize them."[82] In the next century, Joseph Story, in his *Commentary on the Law of Bills of Exchange*, observed that "the Law of Bills of Exchange and Promissory Notes and other negotiable paper, has mainly grown up since Lord Mansfield came upon the Bench, and we owe more to his labors on the subject than we probably do to any other single judicial mind."[83]

In 1787 two treatises appeared on the law of insurance: John Millar's *Elements of Law relating to Insurance* and James Allan Park's *A System of the Law of Marine Insurances*. Both authors emphasized the personal nature of Mansfield's contributions. Millar began by observing that it was not surprising that no previous work had supplied a systematic account of this area of law, since it was "principally from the abilities of an eminent judge still living" that "we have acquired a great number of systematic decisions." His "first object" had been "to make a complete collection of practical cases," and for this "undoubtedly the decisions of Lord Mansfield ought to hold the chief place."[84] Park also maintained that no previous work had "attempted to form this branch of jurisprudence into systematical arrangement." And he likewise highlighted Mansfield's special contributions, dedicating his publication to the Chief Justice and maintaining that "when the many admirable improvements which you have made in that branch of law ... are considered, any treatise upon the subject must be admitted to be the exclusive property of your Lordship."[85]

Those legal writers who advanced more general evaluations of his career also stressed the extent to which he had settled large areas of law on a systematic basis. George Joseph Bell noted that "in an uninterrupted period of thirty years," Mansfield had "devoted the strength of his great talents" to the "duty of building up, in a series of determinations, a system of mercantile jurisprudence."[86] Charles Butler maintained that considered "collectively" his decisions "will be found to form a complete code of jurisprudence on some of the most

---

[82] John Bayley, *A Short Treatise on the Law of Bills of Exchange, Cash Bills and Promissory Notes* (London, 1789), p. iii.

[83] Joseph Story, *Commentaries on the Law of Bills of Exchange, Foreign and Inland* (Boston, Mass., 1843), p. 15n.

[84] John Millar, *Elements of the Law relating to Insurance* (Edinburgh, 1787), p. vii and see p. 17.

[85] Park, *System of the Law of Marine Insurances*, p. iii.

[86] Bell, *Mercantile Jurisprudence*, pp. ix–x.

important branches of our law."[87] One such attempt actually to form his decisions into "a code of jurisprudence" was published in 1801. In his introduction to *A General View of the Decisions of Lord Mansfield*, William David Evans endorsed the contemporary consensus: "His decisions will be resorted to not merely as individual precedents in cases having a direct coincidence of circumstances, but as important guides in investigating the grounds and rudiments of the law."[88]

Not only had Mansfield founded a "system of mercantile jurisprudence," but this had been effected without major contribution from parliamentary legislation. This striking legislative lacuna was mentioned by several authors in their characterization of the Chief Justice's accomplishments. John Millar, for example, found it "pretty remarkable" in the light of England's commercial status, that "we have few statutory regulations" on insurance. He could only explain this by suggesting that the legislature of a "great and extensive empire" was unlikely to direct its attention "to the improvement of private jurisprudence."[89] Campbell too reflected on the manner in which Mansfield's efforts operated in legal territory largely unoccupied by statute law. But he explained this by attributing to the Chief Justice the same motives Blackstone had perceived in the reforming enterprises of earlier common law judges. In his attempt to advance English law for "the concerns of a trading population," he had consciously avoided parliament. "Instead of proceeding by legislation," Mansfield "wisely thought it more according to the genius of our institutions to introduce his improvements gradually by way of judicial decisions." The crucial feature of Mansfield's "complete code of jurisprudence" was that it did not need to take the form of legislation:

> It has been said reproachfully, that, although he was a member of the legislature for half a century, we have no "Lord Mansfield's Act". Yet when our CIVIL CODE shall be compiled, a large portion of it, and one of the best, will be referred to his decisions. The observation has been truly made that "he has done more for the jurisprudence of this country, than any legislator or judge or author who has ever made the improvement of it his object."[90]

---

[87] *Reminiscences of Charles Butler*, p. 136; see also Blackstone's remarks at 2 *Comm* 460 that, "The learning relating to these insurances hath of late years been greatly improved by a series of judicial decisions; which have now established the law in such a variety of cases, that (if well and judiciously collected) they would form a very complete title in a code of commercial jurisprudence."

[88] William David Evans, *A General View of the Decisions of Lord Mansfield*, 2 vols. (Liverpool, 1810), p. iii.

[89] Millar, *Elements of the Law relating to Insurance*, pp. 12–3.

[90] Campbell, *Chief Justices*, II, 566.

6

◁ ══════════════════════════════════════ ▷

Common Law, principle and precedent

The success of Mansfield's court in refining and settling England's commercial law provided a most forceful vindication of the common law's continued capacity to develop legal remedies in response to new social needs. English legal theory, as authoritatively elaborated by Hale, explained how the incremental growth and steady process of correction in the methods of common law had produced in England an unmatched legal fabric, one in Blackstone's formula "now fraught with the accumulated wisdom of ages."[1] Classical doctrines of equity further revealed the discretion judges enjoyed to operate general rules of law in such a fashion that justice always occurred in each particular case before the court.[2] Yet, in its extent and speed of accomplishment Mansfield's judicial achievement went beyond the expectations raised by these established orthodoxies. Through a masterful and programmatic utilization of the technical resources of the common law system, a "period of thirty years" had proved sufficient for the Chief Justice to consolidate an entire "system of mercantile jurisprudence." "His decisions" were not of value "merely as individual precedents" – considered "collectively," they were found "to form a complete code of jurisprudence."[3]

"The period during which Lord Mansfield presided in the Court of King's Bench," William David Evans explained, "will ever be regarded as an important era in the annals of English jurisprudence."[4] The commercial code was not the only branch of law where the accomplishments of Mansfield's court seemed to mark a new era.[5] Still,

---

[1] See the discussion above, chapter 1, at nn58–64.
[2] See the discussion above, chapter 3, at nn6–17.
[3] See the comments of George Joseph Bell, William David Evans and Charles Butler discussed above, chapter 5 at nn86–8.
[4] Evans, *Decisions of Lord Mansfield*, I, iii.
[5] See, for example, the praise of Mansfield's work in consolidating the settlement law offered by Thomas Gilbert, *Plan for the better Relief and Employment of the Poor* (London, 1781), p. 14, and by Richard Burn, *Bill for the Better Relief of the Poor*, pp. 25–6.

the commercial law was altogether exemplary: the area of law believed to have received the most dramatic improvements and the area of law associated most directly with the nation's distinctive economic and social circumstances. In 1759 when Lord Chancellor Hardwicke had occasion to identify the major challenges for law and equity "since the Revolution," he naturally remarked upon the "new discoveries and inventions in commerce" which had produced "new species of contracts" and "new contrivances to break and elude them," and "for which the ancient simplicity of the common law had adapted no remedies."[6] By the end of the century and in result of the labors of the "eminent man who has been called the father of the commercial law of England," even foreign legal writers found in English sources abundant "authorities and decisions" for "cultivating the subject of mercantile law."[7] Mansfield's chief justiceship, Charles Butler enthused, was "admirably suited to the genius and circumstances of the age."[8]

This achievement warns against any straightforward reading of the eighteenth-century constitution in the manner implied by Lord Camden in his repudiation of Mansfield's ruling in the case of Literary Property.[9] Camden suggested that parliament's legislative sovereignty meant that only parliament could supply new legal rules, while the courts were empowered to apply those rules which had been constituted by historical precedents or enacted by the legislature. This view was frequently conveyed through the canonical maxim invoked by Bacon and many others that the office of the judge was *jus dicere* and not *jus dare*.[10] Constitutional orthodoxy, however, also allowed a more complex reading of the relationship between parliament and the courts over the matter of legal change. The point of legislative sovereignty, according to this interpretation, was that no other power could challenge or alter parliament's legislative will. But such omnipotence did not mean that only parliament could effect legal change. The common law was not simply a bundle of historic precedents, and the common law system retained the capacity and authority to accommodate new cases. When in 1774 Edward Wynne encountered the alleged maxim that "the bare want of a Precedent is a great argument" of a case "being against law," he briskly reported, "that opinion is now disregarded; every day new cases arise and are determined on their own reasons."[11]

---

[6] Yorke, *Life of Hardwicke*, II, 554–5.
[7] Bell, *Mercantile Jurisprudence*, pp. ix–x.
[8] *Reminiscences of Charles Butler*, p. 136.
[9] See the discussion above, chapter 4 at n31.
[10] See the discussion above, chapter 1 at nn108–12 and chapter 3 at nn30–2.
[11] Wynne, *Eunomus*, III, 178.

For all these reasons, and notwithstanding the recent scholarly qualification of contemporary judgments, it is important to take the full measure of the late-eighteenth-century opinion which recognized Mansfield's "founding" of the commercial law as an inspired and instructive instance of legal innovation. At the same time, it must be stressed that this was not a particularly disruptive form of innovation. Mansfield had successfully settled the law-merchant, which was already recognized as part of English law, in such clear and comprehensive terms so as to provide an effective legal guide for future affairs. He reformed the law by refining and consolidating one of its acknowledged but inadequately developed branches. However, in other areas to which we now turn, his reforming efforts involved a more direct confrontation with the settled rules of common law. Mansfield in these situations appealed to the law's rational principles which again might serve to advance and refine the law, even on occasion at the expense of established precedents. The conception of common law this entailed appears also to have informed the Chief Justice's often critical attitude to parliamentary legislation.

It is easiest to begin by examining Mansfield's comments on the statute law. Something of his attitude has been noticed already. John Rayner included him in his distinguished canon of statute law critics. In his arguments in *Omychund* v *Barker*, the future Chief Justice insisted upon the superiority of common law over legislation as a mechanism for developing the rules, there presenting an argument that was later received as a classic pronouncement on the wisdom of the common law.[12] On the bench Mansfield supplied further observations on the failures of parliamentary legislation. Many of these took the familiar form of complaints against the careless drafting and technical flaws in many acts of parliament.[13] In a ruling of 1767, though, he returned to the broader issue of the rival claims of common law and statute, and again presented the record of the past as a clear demonstration of the superiority of common law.

The ruling was given in the House of Lords in the famous case "between the City of London and the Dissenters."[14] The dispute arose over the legality of a 1748 London corporation by-law which imposed

---

[12] Rayner's work is discussed above, Introduction at n79. For the later utilization of Mansfield's arguments in *Omychund* v *Barker*, see the treatments by Edmund Burke (discussed above, chapter 4 at nn19–20), and by Samuel Romilly in "Papers relative to Codification ... by Jeremy Bentham," *Edinburgh Review*, XXIX (1818), 223.

[13] See *Windham* v *Chetwynd*, (1757) 1 Burrow 414, 417 on the Statute of Frauds, *Janson* v *Willson*, (1779) 1 Douglas 257, 259 and *Wyllie* v *Wildes*, (1780) 2 Douglas 519, 523 on the Bankruptcy Acts.

[14] The history and decision of the case is reported in Philip Furneaux, *Letters to the Hon. Mr Justice Blackstone, concerning his Exposition of the Act of Toleration ... in his Celebrated Commentaries on the Laws of England*, 2nd edn (London, 1771), pp. 221–84.

heavy fines on corporation members who refused to serve or be nominated for corporation offices. The by-law was enacted as part of the fund-raising schemes used to finance the building of the Mansion House, and it was aimed at the Dissenters. Under the terms of the Corporation Act, Dissenters were barred from such offices. Once nominated by the corporation they would automatically incur the fines established in the 1748 by-law. The legality of this tactic turned on the legal effects of the Toleration Act. The Lords interpreted the Toleration Act to have made Protestant dissent legal, rather than to have merely removed the penalties for such dissent, and on this basis ruled against the corporation by-law. Thus the decision of the case centered on the relation between the Corporation Act and the later Toleration Act. Mansfield, however, used this case to defend the cause of religious toleration generally, and fashioned his defense through a comparison of the rival merits of common law and statute on this question. He began by claiming that if nonconformity was "a crime by common law," it must be sanctioned either by "Usage or Principle." He then declared there to be "no usage or custom" making "Nonconformity a crime." Accordingly, the common law position turned on the criterion of "Principle," and here Mansfield simply stated the contemporary moral arguments for religious toleration:

> It cannot be shown from the principles of Natural or Revealed Religion that independent of positive law, temporal punishments ought to be inflicted for mere opinions with respect to particular modes of worship. Prosecution for a sincere, though erroneous conscience, is not to be deduced from reason or the fitness of things.[15]

Since religious persecution could not be deduced "from reason," the common law, which Mansfield declared to be "only common reason or usage," could not view nonconformity as criminal.[16] It could only be supported through "positive law." The disgraced and morally reprehensible policy of religious persecution thus became yet another example of the failure of England's legislators:

> What bloodshed and confusion have been occasioned from the reign of Henry IV when the first penal statutes were enacted, down to the Revolution in this kingdom, by laws made to force conscience. There is nothing certainly more unreasonable, more inconsistent with the rights of human nature, more contrary to the spirit and precepts of the Christian religion, more iniquitous and unjust, more impolitic, than Persecution. It is against Natural Religion, Revealed Religion and sound Policy.[17]

---

[15] *Ibid.*, 263–4.   [16] *Ibid.*, 278.

[17] *Ibid.*, 278. See also Mansfield's comments on the statutes against Catholics in *Foone* v *Blount*, (1776) Cowper 464.

Through these arguments Mansfield endorsed the cause of religious toleration by accommodating it within the English lawyer's conventional contrasting of the wisdom of common law with the tainted record of statute. Here, as in *Omychund* v *Barker*, Mansfield's celebration of the superiority of common law turned critically on this law being founded in "reason" and "principle." This was an understanding of common law frequently invoked and much embellished in Mansfield's court.

Mansfield, despite contemporary complaints to the contrary, never entirely ignored precedents. But he was clear that the essence of England's law was principle. As he observed in 1774, "the Law would be a strange Science if it rested solely upon cases, and if after so large an increase of Commerce, Arts and Circumstances accruing, we must go to the time of Richard I to find a Case and see what is Law." Such cases and precedents served "to fix Principles," but "precedent, though it be Evidence of law, is not Law itself, much less the whole of the Law."[18] The same argument was advanced in a bankruptcy suit which appeared at King's Bench three years later. There the Chief Justice admitted that he could find "no case exactly parallel," but the difficulty was overcome by the appeal to principles. "The law," he explained, "does not consist in particular cases, but in general principles which run through cases and govern the decision of them."[19]

In addition to placing emphasis on the principles of common law, Mansfield tended to treat the law's historical character by stressing the continual process of legal change and adaptation which properly occurred in response to altered social conditions. This attitude to legal custom was best revealed in a series of cases the Chief Justice determined on the question of a *feme covert's* powers of contract. As Mansfield noted in one such case, "it has been truly stated that by the common law the wife has no separate power of contracting." But notwithstanding this historic rule, "within the last century a great change" had "been introduced into the law relating to married persons," as was appropriate, since "general rules" had to be "varied by change of circumstances." It now became possible to construe these changes as settling a new rule of law: "cases arise within the letter, yet not within the reason, of the rule; and exceptions are introduced, which grafted upon the rule, form a system of law."[20] In a later ruling on the

---

[18] *Jones* v *Randall*, (1774) Lofft 383, 385 and Cowper 37, 39.

[19] *Rust* v *Cooper*, (1774) Cowper 629, 632. For similar comments, see R v *Inhabitants of Weston*, (1770) 4 Burrow 2507, *James* v *Price*, (1773) Lofft 219, R v *Bembridge*, (1783) 3 Douglas 327.

[20] *Ringsted* v *Lady Lanesborough*, (1783) 3 Douglas 197, 199, 202–3.

same point, Mansfield again pointed to this understanding of an historical law:

> ... *quicquid agunt homines* is the business of Courts, and as the usages of society alter, the law must adapt itself to the various situations of mankind.[21]

In the light of this conception of common law, many of Mansfield's more controversial practices at King's Bench can be readily characterized. The same social developments which required the settling of England's mercantile law also demanded advancement of the common law itself. Such legal change could legitimately be encouraged by the courts because the common law itself was not constituted by particular cases and aways retained its capacity to draw directly "from the fountain of justice."[22] A leading example of such reforming enterprise is found in the Chief Justice's controversial treatment of the common law action of *indebitatus assumpsit*, the action for "money had and received." Here Mansfield has often been thought to have attempted to reformulate the English law of quasi-contract according to the equitable principles of Roman and continental jurisprudence.

The background to this episode lies in the complex and not fully revealed historical process by which money claims at common law came to be adjudicated under the action of *assumpsit*.[23] Originally, such claims were tried by the action of debt, *assumpsit* being restricted to cases involving positive wrongdoing which resulted in physical damages. *Assumpsit*, however, had the procedural advantage of providing for trials by jury, whereas the older action of debt on a

---

[21] *Barwell v Brooks*, (1784) 3 Douglas 371, 373.
[22] *Omychund v Barker*, (1744) 1 Atkyns 21, 33; cited above, chapter 4 at n10.
[23] There is an abundance of recent literature on the action of *assumpsit* and the early history of contract. For accounts and responses to the book-length discussions by A. W. B. Simpson, S. J. Stoljar, Morton J. Horwitz and P. S. Atiyah, see J. H. Baker, "Review of A. W. B. Simpson, *A History of the Common Law of Contract*; Volume 1: *The Rise of the Action of Assumpsit* and S. J. Stoljar, *A History of Contract at Common Law*," *American Journal of Legal History*, XXI (1977), 335–41; A. W. B. Simpson, "The Horwitz Thesis and the History of Contracts," *University of Chicago Law Review*, XLVI (1979), 533–601; and J. L. Barton, "The Enforcement of Hard Bargains," *Law Quarterly Review*, CIII (1987), 118–47. In addition to this material, I have benefited from the following studies: J. H. Baker, "New Light on *Slade's Case*," *Cambridge Law Journal*, XXIX (1971), 51–67, 213–36, and "Origins of the 'Doctrine' of Consideration, 1535–1585," in M. S. Arnold, T. A. Green, S. A. Scully and S. D. White, *On the Laws and Customs of England: Essays in Honor of S. E. Thorne* (Chapel Hill, 1981); H. K. Lücke, "*Slade's Case* and the Origin of the Common Counts," *Law Quarterly Review*, LXXXI (1965), 422–45, 539–61 and LXXXII (1966), 81–96; R. H. Helmholz, "Assumpsit and *Fedei Laesio*," *Law Quarterly Review*, XCI (1975), 406–32; David Ibbetson, "Assumpsit and Debt in the Sixteenth Century: the Origins of the Indebitatus Count," *Cambridge Law Journal*, XVI (1982), 142–61, and "Contract Law: *Slade's Case* in Context," *Oxford Journal of Legal Studies*, IV (1984), 295–317.

contract was tried by wager of law. It became possible to use the action of *assumpsit* for money claims once the courts came to view simple contracts as necessarily containing a separate promise to pay the sum due. The *assumpsit* was thus grounded on this implied promise to pay. This development was consolidated in Slade's case in 1602, following which the action of debt on a contract fell out of use. This process of replacing older actions with *assumpsit* was extended later in the century to cover cases of indebtedness occurring outside the field of contractual agreements. A clear instance of this was in suits for the recovery of feudal dues or customary impositions. In such situations one party's indebtedness was established in law, without any actual agreement or promise having occurred between the creditor and the debtor. What was originally an implied promise in an actual contract, as in Slade's case, became a purely fictitious promise in an implied contract.[24]

This extension of the action to non-contractual cases was particularly important for the growth of the action of *indebitatus assumpsit* for 'money had and received,' one of the so-called 'common counts' in *assumpsit*. This form of the action had considerable technical advantages for a plaintiff in that he merely had to claim the defendant's indebtedness, rather than set out at length the circumstances which led to the transfer of money under dispute. The action was available in situations where money had been transferred by mistake, or where money had been given to the defendant for transfer to the plaintiff. In these cases, the parties concerned rarely had reached any specific agreement or undertaking, and the courts again allowed the fictitious promise on which to base the action. Given the generality of the action and the advantages it provided for plaintiffs, it was possible for *indebitatus assumpsit* to replace a wide range of standard common law actions in tort. The courts, however, resisted any blanket duplication of common law remedies, and Sir John Holt was especially eager to prevent the action being employed in such a way that "the defendant can't tell how to make his defence." He condemned the previous latitude of the courts in raising fictitious promises, and generally resisted the extension of the action beyond those cases where the courts had already permitted it.[25] As a result, the scope of the action did not conform to any simple principle regarding the law's attitude to debt. Instead, it had to be explained in terms of the somewhat unsystematic category of cases in which the courts were prepared to allow the

---

[24] See Simpson, *Common Law of Contract*, pp. 489–505; Baker, *Introduction to English Legal History*, p. 307.

[25] See Simpson, *Common Law of Contract*, pp. 504–5; Baker, *Introduction to English Legal History*, pp. 308–12.

necessary fictitious promise. Despite these technical limitations, by mid-century the action for money had and received was already emerging as one of the most popular actions in the courts. This was the result of its procedural advantages, and a reflection of the increasing number of informal transfers of money and credit which underlined England's commercial growth during the period. And it was a development to which Mansfield sought to contribute.

Mansfield's approach to *indebitatus assumpsit* reveals many of the same objectives found in his commercial law rulings. He clearly recognized the advantages of the action as a legal remedy suitable to a large number of commercial transactions. In contrast to Holt's restrictive attitude, he supported "a liberal extension of the action," and declared himself "a great friend to the action." He would not allow a defendant "to be surprised by it," but "consistent with that guard" he did not believe "the action can be too much encouraged."[26] As in the case of the law-merchant, the Chief Justice sought to strengthen the action by settling some clear general principle to characterize its scope and nature, and thereby provide an effective guide for future determinations. Thus, in what was probably his most famous ruling on *indebitatus assumpsit*, in the 1760 case of *Moses* v *Macferlan*, the Chief Justice did not dwell on the technical matter of implied contracts and fictitious promises. Instead, he introduced his judgment by listing the various situations for which the action was available and "much encouraged," and then advanced a general equitable explanation of the action to "recover back money":

> In one word, the gist of this kind of action is that the Defendant, upon the circumstances of the case, is obliged by the ties of natural justice and equity to refund the money.[27]

This understanding of *indebitatus assumpsit* was rehearsed regularly by Mansfield. The action was "founded on principles of eternal justice"; it lay "only for money which *ex aequo et bono* the defendant ought to refund"; it was available "to recover what in conscience ought not to be kept from you"; and the adjudication of such actions was "governed by the true equity and conscience of the case."[28]

In these comments, the Chief Justice sought to free the action from the procedural technicalities which had occasioned its first formulation. This concern was further served by his attempt to define the scope of

[26] *Longchamp* v *Kenny*, (1779) 1 Douglas 137, 138, and *Towers* v *Barrett*, (1786) 1 Term Rpts 133, 134–5.

[27] *Moses* v *Macferlan*, (1760) 2 Burrow 1005, 1012.

[28] *Towers* v *Barrett*, (1786) 1 Term Rpts 133, 134; *Moses* v *Macferlan*, (1760) 2 Burrow 1005, 1012; *Clarke* v *Johnson*, (1774) Lofft 756, 758; *Longchamp* v *Kenny*, (1779) 1 Douglas 137, 138.

the action by describing it as "an action in nature of a bill in equity."[29] The range of *indebitatus assumpsit* was thereby shifted from the common law standard of fictitious promises to the more substantive principles of legal liability adopted in the equity courts. The advantages of this tactic were exploited by Sir Francis Buller in a case which came before King's Bench in the final year of Mansfield's judgeship. Buller began his ruling by noting that "of late years this court has very properly extended the action for money had and received." This extension was based "on the principle of its being considered like a bill in equity." Accordingly, the most direct manner of settling the boundaries of the action was by reference to the practice of the equity courts: "in order to recover money in this form of action the party must shew that he has equity and conscience on his side, and that he could recover it in a court of equity." Hence, in cases where "a court of equity" would not relieve the plaintiff, "we ought not to permit him to recover in a court of law in an action founded upon equitable principles."[30]

By so emphasizing the equitable character of the action, Mansfield has been alleged to have borrowed principles found in the Roman law of quasi-contract or in the French doctrine of *enrichissement illegitime*. This has made his handling of the action often appear essentially antithetic to common law conventions, although other commentators have discerned a less radical and unorthodox approach in the Chief Justice's enterprises.[31] What is clear is that Mansfield himself did not go out of his way to supply his rulings with the more technically orthodox glosses that have been proffered in his defense, and in celebrating the resources of the common law he did not mean to praise past technicality. Instead, his approach to the action of *indebitatus assumpsit* can be related to his understanding of common law in general and his attitude to commercial law in particular. His declared goal, as we have seen, was for mercantile disputes to be settled according to clear and certain rules, in accordance with principles of "natural justice" and not hampered by "niceties of law."[32] In most instances, this involved

---

[29] *Clarke* v *Johnson*, (1774) Lofft 756, 758, and see *Jestons* v *Brooke*, (1778) Cowper 793.

[30] *Straton* v *Rastall*, (1788) 2 Term Rpts 366, 370–1.

[31] Compare the discussions by H. G. Hanbury, "The Recovery of Money," *Law Quarterly Review*, XL (1924), 31–42; H. C. Gutteridge, "Does English Law Recognize a Doctrine of Unjustified Enrichment?" *Cambridge Law Journal*, V (1934), 223–9; and by R. M. Jackson, *The History of Quasi-Contract in English Law* [in H. D. Hazeltine (gen. ed.), *Cambridge Studies in English Legal History*] (Cambridge, 1936), pp. xiv, 117–21. For a more recent treatment of the issue, see Simpson, *Common Law of Contract*, 316–23, 327–74, and Atiyah, *Freedom of Contract*, pp. 162–4.

[32] "The most desirable object on *all* judicial determinations, especially in *mercantile* ones (which ought to be determined upon natural justice and not upon niceties of law) is to do substantial Justice," *Alderson* v *Temple*, (1768) 4 Burrow 2235, 2239. See also Mansfield's ruling in *Hamilton* v *Mendes*, (1761) 2 Burrow 1198, cited above, chapter 5 at n20.

adjudication under the law-merchant, itself based on merchant usage and the law of nature and nations. But Mansfield conceived the common law to be a system of legal usage which also encompassed among its sources the law of nature and nations and which, when properly "looked into," revealed its foundations "in equity, reason and good sense."[33] Accordingly, it was possible to view common law remedies in an equitable light, and particularly appropriate to do so in areas of law, such as actions for money claims, which were vital to the concerns of a commercial society. The substance of Mansfield's doctrines owed more to Roman jurisprudence than to the English standard of implied and fictitious promises. None the less, the rationale of his encouragement of the action to "recover back money" followed directly from his conception of common law and its distinctive strengths.

The same attitude to common law figured in those cases where Mansfield's court adopted practices developed in Chancery or provided remedies previously available only in equity. This development was remarked upon by Sir William Ashhurst in a King's Bench ruling of 1787. Ashhurst observed "that formerly the Courts of Law did not take notice of an equity or a trust, for trusts are within the original jurisdiction of a court of equity." Nevertheless, "wherever this court have seen that the justice of the case has been clearly with the plaintiff, they have not turned him round," since it was "productive of great expense to send the parties" to Chancery. As a result, King's Bench had to come to "take notice" of trusts and other equitable rights.[34]

Once more, Mansfield's innovations have often appeared as a foreign-inspired assault on English orthodoxies, threatening in this instance to undermine the separation of law and equity.[35] There is indeed evidence to suggest that the Chief Justice had less than full sympathy for the institutional division of law and equity which, in correspondence with Lord Kames, he acknowledged to be "proper, beneficial, and necessary in England," albeit for "local and peculiar" reasons.[36] Nonetheless, there is no need to see in these maneuvers at King's Bench anything so visionary as the attempt to fuse the two jurisdictions. Instead, his enterprises can again be readily understood

---

[33] *James* v *Price*, (1773) Lofft 219, 221.

[34] *Winch* v *Keeley*, (1787) 1 Term Rpts 619, 622–3. For similar cases, see *Robinson* v *Bland*, (1760) 2 Burrow 1077, *Darlington* v *Pluteney*, (1775) Cowper 260, *Rice* v *Shute*, (1770) 5 Burrow 2611. Also see 4 *Comm* 442, where Blackstone presents this as one of the major developments in the law since 1688.

[35] See the criticisms raised by Powell, *Law of Contracts and Agreements*, II, vii–x, and by Mitford, *Pleadings in Chancery*, p. 2, and those discussed by Campbell, *Chief Justices*, II, 437–8.

[36] Letter of 1766, cited in Ian Simpson Ross, *Lord Kames and the Scotland of his Day*, (Oxford, 1972), pp. 241–2. See also his comments cited in Campbell, *Chief Justices*, II, 554.

by returning to his most general conception of common law. His theory of the common law allowed for little distinction between English law and English equity as systems of customary law, notwithstanding their dramatic differences in procedures and administrative forms. As for Blackstone, both law and equity were equally settled systems of legal art, where precedents served as evidence of law and where the application of settled rules was not suffered to violate the principles of reason and justice. Of course, as we have seen, this view of the similarity between English equity and common law was most often drawn in order to insulate the common law from interference by courts of equity.[37] However, the same theory could also legitimate the common law's adoption of remedies consolidated within Chancery practice. As Mansfield characterized the institutional relationship (again in his private correspondence with Lord Kames), "The Idea of a Court of Equity distinct from a Court of Law subsists only in England...But in most cases, the Rule of Decision in both Courts depends upon the nature of the question. The merits of the same question would generally in both Courts be decided by the same reasons."[38]

In both these areas, Mansfield's reforming efforts were soon curtailed by his successors. The more radical implications of his interpretation of *indebitatus assumpsit* were resisted by recourse to the orthodox standard of fictitious promises.[39] Under Lord Kenyon in King's Bench and Lord Eldon in Chancery, the separateness of law and equity in England was sharply reaffirmed.[40] These counter-developments point to the more controversial aspects of Mansfield's approach to common law, and they also raise important issues concerning the limits of judicial law reform. Many of these issues had in fact already been brought into sharp focus during Mansfield's own tenure in King's Bench, when his innovative appeal to legal principle against precedents conflicted with the settled forms of real property law. In this instance, his efforts floundered, the foundations of England's gothic castle remained unshaken, and precedent triumphed comfortably over principle. Yet although this episode was of only marginal significance for the development of the law, it provided an occasion for a fairly sustained discussion of the nature of common law and the general capacity of the courts to effect legal change.

---

[37] See above, chapter 3 at nn38–45.
[38] Ross, *Lord Kames*, p. 242.
[39] See Jackson, *Quasi-Contract in English Law*, pp. 121–2.
[40] See Holdsworth, *History of English Law*, XII, 595–605.

These issues arose in the context of the controversial King's Bench decision in the case of *Perrin* v *Blake*.[41] The suit originated in Jamaica in 1758 and did not complete its inauspicious career in the English courts until 1777, by which time the dispute had been settled by private compromise. The determination of the case involved the legal construction of a technically flawed will. Such cases were the common currency of the courts, and at the level of legal principle the position of the law to them was plain. As Blackstone maintained from the bench, "the great and fundamental maxim upon which the construction of every devise must depend, is 'that the intention of the testator shall be fully and punctually observed, *so far* as the same is consistent with the established rule of law and *no farther*.'"[42] "The first rule of law in expounding wills," Hardwicke explained, meant that "the law will help an improper and unapt expression" where "the testator's intent appears plain."[43] Thus the courts were empowered to follow the testator's intention even in those cases where the legal instrument under dispute had been inaccurately or imprecisely drawn. "Courts of justice," Mansfield maintained, "are to construe the words of parties so as to effectuate their deeds, and not to destroy them."[44]

This legal principle, while allowing the courts considerable flexibility in interpreting the terms of a particular will or devise, restricted the courts to doing only what was "consistent with the established rule of law." In the first place, this simply indicated that the courts could never effect an illegal intention. Thus the courts would not support "an intention in the testator to create a perpetuity, or to limit a fee upon a fee, or to make a chattel descend to heirs," since in all these cases the avowed intention was "contrary to the rules of law."[45] But included under the rubric of the rule of law were also the more technical rules by which the courts construed those standard terms of legal art commonly employed in wills and conveyances. Such standard rules of construction were required to preserve the certainty of property law, since otherwise the authentic meaning of any particular instrument could only be established by individual judicial decision.

Unfortunately in the case of English law, these standard rules for

---

[41] The case is fully reported by Francis Hargrave in *Collectanea Juridica*, I, 283–322, and in *A Collection of Tracts, Relative to the Law of England* (London, 1787), pp. 487–510. See also the discussion in Fifoot, *Lord Mansfield*, pp. 158–83.

[42] Hargrave, *Collection of Tracts* (London, 1787), p. 489–90.

[43] *Bagshaw* v *Spencer*, (1743) 2 Atkyns 570, 580.

[44] *Pugh* v *Duke of Leeds*, (1777) Cowper 714, 725. For similar rulings, see *Robinson* v *Robinson*, (1756) 1 Burrow 38, *Hayward* v *Whitby*, (1757) 1 Burrow 228, *Ordiarne* v *Whitehead*, (1759) 2 Burrow 704, *Long* v *Laming*, (1760) 2 Burrow 1100, *Evans* v *Astley*, (1764) 3 Burrow 1570, *Fen* v *Lowndes*, (1768) 4 Burrow 2246.

[45] Mansfield's examples in *Long* v *Laming*, (1760) 2 Burrow 1100, 1108.

interpreting devises had been formulated as part of the elaborate web
of legal fictions through which the courts had gradually extended the
individual's power to alienate property. As a result, they were
enormously complex and technical, if not entirely unintelligible to the
uninitiated. Blackstone had argued in the *Commentaries* that given the
proper historical learning, it was not difficult to perceive the "clew" to
this "labyrinth." Other legal writers proved more skeptical. Richard
Wooddeson acknowledged that the "necessary shifts and contrivances
used in conveyancing" were "frequent and popular matters of
complaint," and Michael Nolan maintained that if the professional
conveyancer mastered the system, for "the rest of mankind it must
remain unaccountable."[46] Barrington even questioned whether most
conveyancers or attorneys fully understood the rules for contructing
devises, and concluded from this that "the testator might as well have
continued to have had no such power" as was first granted him under
the Henrician statute of wills.[47] Even the most basic rules of
construction, such as those relating to the distinction between real and
personal property, were frequently unknown. As Mansfield observed in
a typical ruling, "generally speaking, no common person has the
smallest idea of any difference between giving a person a horse and a
quantity of land. Common sense alone would never teach a man the
difference."[48] In the light of so "many technical words and forms,"
Bentham compared the law to "the lying boy in the Fable: the abuses
of language though not perpetual are yet so frequent and their existence
so notorious, that where any part of language presents itself, men never
can think themselves in security."[49] In the multitude of provisions for
a reformed legal policy Bentham canvassed in the 1770s, he particularly
recommended that judicial decisions "concerning the construction of
words" never be preserved.[50]

Given the technical demands of the conveyancing system, mistakes
were easily made, and in the many cases concerning wills and devises
which entered Westminster Hall, the courts were forced to determine
between an interpretation which followed the testator's intent and one
conforming to the technical rules of construction. The general policy of
the courts was to sacrifice the rules to the intent where that intent was
clearly stated, but to supply a more technical construction where the
intent was unclear. In *Perrin* v *Blake* the testator had stated in his will

---

[46] Wooddeson, *Elements of Jurisprudence*, p. 106, and *Coulson* v *Coulson*, (1743) 2 Strange 1125
(Nolan's note).
[47] Barrington, *Ancient Statutes*, pp. 446–7.
[48] *Hogan* v *Jackson*, (1775) Cowper 299, 306. Also see *Hope* v *Taylor*, (1757) 1 Burrow 268, *Massey*
v *Rice*, (1775) Cowper 346.
[49] UC xxvii. 91. Also see UC lxxa. 35.   [50] UC lxix. 36.

that "it is my intent and meaning that none of my children shall sell or dispose of my estate for a longer time than his life." He then left the estate to his son "for his natural life" with the remainder "to the heirs of the body of my said son."[51] By using this formula the will fell under the so-called "rule in Shelley's case," laid down in Coke's *Reports*.[52] According to this rule, the son received the estate as a tenant in tail in possession. He thereby enjoyed effective power to alienate the estate as he pleased, in violation of the testator's intention to limit his powers over the estate to his own lifetime. The rule in question had been formulated to prevent the evasion of feudal dues, and even when it appeared as a rule of construction in the sixteenth century, it represented a restrictive interpretation of rules originally designed to facilitate powers of alienation. By the eighteenth century, the application of the rule in cases like *Perrin v Blake* virtually always prevented the testator's intention from being effected, even though the intention itself was perfectly legal.[53]

Perrin v Blake came before the court of King's Bench in 1769, where it was decided in favor of the testator's intent. The court argued that in this particular case the testator had expressed his design so clearly that it was proper to exempt the devise from the rule in Shelley's case. In his judgment, Mansfield admitted that there were doubtless "lawyers of a different bent of genius" who would have "chosen to adhere to the strict letter of the law." But he insisted upon upholding the principle of law which "allowed a free communication of intention to the testator," stressing that "it would be a strange law to say, 'Now you have communicated that intention so as everybody understands what you mean, yet because you have used a certain expression of art, we will cross your intention...though what you mean to have done is perfectly legal, and the only reason for contravening you is because you have not expressed yourself as a lawyer.'" He further warned that if the common law courts neglected this legal principle and simply adhered "to the mere letter of the law," "the great men who preside in Chancery" would "devise new ways to creep out of the lines a law,"

---

[51] Hargrave, *Collectanea Juridica*, I, 285.

[52] For an account of the rule, see Simpson, *An Introduction to the History of Land Law* (Oxford, 1962), pp. 89–96. For contemporary discussions, see Edward Coke, *The First Part of the Institutes of the Laws of England, or, a Commentary upon Littleton*, 13th edn by Francis Hargrave and Charles Butler, 2 vols. (London, 1775–88), II, 276–80 (Butler's note) and Hargrave, *Collection of Tracts*, pp. 549–78.

[53] "In the cases in which the question arises, whether the rule shall govern or not, it almost ever occurs that the author of the entail doth not mean that the tenant for life, to the heirs of whose body the remainder is limited, should have power to defeat the succession to them by an alienation to their prejudice," Hargrave, *Collection of Tracts*, p. 556.

a situation which only threatened even more "confusion in the titles of owners."[54]

This decision had been reached only over the objections of Sir Joseph Yates, and a writ of error was brought against the King's Bench judgment. The suit was reheard in 1772 in the Exchequer Chamber where the King's Bench ruling was reversed. Blackstone, then a judge in the court of Common Pleas, supplied the judgment in reversal. He argued that the disputed devise did not in fact provide "any such plain and manifest *intent* of the divisor" as was needed to exempt the will from the rule in Shelley's case.[55] Accordingly, the technical rule of construction prevailed.

In terms of these arguments the decisions of the two courts occupied rather narrow legal ground. What was disputed was whether the testator had recorded his intentions with sufficient clarity, both courts accepting that if this had been achieved, the intention was to override the relevant rule of construction. But in support of their rulings, the two courts also addressed other questions. These raised more general issues regarding the relationship between precedents and principles, and highlighted the divergent implications of an historical under-standing of England's legal inheritance.

Those judges and lawyers who opposed Mansfield's determination were quick to point out the long series of precedents which stood against him. As Yates maintained in his dissenting judgment, there were many "cases to be met with" where the courts had given way "to the superior influence of law" even though the testator had "holden forth strong marks" of a contrary intention. Given the need to preserve the stability of law it was better to adhere to "the established rules" even if "a thousand testators' wills be overthrown."[56]

Despite the importance of this argument, none of the supporters of Yates' position sought to establish the case for legal certainty through any simple appeal to previous precedents. In the first place, the record was not conclusive. As Serjeant Glynn acknowledged in his arguments, it was impossible to "contend" that the rule in Shelley's case had "not been broken in upon."[57] The argument from precedents also required further elaboration because the common law as a legal process did not achieve certainty solely on the basis of strictly adhering to precedents. Such precedents only provided evidence of common law, and as Hale had explained in his history of the law, in most cases legal certainty was attained by virtue of the general consensus among the judges as to the

---

[54] Hargrave, *Collectanea Juridica*, I, 318, 321–2.
[55] Hargrave, *Collection of Tracts*, p. 502.
[56] Hargrave, *Collectanea Juridica*, I, 310.   [57] *Ibid.*, 288.

law's true substance.[58] Hale's teaching had received dramatic confirmation in Mansfield's achievement in settling the commercial law. In this legal field there were few adequate precedents or English law authorities to guide the courts, and the necessary certainty, which Mansfield held to be the special object in commercial law, was achieved through the judiciary's support for Mansfield's rulings. This support had been purposely cultivated, particularly in the court of King's Bench. It was not until the thirteenth year of Mansfield's chief justiceship that the court reached a split decision. As he explained on that occasion, the previous unanimity "never could have happened if we did not among ourselves communicate our sentiments with great freedom; if we did not form our judgments without any prepossession to first thoughts; if we were not always open to conviction and ready to yield to each other's reasons."[59]

In the case of *Perrin* v *Blake* this judicial consensus collapsed, with the consequence of dramatically reducing the opportunity for judicial flexibility. Still, it was not the contrary precedents which led to this judicial opposition so much as the belief that the proper process of judicial consultation used to settle rules of common law had already occurred some thirty years earlier in the case of *Coulson* v *Coulson*.[60] In this sense, the trouble with Mansfield's attempt to secure a judicial re-examination of the rule was that it had come too late. The case of *Coulson* v *Coulson* appeared before Hardwicke in Chancery, and was sent to King's Bench to determine the status of the rule in Shelley's case. The common law judges supported the application of the rule against the testator's intent, and Hardwicke adhered to this judgment. As Glynn stressed in his pleadings, "all the cases" relevant to the rule were "considered by this court in the case of *Coulson* and *Coulson*," and the court's decision "was delivered on the most weighty and deliberate thought." On the basis of this ruling, "the rule laid down by Lord Coke is revived," and it was now too late to reopen the issue.[61] Yates and Blackstone also emphasized the particular importance of this case, Blackstone noting that "half the titles in the kingdom are by this time built upon its doctrine."[62]

In addition to the absence of judicial consensus, Mansfield also faced the opposition of the professional conveyancers. This again contrasted with the experience in commercial law, where the courts reforming

---

[58] Hale, *History of Common Law*, p. 162.
[59] *Millar* v *Taylor*, (1769) 4 Burrow 2303, 2395. Also see Mansfield's use of judicial conference in *Belitber* v *Gibbs*, (1767) 4 Burrow 2117 and *Bidleson* v *Whytel*, (1764) 3 Burrow 1545.
[60] *Coulson* v *Coulson*, (1741) reported at 2 Atkyns 246 and 2 Strange 1125.
[61] Hargrave, *Collectanea Juridica*, I, 288.
[62] Hargrave, *Collection of Tracts*, p. 508, and see *Collectanea Juridica*, I, 317.

efforts depended upon the support and co-operation of the community affected by its actions. In *Perrin* v *Blake*, the conveyancers, who operated the technical system under examination, actively pursued the reversal of the King's Bench determination. Indeed, of all of the contemporary critics of Mansfield's judicial style, none was so effective in damaging the Chief Justice's reputation as the conveyancer Charles Fearne in his vituperative condemnation of the King's Bench ruling in *Perrin* v *Blake*.[63]

In the face of these objections, it became crucial for Mansfield and his supporters to counter the leading authority of *Coulson* v *Coulson*. This was attempted through two principal arguments. In the first place, Mansfield simply denied that the case enjoyed the status that was being ascribed to it. He claimed that the decision had been compromised by later cases, and particularly stressed that it was incorrect to view the ruling as "the unanimous opinion of the courts." Sir Thomas Denison, he maintained, "certainly did not agree with his brothers at first," and Hardwicke himself was "little satisfied with it." This was certain because the Chancellor had later sent the similar case of "*Sayer* and *Masterman*" over to King's Bench, "and he told me he did it to have *Coulson* and *Coulson* reconsidered."[64]

This argument, however, was scarcely compelling. The case of *Coulson* v *Coulson* had received considerable publicity and was within the living memory of the courts. Hardwicke, whatever the doubts he had privately shared with Mansfield, had clearly decided the issue in support of the rule in Shelley's case, and Mansfield was even accused of dissembling in his account of the judicial attitude to the decision.[65] Blackstone, moreover, suggested that even if *Coulson* v *Coulson* had been determined "on dubious grounds," he would still "tremble at the consequences of shaking its authority," since the decision was taken as authoritative by the conveyancers.[66] Thus in order to overcome the case, the judges in King's Bench needed to proceed a step further. Their second argument involved a more systematic analysis of the rule in Shelley's case itself.

Mansfield and his supporters on the bench readily acknowledged that the rule in Shelley's case was "clear law." Their concern was to demonstrate that the rule did "not constitute a decisive uncontrollable rule" equivalent to a "general proposition" of law. If this could be

---

[63] See Campbell, *Chief Justices*, II, 434–7.

[64] Hargrave, *Collectanea Juridica*, I, 320–1; see also Aston's comments at I, 308.

[65] See Charles Fearne, *Copies of Opinions ascribed in Eminent Council, on the Will which was the Subject of the Case of Perrin v Blake ... Addressed to the Right Honourable William, Earl of Mansfield* (London, 1780).   [66] Hargrave, *Collection of Tracts*, p. 508.

shown, then it was proper for the courts to sacrifice the rule to the testator's intent. The judges pursued this objective by supplying an historical anaysis of the rule so as to establish its anachronistic nature. Mansfield's colleagues, Sir Richard Aston and Edward Willes, developed this position at length. Aston described the rule in Shelley's case as "an old rule of feudal policy, the reason of which is long since antiquated," and which accordingly "must not be extended one jot."[67] Willes echoed these comments in stressing that the rule "grew with feudal policy, and the reasons of it are now antiquated." He went on to insist that the strictness of feudal property law was essentially antithetic to the needs of contemporary society. "It is an universal notion," he claimed, "that in a commercial country all property should be freed from every clog which may hinder its circulation." In accord with these "motives of policy," he would "ever discountenance" as much as possible "anything which favours of ancient strictness" and "depart with justice from an old maxim the policy of which is now ceased." He went on to invoke Lord Cowper's telling formula that should the courts simply adhere "to the technical expressions without any deviation," then common law would be reduced to "mere matter of memory, instead of being a system of judgment and reason."[68] Mansfield himself did not explore this argument, aside from recording his complete agreement with Aston and Willes.[69] In previous cases, though, he had embraced the same position and treated the rule in Shelley's case as "an ancient maxim of law" to be restrictively applied because "the reason of this maxim has long ceased."[70]

Blackstone's judgment reversing the King's Bench decision contained a direct response to this argument. He admitted that the rule was not "to be reckoned among the great fundamental principles of juridical policy," and therefore would "give way" to the "plain intention of the testator." But while agreeing with the King's Bench judges over the status of the rule, he was careful to eschew the historical reasoning through which they had contained it. What Blackstone clearly perceived was that the logic of this argument threatened the entire structure of common law. Hence, he examined the historical character of the rule in order to demonstrate its continued importance, and thereby provided an elegant statement of the conservative implications of an historical approach:

> There is hardly an ancient rule of real property but what has in it more or less of a feudal tincture. The common law maxims of descent, the

---

[67] Hargrave, *Collectanea Juridica*, I, 305.
[68] *Ibid.*, 297–8, 301.   [69] *Ibid.*, 318.
[70] *Long* v *Laming*, (1760) 2 Burrow 1100, 1106–7.

conveyance by livery of seisin, the whole doctrine of copyholds, and a hundred other instances that might be given, are plainly the offspring of the feudal system: but whatever their parentage was, they are now adopted by the common law of England, incorporated into its body, and so interwoven with its policy, that no court of justice in this kingdom has either the *power* or (I trust) the *inclination* to disturb them... The law of real property in this country wherever its materials were gathered, is now formed into a fine artificial system, full of unseen connexions and nice dependencies; and he that breaks one link of the chain, endangers the dissolution of the whole.[71]

The determination of *Perrin* v *Blake* in the Exchequer Chamber proved decisive. In later cases on the same point of law, Mansfield's court adhered to the technical rule in Shelley's case, and the rule never again underwent judicial examination.[72] Blackstone's judgment had not relied on the appeal to precedents alone, but it was not difficult to treat the episode as a straightforward triumph of precedents over the reforming enterprises of the Chief Justice. This reading was proffered with considerable relish by Charles Fearne in his authoritative treatise on the law on contingent remainders. Fearne sharply lampooned Mansfield's judicial style, offering the hope that his own discussion of accepted judicial precedents would not "appear *quaint* or *absurd*," or expose him "to ridicule for his affectation of *obsolete* terms." "For PRECEDENTS," he confessed, "seem now to be quite *out of fashion*."[73] In treating *Perrin* v *Blake* he promptly admitted that "the reader's curiosity" would have to be "on the stretch" to comprehend how King's Bench had managed "to get rid of so strong a system of authorities" as the precedents supporting Shelley's case. The answer was provided in a brisk caricature of the court's ruling, in which Fearne laid special stress on the programmatic employment of history favored in Mansfield's court. "Old cases," the judges claimed, "did very well for old times," but "those cases and those times" grew "*antiquated* together" and "new times called for new decisions." "The heard of mankind" did "well to adhere to old rules," but "men endowed with superior talents" needed "to look higher" and "to exert their abilities in the great field of improvement." Accordingly, the court "expressly held that precedents are in general to be discarded," and that

---

[71] Hargrave, *Collection of Tracts*, pp. 494–5, 498. Also see Yates's comment: "I admit that the original reason of it has long since ceased, but I deny that for that reason it must be discountenanced," in Hargrave, *Collectanea Juridica*, I, 312.

[72] See *Hodgson* v *Ambrose*, (1780) 1 Douglas 337.

[73] Charles Fearne, *An Essay on the Learning of Contingent Remainders and Executory Devises*, 3rd edn (London, 1776), p. xii.

"every thing which favours of ancient strictness ought to be discountenanced and exploded."[74]

It is in the context of this conservative attack on Mansfield's approach to common law that English law begins to assume the appearance of that unfortunate legal entity condemned by Bentham in *A Fragment on Government*.[75] Common law appears as a body of arcane technicalities, incomprehensible to all but a professional caste, its sole justification lying in its status as a system of established practice. The common law system appears incapable of achieving legal certainty except through a blind adherence to these technicalities. And common law precedents appear as the substance of the law, rather than as illustrations of the law's guiding principles. As even more sympathetic commentators observed, this branch of English law had to be explained in terms of precedents and not principles. The standard defence of Shelley's case based on the need to preserve the stability of real property, Francis Hargrave shrewdly noted, contained "a sort of implied admission" that were it not for "the accumulation of authorities and practice," the "technical and artificial sense" of the rule could never be sustained.[76] Wooddeson likewise acknowledged that "in framing laws *de novo* for a people," it would "be very superfluous to transcribe into their code some of those complex rules which here absolutely govern the title to estates." These had to be regarded as among those "excrescences" which "in process of time all civil institutions... unavoidably acquire."[77] Charles Butler conceded that Shelley's rule was but one of "many other rules of construction" whose "reason or foundation" was "not now discoverable." Such rules indeed were "arbitrary and some of them not reconcileable to plain reason." Yet, the courts considered "themselves bound to submit to them," though "sometimes ever with an avowed reluctance."[78]

One important implication of the rigidity with which the courts operated this most distinctive branch of common law was that any legal change in this area would necessarily have to come from parliament. This implication, however, was almost universally resisted by the common lawyers and conveyancers. If the courts could not invade this "fine artificial system" without endangering "the dissolution of the whole," so much less likely of success was an invasion launched by England's untutored legislators. As Blackstone affirmed in the *Commentaries*, the judges in developing this system had "wisely avoided

---

[74] *Ibid.*, 125–7.   [75] See the discussion below, chapter 11.
[76] Hargrave, *Collection of Tracts*, p. 560.
[77] Wooddeson, *Elements of Jurisprudence*, pp. 106–7.
[78] Coke, *Commentary upon Littleton*, II, 380 (Butler's note).

soliciting any great legislative revolution." Yet, in his judgment in *Perrin* v *Blake*, he suggested that the process of judicial adaptation had to be arrested. Thus it seemed that this area of law, because of its very complexity and artificiality, might be altered successfully by no one – a state of affairs which provided further grist for the Benthamic mill. On the other hand, when in the next century parliament did first attempt law reform in this area, their creation did little to call into question Blackstone's fears.[79]

The controversy surrounding *Perrin* v *Blake* offers a valuable insight into the nature and limits of judicial law reform during the period. The dispute neatly exposed the potentially antagonistic claims of precedent and principle, and occasioned an unusually direct confrontation between the rival implications of an historically informed legal consciousness which distinguished Blackstonean conservatism and Mansfield's reformism. On the basis of this protracted legal episode, Mansfield's reforming efforts can be seen as based upon an orthodox theory of common law, whose programmatic application could succeed only in those instances when the legal community was prepared to endorse "the recurrence to principle." But even when the lawyers refused to follow Mansfield's lead, they were furnished with more evidence of his devotion to the "great field of improvement."

Nowhere was the contemporary image of Mansfield as the period's most ardent and accomplished legal improver better displayed than in the enthusiastic response of other self-conscious law reformers to the Chief Justice. Lord Kames (to whom we next turn) dedicated the second edition of his treatise on the *Principles of Equity* to Mansfield, declaring himself a "zealous friend" and tendentiously identifying his own scheme for judicially-orchestrated law reform with the Chief Justice's triumphs at King's Bench. "The ambition of gaining Lord Mansfield's approbation," Kames devotedly recorded, "has been my chief support in this work."[80] Far more dramatic was his impact on the young Jeremy Bentham at the outset of his career in the 1770s. Bentham attended King's Bench as a law student, defended the Chief Justice in the public press, and was clearly delighted by the public speculation that his anonymous *A Fragment on Government* might have been penned by Mansfield himself.[81] During this period, he actively

---

[79] See Simpson, *History of Land Law*, pp. 249–51, on Lord Tenterden's Prescription Act of 1832.

[80] Henry Home (Lord Kames), *Principles of Equity* (1760), 2nd edn, corrected and enlarged (Edinburgh, 1767), "Letter to Lord Mansfield." For Kames's dedication of the work to Mansfield, see Ross, *Lord Kames*, pp. 226–8.

[81] See *Memoirs of Jeremy Bentham; including Autobiographical Conversations and Correspondence*, edited

exploited his friendship with John Lind and his rather more tenuous connection with David Martin in the hopes of gaining entry into Mansfield's circle.[82] Indeed, so profound was Bentham's "idolatry" that he kept "as a great treasure" a picture of the Chief Justice, and would regularly travel to his home at Kenwood, "as a lover to the shrine of his mistress."[83]

For others, however, Mansfield's judicial style appeared more like a problem, and under the impact of his judgeship, several writers were moved to reconsider traditional legal thinking of the question of legal change. Their perplexity and unease provide a not insignificant measure for Mansfield's achievement. John Mitford observed that it was usual to fear disruptive judicial innovation from the equity courts and to seek to prevent them from undermining the common law. But after Mansfield this situation seemed to have been reversed, for "of late years" any doubts which remained regarding the relationship between the two systems had "principally arisen from the liberality with which the common law courts have noticed and adopted principles of decision established in courts of equity."[84] Far more serious was the challenge Mansfield posed regarding the proper relationship between the courts and parliament. By the time of Mansfield's retirement and the "founding" of commercial law by the courts, it was no longer easy to interpret that relationship unambiguously on the basis of the favored maxim that the judge's office was *jus dicere*, not *jus dare*. John Joseph Powell acknowledged that it was proper for a judge "to model and adapt" the "rules of justice" according to "the exigencies of mankind." Still it was necessary to distinguish this from a power "to create or annihilate" which belonged solely to the "legislature."[85] And Butler more openly confessed that he had "long thought that no work would be more useful than one which would show where interpretation should stop and legislation begin."[86]

---

by John Bowring, in *Bowring*, X, 45–6 and *Corr.* I, 149n (on Bentham's letters in defence of Mansfield); *Corr.* I, 366 and II, 102 and *Bowring*, X, 78–9 (on the authorship of *Fragment*). Bentham was attending Mansfield's court as late as 1784; see *Corr.* III, 263.

[82] See *Corr.* II, 147–8, and *Fragment* (1823 Preface), pp. 517–21.

[83] *Bowring*, X, 46. For Bentham's later hostile attitude to Mansfield, see *Bowring*, V, 248–9, 542, and *Fragment* (1823 Preface), pp. 517–23.

[84] Mitford, *Pleadings in Chancery*, p. 2. See also the more explicit criticisms by John Mitford (Lord Redesdale) cited in Campbell, *Chief Justices*, II, 437–8.

[85] Powell, *Law of Contracts and Agreements*, I, viii.

[86] *Reminiscences of Charles Butler*, p. 41n.

◁ ═══════════════════════════════════════ ▷

7

Kames, legal history and law reform

The legal writings of the Scottish judge and philosopher, Henry Home, Lord Kames, contain, amongst much else, one of the eighteenth century's most ambitious and articulate programs of judicial law reform. Kames's elaborate defense of the judicial route to legal improvement, as well as his more general approach to legal theory, owed much to the specifically Scottish setting in which he trained and professionally served, and no account of his career and corpus could afford to neglect this Scottish context. His inclusion provides an opportunity to relate the themes of this study to the rich corpus of Scottish social speculation which offered some of the most profound and innovative legal philosophy produced in Britain in the period preceding the appearance of Benthamic analytic jurisprudence. Nonetheless, it is perhaps best to begin with a caution against any narrowly parochial interpretation of the contribution to eighteenth-century legal speculation now under consideration.

Kames belonged to a generation of Scottish lawyers eager to create a British audience for their scholarly productions. In his most famous legal publication he urged the cultivation of a legal literature devoted "to subjects common to the law of England and Scotland," and presented his own researches as the first steps towards the construction of a "regular institute of the common law of this island."[1] In the program of law reform he pressed upon the Scottish courts, he invoked Mansfield's example and expressly drew upon the tendentiously formulated lessons of English legal development.[2] At the same time he took every effort to gain notice for his scholarship and proposals in

---

[1] *Historical Law Tracts*, I, xii − xvi. For other important contemporary instances of this concern, see Andrew McDouall (Lord Bankton), *An Institute of the Laws of Scotland in Civil Rights: with Observations upon the Agreement or Diversity between them and the Laws of England*, 3 vols. (Edinburgh, 1751 − 53), I, ix, and John Dalrymple, *An Essay towards a General History of Feudal Property in Great Britain*, 2nd edn (London, 1758), pp. vii–ix.

[2] Kames's law reform program is discussed below, chapter 8; for his citing of Mansfield, see above, chapter 6 at n80.

England, corresponding with Hardwicke and Mansfield over his legal writings and lobbying for English patronage of his schemes of improvement. Nor were these endeavors to introduce Scottish legal science "into England," where it might "be studied...for curiosity as well as profit," without effect.[3] Blackstone, for example, utilized Kames's historical researches in the *Commentaries*, and singled out Kames as a special target for criticism in his account of English equity.[4] The young Bentham, in turn, viewed Kames as a vital corrective to Blackstonean apologetics.[5] Joseph Parkes, in his *A History of the Court of Chancery*, pronounced Kames's *Principles of Equity* to be a work of "profound legal erudition," and reported that it had "excited considerable attention throughout the kingdom."[6] John Huntingford and William David Evans both referred to Kames for canonical statements and illustrations of the need for an historical approach to the study of legal institutions.[7]

The Scottish jurist who thus earned the attention of English lawyers and who was celebrated at home as the figure who "did more to promote the interests of philosophy and *belles lettres* in Scotland than all the men of law had done for a century before," began his career in distinctly unpromising circumstances.[8] Deprived by lack of financial means of either a native university education or an academic legal education abroad, Kames embarked on his professional studies in a "Writer's Chamber," and by his own account, was "just a mechanical student and got law by rote." He spent "ten years at the bar without making ten pounds," and his first venture in legal letters, the 1728 *Remarkable Decisions of the Court of Session*, was a technical collection of law reports originally designed to supplement a new edition of Stair's *The Institutions of the Law of Scotland*.[9] Yet, by the end of his publishing

---

[3] *Historical Law Tracts*, I, xv.
[4] 4 *Comm* 308 and 3 *Comm* 433; and see the discussion below, chapter eight at n52.
[5] Bentham, *Comment*, p. 330.   [6] Parkes, *History of the Court of Chancery*, p. 334.
[7] Huntingford, *Statute Laws Considered*, p. 23, and Pothier, *Treatise on the Law of Obligations or Contracts*, I, 44 (Evans' editorial introduction). See also Eden, *Principles of Penal Law*, pp. 70, 184.
[8] John Ramsay of Ochtertyre, *Scotland and Scotsmen in the Eighteenth Century*, ed. Alexander Allardyce, 2 vols. (Edinburgh, 1888), I, 179. Kames has been the subject of two valuable recent biographies: William C. Lehmann, *Henry Home, Lord Kames, and the Scottish Enlightenment* (The Hague, 1971) and Ross, *Kames*. For further details on his career, see the contemporary portrait by Alexander Fraser Tytler (Lord Woodhouselee), *Memoirs of the Life and Writings of the Honourable Henry Home of Kames... Containing Sketches of the Progress of Literature and General Improvement in Scotland during the greater part of the Eighteenth Century*, 2 vols. (Edinburgh, 1807), and Boswell's "Materials for Writing the Life of Lord Kames" (1778), in *Private Papers of James Boswell from Malahide Castle*, prepared for the press by Geoffrey Scott, 18 vols. (private printing, Mount Vernon, N.Y., 1928–34), XV, 267–87, 306–16.
[9] "Materials for Writing the Life of Lord Kames" (1778), *Private Papers of James Boswell*, XV, 269–72, and Ross, *Kames*, p. 31.

career in 1781, when at the age of eighty-five he produced his *Loose Hints on Education, chiefly concerning the Culture of the Heart*, he had assembled a massive, if rather prolix, corpus of over twenty volumes that could serve as an index to nearly all of the intellectual pursuits of the Scottish Enlightenment, encompassing such topics as morals, religion, law, government, natural philosophy, political economy, education, aesthetics, and of course history.

As befitted the virtuous citizen, Kames not only philosophized, but was also immersed in public affairs and social improvement. In addition to his judicial appointments to the Court of Session and High Court of Justiciary, he served on the boards for the promotion of trade, fisheries and manufactures, and as a commissioner for the annexed estates following the '45 Jacobite rebellion. His own estate at Blair Drummond furnished a notable specimen of that "fever of improvements" which he urged on other "gentlemen farmers." He effectively promoted the academic fortunes of Adam Smith and John Millar, and along with his kinsman, David Hume, weathered the threat of excommunication at the hands of the Evangelical Party in the General Assembly. He was an active participant in Edinburgh's cultural life, and a moving spirit behind the founding of the Physical and Literary Society (later the Royal Society of Edinburgh).[10] When Adam Smith observed that "we must every one of us acknowledge Kames for our master,"[11] he may not have been referring so much to the judge's intellectual gifts, as to his political prowess and success as a patron of the literati.

At the same time, Kames's efforts to combine the vocations of philosopher and judge, jurist and patriot, scholar and activist often proved a good deal less inspiring than he wished. His legal brethren were at times openly contemptuous of his readiness on the bench to embark upon abstruse, speculative disquisitions.[12] His philosophic betters clearly grew impatient with the vain auto-didact who in later years seemed prepared to pass judgment on virtually any subject at virtually uncontrollable length. As David Hume crushingly put it, "when one says of another man he is the most arrogant man in the world, it is only to say that he is very arrogant. But when one says it of Lord Kames, it is an absolute truth."[13] There were even those among his countrymen who remained unmoved by Kames's exemplary devotion to scientific improvement. "Some malicious rogues would

[10] For these episodes see Ramsay, *Scotland and Scotsmen*, I, 197, 207; *The Letters of John Ramsay of Ochtertyre*, ed. Barbara L. H. Horn (Edinburgh, 1966), p. 121; and Ross, *Kames*, pp. 154–65, 315–32, 362–4.

[11] Cited in Ross, *Kames*, p. 97.

[12] See the criticisms reported in Ramsay, *Scotland and Scotsmen*, I, 186–7 and 186n, and in *Boswell, Laird of Auchinleck 1778–1782*, ed. Joseph W. Reed and Frederick A. Pottle (New York, 1977), pp. 184–5.   [13] *Boswell, Laird of Auchinleck*, p. 385.

persuade us," Boswell recorded, "that he has tasted all sorts of dung with a truly philosophical palate, in order to acquire a perfect knowledge of the most effective ways of fertilising the soil."[14]

As in the case of other contemporary Scottish philosophers, jurisprudence provided the disciplinary context and much of the structure for Kames's explorations in social theory.[15] It was in his essays on law that he first revealed many of the same general sociological interests displayed by Adam Smith in his *Lectures on Jurisprudence* or by John Millar in *The Origin of the Distinction of Ranks*. The distinctive concern of this body of eighteenth-century legal speculation, according to the testimony of John Millar in his *An Historical View of English Government*, was the attempt to reformulate the natural law jurisprudence of Grotius and his successors as a "natural history of legal establishments." To this end, "speculative lawyers" were led to examine the formation and growth of "civil society," the "cultivation of arts and sciences," the "extension of property in all its different modifications," and their combined influence "upon the manners and customs, the institutions and laws of any people."[16] In Millar's judgment, the leading practitioners of this genre of "natural history" were Montesquieu, Smith and Kames – Montesquieu having first "pointed out the road" and Smith representing "the Newton" of "this branch of philosophy."[17]

Kames was fully committed to what Millar thus identified as the "natural history of legal establishments." To cite a characteristic pronouncement, when Kames called for law to be pursued as a "rational science" suitable for "every person who has an appetite for knowledge," he referred to the dual tasks of having the law's "principles unfolded" and "its connection with manners and politics" displayed.[18] What distinguished his legal writings from those of his fellow *philosophes* was his special concern to bring their historical approach and analysis of societal development to bear on the technical detail of Scottish legal practice – an enterprise Hume described

[14] *Boswell in Holland 1763–1764*, ed. Frederick A. Pottle (London, 1952), pp. 84–5.
[15] The recovery and elucidation of the jurisprudential background to the social and moral theory of the Scottish *philosophes* has been a major accomplishment of recent historical scholarship on the Scottish Enlightenment. In addition to the literature cited above, Introduction at n46, I have learned most from Forbes, *Hume's Philosophical Politics*, pp. 3–90; Donald Winch, *Adam Smith's Politics. An Essay in Historiographic Revision* (Cambridge, 1978), pp. 46–69, and "Science and the Legislator: Adam Smith and After," *Economic Journal*, CXIII (1983), 501–20; Peter Stein, *Legal Evolution. The Story of an Idea* (Cambridge, 1980), pp. 23–50; and Knud Haakonssen, *Science of a Legislator* and "John Millar and the Science of a Legislator," *Juridical Review*, XXX (1985), 41–68.
[16] John Millar, *Historical View of English Government* (1803), 4 vols. (London, 1812), IV, 284–5.   [17] *Ibid.*, IV, 284 and II, 428n.
[18] Kames, *Elucidations respecting the Common and Statute Law of Scotland* (Edinburgh, 1777), p. xiii.

sceptically as an attempt to make "an agreeable Composition by joining Metaphysics and Scotch Law."[19] This emphasis in turn related Kames's legal scholarship to another major intellectual project of eighteenth-century Scotland. This was the systematic exposition of Scottish law in text book form, or what legal historians conventionally describe as the "classical" or "institutional" phase of Scots legal development.[20] As Peter Stein points out, although the philosophers and institutional law writers occupied overlapping scholarly provinces, and regularly relied on the same legal authorities in their works, there appears to have been little intellectual cross-fertilization between the groups. Kames, however, ignored this division of labor and contributed prolifically to both traditions.[21] The point was nicely captured by William Smellie, when he included Kames along with Hume and Smith in his *Literary and Characteristical Lives*, and then went on to praise the judge's "law writings" by claiming, inaccurately, that they enjoyed the same status "as those of Coke and Blackstone in the courts of England."[22]

Kames brought to the study of the law two general methodological principles, and their application gave a general unity to his diverse and voluminous legal texts. First was his insistence that law had to be studied as an historical subject. He introduced his *Historical Law Tracts* by stressing that "law in particular becomes then only a rational study when it is traced historically, from its first rudiments among savages, through successive changes, to its highest improvements in a civilized society."[23] As we have seen in the case of eighteenth-century English legal writing, it was not unusual to claim that numerous questions of law "receive the only light they are capable of from the reflection of history," particularly since so much contemporary legal process was incomprehensible without an understanding of feudal land holdings.[24]

---

[19] Hume to Adam Smith, 12 April 1759, *Letters of David Hume*, ed. J. Y. T. Greig, 2 vols. (Oxford, 1932), I, 304.

[20] For a survey of Scottish institutional law writing, see *An Introductory Survey of the Sources and Literature of Scots Law, Stair Society Publications*, I (Edinburgh, 1936), pp. 59–69, and David M. Walker (ed.), *Stair Tercentenary Studies* (Edinburgh, 1981), pp. 201–52. John W. Cairns offers an important re-examination of the historical character of this literature in "Institutional Writings in Scotland Reconsidered," *Journal of Legal History*, IV (1983), 76–117. On the issue of Kames's alleged authority as an institutional writer, see T. B. Smith, *Scotland, The Development of its Law and Constitution* [volume 2 of *The British Commonwealth: The Development of its Laws and Constitution*, general editor, George W. Keeton], (London, 1962), p. 32, and David M. Walker, "Equity in Scots Law," *Juridical Review*, LXVI (1954), 115–25.

[21] Peter Stein, "The General Notions of Contract and Property in Eighteenth-Century Scottish Thought," *Juridical Review*, VIII (1963), pp. 1–2, 10, and "Law and Society in Eighteenth-Century Scottish Thought," in N. T. Phillipson and Rosalind Mitchison (eds.), *Scotland in the Age of Improvements* (Edinburgh, 1970), p. 159.

[22] William Smellie, *Literary and Characteristical Lives of John Gregory, Henry Home, David Hume and Adam Smith* (Edinburgh, 1800), p. 128. [23] Kames, *Historical Law Tracts*, I, v.

[24] See Wynne, *Eunomus*, I, 59, cited above, chapter 1 at n50.

Kames, however, was advancing a more ambitious claim, and referred to a type of legal scholarship that sought to relate entire systems of legal practices to the general progress of society as a whole. It was in the context of *Historical Law Tracts* that he provided perhaps the earliest account of the more conjectural techniques of philosophical history, which the philosopher was forced to employ in dealing with "dark ages unprovided with records." In the same setting Kames presented one of the first published versions of the "four stages" theory of societal development which viewed social change in terms of four distinct historical periods, each distinguished by a particular mode of subsistence and each characterized by its peculiar customs, manners and legal establishments.[25] When Dugald Stewart described the Scottish advances in "theoretical or conjectural history" which had followed Montesquieu's seminal contributions, he could confidently point to the "excellent specimens" of the genre produced by "Lord Kames in his *Historical Law Tracts.*"[26]

In addition to maintaining that history alone could make law studies rational, Kames advanced the more radical proposition that the rationality of the law itself had to be assessed in historical terms. In this sense, the lawyer needed to be sensitized to history since this provided the proper means for assessing the merits of particular legal arrangements:

> The law of a country is in perfection when it corresponds to the manners of the people, their circumstances, their government. And as these are seldom stationary, the law ought to accompany them in their changes. An institute of law accordingly, however perfect originally, cannot long continue so... The knowledge, therefore, of the progress of law and of its innovations is essential;...[27]

Something of the considerable heuristic advantage Kames perceived in this approach to law was revealed in his response to one of the period's most frequently aired issues in legal theory. It was orthodox, as we have seen, to treat questions of legal legitimacy in terms of ethical theory, and most often by reference to those laws of nature through which God ordered the physical universe and the social relations of man.[28] But straightaway this approach seemed to falter, for the sort

---

[25] *Historical Law Tracts*, I, 36–7, 77–80n. Meek argued that although Kames published his account of the "four stages" theory earlier, he probably learned the theory from Smith's lectures on jurisprudence; see Ronald L. Meek, *Social Science and the Ignoble Savage*, (Cambridge, 1976), pp. 102–7.

[26] Dugald Stewart, *Account of the Life and Writings of Adam Smith*, LL.D. (1793), reprinted in Adam Smith, *Essays on Philosophical Subjects*, ed. W. P. D. Wightman and J. C. Bryce (Oxford, 1980), pp. 294–95.

[27] Kames, *Select Decisions of the Court of Session, from 1752 to 1768* (1780), 2nd edn (Edinburgh, 1799), p. iii.   [28] See the discussion above, chapter 1 at nn23–35.

of claims which were made for these moral principles, and often the very point of conceiving these principles as laws of nature, appeared strikingly at odds with the regular operation of existing legal systems. Natural laws were timeless and universal. Human laws varied from nation to nation. In the case of Britain, they varied within a single nation, and on occasion, from county to county. Natural laws were easily recognized and discerned by all rational agents. Kames himself held that the dictates of natural justice were "so simple and clear" even to the "most ignorant."[29] Human laws were complex and often contradictory. It required volumes to present them, and the daily practice of the courts testified to the continual disagreement over their actual content. The disjunction between moral norms and legal obligations could be made to appear profound, and for many moralists the disjunction stood out as a major problem demanding careful scrutiny. As William Paley observed, "why, since the maxims of natural justice are few and evident" and "the principles of the law of nature be simple" and "sufficiently obvious, there should exist nevertheless in every system of municipal laws ... numerous uncertainties and acknowledged difficulty."[30]

Kames insisted that the matter demanded historical analysis. The progress of society provided the basis for explaining the various ways in which particular nations had translated moral imperatives into positive duties, and the particular history of any given state could account for the disparate and contradictory elements in its legal system. He developed the point in one of his first editions of Court of Session decisions, an appropriate setting since few legal sources provided such vivid evidence of the complexity and occasional irregularity of positive laws as a collection of law reports. Kames maintained that there was "little clashing among our decisions," particularly in light of the fact that Scots law was "scarce past its infancy." To support the claim he distinguished between genuine "*antinomies* of the law" and those "opposite decisions in different ages" which resulted necessarily from "an alteration of circumstances." To adopt his own example, in former periods the courts refused to admit the testimony of "moveable tenants" on behalf of their masters, whereas "at present they are admitted." The apparent inconsistency simply reflected the fact that in earlier periods the "common people in Scotland were little better than slaves." Now they were "somewhat more independent," and thus their testimony was no longer impugned by their "want of safety." Such

---

[29] Kames, *Sketches of the History of Man* (1774), 4th edn, considerably enlarged by the Last Additions and Corrections of the Author, 4 vols. (Edinburgh, 1788), IV, 80–1.

[30] Paley, *Moral and Political Philosophy*, p. 511, and see also Wynne, *Eunomus*, II, 52–7.

cases, he concluded, "cannot be ranked among the *antinomies* of the law; on the contrary, the law of that country is wrong which does not accommodate itself to the fluctuating manners of the people."[31]

Kames's final point was aimed directly at the law of Scotland, and disclosed another purpose served by legal history. This was to indicate the need for legal change by demonstrating the antiquated nature of inherited legal practices. Pocock has observed in general of the Scottish "sociological historians" that their "great achievement" lay in "the recognition that a commercial society had rendered obsolete much that had been believed about society before."[32] The corollary to this in Kames's case was the recognition of the inadequacy of the historic Scots law to accommodate the legal needs of contemporary society. Kames's contemporary biographer and protégé, Alexander Fraser Tytler (Lord Woodhouselee), drew attention to the point in emphasizing that Kames "was sensible that the law of Scotland was in many of its branches in a state of great imperfection" because he perceived that many of its doctrines "which originally had their foundations in expediency, were, in the lapse of time... both inexpedient and contrary to material justice."[33] In contrast with the later nineteenth-century association of historical jurisprudence and legal conservatism, Kames marshalled his historical understanding of the law to the cause of legal improvement. His legal studies provide a formidable example of the more practical, if cruder, uses of Scottish philosophical history, for the limits of his historical vision were generally set by his reforming objectives.[34] As he declared in one such discussion of Scots law, in phrases more often associated with Bentham, "my intention is only to give examples of reasoning, free from the shackles of authority. I pretend not to say what our law actually is, but what it ought to be."[35]

In order to chart the content of Kames' legal doctrines some account of his moral philosophy is required. He advanced an essentially Hutchesonian ethical theory.[36] Man was viewed as an hedonistic creature for whom morally correct actions were agreeable and vicious

---

[31] Kames, *The Decisions of the Court of Session, from its First Institution to the present Time. Abridged and digested under proper Heads, in Form of a Dictionary* (1741), 2 vols. (Edinburgh, 1797), I, iii.

[32] Pocock, "Machiavelli, Harrington and English Eighteenth-century Ideologies," in *Politics, Language and Time*, p. 146.   [33] Tytler, *Memoirs of Kames*, I, 156.

[34] See Stein, "Law and Society in Eighteenth-century Scottish Thought," 158.

[35] Kames, *Elucidations respecting the Common and Statute Law*, p. xiii.

[36] Kames presented three versions of his moral theory, in *Essays on the Principles of Morality and Natural Religion* (Edinburgh, 1751); *Principles of Equity* (2nd edn, Edinburgh, 1767); *Sketches of the History of Man* (1774). The account here is taken from the final version in the fourth edition of *Sketches of the History of Man* (1788).

actions disagreeable. Man discerned the moral character of action through his "*moral sense* or *conscience*," and the dictates of this moral sense could be construed as laws of nature, which for Kames included notions of divine purposes and final causes.[37] The content of morally correct actions, moreover, could be specified in consequentialist terms:

> ...the general tendency of right actions is to promote the good of society, and of wrong actions, to obstruct that good. Universal benevolence is indeed not required of man...But for promoting the general good, everything is required of him that he can accomplish.[38]

It was on the basis of these considerations of social utility that Kames discussed such political questions as the nature of obligation, the right of taxation, and the rival merits of different forms of government.[39]

One of the most important features of this ethical theory for his jurisprudence was the distinction drawn between actions which were morally just and those which were simply morally correct. Justice related to situations of perfect rights and correlative duties, and entailed a precise moral imperative. According to Kames, "right actions are distinguished by the moral sense into two kinds, what *ought* to be done and what *may* be done, or left undone." In the former case, the individual found himself under "the necessity" to act which "is termed *duty*." Such duties implied "a *right* in some person to exact performance of that duty," and this, in turn, distinguished just actions from other virtuous actions: "Duty is twofold; duty to others and duty to ourselves. With respect to the former, the doing what we ought to do is termed *just*: the doing what we ought not to do, and the omitting what we ought to do, are termed *unjust*."[40]

The best known, and indeed most articulate, presentation of this doctrine of justice was furnished by Adam Smith in *The Theory of Moral Sentiments*, and it is of some interest that Smith generously alluded to Kames's theory when developing his own contrast between justice and beneficence.[41] The distinction impinged upon legal theory at several crucial points. First, because justice was unlike other moral virtues, the

---

[37] *Sketches of the History of Man*, IV, 10–14, 78–94.   [38] *Ibid.*, IV, 46.

[39] See *Essays on Several Subjects Concerning British Antiquities, Composed Anno 1745* (1747), 3rd edn (Edinburgh, 1763), pp. 193–216 (on obligation); *Sketches of the History of Man*, II, 361–8 (on taxation); *Essays on British Antiquities*, p. 197 (on forms of government, but compare with *Sketches of the History of Man*, II, 230–59).

[40] *Sketches of the History of Man*, IV, 14–15.

[41] Adam Smith, *The Theory of Moral Sentiments* (1759), ed. D. D. Raphael and A. L. Macfie (Oxford, 1976), p. 80. For a more extensive account of the development of this doctrine by the Scottish moralists, see Haakonssen's excellent discussion in *Science of a Legislator*.

rules of justice were susceptible to precise formulation in a manner inapplicable to other moral precepts. Thus Kames presented the dictates of justice as three specific rules derived from the fundamental principle of justice not to harm the innocent: the duty of veracity; the duty to perform promises and covenants; and the duties created by special relationships, like those between a parent and child.[42] In legal theory, it was vital to observe this distinction, and not treat all ethical questions in terms of those precise rules which were relevant only to the consideration of justice. The failure to observe this distinction, Smith observed, had undermined all previous attempts to construct natural systems of jurisprudence, which in consequence had degenerated into casuistry.[43]

The distinction between justice and other virtues was also relevant to the historical treatment of legal establishments. Although justice, in Smith's famous phrase, was merely a "negative virtue" which could often be fulfilled "by sitting and doing nothing," it was indispensable for any social existence.[44] "Without it," wrote Kames, "society could never have existed," and "here the moral sense is inflexible."[45] Thus, any society would provide some mechanism, if only a natural one, for the preservation of justice. But with regard to other moral actions, the moral sense was more pliant and did itself develop with the progress of society. "The moral sense is born within us," Kames maintained, but "require[s] much cultivation." "Among savages" the moral sense was "faint and obscure," and only slowly and never inevitably progressed "toward maturity."[46] Accordingly, the standards for morally correct behavior would vary considerably between nations, and between the historical epochs of a single nation. And the law, which had "to accommodate itself to the fluctuating manners of the people," would likewise vary according to the gradual refinement of the moral sense.

Finally, because justice was absolutely required for any social relations, and because the maintenance of justice furthered "the general good of mankind" more effectively than any other virtue, it acquired a distinctly utilitarian character. But for Kames, as for Smith and in contrast to Hume, this did not mean that justice could be explained purely in utilitarian or consequentialist terms. Doing justice remained an immediate and uncalculated response to the moral sense.[47]

[42] *Sketches of the History of Man*, IV, 31–9.
[43] Smith, *Moral Sentiments*, pp. 329–33, 340, and also see Millar, *Historical View of English Government*, IV, 235–6, 267–72.   [44] Smith, *Moral Sentiments*, pp. 82, 85–7.
[45] Kames, *Sketches of the History of Man*, IV, 33.
[46] *Ibid.*, I, 196–7; also see IV, 127–90, on "Progress of Morality."
[47] *Ibid.*, IV, 45–6, 80–3.

Kames approached the matter of legal improvement thus armed with two main philosophical doctrines. He was equipped with an ethical theory which indicated the need to promote the general welfare, and a theory of historical development which enabled him to evaluate the relative suitability of legal practices for a particular society. A cogent example of how these positions worked out in application was provided in his "History of the Criminal Law," which Bentham in a splendid piece of misprediction described as that "ingenious and instructive essay" which would probably enjoy "permanent currency."[48]

Kames began the history by maintaining that the criminal law must ultimately derive from some law of nature. This he identified with the natural passion for "revenge" which always followed "injury or voluntary wrong." The right of the injured to "revenge" such wrongs was "a privilege" bestowed "by the Law of Nature." Since this privilege obtained in cases of injustice, "the first Law of Nature regarding society, that of abstaining from injuring others" was "enforced by the most efficacious sanctions."[49]

The natural system for revenging wrongs could operate because of the shared moral consciousness of the offender and his victim. Indeed, for the "passion" of resentment to be "fully gratified," "the person injured must inflict the punishment" and "the criminal must be made sensible not only that he is punished for his crime, but that the punishment proceeds from the person injured."[50] But while man's shared moral or common sense made this possible, the natural system itself was deeply flawed, particularly when viewed in terms of social harmony. It was likely that the morally conscious offender and his morally conscious victim would disagree over the infamy of a crime and the appropriate degree of revenge. Even if such disputes did not occur, there was always something socially disruptive about this sort of natural vigilantism. Hence Kames argued that government "can never fully attain its end where punishment in any measure is trusted in private hands." But given the essentially private character of natural punishment the required shift from personal revenge to criminal law involved "a revolution so contradictory to the strongest propensity of human nature." It could only occur through "slow" and "gradual"

---

[48] UC xcvi, 175. The "History of the Criminal Law" comprised the first chapter of *Historical Law Tracts*. Kames's account closely parallels Smith's treatment in his lectures on jurisprudence; see *Lectures on Jurisprudence*, pp. 106–10, 126–31, 209–10. For the relationship between Kames's *Historical Law Tracts* and Smith's lectures, see above, n25.

[49] *Historical Law Tracts*, I, 6–7.   [50] *Ibid.*, p. 10.

"progressive steps," and could only be explained historically in terms of general social development.[51]

Kames pointed to two particular steps which enabled governments to appropriate the business of punishing. The first related to the several expedients adopted for the direction of personal revenge. Most noteworthy among these was the appearance of "primitive magistrates" who assisted in the identification of criminals. Punishment itself remained the exclusive right of the injured party.[52] More important was the second step: the emergence of fluid forms of property which accompanied the economic advance of agrarian societies. This enabled individuals to substitute pecuniary compensation for corporal punishments, a process which greatly facilitated the socialization of revenge. By "the temptation of money, men were gradually accustomed to stifle their resentments," and this "was a fine preparation for transferring the power of punishment to the magistrate."[53] The magistrate began punishing still later, when a positive sense of a community interest allowed for the recognition of social crimes, such as disturbing the king's peace, for which there was no assignable victim. Since these offences lacked individual victims, the magistrate himself punished the criminal.[54] Once this was achieved, the magistrate's role was extended to punishing purely private wrongs "by imagining every atrocious crime to be a public as well as a private injury."[55] Thus punishment ceased to be a matter of private action altogether.

With regard to the public administration of punishment, Kames again pointed to several separate stages of historical development. At first magistrates inflicted light pecuniary fines because of the weakness of public government. Then, as government gained in authority, it exacted heavier penalties including corporal punishments. Finally, "when a people have become altogether tame and submissive, under a long and steady administration, punishments being less and less necessary, [they] are generally mild and ought always to be so."[56] Moreover, since punishment had now fully evolved into a public institution with primarily social purposes, and since Britain was "tame and submissive," it became proper to model the criminal law (and generally to reduce penalties) in accordance with these social circumstances. Hence Kames concluded his history by rehearsing the arguments for criminal law reform presented by Montesquieu, and soon to be developed systematically by Beccaria and Bentham:

[51] *Ibid.*, p. 31 and see p. 64.   [52] *Ibid.*, pp. 37–40.
[53] *Ibid.*, pp. 54–5.   [54] *Ibid.*, pp. 56–61.
[55] *Ibid.*, p. 60.   [56] *Ibid.*, pp. 72–3.

...to preserve a strict proportion betwixt a crime and its punishment is not the only or chief view of a wise legislator. The purposes of human punishments are, first, to add weight to those which nature has provided, and next, to enforce municipal regulations intended for the good of society...Hence, in regulating the punishment of crimes, two circumstances ought to weigh, *viz.* the immorality of the action, and its bad tendency, of which the latter appears to be the capital circumstance; for this evident reason, that the peace of society is an object of much greater importance, than the peace, or even life, of many individuals.[57]

A similar strategy of historical and ethical argument was used to advance what Kames considered the single most important law reform required in eighteenth-century Scotland: the abolition of entails. For Kames, entails had converted "one of the greatest blessings of life," landed property, "into a curse," and constituted the most easily identifiable obstacle to Scottish improvement.[58] The continuation of the law supporting entails represented an unpardonable retreat of reason before legal authority, and sharply contrasted with the pragmatic manner in which the English judges had manipulated this area of their law.[59] It was easy to prove that entails were contrary to nature and reason, and a source of profound social mischief. Kames, however, was equally eager to show that Scottish entails constituted an historical anachronism – a pernicious vestige of feudalism, that "violent and unnatural system."[60]

The first part of Kames's case was to characterize entails as a perverse extension of the principles of feudal property law. In many instances Kames implied that the label "feudal" was sufficient condemnation in itself, but here he was concerned to go further.[61] Entails, which enabled individuals "to preserve their names, families and possessions in perpetual existence," followed directly "from the very nature of the feudal system." The feudal system not only provided for "a perpetual succession" to a single heir, but also prevented the "dilapidation" of the estate by heirs because the "vassal's right" was a "life-rent and usufruct only."[62] This system, in turn, "unluckily suggested a hint for gratifying this irrational appetite" to control the inheritance of an

---

[57] *Ibid.*, pp. 73–5. The consequentialist features of this utilitarian formula are mitigated by Kames's distinction between "punishment" and "reparation" which turned on the question of intentionality; see *Sketches of the History of Man*, IV, 66–78.
[58] *Historical Law Tracts*, I, 219.
[59] Kames, *Elucidations Respecting the Common and Statute Law.*, pp. 378–9, and *Sketches of the History of Man*, IV, 450.
[60] *Historical Law Tracts*, I, 198.
[61] See *Sketches of the History of Man*, II, 83; III, 11; IV, 157.
[62] *Historical Law Tracts*, I, 197–9.

estate forever.[63] This was attempted in the 1685 statute of entails, which even at the very moment of its enactment represented a reactionary move by the land owners to resist the pressures of commercial exchange.[64]

Once the feudal character of entails was perceived, it became possible to appreciate how antithetic they were to the property relations required by a commercial society. The rationale of feudal land tenure, Kames argued, related entirely to the peculiar techniques by which political authority and military service were identified with the possession of land.[65] The cost of this often unstable system of authority was to withdraw "land from commerce."[66] This "hardship" went unnoticed "in times of war," but became apparent with the emergence of "regular government" in Britain "which made the arts of peace prevail."[67] Once the political reasons for a strict succession of estates to a single heir had been rendered obsolete by the passing of feudal society itself, the only remaining consequence of such forms of land holding was to hinder commerce and improvement. This occurred because the heir to an entailed estate was unable to improve his land efficiently, and more especially because entails removed large amounts of property from circulation.[68] As Kames insisted, "no circumstance tends more to the advancement of commerce than a free circulation of the goods of fortune from hand to hand."[69] In the case of the law of real property, these economic conditions required provisions for "splitting land property" into "many parts" as was "favourable indeed to commerce." Kames admitted that the necessary legal powers made the "law intricate," but these "inconveniences are unavoidable in a commercial country."[70] Accordingly, when entails were judged by the standards of social welfare, they appeared as a fundamental economic liability. And when they were judged in terms of historical development, they appeared as an antiquated relic of feudalism inappropriately maintained in a commercial country. As Kames stressed

---

[63] *Ibid.*, p. 218.

[64] *Ibid.*, pp. 218–19. As the Scottish entail law was based on statute, Kames was also able to argue that the poor wording of the law had led the judges to interpret the measure too broadly and against equitable principles; see *Elucidations respecting the Common and Statute Law*, pp. 341–61.

[65] Kames, *Essays on British Antiquities*, pp. 135–41.   [66] *Ibid.*, pp. 156–8.

[67] *Ibid.*, p. 157 and *Historical Law Tracts*, I, 198.

[68] See *Sketches of the History of Man*, IV, Appendix 1, pp. 447–63. Here again Kames's historical and economic analysis parallels Smith's treatment of entails and primogeniture; see *Lectures on Jurisprudence*, pp. 49–56, 68–71, and *An Inquiry into the Nature and Causes of the Wealth of Nations* (1776), ed. R. H. Campbell, A. S. Skinner, and W. B. Todd, 2 vols. (Oxford, 1976), pp. 383–7.

[69] Kames, *Principles of Equity*, p. 259.

[70] Kames, *Historical Law Tracts*, I, 223–4.

in discussing another remnant from feudal law, "when the substantial part of the feudal law has thus vanished, it is to be regretted that we should still lie under the oppression of its forms..."[71]

Kames reserved his heaviest guns for his 1774 *magnum opus*, the four-volume *Sketches of the History of Man*, which contained an appendix on "Scotch entails considered in Moral and Political Views." He first argued that entails were contrary "to nature and reason," since the desire to control property "for ever to certain heirs" was the work of a "diseased fancy" and "distempered appetite," utterly "repugnant to the frail state of man."[72] He explored at length the vicious economic consequences of entails, displaying how they undermined commerce, industry, improvement and population.[73] Lastly, he claimed that entails threatened the very fabric of social and political life in Britain. In this context, he advanced a new set of arguments which again were drawn from the Scottish social and historical reading of the recent past. Here he highlighted the implications of the fact that large entailed estates threatened the economic position of "gentlemen of a moderate fortune." These gentlemen had not only brought opulence to Britain, but had also improved "manners" and furthered "arts and sciences." More importantly, the constitution and present system of political liberty were dependent on such gentlemen. "In such only," maintained Kames, "resides the genuine spirit of liberty." In contrast, the owners of entailed estates were likened to a "feudal oligarchy," whose immoderate land holdings produced "an irregular and dangerous influence with respect to the House of Commons."[74] Entails were thus an historical anachronism, an economic disaster and an ominous political hazard. "In a word," Kames warned, "the distribution of land into many shares, accords charmingly with the free spirit of the British constitution; but nothing is more repugnant to that spirit, than overgrown estates in land."[75]

Once more, Kames's historical researches revealed a body of Scots law which had demonstrably failed to "accommodate itself" to altered social circumstances. Given such findings, it was altogether appropriate that in his *Principles of Equity*, the legal treatise which followed *Historical Law Tracts*, Kames turned his attention to the elaboration of a constructive strategy for legal improvement.

[71.] *Ibid.*, p. 246. Kames is here discussing the adaptation of "infeftment of rent" as a security for debt, which he criticized as historically antiquated (pp. 244–58).

[72] *Sketches of the History of Man*, IV, 448–9.

[73] *Ibid.*, pp. 452–9.   [74] *Ibid.*, pp. 460–2.   [75] *Ibid.*, p. 461.

◁ ══ ▷

8

Kames and the principles of equity

For Kames the lessons of legal history and the claims of social welfare both pointed to the need for legal change. The most startling feature of his program for law reform was that it was to be put into effect by the judiciary. Kames based his endorsement of this judicial route to legal improvement on a novel theory of legal equity and a trenchant analysis of the legal implications of recent social development. But the notion of the judicial office this program entailed also reflected less theoretical matters, and these relate largely to Scotland's political circumstances in the period following the 1707 Act of Union.

Many of these more practical considerations can be viewed as a Scottish version of the problems regarding parliamentary legislation which Blackstone diagnosed in the *Commentaries*. Blackstone, as we have seen, recognized parliament's constitutional authority as an "absolute despotic power" for making and changing law. At the same time, though, he remained deeply pessimistic over the quality of parliament's enactments, and explicitly resisted the notion that the legislature might be called upon to exercise its constitutional authority by implementing major changes in English law.[1] Blackstone did not, in any case, believe common law required major improvements, and on this important matter his position contrasts with that of Kames. Nevertheless, the difficulties he discerned in the practicalities of parliamentary law-making were even more dramatic when applied to Scotland.

Following the Union, Scotland lacked a native legislature and had to depend upon Westminster for new statute law. On the basis of the Blackstonean analysis there could be little comfort in this situation. If England's untutored legislators had proved themselves incapable of legislating effectively with regard to English law, they were even less likely to succeed in dealing with a foreign system of law which few

---

[1] See the discussion above, chapter 2.

English lawyers, let alone members of parliament, adequately understood. Scotland, moreover, was significantly under-represented in the British parliament, and important Scottish legislation depended for its passage on ministerial support. This made legislating for Scotland an especially precarious business, of which Kames had direct personal experience. Despite his confidence in judicial law reform, Kames realized that the law of entails could only be altered by statutory amendment. Accordingly, he drafted legislation for their abolition, had his bill published, and solicited the support of several political leaders in England, particularly Lord Chancellor Hardwicke in 1759. However, in the absence of any active English sponsorship, his legislative effort never moved forward. Even when in 1764 the Faculty of Advocates assumed the leadership of the campaign against entails, and produced a bill virtually identical with that drafted by Kames, their enterprise quickly collapsed once the Scottish members of parliament divided at Westminster.[2]

This particular instance of legislative frustration reflected the more general problems Scottish lawyers experienced in looking to West-minster for legal assistance. In the winter of 1737, for example, Duncan Forbes, the newly appointed Lord President of the Court of Session, wrote to Hardwicke on the question of Scots law reform. He noted that "thirty years experience since the Union" had revealed "many blemishes" in the law, and proposed that the Session judges produce a bill to remove these defects which then could be placed under Hardwicke's supervision at Westminster. But, he also shared Hardwicke's fears that such a bill might be vulnerable in parliament to "alterations from hands that may not be so well acquainted with the subject," and stressed that the proposition would depend on the likelihood of these fears being realized:

> If I could with reason hope that a bill so settled there would pass unaltered, I would set about it without loss of time... but if I may not rely on that, I should rather choose to jog on as we are, than to risk amendments... by unskilled hands.[3]

Hardwicke replied within a fortnight, announcing his support and willingness to serve. Yet notwithstanding his own success as a

---

[2] For Kames's correspondence on entails and legislative proposals, see Tytler, *Memoirs of Kames*, I, 210–14, 222–8. One of the letters to Hardwicke, as well as the text of his proposals, is printed in Lehmann, *Kames*, pp. 327–32. Kames also published some of his correspondence with Hardwicke in *Elucidations Respecting the Common and Statute Law*, pp. 381–8, and outlined his bill in *Sketches of the History of Man*, IV, 462–3. For the Faculty of Advocates' legislative effort of 1764, see Nicholas T. Phillipson, "Lawyers, Landowners and the Civic Leadership of Post-Union Scotland," *Juridical Review*, XXII (1976), 97–120.

[3] Cited in Yorke, *Life of Hardwicke*, II, 532.

legislative manager, he could provide no reassurance on the problem which most disturbed the Scottish judges:

As to the Bill passing *without alterations*, your Lordship, who [has] had long experience of our parliament's genius, of the disposition to amend the English law, and of some attempts relating to your own, can judge, as well as I, of the probability of such an event.[4]

He went on to mention a further problem that "unless some of your countrymen here are taken in to the original project, many obstacles may arise." In the end no such bill was produced, and the Scottish courts were left to "jog on" as before. Kames, however, insisted that another option remained for reforming Scots law, one resting on the equitable authority of the Court of Session itself.

The same institutional arrangement which deprived Scotland of any untroubled access to legislative law reform, also enhanced the institutional importance of the Scottish courts. Aside from the church, the most socially potent survivor of the union with England was the Scots law and legal establishment, and it is clear that the Scottish courts served a much broader political function than their counterparts in England. Kames's presentation of the Session Court as an authority competent to reform Scots law in some sense exploited the ambiguities in this situation. If English lawyers such as Blackstone viewed his doctrines as violating constitutional norms, then this in part reflected the difficulty in applying these norms, especially any notion of a strict separation of powers, to the actual governing of contemporary Scotland. At this level, Kames's reforming advocacy exemplifies a more general pattern of concerns that scholars have discerned in the Scottish Enlightenment as a whole. Nicholas Phillipson, for example, has suggested that many of the distinctive ideas and activities of the Scottish intelligentsia should be read as part of a process whereby a provincial society which had lost its political identity with the abolition of the Scottish Parliament turned to other institutions to further an already established program of improvement – a process evinced in the creation of new bodies like the polite societies of Edinburgh and the strengthening of older institutions like the universities, and in the moral values and social goals these institutions were hoped to further.[5] Kames's proposals present a legalistic variation on this

---

[4] *Ibid.*, II, 534.

[5] Nicholas T. Phillipson, "Culture and Society in the Eighteenth-Century Province: The Case of Edinburgh and the Scottish Enlightenment," in Lawrence Stone (ed.), *The University in Society*, 2 vols. (Princeton, 1974), II, 407–48; see also his "The Scottish Enlightenment," in Roy Porter and Mikuláš Teich (eds.), *The Enlightenment in National Context* (Cambridge, 1981), pp. 19–40.

theme – a program of legal improvement which urged Scotland to follow an English lead, and a program whose realization depended on the initiative of a native institution, in this case Scotland's premier civil court.

Kames, however, did not seek to defend his notion of the judicial office on the basis of mere political necessity. In the first place he was confident of the substantive superiority of law produced through judicial deliberation. He defended this position in his most important collection of law reports, the 1741 *Dictionary of Decisions*, when commenting on the relative paucity of statute in Scots law. This, he acknowledged, "certainly was once our misfortune," as the absence of legislation allowed the judges too much freedom. The problem, however, was removed as the "law came to be more and more ascertained in the course of practice," and by comparing the relative merits of common law and statute it became obvious that "what was originally our misfortune, will turn out to our advantage":

> Statutes, though commonly made with a view to particular cases, do yet enact in general upon all similar cases; and as man is but short sighted with regard to consequences, 'tis odds but, in remedying one evil, a greater is produced. A court of justice determines nothing in general; their decisions are adapted to particular circumstances. If upon any occasion they chance to stray, 'tis but to return again, with greater certainty of the road. They creep along with wary steps, until at last, by induction of many cases...a general rule is with safety formed.[6]

Kames's remarks deserve some expansion, not least because his summary statement evoked a range of claims that informed much of the contemporary scepticism over the efficacy of legislation as a vehicle for developing legal rules. Part of his argument referred to that orthodox premise of equity theory which held that the legislator was necessarily "short sighted with regard to consequences" in that he could never produce a set of legal rules which would fulfill its desired goals or the demands of justice in every possible case.[7] Part of the argument drew on the equally orthodox and influential account of the unique strengths of customary law. Unlike the legislature, Kames explained, the courts only arrived at "a general rule" through the "induction of many cases," each "adapted to particular circumstances." Through such a steady and gradual process of legal growth, customary law achieved a standard of excellence unavailable in other forms of law-making. According to the frequently invoked formulas of English common

[6] Kames, *Dictionary of Decisions*, p. iii, and see Tytler, *Memoirs of Kames*, III, iii.
[7] See above, chapter 3 at nn6–12.

lawyers, by such means England's unwritten law (in Mansfield's words) "work[ed] itself pure" by refining rules "drawn from the fountain of justice." And the natural result was a body of common law "superior to an act of parliament."[8]

This conventional celebration of the wisdom of the common law formed such a dominant and pervasive theme of English legal orthodoxy that it has often come to seem a peculiarly English doctrine of historical traditionalism.[9] Still, it would be a mistake to limit its relevance to the English legal tradition. An eighteenth-century Scottish lawyer, for example, would have encountered much the same doctrines in Stair's *Institutions*. There Stair likewise stressed the superior virtues of legal custom "wrung out from... debates upon particular cases," in which "the conveniences and inconveniences thereof, through a tract of time, are experimentally seen." And as Kames was later to do, Stair immediately contrasted this with the situation in statute law, where "the law-giver must at once balance the conveniences and inconveniences," and therefore "may, and often doth, fall short."[10]

At the same time, Kames's arguments in favor of common law referred to the immediate experience of eighteenth-century legislating, and especially to the retrospective character of so many parliamentary statutes. On most occasions the legislature acted "with a view to particular cases," and in this sense functioned in a manner similar to a judge. The difficulty with statute was that although the legislature looked to a particular case, it automatically created a general rule which determined future cases. The effects of its actions thus extended well beyond the circumstances which guided its original deliberation. One solution to this problem, which Bentham began to explore in the 1770s, was to seek a comprehensive arrangement for legislation which would enable the legislator to see all the potential consequences of his legislative actions immediately. Kames, however, raised the issue only to indicate the inherent superiority of judicial practice as a mechanism for refining legal rules. The judiciary responded to particular cases with particular decisions, all equally corrigible, and only later "with safety" produced a general rule. And like Blackstone, Kames believed this reasoning could be readily vindicated through a simple appeal to the existing state of the law:

Let any one who is curious run over our law in this view, and he will find

---

[8] Mansfield's comments are discussed above, chapter 4 at n10.

[9] See, for example, Pocock's discussion in "Burke and the Ancient Constitution: a Problem in the History of Ideas," *Politics, Language and Time*.

[10] James Dalrymple, Viscount of Stair, *The Institutions of the Law of Scotland*, (1693), ed. D. M. Walker (Edinburgh, 1981), pp. 84–5 (I.I.15).

that those branches of it which have been modelled by the court are, generally speaking, brought nearer a standard than those upon which statutes are most frequent.[11]

Kames also sought to restrict the scope for legislation through another set of arguments, those which Pocock has construed as the civic humanist themes in Scottish social theory.[12] There is no doubt that Kames shared the preoccupations of civic humanism. His *Sketches of the History of Man* contain incessant warnings on the need to maintain patriotism, on the threats to virtue posed by commercial life, and on Britain's desperate vulnerability to the forces of luxury, corruption and profligate manners.[13] Kames was hardly at his most original or most compelling in these contexts, but it is worth noting how he invoked these claims at the expense of legislation. Initially, of course, his very commitment to the "important doctrine that patriotism is the cornerstone of civil society" entailed a devaluing of legislation and public institutions generally as a source of social welfare.[14] Thus he maintained that though "good government will advance men to a high degree of civilization," not even "the very best government" could "preserve them from corruption."[15] The point was further strengthened by his adoption of Montesquieu's insight that legislation represented only one of many causes which determined the moral character of any community.[16] This again tended to limit the area for legislation since the legislator needed to recognize the large number of social practices which could only be altered by customs, manners, education and the like. As Kames observed in his principal didactic tract, "manners, depending on an endless variety of circumstances, are too complex for law; and yet upon manners chiefly depends the well-being of society." In such areas legislation could "do little" and the sovereign had to work by "example and precept."[17] On this basis, in *Sketches of the History of Man*, he condemned a wide range of recent statutes as misguided attempts to solve problems incapable of legislative

[11] Kames, *Dictionary of Decisions*, p. iii.
[12] Pocock elaborated this interpretation in *The Machiavellian Moment*, pp. 486–505. For more recent discussions, see his "Cambridge Paradigms and Scotch philosophers," in *Wealth and Virtue*, pp. 235–52, and "Varieties of Whiggism," in *Virtue, Commerce and History*, pp. 230–52.
[13] See Kames, *Sketches of the History of Man*, I, 186–95, 342–8, 401–23; II, 152–4, 294–316, 317–51; III, 1–65; IV, 164–82.   [14] *Ibid.*, II, 155.
[15] *Ibid.*, I, 402, and see IV, 180.
[16] Montesquieu, whom Kames honored as "the greatest genius of the present age," was the principal source for most of his social theory in the *Sketches of the History of Man*; see I, 314–15 and II, 249.
[17] Kames, *Loose Hints on Education, Chiefly Concerning the Culture of the Heart* (Edinburgh, 1781), pp. 21–2.

cure.[18] Such laws, even if they went unenforced, were "never innocent with regard to consequences," since "nothing is more subversive of morality as well as of patriotism than a habit of disregarding the laws of our country."[19]

Kames's utilization of this argument, in fact, sits somewhat uneasily alongside his own devotion to projects for social improvement. Whatever his sensitivity to the complex and organic nature of social life, it did not prevent his proposing such visionary pieces of social engineering as, for example, a plan to close down most of London in the interests of public morals.[20] Nonetheless, this social theory was obviously of use for censuring parliament, and these criticisms dovetail with his general insistence on the superiority of judge-made law. According to his social theory, any judicial attempt to create patriotism through legal rules would likewise be doomed to failure. However, the procedures of customary law, as understood by Kames, were unlikely to generate this sort of misguided and pernicious law-making. The statute book, in contrast, testified to the fact that the legislature had frequently succumbed to the temptation to intervene in areas of social life beyond the reach of law.

At all events, Kames was confident of the advantages of judge-made law. "Matters of law," he stressed, "are ripened in the best manner by warmth of debate at the bar and coolness of judgment on the bench."[21] And he was equally certain of the need for all legal rules to keep pace with historical development and social change. Hence it became especially vital for him to explain the manner in which the courts developed systems of legal custom in harmony with the "fluctuating manners of the people." Part of the answer was found in the conception of precedent, embraced by Blackstone and Mansfield, which distinguished common law itself from particular judicial decisions, and thereby indicated that this type of law was not to be reduced to a mere collection of historical precedents. Given Kames's preoccupation with legal change and adaptation, it was appropriate that he, no less than Mansfield, developed a particularly unequivocal account of the primacy of legal principle over precedent in the practice of customary law. He maintained that in cases concerning "principles" (as opposed to "arbitrary questions"), earlier decisions "ought there to have authority." If the decision was found to be "just," "then reason

---

[18] See *Sketches of the History of Man*, I, 381 (laws against swearing); II, 396–9 (laws multiplying legal oaths); III, 87–8, 95–100 (poor laws).   [19] *Ibid*, IV, 177.

[20] *Ibid.*, III, 120–37, especially 135–7.

[21] *Historical Law Tracts*, I, 324, and also see Kames, *Remarkable Decisions of the Court of Session, from 1716 to 1728* (Edinburgh, 1728), preface (n.p.).

is the authority, not the decision," whereas "if the decision be founded on wrong principles, it can signify nothing."[22]

This position ensured that the judiciary was not confined merely to perpetuating an historic body of precedents, which, as in the case of eighteenth-century Scotland, might demonstrably be antiquated. But the doctrine in itself provided no direct guidance as to how the courts were to direct the operation of principle in a manner appropriate to current social and historical conditions. This task was undertaken in 1760 in the *Principles of Equity*.[23] Kames's treatise on equity jurisprudence, perhaps due to the current scholarly emphasis on his contributions to philosophical history, has received relatively little attention.[24] Yet, Kames himself (who admittedly was never disposed to underestimate the value of any of his publications) regarded the text as among his greatest achievements, viewing it as the work that would ensure his posthumous fame. As his critics on the bench bluntly noted, "Kames thinks nothing of any law book but [his own] *Principles of Equity*."[25]

The *Principles of Equity* offered an account of the equity practice of the Court of Session, which Kames believed to require not only systematic ordering, but also expansion on the lines of the jurisdiction of the English court of Chancery. To this end, he constructed an elaborate and remarkable theoretical explanation of the peculiar nature of equity in modern English and Scots law. This ground had been prepared two years earlier in the *Historical Law Tracts*, when Kames in an essay on the "History of Courts" explored the origins and nature of the Court of Session's judicial authority. His historical investigations revealed that "no defect in the constitution of a state" deserved "greater reproach than the giving license to wrong without affording redress," and that therefore "the power to redress wrongs of all kinds must subsist somewhere in every state."[26] In Scotland, this power had first been lodged in the privy council. When that court was abolished, its authority "devolve[d] upon the court of session," and gave it a "new branch of jurisdiction" distinct from its original status "as a

---

[22] Kames, *Dictionary of Decisions*, p. ii. For an assessment of the orthodoxy of Kames's view, see T. B. Smith, *The Doctrines of Judicial Precedent in Scots Law* (Edinburgh, 1952), pp. 1–10. For Blackstone and Mansfield's treatments, see the discussions above, chapter 1 at n66, chapter 3 at n63 and chapter 6 at n19.

[23] Quotations below are from the expanded second edition of 1767.

[24] The important exception among recent commentators is D. M. Walker, whose "Equity in Scots Law," *Juridical Review*, LXVI (1954), 103–47, remains the most substantial treatment of the work.

[25] See "Materials for Writing the Life of Lord Kames" (1778), in *Private Papers of James Boswell*, XV, 274, and *Boswell, Laird of Auchinleck*, 239n.

[26] *Historical Law Tracts*, I, 321, 325.

court of common law." Its resulting "extraordinary power" was to be compared with the "English court of chancery," which redressed "every sort of wrong occasioned by the omission or transgression of any duty... where a remedy is not otherwise provided by common or statute law."[27]

These arguments were revived and expanded in the introduction to the *Principles of Equity*, where Kames again sharply contrasted the Session's expansive authority as an equity court with its original function under common law. "One operation of equity universally acknowledged," he maintained, "is to remedy imperfections in the common law, which sometimes is defective and sometimes exceeds just bounds." In this sense, "equity is constantly opposed to common law" in that it "commences at the limits of the common law."[28] Since equity "in its proper sense" comprehended "every matter of law that by the common law is left without remedy," the only way to ascertain its jurisdiction was by "historical deduction"; that is, by an historical examination of the contents of the original common law so as to determine which legal remedies were in operation prior to equity's intervention.[29] Accordingly, Kames embarked on a brisk assessment of the Scots common law, promptly declaring it the law of "our rude ancestors," which provided only "regulations to restrain individuals from doing mischief and to enforce performance of covenants," and which altogether disregarded "the more refined duties of morality."[30] Hence, in the case of Scotland, common law demanded a massive dose of equitable correction:

> But law, in this simple form, cannot long continue stationary; for in the social state... law ripens gradually with the human faculties... [and] many duties formerly neglected are found to be binding in conscience. Such duties can no longer be neglected by courts of justice; and as they made no part of the common law, they come naturally under the jurisdiction of a court of equity.[31]

Kames next examined those legal principles which were to guide the actions of the equity court, and which had their source in the "moral laws of society."[32] The first principle enforced by the equity court was the principle of justice, which meant that it was the court's

---

[27] *Ibid.*, I, 324–6.
[28] Kames, *Principles of Equity*, pp. 38, 42. Throughout the discussion Kames uses the term "common law" as in England, though this was not the sole or original usage in Scots law.
[29] *Ibid.*, pp. 38, 40. [30] *Ibid.*, p. 40. [31] *Ibid.*, p. 41.
[32] A separate discourse summarizing Kames's moral theory under this title was added in the second edition, pp. 1–37.

responsibility "to make right effectual" and "to redress wrong."[33]
This was fairly orthodox, as equity was regularly identified with
"natural justice" and treated as a species of judicial discretion designed
to prevent the application of legal rules from producing injustice in
particular cases.[34] But Kames's ethical system, as we have seen, also
contained distinct utilitarian features. On the basis of these he presented
another, often neglected principle guiding the equity court:

> All the variety of matter hitherto mentioned is regulated by the principle
> of justice solely ... But, upon more narrow inspection, we find a number
> of law cases into which justice enters not, but only the principle of utility.
> Expediency requires that these be brought under the cognizance of a
> court; and the court of equity gaining daily more weight and authority,
> takes naturally such matter under its jurisdiction.[35]

Moreover, given the fundamental social purposes of the legal system,
when these two principles were found "in opposition," the court was
to sacrifice justice to utility. "Equity," Kames reasoned, "when it
regards the interest of a few individuals only, ought to yield to utility
when it regards the whole society."[36]

The purposes served by this theoretical construction were made
clearer when Kames turned to the actual practice of the equity court
and to those areas of Scots law requiring equitable amendment. He first
considered those areas where equity was guided by the dictates of
justice. At the center of the discussion was the law of contract and
quasi-contract, and here Kames presented traditional points of contrast
between common law and equity procedure. Thus, equity was able to
direct the specific performance of a contract, where common law could
only provide pecuniary damages. Similarly, equity enjoyed a more
extensive authority for construing deeds and covenants. Common law
was confined to adhering strictly to the letter of an agreement, even in
the case of feigned instruments like "double-bonds."[37] But equity was
authorized "to follow the dictates of refined justice" and to interpret
every contract "in its true light of a means employed to bring about
some end."[38]

A second category of cases comprised legal matters for which the
principle of justice proved an indecisive guide, leaving the court's
decisions to be determined by considerations of utility. A leading

---

[33] *Principles of Equity*, p. 249.
[34] See the discussion above, chapter 3 at nn7–15.
[35] *Principles of Equity*, p. 44.
[36] *Ibid.*, p. 47; also see Kames, *Elucidations Respecting the Common and Statute Law*, p. 266.
[37] *Principles of Equity*, pp. 42–4, 118–21.   [38] *Ibid.*, pp. 151–2.

illustration was found in the question of a *bona fide* payment of debt to the wrong creditor. This situation resulted from the basic need in a commercial country to allow "a free and expedite currency" of property as was required for "the advancement of commerce." The cost of this system of fluid property exchange was the difficulty created for a debtor, particularly in the case of bonds or other negotiable notes, in identifying the true creditor to his debt. Often the debtor might make payment to the wrong individual, a situation, Kames observed, "extremely nice in point of equity." If the court refused to sustain the mispayment, then the debtor would suffer by having to pay twice on the same debt. But if the payment was sustained, the creditor would sacrifice his right through no fault of his own. As Kames put it, "here the scales hang even" as the principle of justice could not determine the issue. The "principle of utility," however, was absolutely decisive and exerted "all its weight" on the debtor's scale. Unless the debtor was "secure by voluntary payment," no debtor would pay anything without going to court, "and how ruinous to credit this would prove, must be obvious without taking a moment for reflection."[39]

Lastly, Kames considered those cases where justice and utility clashed and where utility had to predominate. Again, the question referred to the special legal demands created by commerce. His example was the case "where a transaction extremely unequal is occasioned by error." In this situation, "the justice of affording relief is obvious," and Kames noted that many legal systems did provide such relief. Nonetheless, the court of equity had to "yield to utility," since the justice of the case violated "the interest of the public." As Kames warned, "if complaints of inequality were indulged, law-suits would be multiplied, to the great detriment of commerce."[40]

This discussion represented only part of Kames's account of the operation of utility in the practice of the equity court. The principle of utility also dominated his treatment of the question, "whether a court of equity be, or ought to be, governed by any general rules."[41] As we have seen, this question was regularly aired by legal writers in England, where equity functioned most often as a system of settled rules.[42] Kames maintained that this was proper and that the equity court should always adjudicate by reference to general rules. He defended this position by

---

[39] *Ibid.*, p. 259.
[40] *Ibid.*, p. 268; and compare with Hugo Grotius, *The Rights of War and Peace ... wherein are explained, The Law of Nature and Nations ... translated in English, to which are added all the large notes of M. Barbeyrac* (London, 1738), Book 2, ch. 12, p. 300.
[41] *Principles of Equity*, p. 46.
[42] See above, chapter 3 at nn41–55.

rehearsing arguments which English authors commonly deployed against the level of judicial discretion classical accounts of equity seemed to license. He noted that "men are liable to prejudice and error," and hence all courts relied on general rules "to preserve uniformity of judgement." Equity was "a happy invention to remedy the errors of common law," but it "must stop some where," and there was no adequate "check upon a court of equity but general rules."[43] Moreover, in adhering to general rules the equity court fulfilled the dictates of utility and the consequent need to sacrifice the "interests of a few individuals" when they opposed "the whole society." "It is for that very reason," Kames maintained, "that a court of equity is bound to form its decrees upon general rules, for this measure regards the whole society in preventing arbitrary proceedings."[44]

Not only was the equity court to employ general rules. Kames argued further that "however clear a just claim or defence may be," the court ought not to intervene "unless the case can be brought under a general rule." This restriction discouraged law-suits, a crucial priority in a commercial country, and it precluded "the hazard of making judges arbitrary." Indeed, it followed "from the very nature of a court of equity" that it adhered to general rules "even at the expense of forbearing to do justice." The court was concerned to perfect the "distribution of justice" because this served to "promote the good of society." But "the means ought to be subordinate to the end." Therefore, if the court found it could provide justice only "by using means that tend to the hurt of society" (that is, by evading general rules), "a court of equity ought not to interpose."[45]

The dictates of utility thus sanctioned those areas of law in which equity ignored individual just claims and also justified the general practice of equity as a system of general rules. And these legal doctrines were buttressed by the utilitarian elements Kames discerned in the "moral laws of society" as a whole. Yet, notwithstanding the consistency of Kames's position, the notion of equity which followed from these commitments was extraordinary, if not simply bizarre. By so introducing "the principle of utility" into equity jurisprudence, Kames had eliminated precisely that legal function which orthodox theories of equity served to explain. This was the judicial authority to grant exceptions to legal rules in those particular situations where their application would result in injustice.[46] Kames denied to the equity judge just this sort of authority, even though he readily conceded that

---

[43] *Principles of Equity*, p. 46.
[44] *Ibid.*, p. 47.   [45] *Ibid.*, p. 268.
[46] See above, chapter 3 at nn6–12.

general rules "must often produce decrees that are materially unjust, for no rule can be equally just in its application to a whole class of cases that are far from being the same in every circumstance."[47] As a result, the Kamesian system of equity ceased to resemble equity at all. Instead, his conception of equity as a separate body of the general rules of law which corrected by supplementing the historic common law came to appear remarkably like a program of legislative law reform.

It is important not to overstate the case. Kames never directly compared his general rules of equity to legislation, and he never suggested, of course, that what his equity judges were doing was legislating. He maintained the proper constitutional norms and insisted upon the court's subservience to parliamentary statute.[48] Nonetheless, there was more than a merely superficial similarity between his general rules of equity and legislation. This became evident in his discussion of the function of statutes "as they regard matters of law." These he divided into two classes: "First, those which have justice for their object by supplying the defects... of common law. Second, those which have utility for their sole object."[49] By describing statute in these terms Kames ascribed to it the same institutional role through which he had first defined the province of equity. Both statutes and equity improved the administration of justice by correcting common law and both promoted social utility. The principal difference between them was that equity could only serve utility by negative means – by preventing acts which produced social mischief. Statute, in contrast, could also effect projects "calculated for promoting the positive good and happiness of society."[50] The equity court, for example, could never undertake such programs as the improvement of the Scottish highways or the reform of the royal boroughs, to name but two of Kames's favored projects.[51] But with regard to private jurisprudence, their functions were clearly analogous, and indeed characterized in almost exactly the same terms.

In the light of this, there was some merit to Blackstone's shrill response, that "if a court of equity did really act" as Kames "from theory" supposed, "it would rise above all law, either common or statute, and be a most arbitrary legislator in every particular case."[52]

---

[47] *Principles of Equity*, p. 46.
[48] See *ibid.*, pp. 177–9, 183–4. However, Kames did maintain that the equity court enjoyed a more extensive authority to interpret and apply the statute law than a court of common law; see pp. 177, 185–6, and his application of the doctrine with regard to the bankruptcy acts at pp. 298–325.
[49] *Ibid.*, p. 185.   [50] *Ibid.*, p. 186, and see pp. 261–6.
[51] See *Sketches of the History of Man*, IV, Appendices 2 and 3, pp. 464–92.
[52] 3 *Comm* 433. Blackstone referred to Kames as "a very ingenious author in the other part of the island"; the reference was dropped in the eighth edition (1778).

Still, Blackstone's reaction demands some unraveling. As Kames's contemporary biographer, A. F. Tytler, correctly perceived, the two authors' treatment of equity shared much common ground. Both rejected classical doctrines of equity as an appropriate description of the practice of the English equity court because both agreed that English equity, in Blackstone's phrase, was "governed by general rules."[53] Tytler in fact thought their positions so close that he could only account for Blackstone's hostility by suggesting that he had perhaps never in fact read the *Principles of Equity*.[54] Fortunately, a better explanation is available, though it has less to do with the issue of equity than with Blackstone and Kames's antagonistic assessments of common law. Blackstone was confident of the enduring competence of the common law, and looked neither to parliament nor to the court of equity for introducing substantial alterations in common law practice. Although equity originally emerged to fill gaps in common law remedies, it had largely developed into a settled body of legal rules. The operation of these rules prevented equity from disrupting common law forms or from undermining the common law's position of primacy within the legal system. Kames likewise recognized equity as a system of legal rules, but the legal area these rules were to occupy was massive. As Kames's historical investigations repeatedly disclosed, Scotland's inherited body of customary law was inappropriate, if not antithetic, to the legal needs of a commercial society. "The imperfections of common law are so many and so various" that Kames believed it scarcely possible "to bring them into any perfect order."[55]

In addition, whereas Blackstone treated the general rules of equity as the end-result of a prolonged process of legal history, Kames defended these rules on the grounds of utilitarian legal principle. This too reflected important points of divergence. For Kames suggested that at a further stage of social development it might again be proper for the equity court to revise the law, and that such reforms would be justified provided they could be formulated as general rules.[56] Kames's general rules of equity thus served to restrict the actions of an individual judge, but did not permanently restrict the equity court as an agent for legal change. Blackstone's account of the general rules of English equity, by contrast, implied that the dynamic period of equity's interventions in the legal system had been completed.[57]

---

[53] See the discussion above, chapter 3 at n57 and n59.
[54] See Tytler, *Memoirs of Kames*, I, 250–7.
[55] *Principles of Equity*, p. 56.   [56] *Ibid.*, p. 47.
[57] A final point of contrast between Blackstone and Kames should be noted. This concerns Kames's criticism of the use of legal fictions as a technique for adapting common law forms to altered social circumstances. See his comments in *Essays on British Antiquities*, p. 147.

Despite Blackstone's certainty that Kames had seriously misunderstood the practice of an equity court in England, the English legal experience was plainly vital for the construction of Kames's theory. He extravagantly identified Mansfield as his great mentor in the work, acknowledging that the Chief Justice "was never out of [his] view" throughout each moment of the work's composition.[58] He made ample use of Chancery precedents in the *Principles of Equity* (a rather curious feature in a treatise ostensibly claiming to state *Scotland's* equity law).[59] Even more important, Chancery furnished a model of an equity court whose practice and legal impact differed so dramatically from the type of particularist judicial discretion described by classical equity doctrines. The jurisprudence he urged upon to the Court of Session, Kames explained in his *Historical Law Tracts*, "seems to be adopted by the English court of chancery in its utmost extent."[60] Moreover, Kames's general concern that the Scottish courts reap the full lessons of English legal development led him to produce an unusually precise and comprehensive summary of these lessons. Not the least of his accomplishments in the *Principles of Equity* concerned this synthetic statement of how legal principles shaped the law of a modern commercial society. The principle of utility sanctioned the general rules in equity practice, and further accounted for the content of these rules as they governed property disputes. In a commercial society, social utility required that the law support that system of rapid exchange upon which commerce and prosperity depended. And this in turn meant that the courts would protect individual just claims of right only to the extent that this maintenance of justice harmonized with the dictates of utility.

Kames, of course, was scarcely alone in finding so much of the change in legal practice engineered by the courts attributable to the impact and requirements of trade and commercial life. Mansfield's "founding" of the nation's commercial law provided one especially dramatic instance of this process, but the process was in no way exhausted by this celebrated judicial achievement. Thus, for example, when Blackstone considered the earlier, historic transformation of the kingdom's "system of remedial law," he explained that the "old feudal actions" had to be altered so as to accommodate the succeeding "commercial mode of property" which required "a more speedy decision of right to facilitate exchange and alienation."[61] When

[58] *Principles of Equity*, "Letter to Mansfield."
[59] See Walker, "Equity in Scots Law," 205–6.
[60] *Historical Law Tracts*, I, 326.
[61] 3 *Comm* 265–8, discussed above, chapter 1 at n78.

Edward Willes sought to clarify those "considerations of policy" which continued to prompt the court's efforts to modify law of real property, he cited the "universal notion that in a commercial country all property should be freed from every clog which may hinder its circulation."[62] And when Hardwicke characterized the most recent developments in English law and equity, he promptly invoked the complex property relations which followed the "new discoveries and inventions in commerce" and "for which the ancient simplicity of the common law had adapted no remedies."[63]

But if Kames's awareness of the importance of commerce was not novel, like other Scottish *philosophes* he commanded an unusually rich conception of the social transformation wrought by commerce and of how extensively commercial society differed from its historical predecessors.[64] One critical implication of this understanding of commercial life, which Kames pursued at length in his historical studies, was the extent to which Scotland's legal inheritance had been rendered obsolete and harmful by current social conditions. In the *Principles of Equity*, Kames constructively surveyed the type of law which did respond successfully to the distinctive challenges of commercial life. This is presented as a legal order in which the court's traditional duty "to make right effectual" had been supplemented and regulated by a new responsibility to "the principle of utility." In a mercantile nation, Kames even suggested, the legal demands of justice might be entirely subsumed within the principles of utility. The two principles were such "good friends" that "utility" was "inseparable from justice," and this "must be always understood when we talk of justice."[65] In a commercial society, the ruling principle of law was the principle of utility.

Thus to encounter in eighteenth-century legal theory the articulation of a distinctly utilitarian jurisprudence deployed on behalf of a program of law reform may, in one sense, occasion little surprise. However, we have become so accustomed to identifying this intellectual development with the utilitarianism and legal positivism of Jeremy Bentham that Kames's *Principles of Equity* provides a crucial historical corrective.[66] For Kames, no less than for Bentham, utility featured as a critical

---

[62] Cited in Hargrave, *Collectanea Juridica*, I, 297–8, 301, and discussed above, chapter 6 at n68.

[63] Yorke, *Life of Hardwicke*, II, 554–5, discussed above, chapter 6 at n6.

[64] See the discussion above, chapter 7 at nn32–35 and nn60–75.

[65] *Principles of Equity*, p. 267.

[66] See, for example, Ronald Dworkin's characterization of "the ruling theory of law" which derives "from the philosophy of Jeremy Bentham," in *Taking Rights Seriously* (London, 1977), p. vii.

principle of legal modernization. But, the reformers to whom Kames directed the principle were enlightened judges and not scientific legislators. Kames reminds us how in this period a commitment to the methods and institutions of customary law need not be taken to indicate any lack of commitment to law reform. Indeed, for Kames as for so many of his English contemporaries, the most important and recently confirmed lesson of English law was the clear superiority of the courts over the legislature in orchestrating legal development. It was this lesson which made Lord Mansfield, the period's most illustrious judicial reformer, the proper figure for Kames to invoke at the outset of the *Principles of Equity*. And it was this lesson which, in turn, suggested that the judges of the Court of Session were the ideal agents for lifting Scots law into the modern order of commercial society. This was a lesson in the wisdom of the common law that scarcely could be lost on a philosopher-judge whose devotion to improvement, in John Ramsay's apt phrase, "was almost apostolical."[67]

[67] Ramsay, *Scotland and Scotsmen*, I, 195.

III

Parliamentary statute

9

Statute consolidation

The vitality of the eighteenth-century common law courts, as evinced in the expansive rhetoric and practical accomplishments of King's Bench under Mansfield's direction, supplied an impressive support to those like Blackstone who insisted upon the primacy of common law within the English legal system. In the *Commentaries*, Blackstone had extolled the common law by invoking the wisdom of England's Saxon ancestors, and had sought to reveal the manner in which this ancient structure was disfigured and its foundation threatened by the rash and dangerous enactments of England's untutored legislators. But to seek to protect the common law from such legislative violation was not to reject the opportunity for change and correction within the legal system as a whole. As was most dramatically displayed in the development of the commercial law, the common law system retained the means to adapt and advance English law as altered social circumstance demanded.

On this basis it might appear not only that the common law had on past occasions attained a degree of certainty and level of excellence unmatched in any contemporary legislation, but that in future "the judgments of Westminster Hall" should properly remain the chief "authority" for "by far the greatest part of the law in England."[1] Indeed, as Kames and Mansfield were quick to point out, past experience and orthodox legal doctrine both confirmed that the law generated through the practice of the courts necessarily surpassed anything that might be achieved by legislation. Hence, while fully endorsing the constitutional reality of parliament's uncontrollable legislative power, they eagerly defended and strove to exploit the authority which survived in the courts to refine and perfect the *lex non scripta*.

If the achievements of Mansfield's court thus seemed to vindicate the Blackstonean assessment of English law, such judicial activism in itself

[1] See the discussion above, chapter 3 at n1.

could never provide a complete solution to the problems diagnosed in the *Commentaries*. London's merchants may have found in King's Bench an effective instrument for redressing many of their legal needs, but this remained an exception to the increasingly established pattern of eighteenth-century political life, whereby business interests, local corporations, provincial magistrates and various individuals turned to parliament for such assistance.[2] As Kames recognized, whatever the considerable powers of even an equity court to correct and expand the common law in accord with altered social conditions and "the more refined duties of morality," there still existed a large number of legal and social improvements which could be effected only through parliamentary intervention.[3]

Furthermore, in the period immediately following the publication of the *Commentaries*, England's legislators showed no signs of curtailing the exercise of their legislative will, as the pace of parliamentary law-making continued to increase. And there was never any assurance that parliament would confine its enterprises to those areas advised by the judges, or would fashion its enactments by heeding the lessons of the *Commentaries*. In fact, it was not difficult to find evidence directly to the contrary. William Eden, remarking on a 1770 statute which gave justices of the peace new powers to inflict corporal penalties under the game laws, found the measure sufficiently reprehensible in itself, being "inconsistent with every idea of English liberty." But the measure was even more "remarkable" in that it was enacted "at a time when 'the commentaries on the laws of England' must be supposed to have been recently perused by every Member of the Legislature." In the event, parliament had plainly ignored Blackstone's warning "of not deviating any further from our ancient constitution, by ordaining new penalties to be inflicted upon summary convictions."[4]

In the face of the often disquieting features of parliament's legislative practice, commentators on English law turned their attention directly to the question of statute law reform. The most important of their schemes for legislative improvement, if the frequency of advocacy can be taken as a guide, was the program for statute consolidation. Statute consolidation addressed the immediate consequence of parliament's legislative activism: the sheer size, jumbled chaos and stylistic irregularities of the statute book, or what Richard Burn described as the "acknowledged disorder and confusion" of English legislation.[5] The

[2] The development is surveyed above, Introduction at nn112–15.
[3] See the discussion above, chapter 8 at nn50–51.
[4] Eden, *Principles of Penal Law*, p. 66n.
[5] Burn, *Justice of the Peace*, III, 568.

advocates of the scheme looked for a comprehensive review of the statute book, designed to reduce its bulk through the repeal of all obsolete and disused acts and to methodize its contents by remodeling the remaining law into "uniform and consistent statutes."[6] In recommending the project, legal writers entertained a variety of objectives, and this no doubt partially explains the popularity of this reform proposal. For some, statute consolidation represented only a necessary preliminary to a more ambitious reform of the substance of parliament's enactments. Others suggested that consolidation might prove a sufficient solution to the problems attending parliamentary lawmaking. But what is perhaps most striking was the extent to which statute consolidation came to be seen as a crucial if rather uncontroversial program for English law – a scheme for legal improvement endorsed by the most fulsome and seemingly complacent apologists for the system of law in England.

The attitude of Edward Wynne can be taken as characteristic. Wynne had no doubt that "as far as it is the power of good Laws" to "make good Subjects," the English "are happy above all others." Throughout the course of his four-volume publication of 1774, *Eunomus: Or, Dialogues concerning the Law and Constitution of England*, he rarely encountered a native legal practice which did not deserve praise or which could not be rescued from reproach. Even the exasperating "multiplicity of our Laws" could be placed in an "amiable light," since any legal system which like the English displayed such a "jealous regard to Liberty...must in its nature be voluminous." Nonetheless, even this most comforting insight could not totally explain the conspicuous "bulk of our Laws," and Wynne therefore "heartily" joined in "the wish" that "our Body of Statute Laws were to be thoroughly and maturely reviewed." The consolidation of the statute book, he roundly declared in a concluding comment, "would perhaps be as great a Service and public Blessing as the Parliament could bestow on the Nation!"[7]

The eighteenth-century schemes for statute consolidation were an essentially Baconian solution to the problem of the statute law. Not only did legal writers regularly cite Francis Bacon's authority in this context, but Bacon's own account of legislative composition and revision – as set out in the third chapter of Book 8 of *De Augmentis*

---

[6] *Ibid.*

[7] Wynne, *Eunomus*, III, 332–4. For similar recommendations of statute reform, not discussed in the text, see: Wood, *Institute of the Laws of England*, p. iii; Wooddeson, *Elements of Jurisprudence*, pp. 35–6; Paley, *Moral and Political Philosophy*, pp. 442–3; Huntingford, *Statute Laws Considered*; Pothier, *Treatise on the Law of Obligations or Contracts*, I, iii (Evans' editorial introduction).

Scientiarum, and in two similar proposals for the "amendment" of English law – remained throughout the period the most comprehensive discussion of statute consolidation and its objectives.[8] As late as 1826, Sir Robert Peel was still appealing to Bacon as the most comprehensive authority on statute reform in England.[9] Peel's claim to the House of Commons echoed eighteenth-century orthodoxies, in which Bacon's legislative teaching, along with Matthew Hale's authoritative statement of the strengths of customary law, ranked among the most influential of inheritances shaping professional attitudes to law reform. The neglect of this specifically Baconian tradition of legislative theory is perhaps the most damaging single omission in existing accounts of eighteenth-century legal and political ideas, which in turn has unduly narrowed and distorted scholarly consideration of the rise of Benthamism as a law reform ideology.[10]

In *De Augmentis Scientiarum*, Bacon considered the problems attending the "regeneration and reconstruction of the laws" as part of a more general analysis of legal certainty, which he viewed as "the Primary Dignity of the laws."[11] He claimed that legal certainty was frustrated either "where no law is prescribed" or "where the law is ambiguous and obscure."[12] It was the latter source of uncertainty which chiefly concerned the legislator, particularly the "obscurity" resulting "from an excessive accumulation of laws" and "from an ambiguity or want of clearness and distinctness in drawing of them."[13]

In considering the matter of the "drawing" of laws, Bacon supplied a few broad guidelines for effective legislative composition. He pointed to the several dangers raised by a "too concise and affected brevity" in legislation, recorded his firm disapproval of the use of legislative preambles, and especially stressed the dangers regarding the common "loquacity and prolixity used in the drawing up of laws." Instead of

[8] For examples of the contemporary usage of Bacon's discussions, see: Barrington, *Ancient Statutes*, pp. 499–500; Wynne, *Eunomus*, III, 333; Eden, *Principles of Penal Law*, pp. 21, 296, 316; Huntingford, *Statute Laws Considered*, p. 9, 26; Samuel Romilly, *Observations of a Late Publication, intitled, Thoughts on Executive Justice* (London, 1786), pp. 41–2.

[9] Bacon, *A Proposition to His Majesty by Sir Francis Bacon…touching the Compiling and Amendment of the Laws of England*, in *Works of Bacon*, XIII, 61 (editorial introduction).

[10] Bacon is better served by the scholarship on the seventeenth century. I have benefited especially from the research of Barbara J. Shapiro: "Sir Francis Bacon and the Mid-Seventeenth Century Movement for Law Reform," *American Journal of Legal History*, XXIV (1980), 331–62; "Codification of the Laws in Seventeenth-Century England" *Wisconsin Law Review*, (1974), 428–65; "Law Reform in Seventeenth-Century England," *American Journal of Legal History*, XIX (1975), 280–312 and "Law and Science in Seventeenth-Century England," 727–66.

[11] Bacon, *De Augmentis Scientiarum*, (English trans.), Book 8, Chapter 3, Title 1, in *Works of Bacon*, V, 90.

[12] *Ibid.*, Aphorism 9, p. 90.   [13] *Ibid.*, Aphorism 52, p. 98.

securing "greater certainty," such verbosity usually generated purely verbal controversies which left the authentic meaning of the law confused by "the noise and strife of words."[14]

The difficulties presented by "an excessive accumulation of laws" were more central to the question of statute consolidation. Here Bacon was more expansive, recommending a variety of devices which would allow for legal change without sacrifice of legal certainty. He first identified the proper procedure for introducing new provisions into the legislative system. Rather than making "a few additions and alterations" to the existing laws, Bacon advised having these "former enactments" repealed and in their place substituting "an entirely new and uniform law." The former method "confused and complicated" the legislative system and thereby corrupted "the body of laws," whereas the latter procedure ensured "harmony in times to come."[15] Bacon next proposed that special legislative "commissioners" be appointed "every three or five years" to review the body of laws. These commissioners would be responsible for introducing new legislation to repeal any "obsolete laws" and to resolve any inconsistencies which might have developed in the legal system.[16] Finally, on those occasions when the laws had "by accumulation" become "so voluminous" or "so confused" that "it is expedient to remodel them entirely," Bacon advocated the production of "a new digest of laws." These Digests were designed to contract the law "to a sound and manageable body" through the cancellation of all disused laws, the removal of any inconsistent, inconclusive or reiterative legal provisions, and the abridgement of all "wordy or too prolix" laws.[17]

In the 1610s, Bacon twice set out the case for undertaking the "heroic work" of producing a "new digest" of English law. He pointed to the large number of "ensnaring penal laws" on the statute book, acts which if ever executed would grind the subject "to powder." The statute law also contained other penal acts, "obsolete and out of use." These produced "a gangrene, neglect and habit of disobedience," which undermined the remaining "wholesome laws." The remaining "wholesome laws," moreover, had been rendered "so cross and intricate" by the "accumulation of statutes concerning one matter" that "the certainty of law" was now "lost in the heap."[18] Bacon's solution to these problems and scheme for the restoration of

---

[14] *Ibid.*, Aphorisms 65–71, pp. 101–3.
[15] *Ibid.*, Aphorism 54, p. 98.
[16] *Ibid.*, Aphorisms 55 and 57, p. 99.
[17] *Ibid.*, Aphorisms 59–64, pp. 100–1.
[18] Bacon, *A Proposition... touching the Compiling and Amendment of the Laws of England*, in *Works of Bacon*, XIII, 65.

certainty lay in a four-part program for the "reforming and recompiling of the Statute Law" – the Digest project, as it was later described in *De Augmentis Scientiarum*. Those statutes which had been made irrelevant "by alteration of time" were to be discharged to "the libraries for antiquities"; all the "sleeping" and disused acts were to be repealed; "the grievousness of the penalty" in the penal laws was to be "mitigated"; and all the other statutes, now "heaped upon one another," were to be systematically refashioned into "one clear and uniform law."[19]

In two important respects, which Bacon took care to make explicit, this proposal represented a restricted program of law reform. First, Bacon directly avoided the question of any substantive change in English legal policy. The purpose of the Digest was to give the law "light" rather "than any new nature," and accordingly the scheme did not address "the matter of the laws," but only "the manner of their registry, expression and tradition."[20] In the second place, Bacon dismissed the idea of using the Digest as a vehicle for transforming the common law into legislation. The common law did require several important reforms, and Bacon accordingly suggested that a separate common law digest be produced which would contain an improved collection of law reports and an authoritative set of legal treatises.[21] But he carefully distinguished this project from the more radical program of "ploughing up" the common law and "planting it again" in the form of statute. This he regarded as a "perilous innovation," scarcely worthy of serious consideration. The aim of the Digest was, after all, to restore legal certainty, and the folly of turning common law into legislation became obvious once it was realized that the *lex non scripta* already enjoyed far greater certainty than the statute law. "Sure I am," Bacon explained, "there are more doubts rise upon our statutes...than upon the common law," and hence, "I dare not advise to cast the law into a new mould."[22]

The eighteenth-century supporters of statute consolidation frequently found that their advocacy was best served simply by invoking "the words of Lord Bacon."[23] They did little to expand on the basic Baconian conception of a methodically revised and contracted statute book. Their chief concern rather was to stress that the arguments Bacon had advanced in support of this project had become all the more

---

[19] *Ibid.*, pp. 70–1.   [20] *Ibid.*, p. 63 and see p. 67.   [21] *Ibid.*, pp. 68–70.
[22] *Ibid.*, p. 67. For his other reform proposal, see Francis Bacon, "A Memorial touching the Review of Penal Laws and the Amendment of the Common Law," in *Works of Bacon*, XII, 84–6.
[23] Eden, *Principles of Penal Law*, p. 316. Eden's debts to Bacon are discussed below, chapter 10 at nn28–30.

cogent in consequence of parliament's subsequent legislative practice. The legislature, it appeared, had altogether ignored Bacon's strictures against excessive "loquacity and prolixity" in the "drawing" of statutes. As Bentham reported with a characteristic note of exasperation:

> Under the necessary burthen of increasing Laws, we suffer a stile of composition to remain perpetuated, by which... that burthen is twice or three times doubled, to the great discomforture of plain sense and reason, to the attracting of contempt and ridicule on what ought to be the subject of veneration, and to the signal frustration of those purposes for which Laws are made.[24]

Even more disturbing was the manner in which parliament's piecemeal and uneven amending of the statute law had rendered the statute book so confused and complicated that, in Bacon's phrase, "the certainty of law is now lost in the heap." In 1785 Samuel Romilly observed that the aggravation of the problem "since the time when Sir Francis Bacon wrote" might easily be "conjectured" from one "single circumstance": that "all the statutes prior to his time are comprised in two volumes, whereas those which have been passed since are hardly contained in eleven."[25] Two years later Francis Hargrave reiterated the point in more despairing terms. Since the time of Bacon "down to the present moment," he noted, "the body of our law has been suffered continually and rapidly to increase, with scarce any other aids to contract its bulk or preserve its consistency than those of an occasional private contribution." The expansion of the statute law had in fact been so dramatic that it now became possible to envisage that "moment" of national "ruin" when "the science of law and the administration of justice shall cease to be practicable."[26]

Whereas most legal writers were content simply to emphasize the enhanced importance of Bacon's recommendations for the eighteenth century, the period did witness several, more substantial, contributions to the literature on statute consolidation. Significantly, these tended to reinforce the more restrictive features of the Baconian project, particularly the basic supposition that statute consolidation did not entail any parliamentary interference with the common law.

Amongst the most prestigious of these works was Daines Barrington's weighty addition to the historical scholarship on English

---

[24] Bentham, UC lxxa. 64.
[25] Romilly, *Observations on Executive Justice*, p. 42n.
[26] Hargrave, *Collection of Tracts*, pp. xl–xli.

law, the *Observations on the More Ancient Statutes*. Barrington's study, which first appeared in 1766 and went through five editions by the end of the century, comprised a series of critical expositions on the principal acts of parliament from Magna Carta to the 1623 Statute of Infanticide. Barrington brought to this project considerable philological skills as well as an impressive command of comparative legal techniques, and much of the work's value lies in his successful treatment of the statute book as an historical source. But like so many other specimens of legal antiquarianism, Barrington's researches were also guided by a more practical objective, in this case, the cause of statute reform. As he announced in his prefatory remarks, his chief purpose "was to take notice of such acts of parliament from which no good effects could be expected."[27] It was this feature of the work which prompted Bentham, in a heavy-handed comparison with the *Commentaries*, to depict Barrington as "an active General in the service of the Public" who "storms the strongholds of chicane...and particularly fictions, without reserve."[28]

Despite Bentham's eagerness to prescribe Barrington's *Observations* as an "antidote" to Blackstone's "poisons," the two authors relied on each other's researches and shared a markedly similar attitude to the statute law, so much so that Barrington's more comprehensive and penetrating scrutiny of the statute book often reads as a detailed demonstration of Blackstone's general claims regarding the character and consequences of parliamentary law-making. This was especially the case where Barrington's researches revealed that parliament's enactments represented altogether superfluous and unnecessary additions to the common law. To demonstrate this was of course to argue the Blackstonean case. Such statutes indicated not only the legislators' failures to understand the common law, but also the common law's capacity to deal with such legal matters without the aid of legislation. On the basis of Barrington's work it appeared that the sort of problems Blackstone identified in contemporary legislation were already a feature of the statute law by the fifteenth century. Thus he remarked of an act of 1455 which made criminal thefts committed by servants at the time of their master's death, "there can be no doubt but that this was punishable by the common law." Another statute of the same year which enacted "that a bond extorted from a woman whilst under confinement shall be void," was questionable on precisely the same grounds: "there can be as little doubt but that any such deed so obtained was clearly void by common law." This type of law-making,

---

[27] Barrington, *Ancient Statutes*, p. iii.　　　　[28] *Fragment*, p. 420n.

he concluded, had "very prejudicial consequences," and could only be explained by supposing that "the drawing of acts of parliament was now in the hands of those who had not studied the law professionally."[29]

The same problem reappeared when Barrington considered the commonplace argument "that the preamble of a statute is the best key to its construction." This, in fact, often proved an extremely misleading "key" to the statute. "The most common recital" in these preambles was "*that doubts have arisen at common law,*" whereas such doubts "frequently never existed." The principal effect of "such preambles" was not to clarify the legislature's intentions, but to disrupt the legal system by "much" weakening "the force of the common law."[30]

Barrington's *Observations* also sharply confirmed the common complaints on the chaotic condition of the statute book as a whole. In the first place, Barrington indicated that the statute book contained material of doubtful authority. The so-called *Statutum Haiberniae de Coheredibus*, his leading example, was plainly not an act of parliament. But since the provision had been "inserted in every edition of the statutes for near three centuries together," it became "a question of some difficulty" now to claim that the measure had no legal force. The situation suggested that "the authority of legislature" had been somehow acquired by "the king's law-printers." This disturbing state of affairs was further perplexed by the fact that the ordinance was regularly marked "as *obsolete*" in printed editions of acts of parliament. However, since English law lacked any such doctrine as the Scottish rule that "a statute is said to lose its force by desuetude," this label of obsolescence was of no less dubious authority.[31] Thus it seemed that included within the statute law of England was obsolete legal material which had never been statute law in the first place.

At the same time, Barrington was even more concerned to draw attention to the large number of statutes which clearly were acts of parliament and which remained in force, even though they were completely antiquated. He singled out as a particularly appalling example the 1357 Statute of Herrings which, among other provisions, barred all inhabitants of Norfolk ("except the lords, masters and mariners") from buying nets or fish-hooks, and empowered the privy council to regulate the price of salted fish. "It is scarcely to be conceived," he impatiently remarked, "that a statute which proceeds upon such recitals should have continued so many centuries un-

---

[29] Barrington, *Ancient Statutes*, p. 370 and see p. 422.
[30] *Ibid.*, p. 353.   [31] *Ibid.*, p. 40.

repealed. "[32] Furthermore, as Barrington later pointed out, as long as these antiquated acts remained on the statute book, they might still be used as instruments for legal harassment, whatever the likely success of such malevolent actions. He was able to substantiate the danger by citing recent examples of vindictive prosecutions brought under the more oppressive and generally disused penal acts of the Tudor period.[33]

The frequent complaints against the careless wording and muddled drafting of acts of parliament received similar confirmation. Barrington's researches disturbingly suggested that basic features of English penal law derived from little more than straightforward mistranslations or dubious constructions of foreign terms.[34] These investigations further revealed the scarcely more comforting discovery "that the complaint of obscurity in the statute law" could not be confined "as it generally is" to the "modern acts of parliament." Indeed, against the standard of the ancient statutes, the modern acts appeared "infinitely more perspicuous and intelligible." Unfortunately, the improvement merely served to disclose all the more clearly the true stylistic fault of the modern acts, their insupportable "prolixity." Barrington ascribed this development to the "use of printing." When the legislature relied on manuscript copies of statutes, parliament was forced to consider the matter of "an unnecessary word." But once this incentive to succinctness was removed, English legislation swelled uncontrollably, since "a page or two additional in print neither adds much to trouble nor expense."[35]

Finally, Barrington's comprehensive review of the ancient statutes offered something of a rejoinder to the "prevailing vulgar errors with regard to what is supposed to be law." Just as his study drew attention to the more antiquated and absurd components of the statute law, so it at least also indicated the utter spuriousness of what was popularly thought to be included among the relics of English legislation. He therefore presented a lengthy catalogue of such "non-laws," which contained such splendid specimens as a penal act against killing crows within five miles of London, a statute prohibiting "the planting of vineyards," and an enactment specifying that Englishmen born at sea belonged to Stepney parish.[36] All these could safely be declared not part of England's statute law. But they were perhaps no more bizarre than the parliamentary provision addressed to the unqualified inhabitants of Norfolk who rashly embarked on the purchase of fish-hooks.

---

[32] *Ibid.*, p. 257. [33] *Ibid.*, pp. 500–2. [34] *Ibid.*, pp. 71–81, 243–47.
[35] *Ibid.*, pp. 174–5. [36] *Ibid.*, pp. 422–3n.

Barrington, of course, derived little comfort from his success at providing such extensive documentation in support of the frequent criticisms of the statute law. The contemporary habit of "treating modern statutes as being ill-penned and not having been properly considered" he regarded as "a very great impropriety." The practice was even "permitted every day in the courts of law;" and was certain to produce grave social consequences. If nothing else, "such ridicule eternally thrown upon" acts of parliament "is surely not inculcating a reverence to the laws."[37]

Maintaining the proper "reverence" to the law, however, was not Barrington's sole or most pressing anxiety. His chief concern was the manner in which the verbose, disorderly, antiquated and, on occasion, unintelligible contents of the statute book all but destroyed legal certainty by making it virtually impossible for the subject to know the law. As he noted with characteristic understatement, "it may almost be said that no man of business can go through life without subjecting himself to many prosecutions, when at the same time he was not conscious of having offended against any law whatsoever."[38]

The implications of all this historical erudition, legal scholarship and final pessimism were unmistakable. In a separate appendix Barrington turned directly to the required "reformation of the law." He advocated the appointment of "two or more serjeants or barristers" responsible for regularly reviewing the statute law and reporting on those statutes "which should either be repealed or reduced into one consistent act." Their report should then be inspected and revised by the privy council, the chancellor and master of the rolls, and the common law judges, before being sent to parliament for enactment. Upon the implementation of this scheme, Barrington estimated that the statute book could be easily reduced to half its size, thereby enabling the subject to "better know the law he is to be governed by."[39]

In the process of unveiling this positive program for statute consolidation, Barrington showed equal concern to make clear exactly what his proposal did not include. "By the term *reformation*" he did not mean "that there should be a new arrangement and institute of the whole body of the law, as in the time of *Justinian*, or a *Code Frederique*." What this analogy amounted to, as Barrington further explained, was that parliament was not to meddle with the common law. Even were such a scheme "practicable," he would not "presume to make any innovation with regard to what is founded in the deepest wisdom."[40]

---

[37] *Ibid.*, p. 116n.
[38] *Ibid.*, pp. 501–2.
[39] *Ibid.*, p. 503.
[40] *Ibid.*, p. 497.

As with Bacon, the case against using statute consolidation as a program for reforming the whole of English law was made by returning to the goal of maintaining legal certainty. It then became clear that the common law already enjoyed a satisfactory level of certainty, making any parliamentary intervention unnecessary if not dangerous. Whatever "ridicule" might be thrown upon "the law of England," this could never apply to "that constant, deliberate, and upright administration of justice" which distinguished the practice of "the different courts of this kingdom since the Revolution." The charge "that the law is uncertain" could scarcely be supported "when there is hardly a difference of opinion between the judges" and when "few writs of error" were brought against their judgments, "but for the purpose of delay." Moreover, it was equally evident that the procedures of the courts likewise required no amendment from the legislature. Although "some years ago" the "reproach" of excessive procedural delay "might have been made with propriety" against the court of King's Bench, now "no suitor ever waits beyond the ensuing term." Whatever problems existed in the practice at Chancery, these also could not "be prevented by any new rules" or "alteration of the practice." The elaborate and tedious progress of equity suits resulted from the special circumstances of each case and the demanding claims of "natural justice." And in any case, Barrington prudently recalled, "what are generally called delays" were in fact "absolutely essential to the liberties of a free country."[41]

These considerations Barrington believed sufficient "to obviate the objection" that "any alteration or new arrangement of the law ... should be of the most extensive nature." The required "alteration" in English law was thus strictly confined to the law of parliament's making:

> The reformation of the Code of Statutes, however, so far as to repeal obsolete and sometimes dangerous laws, as well as the reducing the different acts of parliament which relate to the same subject into one consistent statute, would be a salutary, nay is almost become a necessary, work.[42]

If Barrington's systematic examination of the bulk of "the more ancient statutes" appeared to rescue the common law from "ridicule" while reinforcing the case for statute law reform, much the same conclusion was reached by those authors who concentrated on individual topics in English law. A particularly pointed example of such research was presented by Richard Burn in his *History of the Poor*

---

[41] *Ibid.*, pp. 497–9, 499n.   [42] *Ibid.*, pp. 499–500.

Laws, with Observations, which was published in 1764, some ten years after the first edition of his famous justices' handbook. No less than Barrington's *Observations,* Burn's discussion proceeded under the firm conviction that the area of law being treated plainly demanded alteration and reform. "Something in the poor laws is wrong," he briskly announced, "which the wisdom of parliament for ages hath not been able to set right."[43] Again, like Barrington, Burn only approached the question of law reform by first exploring the history of the law in question, devoting the first part of his work to a lengthy survey of "what the laws for the poor were anciently in this kingdom." He anticipated his conclusions at the very outset, noting in the preface that the maxim "there is a time when old things shall become new" would be fully "verified" in the "following historical deduction."[44]

Burn's analysis of how the common law and ancient statutes regarded "vagrants," "servants, labourers and artificers," and "the impotent poor" produced what he considered the dramatic revelation "*that the statute of the* 43 Elizabeth *was not the first compulsive law for the maintenance of the poor.*" It had "been generally supposed" that the Elizabethan poor law "established an entirely new plan"; and owing to the "known abilities of Cecil and Walsingham and other great men of that age," many "arguments" were frequently advanced "in favour of the excellence of that scheme" and of "the difficulty" in "proposing a better." "But," Burn explained, "the matter lies still deeper." For the achievement of the Elizabethan poor law did not derive from its being "a sudden unpremeditated project of Queen Elizabeth's ministers." Rather, the statute succeeded because it was built on "the work of ages before, dictated by necessity and experience."[45] The same mistaken supposition could be shown also to obtain with regard to the alleged novelty of the Carolinian statute concerning settlements and removals.[46]

Repudiating the case for past legislative innovation, however, was not the only discovery afforded by Burn's historical researches. "Another thing very remarkable" became apparent: "*that almost every proposal which hath been made for the reformation of the poor laws hath been tried in former ages, and found ineffectual.*"[47]

The value of these historical insights was promptly exploited in the next section of the work, where Burn considered "the several schemes" for poor law reform advocated "by many private persons." Here he set out at length ten separate reform proposals, beginning with

---

[43] Richard Burn, *The History of the Poor Laws, with Observations* (London, 1764), p. 134.
[44] *Ibid.*, preface (n.p.).   [45] *Ibid.*, p. 104.
[46] *Ibid.*, pp. 106–9.   [47] *Ibid.*, p. 106.

the late seventeenth-century suggestions of Matthew Hale, including two parliamentary bills of 1753 and Henry Fielding's poor law tract of the same year, and concluding with Samuel Cooper's 1764 work, *Definitions and axioms relative to charity, charitable institutions and the poor laws*. As Burn pointed out in his observations, the shortcomings of all these programs were now immediately obvious. In the first place, virtually all the authors began improperly by taking "it for granted" that the Elizabethan poor law "was the first compulsory statute." This mistake was then compounded by their ignorance of the many unsuccessful measures parliament had already attempted in this area of law. Hence, their recommendations frequently comprised little more than "expedients" which "indeed had occurred to the legislature before."[48] Finally, where they did break new ground, these authors most often committed the crucial error, wisely avoided by Elizabeth's able ministers, of seeking to dismantle the ancient foundations of the poor law altogether. Thus, some entertained the repeal of "all the present laws relating to the poor," while others proposed "to abolish the whole doctrine of settlements." Such schemes were all "liable" to "one objection" – "that they aimed at too much at once" and "put too much to the hazard," in effect presenting parliament with an untested "remedy" which threatened to prove "worse than the disease."[49]

Burn accordingly thought it best to "let the present laws stand as to the main." Instead of attempting any radical program of poor law reform, he suggested two limited "alterations." He first urged parliament to enact a specific measure "to prevent the nuisance of *common begging*," and second, he recommended stronger local supervision of the "*overseers of the poor*."[50] But while these self-consciously moderated reforms would improve the policy of the poor laws, Burn maintained that it was "reasonable to advance further still speculation" and consider another implication of his researches. "The laws concerning the poor," he reported, "may not improperly be compared to their apparel." When the legislature detected a "flaw" in the law, "a patch" was "provided for it," and these patches had been so multiplied "till the original coat is lost amidst a variety of patch-work." Parliament had expended "more labour and time" on patching the poor law "than would have made an entire new suit." Burn accordingly also hoped that the opportunity would be found "to *reduce all the poor laws into one*."[51]

[48] *Ibid.*, p. 134.   [49] *Ibid.*, pp. 202–3.
[50] *Ibid.*, pp. 203, 210. For Burn's later thoughts on reform measures, see his *Bill for the Better Relief of the Poor*.   [51] Burn, *History of the Poor Laws*, p. 236.

Once Burn turned from the policy of the poor laws to the problems attending their registry on the statute book, he immediately went on to stress that the situation was by no means peculiar to this body of law. "The case," he explained, "is the same in almost all other instances, especially in those of greatest moment and most ordinary occurrence."[52] The laws "for making of good roads," for example, were now contained in "five and thirty" different acts of parliament, nearly "worse clouted and patched" than the roads they were designed to maintain. These acts were in such an "incredible" state of "confusion" that it was only by "laying all the statutes upon that subject together" that one could discover "what the law really is at present." Moreover, until these statutes were methodized or until someone conducted a careful investigation of the legislative history of the highway laws, such as that Burn undertook for the poor laws, it was not unlikely "that an act of parliament may be made to enact what is the law already, or to propose an expedient which has been already exploded."[53]

The acts "relating to the duties of excise" were likewise "confused beyond imagination." They comprised "about 130" separate statutes, "some of them extremely long and treating many different subjects at once." This law had also undergone "so many alterations" that it was now "exceeding difficult, if not altogether impossible precisely to determine" the excise duties "in many instances." The same strictures applied to the game laws, which equally needed to be revised and reduced "into some order and compass." Again, there was now an "abundance of statutes regulating matters between masters and their workmen," and these too "might easily be reduced into one general law."[54]

In presenting the case for such statute consolidation, Burn joined Barrington in explaining how the accumulation of statutes and the resulting complexity of law frequently frustrated the very purposes of parliament's enactments. But whereas Barrington pointed to the difficulties created for the subject in knowing the law, Burn concentrated on the no less daunting problems facing those responsible for its execution. Parliament, for instance, had passed so many acts expanding the powers of summary conviction possessed by justices of the peace that now "there is not one [justice] in ten who knows how to draw up a conviction in form, without a special precedent before him in every particular case."[55] The uneven progress of the legislature's enactments had left the justices further confused as to their powers "to compel witnesses to appear and give evidence in matters depending

[52] *Ibid.*, p. 236.   [53] *Ibid.*, pp. 236–7.
[54] *Ibid.*, pp. 268, 274, 288.   [55] *Ibid.*, p. 249.

before them."[56] The multitude of recent acts bearing on the vagrancy law presented the same problems, and Burn warned his fellow justices to be especially "cautious" in distinguishing "between what the law once was and what the law now is."[57] He himself had seen a tinker's license "solemnly signed and sealed by justices of the peace," that was "founded upon an act of parliament repealed above a hundred and fifty years before."[58]

Given these pressing difficulties, it was appropriate that Burn rehearsed the same argument for statute consolidation as the conclusion to his justices' handbook, noting that "the possibility and expediency of reforming the statute law" would have occurred "to every reader in perusing almost every one of the larger titles of this book." Each of these titles fully revealed how "very cumbersome and very intricate" the statute law had become "in process of time." Burn knew "but of one material objection" to the program, that it "would tend to unsettle all again, by breaking the connexion which there is between one statute and another." But this charge was scarcely compelling. The whole point was "that for the most part there is no connexion," and where it did exist, it might "easily be preserved." The project, he concluded, "seemeth no way impossible to be done," it merely required "a clear head and much patience."[59]

Both Barrington and Burn were at pains to emphasize the limits of their proposals for legal improvement. Barrington expressly excluded the common law from his program of legal "reformation," and Burn warned against any major innovations in the poor laws while pointing out that previous enactments proved most effective where they were rooted in the foundations of the ancient law. Moreover, in their pleas for statute consolidation both echoed Bacon's point that the scheme would not affect the "matter of the laws," but only the "manner of their registry." In addition to these points of restraint, a further, formidable dose of caution was introduced into the literature of statute law reform through Matthew Hale's *Considerations touching the Amendment or Alteration of Laws*. Hale's *Considerations* had, of course, been composed in the previous century, but they only reached publication in 1787 as part of Francis Hargrave's *A Collection of Tracts, Relative to the*

---

[56] *Ibid.*, p. 251 and see pp. 266–7.   [57] *Ibid.*, pp. 125–6.   [58] *Ibid.*, p. 117.

[59] Burn, *The Justice of the Peace and Parish Officer* (1754), 9th edn, 3 vols. (London, 1764), III, 567–8, and see I, viii. The difficulties created by parliament's expansion of the justices' duties was a common point of concern; see the discussion above, Introduction at nn62–4. Burn's argument for statute consolidation in order to ease the burden on the justices was later repeated in Thomas Gilbert, *Plan for the better Relief and Employment of the Poor* (London, 1781). I am indebted to Joanna Innes for this reference.

Law of England. And despite Hale's having failed to complete the work, his eighteenth-century editor still believed these "reflections" sufficient to "almost exhaust the subject."[60]

Hale's discussion centered on the claim that the same qualities which gave any system of customary law its special strength, in turn made the task of legal amendment and alteration a particularly taxing enterprise. "Antient laws," he explained, could not be considered the work "of this or that council or senate," but as "the production" of "various experiences and applications." "Day after day," "new remedies" had been applied to successive "new inconveniences," until these laws acquired "a kind of aggregation of the discoveries, results and applications of ages and events." Hence it became "a great adventure to go about to alter" them, unless this was done under a "very great necessity" and with "the greatest demonstration of safety and convenience imaginable."[61]

The same process of legal development also strengthened the cohesion and interdependence of the various parts of the legal system. It resulted in what Hale described as "a kind of aggregation and contignation in the fabrick of laws," in which "one piece" was "for the most part subservient unto and mortified in another." This again meant that "great knowledge" and "vast circumspection" was required "in every considerable alteration of the law." For if "the business were only to provide a plaister" to an isolated "sore," "the reformation of any law were very easy." But the "greatest business of a reformer" was "not only to see that his remedy be apposite," but that it "doth not introduce some other considerable inconvenience" or "takes not away some other considerable convenience" which "the former constitution" enjoyed. Thus, "the estimate that is to be made" had to be placed "upon the whole cargo," and "not upon this or that particular commodity."[62]

Hale did not intend these remarks to signify that the "laws of men" had to remain "fixed and unalterable." His concern was to explain why the law reformer needed to proceed "with great prudence, advice [and] care," and above all with "a full and clear prospect of the whole business."[63] Beyond these general insights, his analysis had two important implications specific to the situation in England. The first was to indicate the advantages of securing legal change through the usual agencies of customary law. In other words, Hale advised that

[60] Hargrave, *Collection of Tracts*, p. xxxvi.
[61] Hale, *Amendment of Laws*, p. 254.
[62] *Ibid.*, pp. 262–3, and see the similar comments in his preface to *Un Abridgment des plusieurs Cases et Resolutions del Common Ley...per Henry Rolle* (London, 1668), p. 3.
[63] Hale, *Amendment of Laws*, p. 270.

"what can be done by the power and authority of the court and judges" to reform "things amiss in the law," should always be undertaken "without troubling a parliament for such things."[64] Secondly, given the exacting demands facing all law reform, any major legislative changes in English law had to be supervised by "the judges and other sages of the law." No other individuals were "so fit to be employed" for this purpose, since none other knew "how far may be gone with safety and convenience." Not only were the judges and legal sages "to be employed in the first digestion of such a business," they should also participate in the parliamentary debates on their proposals. Otherwise, Hale warned, "it many times falls out, that a very good and profitable bill is suddenly spoiled with a word inserted or a word expunged, which would be prevented if the contrivers of the bill were first heard to it."[65]

In his own presentation, Hale did not dwell on the manner in which this analysis of law reform bore on the program for a consolidation of the statute law. Significantly, however, Francis Hargrave read his remarks precisely in these terms, and his particular contribution to the discussion was to yoke together Hale and Bacon as the posthumous collaborators behind an authoritatively endorsed program of legislative renewal. In his introduction to the tract, Hargrave immediately identified Hale's discussion with Bacon's account of legislative renewal in *De Augmentis Scientiarum*, and placed special stress on Hale's having "convinced himself" that "some remedy" had "become requisite" to "reduce and simplify our system" by "curing" the "disease of infinite accumulation." Like Bacon, Hale saw that the cure meant "lopping off antient redundancies" and "encouraging an orderly digest and a correct elucidation of all the remaining matter." His particular contribution was to identify the procedure and personnel required for this operation. Such a digest "could not be attained without the sanction of the legislature," but Hale properly recognized that neither could it "be effectuated in the best manner without an union of private labour in the extended vineyard of juridical learning." All that Hargrave needed to add was the reminder of how desperately more pressing Hale and Bacon's recommendation had since become:

> What would a Bacon or a Hale have said, what would they have advised, had they lived to have seen our statute law not only swelled already into more than tenfold size beyond that which so alarmed their apprehensions, but still yearly extending its dimensions by such a ratio as must soon

[64] *Ibid.*, p. 272.   [65] *Ibid.*, p. 273.

terminate in a bulk immeasurable by the most industrious and accomplished of legal understandings?[66]

In his analysis of legal certainty, Bacon had specified that legal value which later proponents of statute consolidation continued to place at the center of their proposals. But in Hargrave's response to Hale's discussion of legal amendment it becomes possible to discern a further set of legal doctrines which made statute consolidation such an attractive option for law reform in the eighteenth century. Here statute consolidation appeared as a programmatic embodiment of those legal assumptions which led common lawyers to question the capacity of the legislative office in the first place. The account of "antient laws" on the basis of which Hale approached the question of legal improvement was the same account deployed by common lawyers and judges to demonstrate the inherent superiority of common law over statute. This was an understanding of customary law for which Hale's other legal writings served as an authoritative source, and Hale had formulated his comments on positive law reform as a corollary to this legal theory.[67] This conception of customary law thus immediately indicated the mistaken "conceit" of imagining that law reform offered an opportunity for establishing a new system of law "as might be faultless, and exquisitely accommodate to the concerns of the whole community and of every member of it."[68] Instead, it showed that the law reformer had to approach his work with an overriding sense of caution and restraint.

As Hargrave readily perceived, the Baconian scheme for legislative improvement could be easily assimilated within Hale's more general and cautious strictures on law reform. For statute consolidation, while presenting the legislature with a positive strategy for law reform, offered parliament no new areas of law upon which to exercise its legislative powers. From this standpoint, the program was entirely backward-looking. Law reform was to be secured by having parliament correct by contracting and ordering the results of its previous legislative practice, but not by enlarging its legislative ambitions. At the same time – and here for Hargrave lay the special value of Hale's discussion – to press the case for statute consolidation was also to raise the question of who would serve as the statute consolidators. Once this question was introduced it became obvious that the individuals best

---

[66] Hargrave, *Collection of Tracts*, pp. xxxix–xli.
[67] See the discussion above, chapter 1 at nn58–64, and chapter 4 at n10.
[68] Hale, *Amendment of Laws*, p. 257.

equipped for the task were Hale's "judges and other sages of the law." As virtually all the supporters of statute consolidation from Bacon onwards agreed, the first stages at least of any systematic review and reordering of the whole statute book would have to occur outside the normal procedures of parliamentary law-making. Hale went further in maintaining that those responsible for drafting such law reforms would also have to share in the parliamentary discussion of these proposals.[69] And when these features of the Baconian program were placed in the foreground, it might seem that in addition to all its other virtues, statute consolidation provided the means for restoring the influence of common law wisdom on English legislation.

These more conservative features of statute consolidation were further disclosed in the concern displayed by so many advocates to stress just what was excluded from their measures of reform. Parliament was not to tamper with the common law, and statute consolidation itself would not affect the "matter" of the law, but only the "manner" of its formulation. Yet even this limited reform program could be thought to promise momentous gains, since so many of the complaints against English law had their source in the statute book's inconsistent terminology, voluminous disorder and perpetuation of obsolete legal relics. However, in one important area – penal law reform – the statute reformers tended to abandon their frequently rehearsed cautious restrictions. Here English lawyers showed greater readiness to look for guidance beyond their native legal authorities, and here any firm distinction between the "manner" and the "matter" of the law proved difficult to sustain. In their arguments for the reform of the penal statutes the traditional Baconian program of statute consolidation began to assume the figure of a Benthamic science of legislation.

[69] Barbara Shapiro points out that among seventeenth-century advocates of statute reform, Hale was atypical in advocating such a large role for the judges in the reform of the statute book; see "Law Reform in Seventeenth-Century England," p. 298.

10

◁ ═══ ▷

Penal law reform

In contrast with much of the material considered thus far, parliament's enactment of a voluminous and savage body of penal law as well as the contemporary criticisms of this legislation are relatively familiar features of eighteenth-century history, which have earned the attention of scholars not directly concerned with the technical history of English law. Radzinowicz began his monumental survey of the criminal law by charting the content of these enactments, the uneven and restrictive manner of their execution and the reformist penal theory which came to be articulated in condemnation of them.[1] More recently, social historians have examined the phenomenon of criminality itself, the law which defined it and the ideology evinced by it, and have found these matters "central to unlocking the meanings of eighteenth-century social history."[2] In these studies, as in the more traditional accounts, "this flood" of criminal legislation survives as "one of the great facts of the eighteenth century."[3]

The approach adopted in this study makes it possible to treat this "great fact" as an element in a larger set of developments in law and legal theory. From this standpoint, parliament's penal acts can be seen as another, clearly the most spectacular, manifestation of its emergence as an active law-making institution, while the doctrines of the penal reformers can be seen as another instance of legal speculation addressing itself to this development. Whatever the insights it might afford for understanding the enactment and enforcement of the criminal law, the perspective of this study is particularly valuable for considering the contemporary criticism it attracted. Against this background, the proponents of criminal law reform cease to appear as isolated figures in a "time of self-complacency."[4] Instead, their weighty attacks on the

---

[1] Radzinowicz, *History of English Criminal Law*, I, parts 1–3.
[2] Hay, "Property, Authority, and the Criminal Law," in *Albion's Fatal Tree*, p. 13. For other recent scholarship, see the studies discussed above, Introduction at n54 and n119.
[3] Hay, "Property, Authority, and the Criminal Law," p. 18.
[4] Maitland's phrase, cited above, Introduction at n26.

penal law can be identified with a more general preoccupation with the failures of the statute law, just as their own proposals for legal improvement can be identified with the traditional Baconian program for statute consolidation. To place the legal criticism of a William Eden or a Samuel Romilly within this broader context of legal orthodoxy is also to explain the extent of the hostility to the penal law among England's legal establishment, and why, for example, penal reform should have provided common cause for such an unlikely partnership as William Blackstone and Jeremy Bentham. In concentrating their objections on this particular area of law all these commentators were agreeing that England's criminal law had to be regarded as a further episode in the blunders of England's legislators. As Blackstone put it, parliament "perhaps inattentively" had enacted "a multitude of successive independent statutes upon crimes very different in their natures,"[5] and the result of such repeated inattentions was a clumsy assemblage of penal provisions distinguished by its bulky disorder, striking inconsistencies, glaring inhumanity and demonstrable ineffectiveness.

The production of this huge volume of penal acts was taken to reflect the same style of law-making as characterized parliament's legislative enterprises generally. Kames maintained that statutes were "commonly made with a view to particular cases," and nowhere did this seem so conspicuously the case as in matters of crime and punishment.[6] Whatever the frequency of the legislature's interventions, parliament's critics charged, this legislation did not result from any prolonged or methodical process of deliberation. Many of the brutal specimens of the penal statutes appeared as little more than reckless and impassioned reactions to particular outbreaks of crime or disorder. According to Samuel Johnson's judgment of 1751, even "a slight perusal" of the criminal law would reveal "such capricious distinctions of guilt" and "such confusion of remissness and severity" as to make it impossible to believe that it had been "produced by public wisdom, sincerely and calmly studious of public happiness." In fact, parliament simply provided "capital denunciations" whenever "any particular species of robbery" became "prevalent and common."[7] Thirty-five years later, Romilly raised the same objection in questioning whether England could be said to have a "system" of penal law in the first place. "System" seemed hardly appropriate for that "mass of jarring and

---

[5] 4 *Comm* 18.

[6] See above, chapter 8 at n6. J. M. Beattie's important recent contribution to the interpretation of the enactment of this capital legislation is discussed above, Introduction at nn118–26.

[7] Samuel Johnson, *The Rambler* (1750–52), ed. W. J. Bate and Albrecht B. Strauss, 3 vols. (New Haven, 1969), II, 242–3.

inconsistent laws" which "for the most part" were "the fruits of no regular design," but the "sudden and angry fits of capricious legislators."[8] Bentham, in turn, took the retrospective and myopic character of these statutes as symptomatic of parliamentary legislation as a whole, and accordingly starkly lampooned the practice of England's legislators:

> ...the Country Gentleman who has had his Turnips stolen, goes to work and gets a bloody law against stealing Turnips: it exceeds the utmost stretch of his comprehension to conceive that the next year the same catastrophe may happen to his Potatoes. For the two general rules...in modern British legislation are: never to move a finger till your passions are inflamed, nor ever to look further than your nose.[9]

In addition to these retrospective acts of legislative ferocity, a further mass of criminal law reached the statute book as a result of the frequent occasions on which parliament responded to legislative initiatives from outside. Not only were numerous penal laws enacted at the behest of particular trades and industries, it was also common for a wide variety of local acts, such as those for bridges or turnpikes, to be supplied with special penal clauses. The immediate impact of such provisions was confined to an individual legislative item, although in some areas these had become so extensive as virtually to constitute a comprehensive body of penal law. When William Eden discussed the offence of forgery in his 1771 *Principles of Penal Law*, he estimated that "there is hardly a case" of forgery "possible to be conceived" which had not "in the course of the present century been made a capital crime." This situation, however, did not derive from the passage of any general law regarding the crime, but from the accumulation of those "special clause[s] of forgery" enacted "upon the issuing of new bills of credit, lottery-orders, army-debencher, &c."[10] Blackstone likewise explained that England, in effect, had a general law declaring forgery a capital offence, for this "punishment is inflicted on the offender in many particular cases, which are so multiplied of late as almost to become general."[11]

As in other areas, these repeated yet independent legislative actions generated a shapeless body of statute law, exceedingly complex and frequently inconsistent. In the first place, as Eden pointed out, parliament's failure to review its legislation regularly meant that the statute book retained many provisions "originally not inconsistent

---

[8] Romilly, *Observations on Executive Justice*, p. 14.   [9] UC cxl. 92.
[10] Eden, *Principles of Penal Law*, pp. 295–6.   [11] 4 *Comm* 248.

with sound policy," but which had "long after" ceased "to be of any consequence to the interests of society." Thus, it was still a capital offence "to give corn, cattle or other consideration to the Scots for protection," or "to bring into the realm a Gally-halfpence," or to "knowingly receive, relieve or maintain Priests or Jesuits."[12] Alongside these legislative relics, Eden placed a large number of more recent enactments which had been adopted "on the spur of the occasion," and which at best might have produced some "temporary advantage." Parliament had again improperly allowed these "temporary" acts to become permanent features of English penal policy.[13] "The accumulation of sanguinary laws," he maintained, "is the worst distemper of a state," and hence no statute should "be suffered to remain a burthen upon the people" when "the grievance for which it was framed hath ceased and is forgotten."[14]

Parliament's episodic and unco-ordinated interventions, moreover, had introduced perplexing confusions and grotesque inconsistencies into the criminal law. Eden reported its being "a clergyable felony" to "destroy or damage the bridges of Brentford or Blackfriars," but it was "death to commit the same offence on the bridges of London, Westminster or Putney."[15] Bentham charged that "if a man kill your pig, you get the value of it," but if he killed your "child," "you get nothing."[16] Romilly pointed to similar anomalies. "To steal a sheep or a horse" or "to pick a man's pocket of the value of only twelve pence farthing" were "all crimes punishable by death." But for "a man to attempt the life of his own father" was "only a misdemeanor." The law made a felony of stealing fruit "ready gathered." But "to gather it and steal it is only a trespass." In sum, England's penal law comprised a "dreadful catalogue" of capital crimes, which included "transgressions which scarcely deserve corporal punishment" while it omitted "enormities of the most atrocious kind." Such laws, he concluded, "proclaim their own absurdity and call aloud for reformation."[17]

Finally, amidst all these difficulties, parliament had created a criminal law so verbose and so voluminous that, as Bacon warned, the "certainty of law" was now "lost in the heap."[18] When Blackstone discussed the mass of statutes which had removed the benefit of clergy from particular types of common law larceny, he immediately conceded

---

[12] Eden, *Principles of Penal Law*, pp. 311, 303–4.
[13] *Ibid.*, pp. 18, 305.   [14] *Ibid.*, pp. 305–6.
[15] *Ibid.*, p. 18.
[16] Bentham, *Essay on the Influence of Time and Place in Matters of Legislation, Bowring*, I, 187.
[17] Romilly, *Observations on Executive Justice*, pp. 16–24; and see Radzinowicz, *History of English Criminal Law*, I, 19–23, for further examples.
[18] See the discussion above, chapter 9 at n18.

that "the multiplicity" of these acts "is apt to create some confusion."[19] Eden condemned the same legislation in stronger terms, noting that the statutes were "so complicated in their limitations" and "so intricate in their distinctions" that "it would be painful" to attempt "the detail of them." Still, he could safely assert "without exaggeration" that, excepting those professionally trained in the law, "there are not ten subjects in England who have any clear perception of the several sanguinary restrictions to which on this point they are made liable."[20]

Legal commentators were already accustomed to acknowledging the singular multiplicity and complexity of English law, and as in other cases, the phenomenon was commonly explained in terms of the special demands on law posed by commercial opulence and the maintenance of English liberties.[21] Nevertheless, as Romilly argued at length, to allow the criminal law to become so intricate that it could be known only "by those who have leisure, capacity and inclination to apply themselves seriously and industriously to so laborious a study" was to defeat the very purposes of penal policy. The chief "objects of criminal laws" were those "hardy crimes which want and ignorance suggest." Thus, although each year "an immense volume of statutes" was "printed and publicly sold," it "might as well not exist." "The multitudes" to whom parliament addressed this legislation, "have not money to purchase it, time to peruse it, or capacities to understand the technical or mysterious language in which it is composed."[22] The legal maxim "that ignorance of the law shall not excuse" might be justified "on the ground of necessity." Yet, those like Romilly who "frequently" attended "the trials of prisoners" would know full well "that the presumption on which this maxim is founded is often contrary to fact."[23] Indeed, as Bentham noted, "the presumption is always so strong that an offender knew nothing of the matter."[24]

In emphasizing the manner in which parliament's legislative enterprises frustrated the certainty and notoriety of the criminal law, these critics were of course rehearsing precisely the same complaints as those advanced by the proponents of statute consolidation. As in the

---

[19] 4 *Comm* 241.   [20] Eden, *Principles of Penal Law*, p. 289.
[21] The commonly perceived relationship between liberty, social development and England's "multiplicity of laws," is discussed above, Introduction at nn66–9. For the more specific description of the effects of trade and opulence on the complexity and severity of the penal law, see Barrington, *Ancient Statutes*, pp. 399–402; Eden, *Principles of Penal Law*, p. 20; and Owen Ruffhead, *The Statutes of the Realm, from Magna Carta to the end of the Last Parliament, 1761*, 8 vols. (London, 1769), I, xxi.
[22] Romilly, *Observations on Executive Justice*, pp. 39–41.   [23] *Ibid.*, p. 45.
[24] UC lxxix. 69; Bentham's further comments are discussed below, chapter 12.

case of Barrington and Burn, much of their own positive strategy for legal improvement derived from the authoritative scheme for legislative correction formulated by Francis Bacon. Penal reform, at this level, constituted a conventional program for law reform as applied to a particular body of the statute law. Moreover, as was the case more generally, the Baconian project of legislative renewal had special appeal for those already convinced of the inevitable superiority of common law over legislation as a vehicle of legal development.[25] The situation was nicely caught in the terms of Michael Foster's 1762 criticism of the Jacobean Statute of Stabbing. Examining the act in the course of his authoritative *Discourses Upon a Few Branches of the Crown Law*, Foster condemned the statute as an unnecessary and excessive supplement to common law remedies. The legislation was, in fact, but one of many "of those Acts which, to borrow an Expression from Lord Bacon, was made *upon the Spur of the Times.*" In contrast, Foster promptly noted, "the Rules of the Common-Law in cases of this Kind may be considered as the Result of the Wisdom of many Ages."[26]

Bacon himself, in making the case in the 1610s on behalf of his own Digest project, had singled out those "obsolete" and "ensnaring" penal acts which disgraced the statute book.[27] This enabled later commentators like Eden and Romilly directly to invoke Bacon's testimony while explicitly subscribing to the principles of *De Augmentis Scientiarum*. Eden expressly joined Bacon in demanding the repeal of all the "obsolete and useless statutes" and all the antiquated and barbarous penalties which "the tacit disapprobation of mankind" had consigned "to disregard and oblivion."[28] He further urged parliament to adopt the "*general rule to give at first a temporary duration only to all new laws which are capitally penal,*" so as to prevent the future accumulation of sanguinary laws.[29] In considering the proper procedure for "the composition and promulgation" of the criminal law, Eden again returned to Baconian strictures. As directly opposed to parliament's present practice, these laws had to be "clearly obvious to common understandings." And this meant, as "was well observed by Lord Bacon," that "the mandatory clause ought always" to introduce "the statute," that "those tedious preambles" should be entirely abandoned, and that the general legislative "stile" should "be clear, and as concise, as is consistent with clearness." It would have been "easy" for Eden

---

[25] See, for example, the contribution of Francis Hargrave, discussed above, chapter 9 at n66–n69.

[26] Michael Foster, *A Report of some Proceedings on the Commission of Oyer and Terminer ... to which are Added Discourses Upon a Few Branches of the Crown Law* (London, 1762), p. 299.

[27] See the discussion above, chapter 9 at n18.

[28] Eden, *Principles of Penal Law*, pp. 19, 67. [29] *Ibid.*, p. 259.

"to pursue this subject to a very considerable length," but he preferred instead to "conclude" with "the words of Lord Bacon."[30]

Romilly equally insisted that before there might be any effective "prevention of crimes," "a total revision and reformation of our penal laws" was "essentially requisite." Like Barrington earlier, he quickly went on to explain that in calling for a "reformation" of the law he had not charged parliament with the task of composing "a perfect criminal code." He looked to the legislature only for the correction "of the grossest absurdities in our laws," by making the penal acts "much less inconsistent, much less obscure and much less inhuman."[31]

At the same time, the penal reformers were even more agitated by a further feature of parliament's criminal legislation: its unbounded enthusiasm for the death penalty. Whenever England's legislators were prompted to intervene in this area of law, their efforts virtually always ended in subjecting another class of actions to what Johnson termed "the severest punishment that man has the power of exercising upon man."[32] Blackstone thus reported the "melancholy truth" that there were now "no less than an hundred and sixty" offences which parliament declared "to be worthy of instant death."[33] Bentham likewise observed that in England "a man may be hanged" for "fifty reasons" which "he never could have thought of."[34] Romilly caustically noted that "every novice in politics" was permitted "to try his talents for legislation by dealing out death among his fellow-creatures."[35] Owen Ruffhead, the publisher of *The Statutes of the Realm*, found he could not avoid the remark "that our Statute Laws" seemed "to breathe too much the Spirit of *Draco*'s, all degrees of offence being confounded and all proportion of punishment destroyed."[36]

In their attacks on parliament's devotion to the death penalty England's penal reformers tended to turn from native legal authorities and instead invoke what Romilly described as the "humane and rational principles" of criminal jurisprudence elaborated in Europe "within the last twenty years."[37] The figure whose "rational principles" they most frequently and extensively embraced was Cesare Beccaria, the celebrated Milanese aristocrat who, according to

[30] *Ibid.*, pp. 306, 312–13, 316; and see pp. 19, 21, 296, for further references to Bacon's discussion.
[31] Romilly, *Observations on Executive Justice*, pp. 105–7.
[32] Johnson, *The Rambler*, II, 243.
[33] 4 *Comm* 18   [34] UC lxxix. 74.
[35] Romilly, *Observations on Executive Justice*, p. 43.
[36] Ruffhead, *Statutes of the Realm*, I, xxi.
[37] Romilly, *Observations on Executive Justice*, pp. 1–2.

Bentham's effusive report of 1776, "was received by the intelligent as an Angel from heaven would be by the faithful."[38]

An English translation of Beccaria's *Dei delitti e delle pene* appeared in 1767, three years after its first publication in Italy. By 1775, the English version had reached a fourth edition, soon to be supplemented by two different "new editions" published in Edinburgh in 1778. The work began with a momentous challenge to Europe's legislators. Hitherto, Beccaria reported, laws had been "the work of the passions of a few" or "the consequences of a fortuitous or temporary necessity." What was now required, in "this enlightened age," were laws fashioned "by a cool examiner of human nature, who knew how to collect in one point, the actions of a multitude, and had this only end in view, *the greatest happiness of the greatest number.*"[39]

Beccaria dismissed the barbarous notion that punishment was designed "to torment a sensible being" or "to undo a crime already committed." Punishment could be inflicted legitimately for "no other" purpose "than to prevent others from committing the like offence."[40] As he went on to show, this principle immediately repudiated a wide range of contemporary penal practices.[41] But that part of his analysis which most concerned English reformers was the demonstration that this deterrence theory did not license an unlimited "severity of punishments." Indeed, such severity not only violated the dictates "of enlightened reason," but also could be shown to prove ultimately "useless."[42]

In the first place, Beccaria maintained that "cruel" and "very severe" punishments had a corrupting influence on society as a whole. "As punishments become more cruel," "the minds of men" grew "hardened and insensible" – within but "an hundred years," the "*wheel*" terrified "no more than formerly the *prison.*" Moreover, where "punishments be very severe," offenders were "naturally led" to the "perpetration" of further crimes "to avoid the punishment due to the first." Accordingly, those nations "most notorious for severity of punishments" were invariably the setting for "the most bloody and inhuman actions and the most atrocious crimes." In such places, "the hand of the legislator and the assassin were directed by the same spirit of ferocity."[43]

In addition to these pernicious social effects, "the severity of

---

[38] *Fragment*, p. 403n. The other continental jurist whose authority was regularly cited in this context was Beccaria's "immortal Montesquieu"; see Cesare Beccaria, *An Essay on Crimes and Punishments, translated from the Italian* (1767), 3rd edn (London, 1770), p. 4.

[39] Beccaria, *Crimes and Punishments*, pp. 2–3.   [40] *Ibid.*, pp. 43–4.

[41] See, for example, his examination of torture at p. 60.

[42] *Ibid.*, p. 12.   [43] *Ibid.*, p. 99.

punishment" proved altogether unnecessary to the successful realization of penal policy. Beccaria's psychological theory revealed that "crimes are more effectively prevented by the *certainty*, than the *severity* of punishment." It was "the nature of mankind to be terrified at the approach of the smallest inevitable evil," and hence "the certainty of a small punishment" made "a stronger impression" than "the fear of one more severe, if attended with the hopes of escaping."[44] Therefore, the wise legislator, who knew how to erect "his edifice on the foundation of self-love," sought to achieve such certainty in the operation of criminal justice that "the two ideas of *Crime* and *Punishment*" came to "be considered, one as the cause and the other as the unavoidable and necessary effect."[45] Once this primary objective of penal certainty was secured, all that was required to prevent offences was that the "*evil*" of the penalty "should exceed the *good* expected from the crime." "All severity beyond this," Beccaria concluded, "is superfluous and therefore tyrannical."[46]

There was much in Beccaria's discussion to flatter an English audience, and this must in part account for the popularity of his treatise. But, more important was the extent to which in England, as elsewhere, Beccaria often preached to the converted.[47] His basic principle that human punishments were designed for deterrence and not retribution was already English legal orthodoxy. Those features of the legal system which Beccaria defended in the interest of legal certainty were already conventionally glorified in England as the guardians of liberty.[48] Moreover, a large body of testimony had already been assembled to condemn what Bacon had styled "the greviousness of the penalty" in England's penal laws.[49] Those, for example, who attacked parliament's readiness to make capital crimes out of mere violations of property made good use of Beccaria's doctrines. But they did not forget also to mention the instructive example of Thomas More's sagacious Utopians.[50]

Thus, it was not the novelty of Beccaria's principles, but the

---

[44] *Ibid.*, p. 98.   [45] *Ibid.*, pp. 176, 76.   [46] *Ibid.*, pp. 99–100.

[47] Contemporary responses to Beccaria's treatise are surveyed by Peter Gay in *The Enlightenment: An Interpretation* (London, 1967–70), II, 438, 445–7, and by Franco Venturi in *Italy and the Enlightenment*, ed. Stuart Woolf (New York, 1972), pp. 154–64. For more detailed treatment, see the recent studies by David Young, "Let Us Content Ourselves with Praising the Work While Drawing a Veil Over its Principles: Eighteenth-Century Reactions to Beccaria's *Crimes and Punishments*," *Justice Quarterly* I (1984) 155–69, and "Property and Punishment in the Eighteenth Century: Beccaria and his Critics," *American Journal of Jurisprudence*, XXXI (1986) 121–35.

[48] See, for example, Blackstone's account at 4 *Comm* 377–8.

[49] See the discussion above, chapter 9 at n19.

[50] See, for example, Johnson, *The Rambler*, II, 247, and Blackstone, 4 *Comm* 238.

comprehensiveness and penetration of his analysis which made his
work so useful and valued. The ease with which his discussion could
be accommodated within English legal conventions was perhaps best
displayed by the author who first made systematic use of his reforming
doctrines: the "learned Commentator" on the Laws of England.

Blackstone's general observations on "crimes and punishments"
comprised a chapter-length introduction to the fourth volume of the
Commentaries on "public wrongs." Here the law's most eloquent
apologist promptly noted that "even with us in England," where the
criminal law had "more nearly advanced to perfection," "we shall
occasionally find room to remark some particulars that seem to want
revision and amendment." These defects had resulted from "too
scrupulous an adherence" to some "ancient common law" rules, from
the failure to repeal what was "obsolete and absurd" in "the old penal
laws," and especially "from too little care and attention in framing and
passing new ones." Nowhere was this lack of care more evident than
in "the enacting of penalties" and in parliament's application of
"the same universal remedy, the *ultimum supplicium*, to every case of
difficulty."[51] Accordingly, much of Blackstone's discussion was
directed to showing that "though the end of punishment is to deter
men from offending, it can never follow from thence, that it is lawful
to deter them at any rate and by any means."[52] He expressly addressed
these comments to "such as are, or may hereafter become, legislators,"
and in so doing he regularly recorded his indebtedness to that
"ingenious writer," Cesare Beccaria, who had "well studied the
springs of human action."[53]

The first part of Blackstone's argument against excessive penal
severity, and the occasion for much the most pointed declamation in
the *Commentaries*, was a reminder to the legislators of the daunting
moral gravity of the death penalty itself. "To shed the blood of our
fellow-creature" required "the greatest deliberation and the fullest
conviction of our own authority," and hence "every humane
legislator" would be "extremely cautious of establishing laws that
inflict the penalty of death, especially for slight offences." He would
certainly demand "a better reason" for doing so, than "that loose one
which generally is given" that "no lighter penalty" was thought
"effectual." If, Blackstone warned, it were found that the legislators
had abused "the extent of their warrant" by sanctioning a needless
"effusion of human blood," then "the guilt of blood" had to "lie at

[51] 4 *Comm* 1, 3–4, 17.   [52] 4 *Comm* 10.   [53] 4 *Comm* 11, 16–17.

their doors," and "not at the doors of the subject" who was but "bound" to the laws "given by the sovereign power."[54]

Happily, these "dictates of conscience and humanity" coincided with prudent penal policy.[55] The most effective means of preventing offences was through the application of "more merciful" penalties, "properly intermixed with due distinctions of severity."[56] Thus, "as a conclusion to the whole," Blackstone presented Beccaria's dictum that what most deterred criminal acts was the "*certainty*" and not the "*severity*" of punishment." This insight further revealed, Blackstone next explained, that parliament's wanton extension of the death penalty was not only, in Beccaria's words, "superfluous and therefore tyrannical," but it actually increased "the number of offenders." For "so dreadful a list" of capital crimes made the certain execution of the penal law altogether impossible, and criminal justice inevitably became an extensive system of evasion and legal disruption. The victims of crime "through compassion" chose not to prosecute, jurors "through compassion" acquitted the guilty, and judges "through compassion" recommended half of those convicted for royal mercy. "Among so many chances of escaping," the "hardened offender" naturally overlooked "the multitude that suffer" and the fitful severity of the law which "long impunity has taught him to condemn."[57]

Once it became apparent, as Blackstone argued, that the very severity of the penal acts precluded the certainty of their execution, then it became necessary for the penal reformers to move beyond the traditional program for statute consolidation.[58] The Baconian Digest could restore legal certainty in regard to the expression and notoriety of the law, but not in regard to its execution. Legal certainty in this latter respect was dependent on the systematic moderation of parliament's legislative excesses. Thus, to adopt Bacon's formula, criminal law reform had to involve both the "manner" and the "matter" of the law.[59] Moreover, as the debate on penal reform developed, controversy focused on what

---

[54] 4 *Comm* 10–12.   [55] 4 *Comm* 11.   [56] 4 *Comm* 16.

[57] 4 *Comm* 16–9. See also Blackstone's bitter condemnation of the game laws at 4 *Comm* 174–5, 415–16, and his strictures against the severity of the acts against smuggling at 1 *Comm* 317.

[58] The relatively infrequent execution of the full severity of the capital statutes has received considerable attention. See the contrasting accounts presented by Radzinowicz, *History of English Criminal Law*, I, 83–164; by Hay, "Property, Authority, and the Criminal Law," pp. 22–3; by Beattie, *Crime and the Courts*, pp. 400–49; and by Thomas A. Green, *Verdict According to Conscience. Perspectives on the English Criminal Trial 1200–1800* (Chicago, 1985), pp. 267–317.

[59] See the discussion above, chapter 9 at n20.

the Rev. Martin Madan in 1785 referred to as this "fashionable" proposal to mitigate "the number and severity" of the penal acts in the interests of legal certainty.[60] This, in effect, meant that it was that part of the reformers' program which fell outside the rubric of statute consolidation which was receiving most attention and which, as a result, came to acquire enhanced importance.

The development can be charted in three accounts of England's system of criminal justice which appeared in 1785 and 1786: William Paley's *The Principles of Moral and Political Philosophy*, Martin Madan's *Thoughts on Executive Justice*, and Samuel Romilly's *Observations* on Madan's tract.[61] Significantly, each of these authors endorsed the same principles regarding the ethics of punishment and the nature of its efficacy. Paley's *Principles* naturally provided the setting for the most elaborate discussion of the utilitarian arguments for the application of punishment, and like other commentators, Paley also held that in preventing crimes "the *certainty* of punishment is of more consequence than the severity."[62] Unlike Blackstone, however, Paley found nothing in these penal doctrines to call into question "the wisdom and humanity" of parliament's penal legislation. By the multiplication of capital statutes, the legislature swept "into the net every crime" which might on occasion "merit the punishment of death." But in passing these laws it did not intend the "indiscriminate execution" of this penalty, only that "a small proportion" of convicted offenders would be "singled out" as "fit examples of public justice." As a result, England's criminal law properly provided the ultimate terror through which to deter virtually every crime, while the selective application of this penalty rescued the law from "the charge of cruelty."[63]

Paley's discussion was especially valuable for its assessment of parliament's intentions in enacting the "bloody code."[64] However, it was not so much the question of legislative motivation as the actual effectiveness of this policy which exercised Paley's contemporary adversaries. Still, it remained perfectly possible to be convinced that the

---

[60] Martin Madan, *Thoughts on Executive Justice, with respect to our Criminal Laws* (London, 1785), p. 7.

[61] As Beattie explains, these publications appeared during a perceived "crisis of violent crime" of the mid-1780s. Paley's *Principles of Moral and Political Philosophy*, based on lectures delivered in Cambridge between 1768 and 1776, had of course been composed earlier; see Beattie, *Crime and the Courts*, pp. 582–92.

[62] Paley, *Moral and Political Philosophy*, p. 549.

[63] *Ibid.*, pp. 533–4. For an earlier, like-minded treatment of England's penal system, see Wynne, *Eunomus*, III, 240, 250–1.

[64] See Hay, "Property, Authority, and the Criminal Law," pp. 25–6, and Beattie, *Crime and the Courts*, pp. 592–601.

random execution of the full severity of the capital acts failed to prevent crime and resist the call for legislative correction. The obvious alternative was pressed with gruesome conviction by Madan in his *Thoughts on Executive Justice*. Madan was certain that England now suffered an epidemic of "the most dangerous and atrocious crimes,"[65] and that "one reason, and only *one*" could account for this. Punishment had been rendered "so *uncertain*" by the regime of judicial leniency laced with royal pardons that the criminal law was reduced to "little more than a *scarecrow*."[66] Since "all writers on the subject of laws," ancient and modern, "all contend for the certainty of punishment," the only reform required for the effective prevention of crime was the rigorous application of all the capital statutes in all possible cases.[67] If parliament had "annexed *death* to the commission of certain crimes," then those constitutionally charged with the execution of the law had to "dispense it" to "all who are the plain, clear and determinate objects of it."[68]

In his reply to Madan, Romilly returned to the doctrines of Beccaria, presenting, as Blackstone had done, the moral and prudential arguments against excessive penal severity, and cataloguing, as Eden had done, the manifest and extensive defects in England's criminal laws. Like Eden, he advocated the systematic consolidation of the penal statutes so as to restore their certainty of expression and notoriety. But in the light of Paley and Madan's recent publications, he dealt with the issues raised by the severity and execution of the capital statutes far more explicitly in terms of a program for the legislature than had previous parliamentary critics. To counter Madan's interpretation of parliament's extension of the death penalty, he adopted Paley's judgment that the legislators had not designed these acts to be "always executed with the utmost severity" in all cases and further claimed that the judiciary's "established usage" in mitigating capital sentences now constituted "the legal and established mode of executing the law."[69] But unlike Paley, Romilly had little patience for the alleged wisdom of a legislative policy which allowed the "same punishment on a pick-pocket as on a parricide," and therefore called for "a more permanent and a more certain correction" than that supplied by judicial recommendations for royal pardons.[70] The chief object of the legislator, he stressed, was "to render laws respected and efficacious," which could only be achieved

---

[65] Madan, *Executive Justice*, p. 4.   [66] *Ibid.*, pp. 34, 18.
[67] *Ibid.*, pp. 131–2.   [68] *Ibid.*, pp. 115–16, 104–5.
[69] Romilly, *Observations on Executive Justice*, pp. 70–73. Romilly abandoned this position in his 1810 proposals for penal reform; see Radzinowicz, *History of English Criminal Law*, I, 320, 325–6.
[70] Romilly, *Observations on Executive Justice*, p. 4.

when those laws were "strictly executed." "But a far more indispensable requisite to that end" was that the laws themselves "be wise and just." Hence, the unmistakable task which lay before England's legislators was to "render" their penal acts in such a condition "that all the wise and honest will join their wishes and contribute their exertions to have them observed, and not leave them armed with such severities that nature tells one it is a virtue to disappoint and to prevent their execution."[71]

In addition to this insistence that penal reform had to address the "matter" of the statute law, Romilly entertained other legal improvements which clearly could not be met by statute consolidation alone. Like earlier commentators, he cited various "defects" in the administration of criminal justice which frustrated legal certainty. He lamented "the great length of time which is suffered to elapse between the crime and the punishment,"[72] while Eden protested against the "extreme of scrupulousness and over-grown nicety" in maintaining technical procedural forms which often obstructed the conviction of the guilty.[73] Romilly also observed that further measures were required to control the "thousand sources of profligacy and encouragement to vice" which surrounded those "helpless creatures" who committed criminal acts.[74]

These observations, at least in their implications, entailed far more radical penal reforms than those only addressed to the "matter" of the penal acts. In questioning the time-consuming intricacies of criminal procedure, these authors challenged what Blackstone had depicted as those "delays and little inconveniences" which lay at the heart of "our constitution" and through which Englishmen paid "for their liberty."[75] In drawing attention to the social conditions which encouraged "vice," they raised the awkward question whether crime could ever be effectively prevented through the mere terror of mild yet certain punishments. Nevertheless, these remarks generally appeared as after-thoughts, and they never blocked the primary objective to secure the ends of penal policy by ridding the criminal statutes of their obscurity, inconsistency and counter-productive severity. Certainly, for example, neither Romilly nor Eden embraced Henry Fielding's argument that the effects of trade had so transformed the "commonalty" of England that lawlessness could now be

---

[71] *Ibid.*, pp. 87–8. For Eden's corresponding analysis of the counter-productive severity of the penal acts, see *Principles of Penal Law*, pp. 13–14, 290–92, 317–20.

[72] Romilly, *Observations on Executive Justice*, p. 109.

[73] Eden, *Principles of Penal Law*, p. 181. See also Barrington, *Ancient Statutes*, pp. 220–1.

[74] Romilly, *Observations on Executive Justice*, p. 94.

[75] 4 *Comm* 350, 280–2, and see the discussion above, chapter 2 at n18.

controlled only through an extensive and co-ordinated scheme of criminal prevention and detection involving substantial alterations in the administration and execution of the criminal law.[76]

It is possible, as Radzinowicz has done, to view the failure of Eden and Romilly to see beyond the immediate defects of the penal statutes as reflecting "important limitations" in "the doctrines of the penal reformers."[77] However, there is no reason to suppose any lack of legal imagination or reforming ambition behind these perceived "limitations." Instead, we should consider what these restraints indicate about the attitude of Eden and Romilly to the legislative office itself. Both reformers engaged in a vigorous and comprehensive critique of English penal law. They began at the very foundations of penal policy, delineated what Romilly termed the "axioms of criminal law" and concluded with a reform program which they laid before their legislators.[78] As on the continent, criminal jurisprudence provided a classic instance of moral and social theory formulated as legislative science, and in England at least, this mode of legal speculation contrasted in important ways with the more traditional forms of statute criticism.

Daines Barrington, as we have seen, also undertook a systematic examination of English legislation. But the practical objective he gave to this investigation was the identification of antiquated legislative provisions. Hence, where Barrington argued against the policy of the statute law, he referred to acts already discarded through obsolescence.[79] The penal reformers, however, condemned statutes of an all too recent vintage so that the statutes whose repeal they urged could not be placed under the convenient category of obsolete legal matter. Moreover, the criteria by which they condemned these acts again contrasted with more conventional forms of legal criticism. Richard Burn, for example, had also attempted a methodical and comprehensive analysis of the existing regulations on the poor. But he followed a familiar route by turning first to the historical foundations of the poor law, finding in the ancient constitution the appropriate standards by which to judge parliament's more recent legislative efforts.[80] Eden and Romilly looked elsewhere for guidance. They derived their "axioms of criminal law" directly from the ethical first principles of punishment

---

[76] See Fielding, *Enquiry into the Late Increase of Robbers*. See also Beattie's account of the eighteenth-century initiatives in support of the "Reformation of Manners," in *Crime and the Courts*, pp. 494–500.

[77] Radzinowicz, *History of English Criminal Law*, I, 318.

[78] Romilly, *Observations on Executive Justice*, p. 3.

[79] See the discussion above, chapter 9 at n27 and n38–n39.

[80] See the discussion above, chapter 9 at n45–n49.

and from the psychology of human nature which determined its effectiveness. They found little instruction in native legal antiquities. Eden introduced his *Principles* with a brief sketch of the "origin" of penal legislation. But for the remainder of his discussion he simply "assumed" a "period of improved civilization."[81] And Romilly more aggressively identified his treatise with those recently discovered "humane and rational principles" of criminal jurisprudence which had altogether "exploded" the "absurd and barbarous notions of justice which prevailed for ages."[82]

Implicit, then, in the investigations of Eden and Romilly was an ambitious and potentially radical conception of the legislative capacity. They freed the legislator from a barbarous past and supplied him with a legal theory on the basis of which he could confidently reconstruct a coherent and humane system of penal jurisprudence. Yet, in their specific proposals to parliament they observed considerable restraint. They noted defects in the procedures guiding criminal prosecutions, but they did not look to the legislature for any fundamental revision of this part of the penal system. Nor did they attempt to apply their more general legal doctrines to other areas of English law. Eden, for example, insisted "that the laws be clearly obvious to common understandings and fully notified to the people."[83] But he did not presume to consider how much of England's customary law could satisfy this requirement. Romilly, moreover, expressly discounted the notion of calling upon parliament "to compose a perfect criminal code."[84] Whatever the breadth and potential of their legal theory, the attention of Eden and Romilly remained firmly fixed on the immediate chaos and severity of the existing penal acts. By concentrating their proposals on the revision of the existing statute law, they joined the advocates of statute consolidation in construing law reform chiefly as a matter of correcting the past mistakes of England's legislators. If their substantive proposals went beyond statute consolidation, this was the product not so much of any desire to broaden the scope of parliamentary legislation as of their acute consciousness of the damage that had already been done by parliament. It was indeed precisely those proposals, which would have demanded more ambitious or novel legislative action, that were conspicuously absent from their program.

Blackstone's own contribution to the critique of England's criminal

---

[81] Eden, *Principles of Penal Law*, p. 3.
[82] Romilly, *Observations on Executive Justice*, p. 2.
[83] Eden, *Principles of Penal Law*, p. 312.
[84] Romilly, *Observations on Executive Justice*, p. 106.

law doubtless most fully reveals the more orthodox features of the reformers' position. His "plea for reform of the laws of crimes and punishments" has frequently seemed a surprising deviation from his "settled and complacent views."[85] But, as should now be plain, there was nothing in Blackstone's disparagement of the penal law to undermine his assessment of the general condition of English law, or to compromise the criterion by which he celebrated the English legal system. The penal acts simply provided another weighty body of evidence to demonstrate the destructive impact of the statute law, while the reforming doctrines of the *philosophes* provided further material for the instruction of England's reckless legislators. Indeed, it was even possible to view the penal law as something of a further triumph for the common law judges. As Romilly observed, whatever humanity and reason obtained in English criminal justice, this was owing to the efforts of the judges in mitigating the barbarity of parliament's enactments.[86] Or, as Blackstone alleged, had "reference" been made to "the learned judges," it was "impossible that in the eighteenth century it could ever have been made a capital crime" to "cut down a cherry-tree in an orchard."[87] Both the criminal law and the contemporary criticism of it thus could be accommodated easily and tidily within the common lawyer's conventional contrast between the wisdom of the common law and the failures of statute.

Nevertheless, soon after Blackstone introduced Beccaria's testimony into the discussion of English penal law in 1768, another of Beccaria's English enthusiasts, Jeremy Bentham, also embarked upon a critical analysis of England's criminal jurisprudence. And by the time that Romilly in 1786 reiterated and expanded Blackstone's arguments, he had developed a scheme for legislation which effectively shattered all the restraints and cautions which parliament's other critics brought to their proposals for legal improvement. The campaign began when Bentham turned their arguments for legal certainty and public happiness against the common law itself.

---

[85] Thomas Green's phrasing in Blackstone, *Commentaries: Facsimile of the First Edition*, IV, iii (editorial introduction). See also Green's valuable discussion of Blackstone's penal doctrines in *Verdict According to Conscience*, pp. 294–7.

[86] Romilly, *Observations on Executive Justice*, pp. 3–4.   [87] 4 *Comm* 4.

IV

Bentham

11

◁ ══ ▷

The critique of Common Law

What of all earthly pursuits is the most important? Legislation was the answer Helvetius gave. "Have I a genius for legislation?" I gave myself the answer fearfully and tremblingly – Yes![1]

The studied melodrama with which the elderly Bentham recalled the original discovery of his "genius for legislation" may well reflect more accurately the temperament of the aging jurist than the actual details of his youthful intellectual development. Nonetheless, it is clear that early in his twenties Bentham embarked on a project which was to occupy more than fifty years' effort, yet remain unfinished when he died in 1832. This was the creation of a "*Pannomion*" – a body of law complete in all its branches.[2]

The rest of this study is addressed to Bentham's early conception of the science of legislation, and the critique of common law around which so much of that conception was formed. From this standpoint, the previous discussion of eighteenth-century legal theory can be viewed as in part designed to recover the correct historical setting for Bentham's own doctrines. Indeed, it now becomes apparent that when Bentham began his legal theorizing in the 1770s by assessing the rival claims of common and statute law, he was entering into a well-rehearsed argument. For him, as for Blackstone and his contemporaries, the relationship between common law and legislation represented a basic problem for legal theory, and a focus for more practical questions regarding the appropriate instruments for legal improvement in England. It is clear that Bentham sought to resolve these problems in a manner strikingly at odds with contemporary legal conventions, and the approach adopted here enables us to chart these departures with considerable precision. However, the first point must be to stress that

---

[1] *Bentham Memoirs, Bowring*, X, 27.
[2] See *Morals and Legislation*, p. 305, for the first published usage.

it was in his projected solution, and not in the problem to which that solution was directed, that Bentham's uniqueness is found.

By the middle of the 1780s, Bentham believed he had produced a satisfactory model of a legislative system which later served as the basis for his unfinished penal, civil and procedure codes. He had reached this position through a rather convoluted and somewhat halting route of intellectual discovery to which his published writings bear scant testimony. The procedure adopted here is to chart Bentham's legislative theory in terms of this development, and since the story is a complex one, it is best to begin by providing an outline of its structure. The starting-point lies in Bentham's positivist critique of common law, which denied that common law could exist as an authentic system of legal rules. The practical conclusion Bentham drew from this was that common law had to be transformed into statute, a proposal which entailed a massive and fundamental reordering of the traditional hierarchy of English laws. However, as will be explored in chapter twelve, the system of legislation which was to supplant common law and also replace the existing statute book, as Bentham recognized, conformed to the traditional program of statute consolidation. This position proved to be a brief interlude in the formation of Bentham's science of legislation. In the early 1780s (as explained in the final chapters), Bentham went on to construct a far more ambitious conception of the ideal system of legislation, which turned on his analysis of the idea of a complete code of laws. It was at this stage, as I shall argue in concluding, that Bentham can be seen to have transcended finally the limits of traditional English legal theory altogether.

Despite the present concern to fix Bentham's relation to English legal theory, it is of course important not to restrict him too narrowly to an English, or even British, setting. Bentham's own reference to Helvetius as his original mentor in the science of legislation warns against this, and already in the 1770s Bentham was looking well beyond England for intellectual stimulus and for outlets for his legislative creations. Thus we find him regularly recording his indebtedness to Helvétius, Beccaria, and Voltaire, drafting correspondence to the French philosophers, and enthusiastically, if rather absurdly, campaigning to become Catherine the Great's codifier.[3] As Bentham liked to put

---

[3] For typical lists of mentors set out by Bentham, and including Helvétius, Beccaria, D'Alembert, James Harris, Voltaire, Montesquieu, DeLolme, Condillac and Adam Smith, see UC xxvii. 144, 148, 173. For the French contacts, see *Corr.* I, letter 192 and *Corr.* II, letters 249–52, 261, 265, 267. For the Russian project, see *Corr.* I, letter 191 and *Corr.* II, especially letters 211, 248, 282, 351.

it, his project addressed the entire field of law in the effort to construct the first authentic system of "universal jurisprudence."[4]

Nevertheless, however unbounded his youthful ambitions, Bentham never departed entirely from the context of English law. As a trained English lawyer based at Lincoln's Inn, he naturally devoted most attention to the legal system and literature over which he had firmest command. Typical of this was a letter drafted to Voltaire in 1776. There Bentham flatteringly observed that he had "taken the counsel" of Voltaire "much oftener than of our own Lord Coke and Hale and Blackstone." But in describing his projected treatise, the "Principles of Legal Policy," he promptly returned to the native terrain – "the object of it is to trace out a new model for the Laws: of my own country you may imagine, in the first place: but keeping those of other countries all along in view."[5]

There is also a more specific reason why so much of Bentham's legal speculation at this time was devoted to the particular issues of English jurisprudence. This was, quite simply, the inexorcisable presence of Sir William Blackstone and the *Commentaries on the Laws of England*, the work Bentham described in 1776 as having "obtained a greater share of esteem, of applause, and consequently of influence" than any other "on the subject [that] has ever yet appeared."[6] Blackstone was Bentham's first instructor in English law, and virtually every major treatise Bentham brought near to completion by 1784 (by which time he could claim that his period of invention was completed) testified to a profound engagement with the *Commentaries on the Laws of England*.[7] This preoccupation with Blackstone was to survive throughout Bentham's long career in legal theory. Still, it was quite contingent circumstances that led Bentham in 1774–6 directly to confront the *Commentaries*, and compose the uncompleted *A Comment on the Commentaries* and the 1776 publication, *A Fragment on Government*.[8] The peculiar literary history of these works produced features relevant to the discussion here. Both were designed as spirited critical performances, initially aimed at drawing a wide readership. Bentham's objective was "to do something to instruct, but more to undeceive," and not "to build up something in its room."[9] His critical purposes did not entail

---

[4] The term "universal jurisprudence" is first used in *Fragment*, p. 418, but was not fully described until *Morals and Legislation*, pp. 6, 294–5. See also UC lxix. 126, where Bentham defines it as "an account of such rights, powers, duties and restraints as subsist ... in every or any state"; and UC xxvii. 45, where he describes his work as "not calculated for the meridian of any one country ... It is adapted to the use of all countries alike."

[5] *Corr.* I, p. 367.   [6] *Fragment*, p. 394.

[7] See *Corr.* III, p. 293 (letter of 1784).

[8] For details of Bentham's early career and his preoccupation with Blackstone, see the editorial introduction to *Comment*, pp. xix–xxviii.   [9] *Fragment*, p. 500 and *Comment*, p 349.

a constructive sequel in these works, with the result that many of the most important parts of Bentham's jurisprudence, notably the presentation of the principle of utility, received at best summary treatment in these texts. Bentham had been constructing the more positive parts of his system for several years before he turned to Blackstone, and the critique of the *Commentaries* was built on these foundations. In considering Bentham's account of common law it is necessary to examine both the negative and positive parts of his system: both the attacks on Blackstone and the manuscript materials from the 1770s, which embody Bentham's own constructive ideas.[10]

Bentham's critique of common law jurisprudence centered on the radical claim that, strictly speaking, common law did not exist.[11] It was only the existence of statute law which made it possible to conceive of common law in misleading terms as a body of laws:

> ...there is no possible means of explaining what it is that shall be understood to make up an article of Common Law of a given description, but by imagining some corresponding article of Statute Law that shall represent it. The Common Law is but the Shadow of the Statute Law, although it came before it. Before the appearance of the Statute Law even the word "Law" could hardly have been mentioned... As a system of general rules, the Common Law is a thing merely imaginary: and the particular commands which are all that (in the way of command) there ever was of it that was real, can not every where, indeed can seldom, be produced... Once more, to give a gross idea of it, what is the *Common Law*? What, but an assemblage of fictitious regulations feigned after the images of these real ones that compose the Statute Law.[12]

Bentham reached this conclusion on the basis of his positivist legal doctrines, which characterized law, properly so called, as a command issued by a sovereign will. Accordingly, the model for law was legislation, or in the case of England, parliamentary statute. "Law and legislation being conjugates in sound," Bentham maintained, they "ought to be kept conjugates in sense." For "Legislation is the act of making Laws" and "Laws are those things which are made by

---

[10] The vast majority of these mss. citations come from two works headed PPI (Preparatory Principles Inserenda) and Crit Jur Crim (Critical Jurisprudence Criminal). Both works appear closely linked to the projected "Principles of Legal Policy." For the dating and subsequent legacy of these mss., see Douglas G. Long, *Bentham on Liberty. Jeremy Bentham's Idea of Liberty in Relation to his Utilitarianism* (Toronto, 1977), pp. xi–xiv.

[11] The issues under discussion here have received extensive exploration in Gerald J. Postema, *Bentham and the Common Law Tradition* (Oxford, 1986), chapters 5–9. In what follows I am heavily indebted to Postema's scholarship and interpretation.

[12] *Comment*, pp. 119–20.

legislation" – "A command given to an individual comes well up to our idea of a Law."[13]

In the next decade, Bentham was concerned to rework the positivist position in a more subtle form, replacing the notion of "command" with "act of volition" and making clear that not all laws had to be the immediate act of a sovereign's volition.[14] But the critical purposes of this approach remained much the same, and in the 1770s Bentham believed that once the legal positivist position was disclosed, it became possible to dismiss preemptively a wide range of "pseudo-laws" under the simple formula that "every thing that is not a Command therefore is not a Law." Accordingly, "a custom" – meaning "an assemblage of acts in some respect or other uniform" – was "not a Law", because "a Law is a Command."[15] Similarly, a "dictate of utility" was "not a Law." A dictate of utility was an "opinion" regarding the utility "in a certain mode of conduct," and an "opinion is an act of the understanding," whereas "a *command* is an *act* of the *will*. And a Law is a Command."[16]

In the case of common law, the positivist position provided the basis for a prompt repudiation of the standard definition of that law, such as adopted by Blackstone, as the *lex non scripta*. Indeed, according to Bentham, "just the reverse of this" was "the truth." Common law was "something written, but that something is not Law."[17] Furthermore, Bentham believed that Blackstone himself had condemned common law in similar terms when he defined municipal law as "rule of civil conduct prescribed by the supreme power in a state." Bentham simply treated the claim that municipal law had to be "prescribed" as a rehearsal of the command theory of law:

> As to Common Law, where is it prescribed?...What is there in it to prescribe? Who made it? Who expressed it? Of whom is it the Will? Questions all these to which he should have had an answer ready before he spoke of Common Law as real Law...[18]

Despite the firmness of Bentham's argument that common law was not "real law," his case for the non-existence of the *lex non scripta* poses several problems. Bentham appears to have adopted a method of criticism he himself regularly condemned in Blackstone and other natural law writers. This was the attempt to overcome undesirable laws

---

[13] UC lxix, 129.
[14] See *Laws in General*, pp. 1–16, and the discussion below, chapter 13 at n54 and nn78–85.
[15] UC lxix. 71, headed "What a Law is." See also UC lxx. 2–13, headed "Intro. A Law what, beginning" and UC lxix. 99 for a list of "non-laws."
[16] UC lxix. 72.
[17] UC lxix. 120 and see *Comment*, pp. 161–4.   [18] *Comment*, p. 43.

by dismissing them as "not law."[19] Bentham elsewhere acknowledged that common law formed a part of every existing legal system.[20] Hence, it is by no means clear how a type of law which existed everywhere could also be said to be non-existent.

Moreover, Bentham's argument against common law rested ultimately on a simple identification of common law with individual judicial edicts. Yet, as we have seen, this identification was eagerly denied by the most influential theorists of common law practice. Blackstone at a crucial point in his account followed Hale in distinguishing the common law from those judicial decisions which furnished evidence of that law. Mansfield likewise clearly insisted that "precedent, though it be Evidence of law, is not Law in itself, much less the whole of the Law."[21] For both jurists, this conception of precedent was closely tied to their understanding of the law's foundations in principles of reason and natural law, which established, as Blackstone explained the orthodoxy, that any particular judicial ruling found "contrary to reason" was simply "*not law.*"[22] What this background indicates is the importance for the success of Bentham's critique of common law of his confronting the "reason " of the law. To overturn common law it was no less necessary to dismiss what Bentham appropriately styled that "formidable non-entity," the law of nature.[23]

Bentham's hostility to natural jurisprudence comes as no surprise, as Benthamic legal positivism is regularly received in Anglo-American jurisprudence as the historically decisive response to natural law theory. What has been less observed is the extent to which Bentham's critique of natural law formed a part of the attack on common law. This in part no doubt follows from the natural law elements of common law theory itself being so often ignored or underplayed. But it must also relate to the relative paucity of natural law discussion in the early Bentham texts. In *An Introduction to the Principles of Morals and Legislation*, where such a discussion was perhaps most likely, Bentham galloped through natural law theory, treating it in a footnote as one of the many variants of the principle of sympathy and antipathy.[24] In the unpublished

---

[19] See *Comment*, pp. 54–6.

[20] See *Laws in General*, p. 235; *Morals and Legislation*, p. 308; *A General View of a Complete Code of Laws*, Bowring, III, 206, for the acknowledgment that customary law existed in all legal systems.

[21] See the discussion above, chapter 1 at n66, chapter 3 at n63, and chapter 6 at n19. See also Bentham's treatment of the doctrine in *Comment*, pp. 194–5, 205–6.

[22] See the discussion above, chapter 1 at n66.

[23] *Comment*, p. 20. Equally characteristic was his description of natural law as a "phantasm of the brain" (at UC lxix. 102) and as "a contradiction in terms" (at UC lxix. 126).

[24] See *Morals and Legislation*, pp. 26–9n.

Comment on the Commentaries, he provided a more sustained analysis, but much of it is given over to Blackstone's shaky attempt to illustrate the content of natural law from Justinian's three maxims of *jus*, rather than to an examination of the doctrine itself.[25] The surviving manuscripts, however, reveal Bentham's concern to construct a more comprehensive critique of natural law jurisprudence and to explain how that critique bore on the argument for the non-existence of common law.

As with common law, the case against natural law generally began by invoking the positivist premise that all authentic law was a species of command. The laws of nature could not be genuine laws since a "real Law is a command, a command...an expression of the will of some person, and there is no person of whose will the Law of Nature can be said to be the expression."[26] Accordingly, it was strictly meaningless to treat "any offence" or "any law" as "contrary" to the "Law of Nature," since "nothing has no contraries."[27] What remained unclear in this reductionist argument was the manner in which the notion of natural law came to be ascribed so extensively by jurists to that which had nothing to do with commands. Equally, it was left unexplained how this general confusion related to the English legal confusion regarding the status of common law. Though none of this survived into his published writings, this question appears to have been of considerable interest for Bentham. He tackled the issue in a series of papers on the "spurious senses" of the term "Law."[28]

Bentham conceded that if one were to trace historically the pattern of rule-keeping in any given society (what he termed "habits of obedience") customary sanctions would precede any formal commands issued by a sovereign will. Nonetheless, it was only the latter which created law, and it was only the presence of this sort of command which could produce a notion of law which might subsequently be misapplied to different kinds of social phenomena. Thus, Bentham maintained that "Law was invented it should seem to denote a General Command of Public Government." Such a command, if effective, would result in "a certain degree of uniformity among the human acts that were the objects of it." And it was this relation between the operation of law and uniformity of actions, rather than the identity between law and commanding, which gave rise to the "spurious senses" of the term law.[29] The term came to be appropriated as an explanation for uniform

---

[25] See *Comment*, pp. 10–21.   [26] UC lxix. 237.
[27] UC lxix. 124; and UC xcvi. 109 on the "state of nature."
[28] See UC lxix. 142–3 and 102.
[29] UC lxix. 142: "[Law] came to be considered as a cause of uniformity among such acts...Looking forward from the Law, men observed an uniformity produced by it: and looking backwards from an assemblage of uniform actions, saw them resulting by a law."

behavior regardless of whether that behavior was the result of a general command of public government.[30]

The first extension was the ascription of the term law to the particular commands of those participating in public government in addition to the government's general commands. In this case the term was transferred "from an article of Statute to an article of Common Law." Bentham believed this likely to occur once "the assemblage of propositions expressive of General Commands of Public Government came to be enumerated," by which he seems to have in mind something akin to institutional law writing. Such writers would want to account for both the uniform actions which resulted from the genuine laws enacted by public government and for those which resulted from "the particular commands of persons bearing a part in public government." Under these circumstances, "it was natural" to adopt the "concise and expeditious" tactic of describing the latter category of uniform behavior "as if it resulted from a Law." This technique had the special attraction of "generating the expectation" of such uniformity "in future," and thereby increasing the efficacy of the legal system as a whole. But it rested on a major intellectual confusion, "by applying to a fictitious entity a name before that peculiar to an object really existing." "Hence followed an obscurity in our ideas," for law being made to signify "now something and now nothing, it became difficult to say what it signified."[31]

This misuse of the term law, in turn, provided the foundation for the next extension "to a supposed Moral Law of Nature, *prescribing* what *ought* to happen." Here the term became divorced from any notion of public commands, and simply referred to "a cause of uniformity." Moreover, in this context the uniformity being explained did not necessarily exist; it was a "uniformity in contemplation," rather than "of observation." In other words, the natural lawyer described a mode of behaviour which he believed ought to prevail. In doing so under the rubric of natural laws, he totally abused the term law, since in this case "there was no such thing as any assignable command at all."[32]

The final extension of the term law occurred when it was adopted by natural philosophers to describe "the existence of uniformity among motions involuntary." The term was again being used to describe a cause of uniformity, but in this context the uniformity being explained no longer referred to the behavior of voluntary agents: "it signified not any act of the will, or any symbol of any act of the will, real or

---

[30] UC lxix. 102: "Men love to know [the] causes of things...Seeing uniformity any where else, they must there also have a cause for it: and this cause must be a law."

[31] UC lxix. 142.   [32] UC lxix. 142–3.

supposed." And precisely because this usage was so "wide from the original one," Bentham believed there was "no danger of [its] being confounded with it," and therefore no danger in its continued currency.[33] While he was convinced that the "Law of Nature" had to be "erased from the vocabulary of Jurisprudence," he refrained from advocating a similar editorial policy for the works of natural science.[34] Grotius and Pufendorf were to be committed to the flames, but Sir Isaac Newton rested in safety.

It is worth highlighting the more radical implications of this account. Bentham's concluding remarks, that natural science could be formulated in terms of laws of nature just because such terminology was entirely divorced from the authentic meaning of law, conveyed a decisive repudiation of the most basic premises of the entire body of natural theology and natural law ethics. For these writers the vocabulary of natural law was appropriate because the moralist and natural philosopher did observe and describe strictly analogous phenomena: the natural laws through which God ordered the material and human world. In the case of jurisprudence, Bentham again suggested a drastic reordering of the traditional lines of discussion. Thus, against English legal conventions, he presented common law as the successor to statute, and natural law as the successor to common law. The result was a hierarchy of legal phenomena assembled exactly in reverse of the traditional picture, such as that presented by Blackstone in the introductory sections of the *Commentaries*.

Once he had demonstrated that natural law theorists never had been treating laws at all, it then became possible for Bentham to turn to the substance of their doctrines. Here his relationship to natural law theory is more complex than he generally was prepared to allow. As a critical jurisprudence designed to provide a reasoned examination of the moral worth of inherited legal practices Bentham's own doctrines had clear affinities with the natural jurisprudence tradition.[35] Furthermore, in this period the laws of nature were being given a distinctly utilitarian cast by such moralists as Cumberland, Hutcheson, Kames, and Paley.[36] Bentham himself on occasion acknowledged the development.

---

[33] *Ibid.*: "Suppose a man were to get up and maintain a Law of the State to be void on pretence of its being contrary to one of Sir Isaac Newton's Laws of Nature: what should we say of such a man? that he was mistaken? no: but that he did not know what he said."

[34] See UC lxix. 125, where Bentham advocates banishing the law of nature from jurisprudence; and see UC lxix. 208, where he suggests replacing it with the "Law of Morality."

[35] On this basis nineteenth-century German jurists treated Bentham's utilitarian jurisprudence as a theory of natural law, see Bryce, *Studies in History and Jurisprudence*, II, 612–17. For a more recent exploration of this theme, see Ross Harrison, *Bentham* (London, 1983), pp. 44–5.

[36] For a valuable elucidation of the first stages of this historical development, see Tuck, *Natural Rights Theories*, pp. 156–72 (on Pufendorf).

He viewed Kames and Price, for example, as two utilitarian moralists who failed to embrace the principal of utility unequivocally,[37] and in another setting described natural law theory as "the resource of those who either tremble to take for the standard of Right and Wrong the Principle of Utility, or meaning in general to take that for their standard, know not how to."[38] In general, however, Bentham's posture was altogether less sympathetic. For him, natural law writers were either describing legal practices or prescribing public policy, and failed to do either satisfactorily in large part because they did not distinguish the two operations.

Probably the best known version of this argument occurs in *A Fragment on Government*, where Bentham treated the rival roles of the censor and the expositor of the law. Blackstone, Bentham argued, had regularly shifted from a description of the law (expository jurisprudence) to a defense of it (censorial jurisprudence), and in so doing violated the epistemological lessons given by Hume in the third book of the *Treatise*.[39] Bentham reworked the argument on numerous occasions in the 1770s, and developed it at length in his *Essay on the Influence of Place and Time in Matters of Legislation*. There Bentham referred to the earlier critique in *A Fragment*, but made plain that the argument was addressed to the whole natural law tradition and not simply to Blackstone. "The question of fact and the question of propriety," he stressed, "are incessantly confounded," and "the books that have been written on the pretended laws of nature have scarce any other foundation than this mistake." Such writers "indiscriminately" produce "two sorts of propositions" under the rubric of natural law: "the one declaring how things are, the other declaring how they ought to be." And Germany was "still full" of these theorists, "who do not know yet what it is they are writing or reading about, history or policy: the moral history of man, or acts of government and legislation." But "expose to light the partition between these two objects" and "the phantom of the law of nature vanishes."[40]

---

[37] UC lxxa. 31, headed, "Utility governs where disavowed. Keymis and Price."

[38] UC lxix. 106. This contrasts with Bentham's repeated observations on the absence of utilitarian principles in other natural law theories; see UC lxxa. 29–30 (on Grotius), UC c. 116–7 (on Grotius, Pufendorf and Coke); *Comment*, pp. 19–20 (on Blackstone).

[39] *Fragment*, pp. 397–9.

[40] The quotation appears in a footnote omitted in the Bowring edition, which should be added to the *Essay on the Influence of Place and Time in Matters of Legislation* at *Bowring*, I, 179, where Bentham notes Montesquieu's confusion on this point. (The essay itself is incorrectly titled in *Bowring* as "*Time and Place*".) See also *Morals and Legislation*, p. 298n (on Grotius, Pufendorf, Burlamaqui and Montesquieu), and UC lxix. 127 (on Grotius, Pufendorf, Heineccius, Vattel, Burlamaqui "and the many others who have hitherto professed to give treatises on Natural Law").

When it appeared as a "moral history of man," natural law theory could easily be overcome. This was particularly the case regarding English law because Bentham believed it was committed to an enormously crude historical theory, particularly when compared with the researches of Barrington and Kames. Thus, in *A Comment on the Commentaries*, Bentham found no difficulty in demonstrating that the formal description of common law as "immemorial" or "ancient" was simply absurd historically.[41] Nor was this merely a matter of Bentham's notorious impatience with arguments drawn from the wisdom of the past. In the 1770s at least, Bentham displayed a decided willingness to adopt the more historically informed arguments developed by the Scottish moralists. His own critique of Blackstone's contract theory and his rival treatment of obligation in terms of "habits of obedience" were explicitly drawn from Hume's *Treatise* and Kames's *Historical Law Tracts*.[42] In *A Comment*, Bentham also followed Kames in arguing that any attempt to defend existing legal practices in historical terms was likely to back-fire by actually demonstrating the antiquated character of those practices.[43] In general, however, he sought to restrict the impact of such historical questions by subsuming them within the doctrine of expectation.[44] Ultimately, the relevance of existing practices referred solely to the expectations men had regarding them. The disturbance of these expectations was just one of the many pains and pleasures the legislator needed to consider in his calculations before effecting legislative change. Although in his actual reform proposals Bentham gave considerable weight to the pain of frustrated expectations, he nowhere implied that this might fundamentally undermine the reforming enterprises of an enlightened legislator.[45]

The second part of natural law theory, that which was addressed to matters "of policy" and "acts of government and legislation," was a more serious challenge to which Bentham devoted much attention. The

[41] See *Comment*, pp. 313–14n, 342–3, on Barrington and Kames, and pp. 164–80, 236–7, on the alleged antiquity of common law.

[42] See *Fragment*, pp. 429–30 and n, 439–40 and n.

[43] See *Comment*, pp. 203–6 (especially p. 205) on the laws of inheritance. See also *Comment*, pp. 317–18, on "Préjugés in favour of Antiquity," and the similar remarks at UC xcvii. 6, 15.

[44] See *Comment*, pp. 196–7, 230–7.

[45] The classic early statement on the limits of historical and social forces is *Essay on the Influence of Place and Time in Matters of Legislation*, *Bowring* I, especially 177–80, 188–92. While Bentham's attitude in the 1770s to the more sociological approaches to legislation is not entirely clear, a revealing statement against such an approach appears at UC xxvii. 95: "It seemed to me that greater advances might be made and surer, by diving at once into the recesses of the human understanding with Locke, and with Helvetius of the human heart, than by wandering about the maze of history in search of particular facts, often ill-authenticated or disguised." The general issue of the relationship between Bentham's legislative program and eighteenth-century social thought is cogently explored in J. W. Burrow, *Evolution and Society* (Cambridge, 1966), pp. 7–42.

essence of his response was that natural law was the last refuge of the indolent and incompetent moralist. The expression, Bentham caustically observed, "makes a man a moralist...at a cheap rate...He has but to take this phrase into his mouth, and the business is done."[46] For to invoke the laws of nature on any question of policy was to proffer disguised and untested private opinion as a public standard: "what is called the Law of Nature is neither a precept nor a Sanction, but the mere opinions of men self-constituted into Legislators."[47] What Bentham was especially concerned to emphasize was that it did not matter under what metaphysical vocabulary such natural laws were framed, nor what substantive doctrines were derived from them. The fundamental failure of this sort of moral argument was that it could never move beyond the level of private assertion:

> When a man disapproves of a mode of conduct considered independently of any actual System of Jurisprudence he says there is a Law of Nature against it...If he can't tell why he disapproves of it, but yet will disapprove, and will have others disapprove of it: he begins talking of a Rule of Right, a Fitness of Things, a Moral Sense or some other imaginary standard which howsoever varied in the description, is from first to last nothing but his own bare unsupported opinion in disguise.[48]

In *A Comment on the Commentaries*, Bentham reproduced this argument whenever Blackstone accounted for English legal practice in terms of the natural law foundations of common law. Thus when Blackstone presented the legal maxim that statutes "contrary to reason" were void, Bentham countered that "contrary to reason" could mean "no more than it is what I readily and strongly disapprove of...use what expressions of positiveness we will, when all comes to all, reasonableness or unreasonableness is nothing but...opinion."[49] The same line of criticism appeared in response to Blackstone's conventional doctrine that judges were to disregard precedents "contrary to reason" or "divine law." There Bentham concluded simply enough that "the most prompt and perhaps the most usual translation of the phrase 'contrary to reason,' is 'contrary to what I like.'"[50]

As a solution to such purely arbitrary and assertive methods of moral argument, Bentham of course paraded the principle of utility. The advantage of the principle was not just that it alone directly addressed the matter of public happiness. More, it alone provided the means for

---

[46] UC lxix. 238.   [47] UC xcvi. 109.
[48] UC lxix. 102. See also UC lxix. 71–2, 106 and UC lxxa, 23, for a rehearsal of the same argument.
[49] *Comment*, p. 159.   [50] *Ibid.*, p. 198.

shifting moral disputes from the sphere of private opinion to an external standard of evaluation. Hence his incessant insistence in the early manuscripts: "Talk of *utility* and of pains and pleasures, this is grounding your doctrine in matter of *fact*... Talk of *right*: – say a man has a *right* to such a thing in such a case, and we have 'no matter of fact to encumber ourselves with. "[51] Or, as he put it in *A Comment* on Blackstone, "had our Author again instead of reason said utility, he would have said something... He would have referred us to calculation founded upon matter of fact: future contingent utility founded upon past utility experienced. "[52]

This argument against natural law theory received its best known formulation in the second chapter of *An Introduction to the Principles of Morals and Legislation*, where the natural law position was contracted under the umbrella principle of "sympathy and antipathy. " According to this, actions were approved or disapproved merely on account of the disposition to approve or disapprove of them, "holding up that approbation or disapprobation as a sufficient reason for itself. "[53] As in the case of natural law, this principle might well sanction actions conforming to the dictates of utility.[54] But the basic inadequacy of the principle, as of natural law, was its incapacity to do more than generate purely personal opinion. Thus Bentham described it as "a principle in name rather than in reality. " For what was required in a principle was "something that points out some external consideration" for "guiding the internal sentiments, " and this "expectation" was "but ill fulfilled by a proposition, which does neither more nor less than hold up each of those sentiments as a ground and standard for itself. "[55]

The way in which the principle of utility furnished an "external guide" for moral judgments resting on "matters of fact" occupied the next eleven chapters of the work, and involved Bentham in the famously dubious enterprise of articulating a mechanism for measuring happiness and projecting a strictly consequentialist account of the moral content of human actions.[56] The enterprise itself, whatever its philosophical impossibilities, followed directly from the contrast between the private character of "sympathy and antipathy" and the "external" standard of public utility. What is of chief interest here is

---

[51] UC lxix. 6–7, and see UC lxix. 72–3, where Bentham illustrates the utilitarian calculation of a "matter of fact" using the traditional natural law example of the duty of parents to care for their children.

[52] *Comment*, p. 199. See also his further remarks on this theme at *Comment*, p. 28, and *Fragment*, pp. 491–2.

[53] *Morals and Legislation*, p. 25. [54] *Ibid.*, p. 29. [55] *Ibid.*, p. 25.

[56] For an interpretation and clarification of these features of Bentham's theory, see Harrison's valuable treatment in *Bentham*, pp. 148–62.

that the position was first formulated by Bentham in response to natural law jurisprudence, and that this, in turn, represented a necessary component in the critique of common law.[57]

Once Bentham had established that the laws of nature were merely private opinions, he was equipped with the proper apparatus for demonstrating common law's actual status as "non-law." To start with, as common law theorists recognized (only to deny the premise), once reason was eliminated as a source of law, all that remained to the common law were individual judicial edicts:

> I hope it is by this time pretty apparent, that what is called the Unwritten Law is made not by the people but by Judges: the substance of it by Judges solely: the expression of it, either by Judges or by Lawyers who hope to be so.[58]

The claim that common law was "judge-made" formed a recurring theme of *A Comment on the Commentaries*, and in subsequent works Bentham substituted the term "*judiciary* law" for common law.[59] It is important not to mistake his point. Bentham was claiming more than that this body of law could be shown to be the instrument of the professional interest of common lawyers and judges, of what he later described as the "sinister interest" of "judge and company."[60] Nor was he simply appealing to the constitutional doctrine that the creation of law by the judiciary undermined the legislative authority of parliament. That argument did appear in *A Comment on the Commentaries*, but it was only introduced through the attack on natural law theory. Once reason was reduced to individual opinion, the constitutional question became simply a calculation as to whether it was more reliable to follow the opinion of "four men appointed by the Crown" or "that of many hundred men chosen the greater part of them by the people."[61]

But the major purpose served by Bentham's equating common law with particular judicial decisions was that this equation enabled him to locate common law within the command theory of law, and thereby indicate its fictitious and unacceptable character as a system of legal management. "We know in general," Bentham again emphasized,

---

[57] Bentham also argued that natural law theory cloaked religious intolerance and encouraged political radicalism; see *Comment*, pp. 55, 345–6, and UC lxix. 145–6, 132–3.

[58] *Comment*, p. 223.

[59] *Morals and Legislation*, p. 8. In *Laws in General*, Bentham used the term "customary law," which he also identified as "acts of autocratico-judicial power"; see *Laws in General*, pp. 152–3, 184–95.

[60] Bentham's early rehearsal of this theme is discussed below, chapter 12 at nn65–70.

[61] *Comment*, p. 159.

"that the office of Law is to command," and hence "that this that is called Common Law must therefore display itself some times or other in commands." The difficulty, completely ignored by other jurists, was "to pick out any portion" of that "greater parcel of what is called Common Law," and "to understand how it contributes to the composition of a Command."[62] Since the judicial act was by its nature an act of judgment (that is, an act of the understanding), and not an act of the will, there was a *prima facie* case for supposing that common law never did "display itself" as a command. Bentham believed that the phenomenon could be explained only by referring to another element in the legal system, the instrument through which virtually all legal commands received their force – punishment. From the standpoint of public punishment, common law and statute could be conceived as two methods for obtaining obedience. "What produces obedience to a Law is the expectation of punishment for disobedience," and therefore it was "not difficult" to understand "how the same expectation should produce the same action or forbearance even without a Law." Thus, to use Bentham's example, one might "command a child to forbear reaching out at the window," and provided the child expected to be punished for disobedience, "he will forbear." But without ever actually issuing a command, it was also possible simply to "punish him whenever he goes to reach out at the window," and "he will in the like manner also forbear."[63]

This, then, exemplified the difference between statute and common law in procedural terms. Statute law, which Bentham at times termed the "enuntiative" method, produced obedience "by command," whereas common law, the "silent" method, produced obedience by punishing "without any command."[64] Common law, however, even from this standpoint, still failed to appear as a system of commands. But, while it did not "enter into it essentially," it was of course perfectly possible for some sort of command to be issued "in the operations of common law." The fact that English common law judges did regularly issue commands was a contingent matter, the consequence of the division of labor which accompanied developed social organization:

> In a numerous and complicated society, the same person who is Judge cannot always be executioner. He issues his Command to another person who is executioner, and it is by means of that command in point of fact that the punishment is inflicted... But the same effect would equally have

[62] UC lxix. 111.
[63] UC lxix. 147; and see UC lxix. 145, 154, 158, 179.
[64] See UC lxix. 159.

been produced, if instead of commanding another, he had inflicted it himself.[65]

Common law commands, therefore, emerged as an accessory to the primary judicial function of judgment. It followed for Bentham that the authentically law-like feature of the common law process was strictly confined to this aspect of judicial action: "When a Sheriff has apprehended a man as he was commanded there is an end of so much Law, if it is to be called Law, as that command amounted to."[66]

By identifying the commands of common law in this way, Bentham could then reveal common law's disqualification as a body of "real law." The "authentic commands" of common law referred to the individual orders of a judge to another judicial agent. This process in itself did nothing to generate those general rules of law required for a system of laws. Those "particular acts of command" a judge issued to another judicial agent could not be said to constitute a body of laws, since "these in their nature...are past and gone. They do not now exist: it is not of them that a system now existent can be composed."[67] Rather, what did now exist was "the assemblage of the respective ideas of those acts" commanded by the judge.[68] It was these "ideas" which gave common law the appearance of an existing system of general rules. But the common law only obtained this appearance of generality and permanence by generating a further, crippling problem. This was the question of whose "ideas" were to be taken as an authentic statement of the general rules of common law. This could not be the judge, because the authoritative, law-like feature of his function was confined to the command and punishment issued with respect to a personal case. And the only answer the common law system allowed was entirely arbitrary: "It is left to every man to compose for himself at his own hazard according to his own ability."[69]

> They are the idea that *you* have formed of the act in question, the idea that *I* have formed of it, the idea that *Titus* has formed of it. These ideas exist...but are...these ideas of one and the same description? Perhaps they are; perhaps not... To serve as ingredients in a system of Law, we must have not ideas of individual articles of conduct, but ideas of sorts of articles of conduct: general ideas taken off from these particular ones; and for these general ideas, words. But who shall take them off? Titus?

---

[65] UC lxix. 147. Hence the appositeness of Bentham's example of the child reaching out the window, since in the case of "domestic government" the same individual served as judge and executioner; see UC lxix. 151.

[66] UC lxix. 120.   [67] UC lxix. 151.

[68] *Ibid.*   [69] UC lxix. 115.

Whose shall be those words? Titus's? Then would Titus be a Legislator. But Legislator, by the supposition, there is none.[70]

It is at this point in his analysis of common law that the significance of Bentham's attendant critique of natural law theory becomes most apparent. For the common lawyer's obvious response to Bentham's emphasis on the inevitably particular and limited character of a judge's commands would be to appeal to those maxims of nature and reason with which common law ultimately harmonized and those general principles of law which a particular judicial ruling in fact only served to illustrate. By reducing reason and principle to mere individual opinion Bentham had eliminated just this option. The appeal to reason and principle was still nothing more than any individual's particular claim about the substance of the law. As he put it in *A Comment on the Commentaries*, "To whose reason?...In Truth it must be the reason, of you, of me, of anyone before whom the determination is supposed to be proposed to judge of."[71] The argument for the non-existence of common law thus rested on the following dichotomy, which the critique of natural law ensured could not be overcome. When common law appeared as an authentic command, it constituted a particular judicial edict. Since this edict was particular and past, it would not constitute an existing general rule of law. When common law appeared as a general rule of law, it represented a conception drawn from a series of particular judicial commands. But unless this was the legislator's idea of these cases, the conception was not authoritative, and hence a general rule of law again was not being described. Bentham developed this position at considerable length in the 1770s in some of his earliest writings in legal theory. In the next decade he was able to formulate the point with a telling clarity and succinctness.

> If in all that has been ever written of [common law]...there be a single paragraph which (not being a passage copied from some statute) is seriously meant to pass for a paragraph of *a* law...it is a forgery. Whether there be anything in it or not that has been marked with the stamp of authority, makes no difference: if authoritative, it is particular; and therefore no law: if general, it is unauthoritative: and therefore again no law.[72]

---

[70] UC lxix. 151.

[71] *Comment*, p. 198. See also UC lxiii. 50: "Ask a Lawyer, what is Common Law?...He knows not what common law is: however he knows what it is *not*...'Whatever is not *reason*, is not Law'...'Is not reason?' what reason?...this man's reason, or that man's reason, or my reason? Oh no, nothing like it: a particular sort of reason – a sort made on purpose – a legal reason...In short would you know precisely what Common Law is? It is Common Law."

[72] *Laws in General*, pp. 153–4 and see *Comment*, pp. 331–2.

On the basis of this analysis, Bentham went on to present a series of conclusions, each indicating common law's inherent defects as a system of legal management. The most important of these was directly entailed in the formal demonstration of common law's status as "non-law." As a "system of general rules," common law was "a thing merely imaginary."[73] Accordingly, it could never receive authoritative formulation, and hence it was literally unknowable and necessarily uncertain. Under common law, the subject's duties were let "loose into the wilds of perpetual conjecture," and law cases remained in a state of "glorious uncertainty."[74] And by failing to achieve certainty, common law undermined "the grand utility" of all law.[75]

Bentham's point here needs to be distinguished from another argument he frequently advanced in this context. This addressed the haphazard and arbitrary process by which reports of law cases came to be preserved in published form. The common law system provided no official mechanism for publishing the record of all the facts and legal arguments relevant to a particular judicial decision. Most of the available law reports actually comprised informal and incomplete notes compiled by lawyers for their private use, which were only published later, usually posthumously, by someone else.[76] Bentham portrayed this as a procedure which enabled a book-seller or an executor to become a legislator, and set out at length the resulting defects contained in the existing reports.[77] Because of the courts' failure to provide an authoritative and comprehensive account of their actions, he compared the practice of the English judges to the legislative techniques of Caligula – a comparison in which the common law came off rather badly.[78]

Bentham, however, was hardly alone in making these protests. Michael Foster in the 1760s had condemned "the indigested things called *Reports of Adjudged Cases*" as "mere fragments of learning, the rummage of dead men's papers, or the first essays of young authors," which were nothing less than "the bane and scandal of the law considered as a science *founded on principle*."[79] Chief Justice Holt

---

[73] *Comment*, p. 119.
[74] *Comment*, pp. 251n, 95. See also *Morals and Legislation*, p. 308: "uncertainty is the very essence of every particle of law so denominated."
[75] *General View of a Complete Code of Laws*, in *Bowring*, III, 206.
[76] The important exception to this pattern, the law reports for Mansfield's chief justiceship, are treated above, chapter 4 at n5.
[77] See *Laws in General*, p. 186–9 and *Comment*, pp. 206–15. Also see UC lxxix. 76: "everything for the sake of which law has been established is left to the sport of fortune."
[78] See *Laws in General*, p. 193 and *Comment*, p. 214.
[79] Foster, *Discourses upon the Crown Law*, pp. i–ii.

confessed his fears that "scambling reports" would "make posterity think ill of his understanding,"[80] and Mansfield often overcame troublesome precedents simply by impugning the law reports in which they were found. In a revealing statement in 1782 he claimed that "the uncertainty of the law of evidence" was owing "to mistaken notes which have turned particular cases into general rules."[81] Indeed, Bentham's own solution to these institutional problems – a systematic program for official law reporting – was, ironically enough, a proposal Blackstone himself had advocated in the *Commentaries*.[82]

The absence of authoritative law reports thus profoundly aggravated the uncertainty of common law. But this particular abuse did not affect Bentham's more basic argument regarding the necessary uncertainty of common law. Even if a particular case was "delineated ever so exactly" in an official record, it was still "but that individual case" which was described. To formulate a general legal rule "a new process" was required, one which the common law system itself could never accommodate.[83] Only legislation could exist as a body of authoritative and general rules. The philosophical analysis by virtue of which Bentham reached this conclusion helps explain what otherwise appears a rather odd position for him to try to defend. As we have seen, an overwhelming body of eighteenth-century legal opinion held that most of the uncertainty in English law was in fact due to the confusions produced by the poorly expressed, misconceived and enormously verbose statute law. The common law, in contrast, had achieved a singular degree of certainty and precision, a point which was easily vindicated, as Kames argued, by a simple examination of the actual condition of the law. Bentham of course recognized the defects of British legislation, and already in the 1770s was engaged in developing techniques for improved legislative style. For him, though, these defects could only represent the abuse of the science of legislation. The uncertainty of common law, however, was basic to its very nature.

Further conclusions followed from Bentham's depiction of common law as a "course of punishing without command." This, for example, eliminated any notion that common law represented a body of customary practices which thereby implicitly contained the freely given

---

[80] Cited in Lofft, p. xii. For similar criticisms, see Burn, *Justice of the Peace*, I, xi, and Douglas, I, iv–viii.

[81] *Crook* v *Dowling*, (1782) 3 Douglas 75, 77. See also his complaints against inaccurate reports in *Miller* v *Race*, (1758) 1 Burrow 452, *Grant* v *Vaughan* (1764) 3 Burrow 1516, and *Heylyn* v *Heylyn*, (1774) Cowper 130.

[82] See 1 *Comm* 72. Bentham's "New Year Books" project is discussed below, chapter 12 at n8.   [83] *Laws in General*, pp. 184–5.

consent of those under its direction.[84] Common law was still a matter
of legal force, a system for the infliction of penalties by judicial agents.
Indeed, for Bentham it was only through such punishment that a
customary practice could ever become a legal entity. Thus in response
to the traditional argument for liberty under common law, he
countered, "with reason precisely equal might it be said, that the
custom of observing statutes was a custom flowing from consent."[85] In
both cases the "custom" of obedience derived from the threat of
punishment.

Common laws' "judge-made" character also meant that it
comprised a body of *ex post facto* commands. The judge declared an
action punishable only after it had been committed. Bentham used the
point to considerable rhetorical effect against Blackstone in response to
the Commentator's conventional praise of English law for its rejection
of all *ex post facto* rulings. "Our author censures against *ex post facto*
law" while he "idolizes Common Law," but "sees not that his censures
cut the throat of his panegyric." "Whatever is done in the way of
Common Law is done *ex necessitate rei* by *ex post facto* acts of
power."[86] There was more to this than Bentham's favorite pursuit of
undermining English legal conventions. The *ex post facto* feature of
common law also revealed its limitations as a creative system of legal
management. The judge's power was dependent on "the concurrence of
the will of a Plaintiff," since the judge could only intervene provided
some other party brought a dispute before him. The legislator, in
contrast, was altogether "free from these restraints."[87]

More importantly, as a "course of punishing without command,"
common law could never be justified on utilitarian grounds. It
inevitably produced an unnecessary surplus of pain – "there is so
much pain wasted as there is produced before the habit of Punishment
is seen to be formed." In contrast, the "enunciative" method of
producing obedience was prompt and economical – "issue a Command, and if the expectation of the pain with which it is supposed to
be backed be strong enough, obedience is obtained *gratis* and at
once."[88] For the utilitarian moralist, then, the method of common law
was essentially inhumane. In later writings, Bentham rehearsed the
point more dramatically, in his famous comparison between common

---

[84] See Blackstone's presentation of this position at 1 *Comm* 73–4.
[85] *Comment*, p. 332; see also pp. 215–24 (on the "abusive application of the term 'assent'"), and
p. 812 (on the relation between a "*legal custom*" and "the idea of Punishment").
[86] UC lxix. 159, and see *Comment*, pp. 49–51n.
[87] UC lxix. 203; and see UC lxix. 202, 144–5.   [88] UC lxix. 154.

law and the law a man makes for his dog. But the equation had been reached as early as the 1770s:

> To be governed by Statute Law belongs only to men. By Common Law it is that even Beasts are governed. A mode of government that is fit only for Beasts and for them fully, because incapable of a better.[89]

As a system of general rules, common law did not exist. It was imprecise and unknowable, "the dark Chaos of Common Law."[90] As a mechanism for obtaining obedience, it was morally indefensible, "fit only for beasts." For Bentham, there was one fundamental solution for this philosophical and moral bankruptcy in English law. What was required was "to mark out the line of the subject's conduct by visible directions," which could only be achieved "by transforming the rule of conduct from Common Law into Statute Law; that is...into Law from no-Law."[91] This project and its objectives were outlined in the only part of Bentham's voluminous writings on common law which reached publication in the 1770s. In a concluding passage of *A Fragment on Government*, he included amongst the several reforms "which public necessity cries aloud for," the "transforming, by a digest, the body of the common law...into statute-law."[92]

Bentham's statutory Digest of the common law represented his initial solution to the problems revealed by his critique of common law jurisprudence. To a great extent, the Digest program reflected the very foundations of that critique itself. According to Bentham, the only means of depicting an article of the fictitious common law was "by imagining some correspondent article of statute law that shall represent it." The Digest, then, was simply an explicit, authoritative version of the mental act which always had to occur in the conventional misidentification of common law as a body of real law.[93] But notwithstanding the programmatic logic of this conclusion, it is difficult not to be struck by the singularity of Bentham's resulting proposal. In his call for a common law Digest Bentham had stood the English legal tradition on its head.

Underlying much eighteenth-century legal speculation was the broad consensus that the primary defect in English law was parliamentary

---

[89] UC lxix. 151, and see *Laws in General*, p. 153. For Bentham's later likening of common law with the law a man makes for his dog, see *Truth versus Ashhurst*, Bowring V, 231–7.
[90] *Comment*, p. 198.   [91] *Comment*, p. 95.
[92] *Fragment*, p. 499.
[93] See UC lxix. 115, where Bentham suggests this reading.

statute. Reforming the law was a matter of controlling legislation, and most often the arguments for such reform were advanced by contrasting statute law's failures with common law's triumphs. As Bentham observed of Blackstone, "he magnifies Common Law at the expense of Statute."[94] Bentham likewise recognized the defective state of the statute book, perhaps in a manner more comprehensive than any of his contemporaries. But in terms of the broader question regarding the relationship between common law and statute, Bentham starkly repudiated the conventional wisdom. Not only was common law bad law, it was "not law." The common law's presumed rival, legislation, was its true savior:

> The truth is, take [common law] all together, it is not yet in a condition to be known. The business is to put it into such a condition. To do this it must be digested by authority: the Common Law must be digested into Statute. The fictitious must be substantiated into real.[95]

[94] UC lxix. 159.   [95] *Comment*, p. 320.

12

◁ ════════════════════════════ ▷

The Digest

In the spring of 1778, Jeremy Bentham, along with his younger
brother, Samuel, embarked on a campaign to attract the patronage of
Catherine of Russia.[1] As part of this effort, the elder Bentham had
occasion to compose a lengthy account of his labors during the past
three years. *A Fragment on Government* and the *View of the Hard Labour
Bill* had already been published, and considerable progress had been
made on his treatises on offenses and punishments. Bentham mentioned
several other projects and singled out for special recommendation his
"plan of a Digest":

> I have lying by me in a rough state a Plan for a Digest of the Laws. This
> concerns the Laws whatever state they may happen to be in for the time
> being, and is applicable to the Laws of one nation as of another. It is what
> I have hinted at towards the conclusion of the Fragment. I have had it
> lying by me these two or three years and am every now and then touching
> it up and making little additions.[2]

In the letter Bentham was particularly concerned to stress the
cosmopolitan potential of his Digest. But his own reference to *A
Fragment on Government* and the dating of the work indicate that he was
describing the project which developed out of his critique of common
law. Further evidence suggests that he was actively engaged in
producing such a Digest during the mid-1770s. Amongst the
manuscripts from this period is a "list of Works projected for the
Improvement of the Law," which is headed by a "Proposal for a
Parliamentary Digest: with a specimen of the work and another of the
mode of operation."[3] In May 1775, Bentham reported to his brother

---

[1] The Bentham brothers' Russian interests, which eventually led to Samuel's service in the
1780s as a naval architect in Krichev (White Russia) and to Jeremy's 1786–87 visit there, are
summarized in the editorial introductions to *Corr.* I, xxvii–xxxi, xxxiii–xxxv, and *Corr.* III,
xxiv–xxix.   [2] *Corr.* II. 114.

[3] UC clxix. 1–2; Bentham concludes the list of projects by noting, "Of almost all of these
[works] the leading principles are fixed upon. In several of them progress has been
made."

the steady progress of both his Digest and *A Comment on the Commentaries*, and announced the completion of the latter work "in three months or so at farthest."[4] As was to become characteristic of Bentham's writing projects, neither work was in fact ever completed, though references to the Digest appear sporadically in correspondence over the next three years.[5]

Much of this "plan for a Digest" survives in the Bentham papers.[6] Unfortunately, these manuscripts present serious problems. Nothing in what survives indicates that the work was anywhere near as complete as Bentham suggested in 1778. Indeed, the 1778 description of the plan as being in "a rough state" appears wildly generous. The material is voluminous, but extremely fragmentary and repetitious, and there is no obvious way to assemble it as a coherent work. More importantly, it is clear that what Bentham described during this period as the "Digest" actually referred to two distinct projects. The first was the project outlined in *A Fragment on Government* and *A Comment on the Commentaries*: the Digest for transforming common law into statute. The second project was a Digest of the statute law itself: what Bentham, following contemporary usage, also discussed as "consolidation."[7] Virtually all the existing Digest materials relate to the statute Digest for consolidation, not the common law Digest.[8] This may of course reflect the accidents of manuscript survival. It is more likely, though, that Bentham embarked on the statute law Digest first, viewing this as the easier operation. Once he had perfected the techniques of "digestion" he could then turn to the more demanding task of "digesting" common law. Thus, in the introductory remarks to his scheme for "personal codes," Bentham observed that he would begin with the "Professional and Official codes," as these were "all statute

---

[4] *Corr.* I, 235.   [5] See *Corr.* I, 241; *Corr.* II. 62.

[6] See UC lxxix, 1–2, for "Digest Plan of a Table of Contents," and UC. xcvi, 72 for "Contents" of another project containing chapters on "composition" and "promulgation." The chapter on "Composition" is further outlined at UC. xcvi. 85, 86, 88–9, 221; another series on composition appears at UC xcvi. 359–62. For Benthan's working plans for statute consolidation, see UC xcvi. 353–8, 363, 364–7 (using Owen Ruffhead, *Statutes of the Realm*); UC xcvi. 369–72 (using Burn, *Justice of the Peace*); and UC xcvi. 373, 374–8 (using *A General Index of the 12–17th Volumes of the Journals of the House of Commons* (1778), compiled by Nathaniel Forster and re-printed by the Order of the House of Commons (House of Commons, 1803). For the actual discussion of composition, see UC lxxa. 60–116, UC lxxix. 4–77; and for promulgation, see UC lxxix. 4–77, UC xcvi. 233–45, UC cvii. 5–13.

[7] See, as an example, UC xcvi. 86.

[8] The only material Bentham assembled for the common law Digest relates to his "New Year Books" program for the publication of authoritative law reports; see *Fragment*, p. 499 and UC lxxa. 118. The relevant material appears at UC x. 1–4, UC lxxa. 117–44; and plans of the work are sketched at UC. xcvi. 244 and UC clxix. 1. Bentham viewed the project as a preliminary to forming the common law Digest, and adopted Sir James Burrow's *Reports* as his model for correct law reporting; see UC lxxa. 132.

law." "The collection of materials under such Titles as are filled principally by the Common Law," he observed, was "yet invisible" and could be "brought together while the other structures are reared whose materials are at hand."[9]

The Digest formed part of a more general conception of the science of legislation in which Bentham sought to distinguish the substantive policy of the law from its verbal expression: "The excellence and efficacy of every system of Laws will depend upon two grand points belonging to it: the policy or matter or purport of the laws, as it may be called; and the form or tenor of them."[10] The two questions of "matter" and "form" had to be separated in order to achieve greater precision in the legislative science. But the two were firmly interconnected in the Benthamic strategy for legal improvement. A perfect system of law could not be produced until a comprehensive scheme for legal arrangement had been constructed. The perfect system of legislation, moreover, would have to be communicated in a perfectly intelligible manner, a problem concerning legal "form." And because of the rarely perceived need to attend to both questions, Bentham smugly distanced himself from other "English Digesters" who ignored the problem of "legal form" or "law metaphysics."[11]

Bentham apparently designed the Digest as a solution to the problems of legal form and expression. This in itself would serve a utilitarian purpose by increasing the knowledge of the law, and thereby the efficacy of the legal system. And Bentham also considered the Digest to be an important preliminary to any substantive reform of the law, since it was easier to identify "defects" and supply "the requisite corrections" once "the scattered Laws" had been digested "into one body." But, initially at least, the Digest was not intended as a vehicle for substantive law reform. As Bentham said of his model of a digested Turnpike Act, the proposed "improvements" had been reached "by the internal comparison of the parts of the present Act," and not "from any external lights" – he had not considered the law "absolutely" as "right or no[t]," but "relatively" in order to render it "consistent."[12]

To the extent that the Digest was solely concerned with questions of legal expression, it enjoyed rather limited objectives, with the result

---

[9] UC lxxix. 11.
[10] UC xxvii. 166, headed "Duo consideranda: policy and form."
[11] See UC xxvii. 122; and the discussion below, chapter 13 at n7 and nn23–32.
[12] UC xcv. 32. See also UC xcv. 10, where Bentham says he has noted only "such defects as arose immediately and solely from Wordiness and the want of System"; and UC lxxix. 1, where he observes, "*Form* of the Law in contradistinction to substance, the subject of consideration in a Digest."

that it is in this context that Bentham appears closest to eighteenth-century law reform conventions. As with so many of his contemporaries, his doctrines regarding legislative method were essentially and recognizably Baconian. Bentham was eager to align himself with the existing movement for statute consolidation and to exploit the well-rehearsed arguments advanced by its supporters. He cited the testimony of Burn, Barrington and even Blackstone, and followed the familiar tactic of appealing to earlier attempts in parliament to methodize the statute book.[13] The title chosen for the proposal, the Digest, evoked Bacon's own terminology, and Bentham appears to have conceived his scheme in terms rather similar to the traditional manuals and abridgements of English law. He was particularly struck by the clarity and synthesis achieved by Richard Burn in his popular justices' handbook, and appropriated the text as an organizing model for his own composition. "A gross conception" of the Digest could be derived from "the Titles in Dr. Burn's *Justice*... The limits of that Book... coincide nearly with those which in our first attempt we propose to prescribe to ourselves."[14]

Where Bentham distanced himself from the tradition of English law manuals was in his insistence that any such work had to be enacted by parliament. This point followed the arguments developed in the critique of common law: only parliament could produce an authentic statement of the law in England. As Bentham noted of the numerous popularizations of English law titled "Every man his own Lawyer" – "Whether it is possible for every man to be made a Lawyer by a book is what I will not be positive about at present; but this I know, that if it be, it must be by a book of the Legislature's writing."[15]

The Digest was defined for Bentham in terms of its objective of "making the Laws to be *known*, to be possessed."[16] This objective provided the point of unity between the two Digests Bentham projected at this time. The Digest was needed in the case of common law because as a fictitious system of legal rules it could never be known. In the case of statute law, it was needed because of the failures of England's legislators. This latter claim had figured in *A Comment on the Commentaries*, where Bentham sought to show that what Blackstone treated as the normal function of the judiciary, as the "interpreter" of English law, was in fact a symptom of the defective state of the statute

---

[13] See UC lxxix. 59, and UC xcvi. 86. See also his use of Bacon's teaching at *Comment*, p. 109.   [14] UC lxxix. 77, and see UC xxvii. 110.

[15] UC lxxxa. 105; and see also UC lxxxa 135, UC lxxix. 23. Although Bentham insisted that parliament had to enact the Digest, he recommended that professional "compositors" be employed for the drafting of the Digest; see UC xxvii. 119 and UC lxxxa. 112.

[16] UC lxxxa. 96.

book. For Bentham virtually all the arguments supporting a liberal or equitable interpretation of the law could be translated into arguments for statute consolidation. It was "the incapacity and inattention of Legislators only" that gave rise to "any such rules" of construction as Blackstone provided.[17]

The "inattention" of England's legislators was regularly invoked throughout the Digest manuscripts. In England, "accident" was "the parent of legislation."[18] "An act of Parliament" was "a piece of work which different persons set about with different tools, none of them Masters of the whole set."[19] It was not the "exigency of the subject matter" which made English jurisprudence "so voluminous," but the "indolence or shortsightedness of the Legislator."[20] It was "only the having been born and bred under this System of elaborate confusion that could have made the burden tolerable."[21]

The chief result of such legislative "indolence" and "incapacity" was to make it impossible for the subject to know that law which was to guide his conduct. Bentham likened the statute law to "a vast Battery, of which the greatest part of the Balls are shot in vain for want of being leveled [at] the object."[22] He estimated that "the greatest part of the people are unapprised of the very *existence* of the 99 parts in a hundred of the Laws that govern them."[23] "In the present state of the laws," he concluded, "the presumption is always so strong that an Offender knew nothing of the matter."[24] In response to this abuse of the legislative office, Bentham (later) advanced his "self-evident axiom" for legislators:

> *The notoriety of every law ought to be as extensive as its binding force...* No axiom can be more self-evident: none more important: none more universally disregarded... Yet till it is attended to and the grievance remedied, the business of legislation is from the beginning to the end of it a cruel mockery.[25]

For the utilitarian moralist, there was a direct correlation between the notoriety of the law and the legitimacy of the legal system as a whole. Since law functioned by coercing individuals through the threat of punishment, the system was effective only to the extent that individuals were aware of which actions the law declared punishable.[26]

---

[17] *Comment*, p. 160. See also p. 116 (marginal heading, "Interpretation the effect of incapacity in Legislators"), and *Laws in General*, pp. 162–4.
[18] UC xcvi. 246. [19] UC lxxa. 112. [20] UC lxiii. 3.
[21] UC lxxix. 54; and see UC cxl. 90, cited above, Introduction at n84.
[22] UC lxxix. 63. [23] UC lxxa. 135.
[24] UC lxxix. 69, and see UC lxxix. 63 and 74.
[25] *Laws in General*, p. 71, and see *Comment*, pp. 44–5.
[26] See *Laws in General*, pp. 63–4.

When such knowledge was lacking, the legislator was simply inflicting pain without the possibility of effecting correct social behavior.[27] Because of this, Bentham argued that the law could be "of use no farther than as it is known."[28] He further insisted that it was possible to double "the sum of obedience" without adding to "the quantity of rewards and punishments." "The way to double the sum of obedience" was "to double the knowledge men have" of the law: "the effect of a body of Laws is to be calculated, not from the quantity of what is *extant*, but from the quantity of what is *known*."[29]

The Digest was to further the "notoriety" of the law by perfecting two distinct legislative operations: composition and promulgation. The first, composition, referred to the "verbal expression given to the ideas which the legislator means should be communicated to the people with relation to the conduct he wishes them to observe."[30] The object of composition was "to qualify that expression in every case for the faithful exhibition of these ideas"[31] in a style comprehensible to the "meanest understanding."[32]

Correct composition, or "the maximum of comprehensive simplicity,"[33] depended on the proper combination and adjustment of four stylistic qualities: "Precision, Apprehensibility, Brevity, and Amplitude."[34] Most of the defects of English statute could be traced to misguided attempts to achieve "precision" and "amplitude" at the expense of "apprehensibility" and "brevity." Thus the legislature retained technical legal terms in the mistaken belief that this furthered precision, whereas its actual effect was to render the law incomprehensible. As Bentham said of the laws restricting "benefit of clergy," "to consider the maneuvers of the Law-Givers on this head, one should almost suppose them to have conceived that the perfection of the Laws consisted in their obscurity and to have regaled themselves with the thoughts that nobody should know what they were doing."[35]

---

[27] See UC lxxix. 74: "A Law, be it never so good in itself, becomes not only useless, but mischievous for want of Notoriety."

[28] UC lxxix. 65: "That a Law may do mischief though it be not known: that it cannot be of use farther than as it is known: that a great part of our Laws are not known: that they cannot as things stand at present be known: and accordingly it is not to be wondered at if many of them are of little use ... that there is a method whereby they might be made known: this method is endeavoured to be explained."   [29] UC lxxa. 119.

[30] Jeremy Bentham, *The Limits of Jurisprudence Defined*, ed. Charles Warren Everett (New York, 1945), p. 193.   [31] *Ibid.*, p. 194.

[32] UC lxxix. 57; and see UC cxl. 129.

[33] UC lxxix. 57.

[34] UC lxxa. 69. Bentham added "Dignity" as another quality of "inferior consideration."

[35] UC lxxa. 67. See also UC cxl. 129 and UC lxxix. 50. Most often at this time Bentham treated the technical vocabulary of English law at a more abstract level, in terms of the need to

In addition to failures of terminology, the great defect of the statute law was its sheer immensity. The legislature sacrificed all other stylistic considerations to "amplitude," leaving English law "smothered amidst a redundancy of works."[36] "To judge from their works," it seemed never to have occurred to the legislature "that words could be too many, that discourse was susceptible [of] such a quality as Brevity...[and] that there were any limits to the capacity of men's understanding."[37] For the most part, Bentham believed the verbosity of England's legislators to be unplanned as well as unnecessary. Hence the repeated emphasis on the legislature's "indolence," "shortsightedness" and "wantonness"; and hence his general claim that it was not "the nature of the subject itself," but the "wanton and deplorable waste of paper committed by Legislators" which rendered the Digest "so voluminous a work."[38] Bentham demonstrated the point graphically in *A Comment on the Commentaries* by reducing a statute against stealing sheep and oxen from 628 words to 46, and concluding from this example that "the whole compass of the Statute Law" could be contracted in "a proportion not very much inferior."[39]

Furthermore, where this voluminousness could be said to have resulted from conscious legislative policy, Bentham argued that the policy was altogether misguided and self-defeating. By amplifying the descriptive phrases in a particular statute, parliament actually confused the import of its will, instead of achieving the desired "precision." Once that will had been fully formulated, Bentham insisted, "every word that comes afterwards is a nuisance."[40] Nor did the legislature's eagerness to multiply the number of laws actually serve to make the law more comprehensive. The leading example of this mistake was found in the penal statutes. Parliament, in an entirely haphazard and impromptu manner, would simply expand the number of particular offences. To adopt Bentham's example, statutes were enacted against stealing turnips, against stealing potatoes, against stealing madder, and the list could be extended to include "every article in Miller's *Dictionary*." But in all this amplification and unnecessary particularity, the crime of Theft itself might never be systematically defined, and the law would fail to achieve actual comprehensiveness. Instead, the mass

construct a natural system of nomenclature for use in "universal jurisprudence"; see the discussion below, chapter 13 at nn19–22.
[36] *A General View of a Complete Code of Laws*, in *Bowring*, III, 208.
[37] UC lxxa. 74. See also UC lxxa. 64 and 69: "all have been sacrificed to Amplitude."
[38] UC lxxa. 62.   [39] *Comment*, pp. 142–4.
[40] UC lxxa. 73. "There are no set of men who have greater occasion to pay so much attention to the precision and force of words, as Lawyers. There are no set of men who give so many words as Lawyers. Hence it becomes a notion [that] the precision of legal words is owing to their multitude."

of penal acts received the "reproach of inordinate severity," while laboring under "all the inconveniences of the opposite effect."[41]

Bentham's principal solution to the problem of volume and verbosity was the traditional one: statute consolidation. "The method of consolidation," he reported in *A Comment*, "has been happily adopted in a few instances and begins to get in use. The Law relating to one subject is gathered out of a number of Statutes ... and reduced into one: the correspondent Statutes or part of Statutes it is gathered out of are then repealed."[42] As Bentham's own description of consolidation acknowledged, he was advocating a familiar stylistic technique already "in use." What distinguished his Digest was not the general notion of a "consolidated" statute book, but rather the format the digest required to achieve "the maximum of comprehensive simplicity."

Many of these suggestions were organized under the heading "mechanical helps to perspicuity," and much of it illustrates Bentham's notorious enthusiasm for the minutiae of law reform projects. Probably the most important of such "mechanical helps" was the construction of a systematic apparatus for the arrangement, cross-reference, and indexing of the Digest. The absence in parliamentary statute of this sort of apparatus compared unfavorably with the better legal texts such as Burn's *Justice of the Peace*. Thus, in response to Blackstone's conventional ordering of English legislation into public and private acts, Bentham charged, "Statutes themselves ... are so thoroughly void of anything that bears the semblance of order or method or regularity, as to be incapable of any classification whatsoever."[43] Not only did parliament fail to provide any satisfactory system for classifying its enactments, it likewise failed to provide any mechanism for distinguishing the separate contents of its enactments. According to the formalities of parliamentary procedure, the legislature enacted one single statute at the end of each session. Any organizing of this statute into separate acts, chapters and sections was the work of parliament's printer, not parliament itself.[44] In the absence of any official system of sectional notation, parliament adopted the verbose expedient of referring to other acts by citing whole passages verbatim in subsequent enactment, or what Bentham described as "jumbling the most heterogeneous matters ... at length in the Belly of a sentence."[45] The result was a chaotic mass "of terrific immensity,"[46] which could

---

[41] UC lxxa. 95. Bentham's examples are hypothetical; he refers to Philip Miller, *The Gardener's Dictionary*, 2 vols. (London, 1731–9). For a recent discussion of the theme, see Langbein, "*Albion's* Fatal Flaws," 117–19.

[42] *Comment*, pp. 154–5.   [43] *Comment*, p. 132.

[44] See *Comment*, pp. 130–1, and *Laws in General*, pp. 103–4n.

[45] UC lxxa. 111.   [46] UC lxxix. 61.

be decisively contracted by applying a comprehensive system of cross-reference. As Bentham put it a few years later (by which time his conception of legal arrangement had advanced dramatically), among the required features of any body of laws was "the ordinary apparatus of divisions and subdivisions, entitled by some such denominations as book, chapter, section, paragraph, article, number, and the like." This apparatus was found in "didactic works of inferior importance" and the "codes of perhaps every civilized nation but one" – "as if everything that savours of method ought to be studiously excluded from a work which stands more in need than any other of such assistances to render it intelligible."[47]

The second function of the Digest was promulgation, "that essential and much neglected branch of administration by the abandonment of which the greater part of the legislative matter that subsists is continually rendering itself worse than useless."[48] Promulgation referred to how a properly composed body of digested statute was to be communicated in order to ensure maximum notoriety.[49] As in the case of legislative composition, Bentham thought he was furnished with a perfect model of how not to proceed in the example of parliamentary law-making. Past experience demonstrated that the English legislator lacked "any more concern... about a Law than to see that it contained his sense upon the matter, was full enough, and was entered in due form upon the Roll."[50] Almost entirely neglected was the second operation of communicating the law. It was this legislative failure that forced the subject to adopt the unsatisfactory expedient of relying upon official legal abridgements and compilations for his knowledge of the law.[51] Bentham believed that parliament's irresponsibility in this regard had received formal and enthusiastic endorsement in the *Commentaries*. Blackstone had maintained that although the law had to be "prescribed," the "manner in which this notification is made is a matter of very great indifference," a phrase which Bentham seized upon with evident relish:

> I must confess it seems a matter of very *great importance*. To notify to the people a Law, is to tell them of it. Now that it is a matter of great indifference... is what I should never have imagined. I should imagine the manner how they are told of it should be such a manner as will answer

[47] *Laws in General*, p. 103n. For the corresponding discussion in the Digest manuscripts see UC lxxa. 82-8 and 135.   [48] *Laws in General*, p. 239.
[49] See UC xcvi. 243: "Composition fits the Law for men's apprehensions. Promulgation conveys it to their organs."
[50] UC lxxa. 74.   [51] See UC lxxix. 5 and 23.

the end of their being told of it ... else that they might as well not be told
of it at all.[52]

Bentham treated Promulgation as a strategy for adjusting two
necessary and antagonistic features of any system of laws. In the first
place, the law required a "brevity" of expression if it was to be capable
of being known. Much of this need would be met by consolidation
which would radically reduce the size of the statute book. But even
after consolidation the law would still require considerable "amplitude" in point of "matter" if it was to achieve its social purposes of
preventing mischief and providing security. Bentham accepted the
common view that the law would have to increase quantitatively with
the increasing complexity of social life, while rejecting this as an
adequate explanation or excuse for the voluminousness of English
law.[53] Promulgation reconciled "brevity" and "amplitude" by
enabling the legislature to impose "upon each man the task of being
acquainted [with] just such a number of [laws] as concerns himself and
no more."[54] This was achieved, as set out in *A Fragment on Government*,
by "breaking down" the Digest "into *codes* or parcels, as many as
there are classes of persons distinguishably concerned in it," and by
"introducing to the notice and possession of every person his
respective code."[55]

Bentham distinguished the production of these "personal codes"
from the process of consolidation itself. The Digest would comprise
"aggregate laws," consolidated according to subject-matter. For the
promulgation of the Digest, the laws were to be re-consolidated into
"personal codes."[56] Provided the first process of "aggregate"
consolidation was performed under Benthamic principles, in a uniform
manner of compositions employing a systematic apparatus for indexing
and cross-reference, it would be a simple procedure to reassemble the
Digest into personal codes for promulgation.[57] These codes were then
to be printed in the form of synoptic "tables" and "charts," and

---

[52] *Comment*, p. 45.
[53] See UC xcvi. 86, where this is treated as an "inadequate" cause for voluminousness; and UC lxxa. 63, where Bentham warns against looking to "the School of Barbarism" for models of legislative simplicity.
[54] UC lxxix. 30; see also UC lxxix. 15–16, 27.   [55] *Fragment*, p. 499.
[56] UC lxxix. 21: "The Laws whose principle of unity is a certain *Subject-matter* or a Certain *End* ... may be stiled the *Aggregate* Laws, in contradistinction to those others whose principle of unity is a certain denomination of *person*; which latter may be stiled the Personal Laws."
[57] See UC lxxix. 118: "the business is so to order these portions of a Code ... whose bond of unity is a *common subject-matter*, that the collecting of them afterwards for the purposes of notification into a Code whose bond of unity is '*person*' may be an affair of mere mechanical juxtaposition." See also UC lxxix. 86–7.

"hung up at places wherever the respective Transactions to which they relate" occur. On this basis, Bentham assembled a cluttered vision of daily life decorated by the utilitarian promulgator:

> Laws relative to Parochial Affairs should be hung up ... in every Vestry. Laws relative to Commercial contracts in general in the Exchange ... in the Halls of the several Companies, and [in] the Compting Housing or shop of every Trader ... Laws relating to Travelling in general at every Turnpike House and every *room* of entertainment in every *House* of entertainment ... Laws relative to the internal economy of Houses to be stuck up in Houses ... [58]

Bentham during this period drafted two specimens of such personal codes: a "Builder's Act" and a "Publican's Law."[59] These are of interest not only as concrete applications of the Benthamic principles of scientific composition and promulgation. They also reinforce the limited character of the Digest project itself, and thereby go some way towards explaining Bentham's perplexing optimism in 1775 that the "plan of a Digest" might be completed in a few months' time. In both cases Bentham was merely refashioning existing examples of consolidation, rather than starting at the beginning with the undigested statute law.[60] His Builder's Act was based on a consolidating act of 1772 (12 Geo III c. 73), and the Publican's Law was composed from the relevant section of Burn's *Justice of the Peace*. What was new in these laws was not the actual "digestion," but the method pursued to achieve maximum notoriety. Thus when Bentham described his Builder's Act in a draft "advertisement" as "digested after a method entirely new," he referred to the fact that it was "printed in the form of a Table whereby persons of that business may see at one view all the Regulations which concern them," a typography designed "to render the contents as concise as easily to be comprehended as possible, both to the eye as well as the understanding."[61]

Given the condition of the relevant manuscripts it is doubtless impossible to arrive at any conclusive picture of the "plan of a Digest of the laws." It is probable that the strategies for composition and promulgation surveyed here were only parts of a larger program.[62] But

---

[58] UC lxxix. 15–6; see also UC lxxa. 138.

[59] The Builder's Act is at UC xcvi. 222–30; the Publican's Law is at UC lxxix. 78–103.

[60] See Bentham's note at UC xcvi. 222: "Analyse thus all the Reducing Acts which have been published ... To go to work upon Acts not reduced would be endless work."

[61] UC xcvi. 222.

[62] Some further features of the Digest program can be identified. See UC lxxix. 57, 115, 35–42, where Bentham discusses the need for a uniform style of expression in legislation; and UC

it does seem reasonably clear that the cornerstone of Bentham's Digest for "making the laws to be *known*, to be possessed" was the consolidation of the statute book, the law reform endorsed by numerous legal writers and the reform which "happily" was beginning "to get in use." It was probably owing to this sympathetic background that Bentham did not find it necessary to explore the concept of consolidation itself at any great length in these materials.

Conspicuously absent in the material examined thus far was any attempt by Bentham to indicate how parliament might be expected to respond to such an enlightened legislative strategy. This was no trivial omission. As we have seen, the perceived limitations of parliamentary law-making exercised a pervasive influence on eighteenth-century attitudes to legal development, and the advocates of law reform displayed special care in their programs of improvement not to expect too much of the legislature.[63] In his own impatient charges against parliament's handiwork, Bentham amply testified to the nature of the difficulty. The "general rules" of "modern British legislation," as we have seen him record in frustration, were "never to move a finger till your passions are inflamed, nor ever to look further than your nose."[64] By insisting that law reform could only be effected by parliament, Bentham rendered all the more substantial the practical matter of how the eighteenth-century parliament could be transformed into a reliable and prescient legislative machine.

The one set of Digest manuscripts in which the question is approached was headed, "Of the obstacles to a reform in Legislation."[65] The material is as revealing in what it neglects as in what it contains. For Bentham nearly all these obstacles were conceived as "resulting from the Interests and Prejudices of various classes of men."[66] They were to be overcome not by any administrative or institutional changes, but through a momentous raising of parliament's legislative consciousness.[67] The first step in this direction was to become a set-piece of the

---

xxvii. 124, where he suggests using the Digest to extend beneficial local acts throughout the kingdom. For promulgation, see UC lxxa. 85–8, where Bentham explores several graphic techniques for printing the personal codes; and UC lxxix. 72–3, where he suggests translating some of the codes.

[63] See the discussion above, chapter 9 at nn40–42 and n60, and chapter 10 at nn82–84.

[64] UC cxl. 92, cited above, chapter 10 at n9. See also his comments in *Laws in General*, pp. 239–40.

[65] See UC xcvi. 72, where "Obstacles" appears as an appendix to a projected work on legislation; and UC xcvii. 1, for a very rough "sketch" of the "Obstacles" section. Most of the material on "obstacles" or "préjugés" is at UC xcvii. 1–54, though Bentham raises similar themes throughout his writings during this period.

[66] UC clxix. 1 (item 20).

[67] The general lack of attention to matters of government administration and management at this stage of Bentham's career is emphasized by Hume in *Bentham and Bureaucracy*, chapter 3.

Benthamic reform advocacy. This was to indicate the extent to which the failures of English law served the professional interests of the legal profession at the expense of the rest of the community. Bentham liked to compare this exposé of the "race of lawyers" and their "jurisprudential superstition" to the *philosophes'* exposing of "priestcraft."[68] Indeed, "the forming a Digest of the Law" was "to Lawyers, what the making a translation of the Bible was to Church men."[69] In law, "the defects of the science" were the "patrimony of the profession," and it could "not be expected that the bulk of the profession should entertain a heartfelt desire to diminish these defects."[70]

Bentham seems also to have appreciated the need for some broader ideological offensive to combat the conventions of legislative complacency. In one draft he isolated a set of popular assumptions he would have to rebut to demonstrate that the "voluminousness" of English law was "not irremediable":

> Inadequate and irremediable causes found out for it: First cause false, increase of vice. Second cause false, amplitude of dominion. Third cause inadequate, increase of trade. Fourth cause inadequate, care taken of liberty.[71]

Several of these points received further elaboration, particularly on the emotive question as to whether the quantity of law better served the liberty of the subject.[72] But, in general, this discussion remained undeveloped, and it was not until the early 1780s that Bentham evolved the proper analytical formula to show that even the most complex social relations could be accommodated within a rigorously ordered system of legal arrangement.

In dealing directly with problems regarding parliament's legislative procedure, Bentham was even briefer, again insisting that the "obstacles" were largely ideological. When faced with the crucial difficulty that the enactment of such a Digest would require procedures "inconsistent with Parliamentary forms," Bentham simply countered that this should not be allowed to be a problem. Parliamentary procedure was merely a matter of "accident" and "inattention," and

---

[68] See UC xcvii. 94–5 (one "Jurisprudential and Ecclesiastical Superstition").
[69] UC xxvii. 124.
[70] UC xxvii. 167; see also UC xxvii. 96, 102 and UC lxxa. 122, 125.
[71] UC xcvi. 86.
[72] See UC xcvii. 35 and UC lxxa. 90: "legislators, content to quiet themselves with the standing apology that complicated laws are a necessary part of the purchase as well as one cause of Liberty, hath hitherto made the simplification of them no part of their concern." On this general issue, see Long, *Bentham on Liberty*, pp. 65–83.

should never have attracted any "prejudice in its favour."[73] Opposition to altering these "forms" came "after all to the old prejudice of an abhorrence to everying new, merely because it is new." Such forms were of value only "as they are subservient to certain ends; and when it can be shown that these ends can better be answered by a new form, must the old one with its inconveniences be entailed on us forever?"[74]

Bentham's impatience with these potential objections probably best explains his apparent insensitivity to the more practical matter of mobilizing parliament's legislative will. For him these practicalities would simply vanish once parliament was shown the way. All that parliament required was a single specimen of legislative perfection. It was not even necessary to produce an entire Digest of the statute book. While he admitted that the pleas of such respected figures as Barrington, Burn and even Blackstone on behalf of comprehensive legislative consolidation had not "hitherto been attended with any effect," Bentham confidently responded:

> I know there is a difference between wishing that a thing were done, and showing in detail how it may be done; and in that difference is founded so much of excuse as hath hitherto been competent.[75]

The example Bentham adopted for "showing in detail" how the Digest was to "be done" was a Turnpike Act.[76] Again, he took a huge shortcut by using a body of law which had already been consolidated by parliament and therefore only required revision. Both the turnpike and highway laws had been consolidated in 1767 (7 Geo III c. 40 and c 42), and were later repealed and re-consolidated in 1773 (13 Geo III c. 78 and c. 84).[77] The surviving materials of this projected Turnpike Act are in an even less complete state than the Builder's or Publican's Acts, but there is enough to indicate the nature of Bentham's objectives.

Bentham's basic point was that the Turnpike Act would serve as a model of consolidation for the entire Digest. "A Treatise on legislation," he observed, "would have been imperfect... without such a specimen as this."[78] Moreover, the availability of such a model would have a direct impact on conditions in parliament. "The supposed immensity" of the task "shrinks into a moderate dimension" once the

---

[73] UC lxxix. 52.   [74] UC lxxa. 104(b).   [75] UC lxxix. 59.

[76] See UC lxxix. 104–37 and UC xcv. 1–20, 22–118.

[77] Bentham appears to have used a draft of the 1773 act, and the recent consolidation of this law may also explain why he chose it as an example.

[78] UC xcv. 15; and see UC xcv. 16: "If my method of Composition be worth learning, there cannot be a more effectual way of teaching it."

legislator came to realize "that in seeing one [specimen], he sees them all."[79] The Turnpike Act also offered a solution to the problems arising from "the prolixity of the proceedings" in parliament which were likely to frustrate any reform effort. Parliament would only have to debate a single time whether to enact a "Digest of every Code" according to the method applied in the Turnpike Act. This achieved, the "general method once agreed upon ... will supersede, and cut off all debates concerning each one in particular."[80] In taking the turnpike law as his example, Bentham had purposely chosen "a fit rich[?] specimen" containing a great "variety of articles" and comprising a "branch of the law complete within itself."[81] Yet, while exploring this one branch of law in detail, Bentham stressed that he was also addressing the statute book in its entirety. "What is here done," he maintained, conformed to "the manner of those Chemists" who investigated a "single parcel" of a mine "for the judgment that may be obtained from it of the whole." " 'Tis the whole map therefore of the Statute Law," and not "this small fragment of it," that was being considered in the "decomposing" of "the old draught, and the recombining in the new one."[82]

The model Turnpike Act thus represented the linch-pin of Bentham's strategy for overcoming parliamentary indolence. This approach, relying as it did on the untested confidence that parliament would "rear the fabric of felicity"[83] once it was shown the way, contained all the ingredients for disaster which confronted Bentham some twenty years later when he presented and tried to erect his model prison. On that occasion, though parliament responded favorably, the British government, it appeared to Bentham, simply failed to act on the model of perfection which had been displayed before it. And Bentham was left to find another solution, which eventually entailed radical politics and comprehensive parliamentary reform.[84] At this stage, however, the legislative will went untested. Like so much else of the material assembled in the 1770s, the "plan for a Digest" and the Turnpike Act remained unfinished and unpublished, so that Bentham, having failed to show "in detail" how the work was to be done, continued to allow "so much of an excuse as hath hitherto been competent."[85]

By about the time Bentham published *A Fragment on Government* in

[79] UC xcv. 9.
[80] UC lxxix. 32. See also UC lxiii. 4–5 and UC xcv. 5.
[81] UC xcv. 4. See also UC xcv. 15–16 and UC lxxix. 104.   [82] UC xcv. 4.
[83] The general "object" of Bentham's system, as described in *Morals and Legislation*, p. 11.
[84] For an account of this development, which corrects Bentham's own often misleading version, see J. R. Dinwiddy, "Bentham's Transition to Political Radicalism," *Journal of the History of Ideas*, XXXVI (1975), 683–700.   [85] UC lxxix. 59, cited above, n75.

1776, he had developed the materials for a reasonably coherent version of the science of legislation. Its most radical feature derived from the philosophical onslaught upon common law jurisprudence: the common law was to be transformed into statute. The statute law itself was to be reformed to produce the maximum notoriety for the law: statutes were to be digested, systematized and re-digested into personal codes. Upon the implementation of these reforms, Bentham could envisage the consummation of the "science of jurisprudence; the art of knowing what has actually been done in the way of internal government."[86] Once the "common law" was "transformed into statute law," "common law jurisprudence" would instantly lose "its object." Once statute law was reformed into "what it ought to be and might be," the rest of jurisprudence would likewise "be at an end." The knowledge of statute law would then no longer demand a separate science: "it would be no more a science of itself than the knowledge of what is contained in newspapers is a science itself."[87]

Even at the very time these remarks were made, Bentham most likely recognized them as exaggerated claims. While many of the specific proposals first aired in the 1770s remained basic parts of Bentham's reform program, the Digest was too constrained a project to survive very long as a principal vehicle of Bentham's legislative science.[88] Within the next five years, the techniques and strategies of the Digest program were to be subsumed within a much grander vision of the legislator's art. And the particular English debate regarding the relationship between common law and statute, from which the Digest first emerged, was effectively transcended. Bentham's model of the ideal system of laws was recast from one in which all law was properly composed statute law, into one in which such statute law satisfied the further goal of constituting a comprehensive and logically complete legal order.

---

[86] UC lxix. 195.   [87] UC lxix. 197.

[88] For Bentham's later and greatly expanded treatment of composition and promulgation, see *Nomography; or the Art of Inditing Laws*, in *Bowring*, III, 231–83.

13

◁ ═══════════════════════════════════════ ▷

From Blackstone to the *Pannomion*

THE IDEA OF A NATURAL ARRANGEMENT

When Bentham published *An Introduction to the Principles of Morals and Legislation* in 1789, it was already some nine years overdue. The work, originally composed for "no other destination than that of serving as an introduction to a plan of a penal code," had been virtually complete (and most of it in print) by 1780. But in correcting some "flaws" in his creation, Bentham "found himself unexpectedly entangled in an unsuspected corner of the metaphysical maze."[1] The process of metaphysical disentanglement led to *Of Laws in General*, which Bentham finished two years later. Bentham entertained several schemes for the publication of this more general and systematic examination of law, but the work ultimately remained in manuscript throughout his lifetime.[2] For our purposes, the most important result of the discussion in *Of Laws in General* was to enable Bentham to depict, in outline at least, the nature of a comprehensive system of legislation. The structure of this legislative system centered on a novel account of a logically unified and exhaustive classification of law, and its elaboration marked the decisive final phase of Bentham's youthful engagement with English legal orthodoxy. It was this intellectual breakthrough which gave substance, if not realization, to his lifelong ambition to construct "a complete body of law; a *pannomion*, if so it might be termed."[3]

The question tackled in *Of Laws in General* originated in the concluding remarks of the final chapter of *An Introduction to the Principles of Morals and Legislation* on the "limits of penal jurisprudence," where Bentham attempted to define precisely the relationship between penal and civil law. This relationship, he argued, could only be assessed by confronting a more fundamental jurisprudential question: "it will be necessary to ascertain what *a law* is; meaning one entire but single

---

[1] *Morals and Legislation*, p. 1.
[2] See the editorial introductions to *Morals and Legislation*, pp. xxxvii–ix, and *Laws in General*, pp. xxxi–v.   [3] *Morals and Legislation*, p. 305.

law."[4] And this question Bentham immediately identified with a larger problem, that of the conceptualization of a complete body of law:

> The idea of a law, meaning one single but entire law, is in a manner inseparably connected with that of a complete body of laws: so that what is a law and what are the contents of a complete body of the laws are questions which neither can well be answered without the other. A body of laws is a vast and complicated piece of mechanism, of which no part can be fully explained without the rest.[5]

In describing how *Of Laws in General* originated (perhaps hoping to justify the long delay in publishing *An Introduction*), Bentham stressed the "unexpected" and "unsuspected" character of the questions which confronted him. Nonetheless, a discernible line of continuity can be perceived between this work and several topics already explored in the 1770s. Particular issues at the heart of *Of Laws in General*, such as "all laws penal" or "law, when complete," had received tentative treatment in the preceding decade.[6] Furthermore, Bentham conceived *Of Laws in General* as addressed to legal "form" as opposed to legal "matter," a distinction first elaborated in the Digest manuscripts. As there, Bentham emphasized that perfecting legal "form" was a necessary preliminary and complement to the reform of substantive law. In contrast to the Digest project, however, Bentham in the 1780s dealt with the distinction at a more abstract and comprehensive level of analysis. His subject, he observed in 1789, was not the law meaning "the statute," but the law meaning "the *logical*, the *ideal*, the *intellectual* whole."[7] Yet even this special concern in *Of Laws in General* with the law as an "intellectual whole" recalls discussions of the 1770s. Here, as in so much else of Bentham's first legal speculations, to trace his interests back to their beginnings is to return to Blackstone's *Commentaries on the Laws of England*.

One of the few compliments Bentham paid Blackstone was the acknowledgment that he had perfected what Bentham termed the "technical arrangement" of English law: "'Tis to him we owe such an arrangement of the elements of Jurisprudence, as wants little, perhaps, of being the best that a technical nomenclature will admit of." According to Bentham, this "business of arrangement" was one of the most demanding tasks in expository jurisprudence, and here Blackstone had not only excelled, but had surpassed "anything in that way that has

---

[4] *Ibid.*, p. 299, and see p. 8.
[5] *Ibid.*, p. 299n.
[6] See UC xcvi. 102–8 and UC lxxa. 8.
[7] *Morals and Legislation*, p. 301.

hitherto appeared."[8] In these remarks, Bentham endorsed what we have seen to be a familiar point of praise for the *Commentaries*, conceding Blackstone's singular achievement in producing a methodical and coherent structure for the system of law in England.[9] But he also used the compliment to introduce by way of contrast a fundamental tenet of Benthamic jurisprudence, "the idea of a natural arrangement":

> That arrangement of the materials of any science, may, I take it, be termed a *natural* one, which takes such properties to characterize them by, as men in general are, by the common constitution of man's *nature*, disposed to attend to: such, in other words, as *naturally*, that is readily, engage, and firmly fix the attention of any one to whom they are pointed out.[10]

The construction of such a "natural arrangement" marked a final stage in the creation of an authentic science of jurisprudence.[11] "In the early ages of jurisprudence," it was impossible to discern any coherent order in legal practices – "when a man proposed a Law he knew not what relation it bore to the whole object of Jurisprudence: he knew not how it connected to the rest of the System."[12] In this, legal learning followed the growth of knowledge generally, for "a methodical and exhaustive arrangement" represented "one of the last improvements a Science can receive."[13] Thus, when Bentham surveyed the "state of the science at present," he pointed not only to the substantive flaws in existing legal systems, but also the general failure of legal writers to present their subject in anything like a methodical or comprehensive form. "Everything" was done "by unconnected sallies and partial views." "All that [was] known" concerning legislation remained "dispersed in a multitude of disjointed aphorisms," and these insights, even if "collected or brought together," would "no more be a regular body or institute of the art of legislation than the aphorisms of Hippocrates are of medicine."[14]

In the development of legal science, Blackstone's efforts could be viewed as a penultimate stage leading to the "natural arrangement." In the first place, the *Commentaries* offered a powerful short-cut for any

---

[8] *Fragment*, pp. 414–15.
[9] See above, chapter 1 at nn20–22, and my "From Bentham to Benthamism," *Historical Journal*, XXVIII (1985), 205.   [10] *Fragment*, p. 415.
[11] The central place of classification, arrangement and definition in Bentham's general understanding of scientific method is helpfully summarized by Hart in his introduction to the Methuen paper edition of *An Introduction to the Principles of Morals and Legislation*, ed. J. H. Burns and H. L. A. Hart (London, 1982), pp. xxxvii–xl.
[12] UC lxiii. 6, which continues: "As speech came before Grammar, so did Laws before Systems of Jurisprudence."
[13] *Ibid.*   [14] UC xxvii. 165.

attempt at a systematic view of English law. It was no longer necessary to consult "Hale, Hawkins, Wood and other systematical writers" whom Blackstone had "left so far behind him."[15] Even more important, by perfecting the system of technical arrangement, Blackstone had demonstrated the very practicability of reducing an entire system of law into manageable form by applying a uniform system of classification. In this context, Bentham was particularly struck by Blackstone's highly compressed, synoptic *An Analysis of the Laws of England*, which set out the structure for the *Commentaries*. Indeed, "from nothing" had Bentham "derived so much advantage as from that most concise and useful composition, the Map of the Science [of] Jurisprudence which stands prefixed to his *Analysis*." Yet, it was only upon discovering "its imperfections" that he began to derive "any benefit."[16]

Bentham retained these observations in *A Comment on the Commentaries*, though his tone was more carping. Blackstone's *Analysis* in fact merely offered "the show of symmetry," a feat which owed as much to Blackstone's printer as to Blackstone himself. Nonetheless, the work was still of value in providing a methodical structure for the arrangement of English law. Its "principal use," reported Bentham, was its "plan of division," a point which Bentham appears to have taken quite literally.[17] Thus, even after his Blackstone campaign of 1774–76, Bentham was still using this "plan of division" as the organizing model for his own projected "Critical Elements of Jurisprudence."[18] For the most part, however, Bentham made use of Blackstone's arrangement not by adopting or perfecting it, but by viewing it as a model against which he could assemble his own system of natural arrangement. As elsewhere, Bentham was far more interested in Blackstone's failures than in his successes, and his own rival notions of legal arrangement can be identified largely in terms of his particular complaints against Blackstone's methods.

No feature of the *Commentaries* received so much censure as Blackstone's overwhelming linguistic imprecision and vacuous terminology. "His nomenclature," Bentham maintained," [is] like a weathercock: you never meet the same term twice together in the same place." "*His definitions*" comprised "strings of identical proposi-

---

[15] UC xxvii. 99. See also UC xcvi. 156, where Bentham adopts Blackstone's account of English penal law and notes, "that celebrated work besides the simple expositions of the several regulations it exhibits contains at once the clearest view of the several regulations it enumerates."   [16] UC xxvii. 99.

[17] *Comment*, pp. 340–1. See also *Fragment*, pp. 418–19, where Bentham concedes that the *Analysis* in parts conforms to the system of natural arrangement.

[18] *Corr.* I, 358–9, and see UC xcvi. 98–127.

tions...explaining *ignotum per ignotius.*"[19] Hence, where Blackstone's teaching was not "evidently false," it proved simply "unmeaning," the result of his reliance upon "declamation" in the place of "definition" which left "the approaches of the science" of law infested with a "flock of chimeras."[20]

At the most basic level, Bentham's charge referred to Blackstone's adherence to the technical vocabulary of English law. His retention of such terms as "misprisions, contempts, felonies, praemunires" ensured that the technical arrangement could never achieve the practical objective of any system of legal classification, "that of enabling the greatest number of persons possible to arrive at a true knowledge of the contents of the body of Laws in being."[21] In a more fundamental way, the abuse of language in the *Commentaries* indicated Blackstone's failure to perceive the proper requirements for an authentically philosophical exposition of law. These requirements had been set by the two "great physicians of the human mind," Locke and Helvetius, and it was only through a rigorous application of their program for "perpetual and regular definition" that legal learning could be transformed into scientific knowledge.

> Nothing has been, nothing will be, nothing ever can be done on the subject of Law that deserves the name of Science, till that universal precept of Locke, enforced...by Helvetius, be steadily pursued, "Define your words."[22]

In the 1770s Bentham most often treated the question of legal definition and nomenclature under the heading of "metaphysics," metaphysics itself being "neither more nor less than this, to examine what ideas we have belonging to the terms we use."[23] Accordingly, "every science" had "its metaphysics," as "every science has its leading terms that are in constant use."[24] But in the case of law, metaphysics was especially critical, for "all questions of Law are no more than questions concerning the import of words."[25] Bentham's concern with "legal metaphysics" was largely instrumental, and many of the claims he made for it replicated the arguments for correct legal

---

[19] *Comment*, pp. 349 and 346n.   [20] *Ibid.*, pp. 64, 18, 69, 7.
[21] *Ibid.*, p. 340.
[22] *Ibid.*, pp. 346–7. It is indicative of the weight Bentham placed on this injunction that he began *A Comment on the Commentaries* by first considering "what the office of definition is"; *Comment*, p. 3.
[23] UC lxix. 152. The important relationship between Bentham's "metaphysics" and his jurisprudence is clarified by Harrison, in *Bentham*, pp. 47–76. I am much indebted to this valuable discussion.   [24] *Ibid.*
[25] UC lxix. 181; and see UC xxvii. 131 and 145 where Bentham explains his inability to "keep clear of metaphysics."

"form" rehearsed in the Digest manuscripts. The legislator, regardless of "how just and comprehensive" his designs might be, still needed to communicate those designs in an effective manner and so was forced to take account of "words," those "awkward and intractable instruments of the mind."[26] Accordingly, Bentham argued that "improvement in point of language" was "almost the necessary concommitant and forerunner of improvements in the law." "To improve the work" of legislation, it was necessary "to improve the instrument" – "Grammar and Legislation must work in concert."[27]

At the same time Bentham also suggested a more extensive role for legal metaphysics in addition to the immediate task of constructing a "suite of terms" to replace the technical terms used in existing legal systems. Here he pointed to the manner in which linguistic precision and regularity bore on the larger question of being able to conceive of a system of law as a single, coherent unit of orderly parts. As he observed in a characteristic passage: "The regularity of the whole plane, the correspondence of the several parts of it, the description of the several offences...every thing in short depends upon the wording."[28]

In addition to its linguistic exactitude, the natural arrangement was further distinguished by its comprehensiveness. Blackstone's technical arrangement, as Bentham bitingly charged in *A Fragment on Government*, may have provided "a sink" which would "swallow any garbage that is thrown into it," but there was nothing in this system of classification to ensure that it comprehended all possible legal matter.[29] The natural arrangement, in contrast, was "methodical" both because it furnished "consistent principles and connected rules" and because it was "exhaustive." What was required was a system of classification which enabled legislators to "take a view of the whole field that lies before them":[30]

> Unless you draw a circle round the whole extent of Jurisprudence you do nothing. While any the least part is left without the circle, the imagination is still distracted and overwhelmed with the idea of immensity. Hide the ends of a fish pond, you fancy it a river.[31]

[26] UC xxvii. 166–7.
[27] UC xxvii. 157, and see *Laws in General*, p. 245 on grammar and legislation.
[28] UC xxvii. 45.   [29] *Fragment*, p. 416.
[30] UC xxvii. 165, "The present is an attempt to give to the art of legislation...something of the form of a science: to furnish it with a set of consistent principles and connected rules."
[31] UC xxvii. 123. See also UC lxix. 182, "Jurisprudence wants an Architect to build up for it a competent[?] suite of terms and expressions to lodge separately those meanings which now either are absolutely without a mansion, or else huddled up by half dozens together in the obscure and ambiguous abodes which the current Nomenclature affords."

In specifying this feature of the natural arrangement, Bentham again took his cue from non-legal sources. Whereas Locke set the requirement for linguistic precision, natural philosophers and philologists established the need for exhaustive systems of classification. Blackstone had sought little more than a stylish version of conventional orderings of the legal system. But Bentham remained certain that the traditional authorities were a positive hindrance – "we must shut up our Law-Books and open those of Natural History: 'tis not Finch or Coke or Hale we are to look to for assistance here, but...Linnaeus and Sauvages."[32]

The first published product of Bentham's search for a natural scheme of legal classification was the elaborate and protracted "Division of Offences" which comprised the sixteenth chapter (and nearly one third of the text) of *An Introduction to the Principles of Morals and Legislation*. The chapter in fact constituted a contracted version of the material Bentham originally assembled for a systematic exposition and analysis of offences in his projected "Principles of Legal Polity."[33] Nonetheless, Bentham believed what survived in *An Introduction* sufficed to make good his claims for the natural arrangement presented thirteen years earlier in *A Fragment on Government*. The connection between his attack on Blackstone's "technical" system and his "natural" Division of Offences was highlighted by Bentham himself, particularly in the fourth section of the chapter on the "Advantages of the present method." There Bentham referred directly to *A Fragment on Government* and lifted whole passages verbatim from that original critique.[34]

These remarks centered on the goal by reference to which Bentham first characterized the natural system of legal arrangement, that which would most "readily engage and firmly fix the attention of any one" examining the laws.[35] This goal had an immediate utilitarian value in that the natural arrangement, by definition, directly served the notoriety of the legal system.[36] But Bentham also specified a more fundamental point of connection between a utilitarian conception of legal practices and the idea of a natural arrangement of law. This derived from the

[32] UC xliii. 71; Bentham's final reference is to the French botanist, Francois Boissier de Sauvages de la Croix. See also UC xxvii. 109 on Linnaeus and arrangement. The other figure frequently referred to in this context is James Harris, author of *Hermes, or a Philosophical Enquiry Concerning Universal Grammar* (London, 1751).

[33] See *Morals and Legislation*, p. xxxviii (editorial introduction).

[34] See *ibid.*, pp. 5 and 272n; compare *Morals and Legislation*, pp. 272–3 (paragraph 57) and pp. 273–4 (paragraph 59) with *Fragment*, pp. 415, 416–17.

[35] *Fragment*, p. 415.   [36] See *ibid.*, pp. 415–16.

claim that the manner in which man most "naturally" perceived the law was in terms of its utilitarian purposes:

> With respect to actions in general, there is no property in them that is calculated so readily to engage, and so firmly to fix the attention of an observer, as the *tendency* they may have *to*, or the *divergency...from*, that which may be styled the common *end* of all of them. The end I mean is *Happiness*: and this *tendency* in any act is what we style its *utility*: as this *divergency* is that to which we give the name of *mischievousness*.[37]

In other words, to arrange laws naturally was to classify them according to the mischievousness of the actions these laws sought to control, and thus a natural arrangement of law coincided with a utilitarian arrangement.

Because of this coincidence, the natural arrangement also "points out the reason of the law."[38] To place an action within the natural division of offences was to indicate the "forms and degrees of *mischievousness*" which led the legislator to turn that "mode of conduct" into a legal offence. Conversely, the natural arrangement also indicated the impropriety of a "bad law" (one prohibiting a mode of conduct in fact "*not* mischievous") because of the difficulty which would necessarily occur in "finding a place for it in such an arrangement."[39] Therefore, the natural arrangement, while specifically designed for expository jurisprudence, also furnished a "compendium" of "*censorial* Jurisprudence": "a slight but comprehensive sketch of what [law] *ought to be*."[40]

The Division of Offences presented in *An Introduction to the Principles of Morals and Legislation* followed from this rubric.[41] The legislator created offences as "the good of the community" required, and the main "classes of offences" were arranged according to the manner in which an offensive action affected the community's good. The mischievous act could either affect an "assignable" person or a group of individually unassignable persons. In the former case, the act was termed a "private offence." Distinguishing further, such a private offence could either affect the "offender himself" (a "self-regarding offence") or an assignable person "other than the offender" (simply a "private offence"). These distinctions formed the basis of the first and third main classes of offences. If the offence was not individually assignable, it could either affect "the whole community" or an assignable "lesser circle" of the community. In the former instance, the offences were

---

[37] *Ibid.*, p. 415.   [38] *Ibid.*, pp. 416–17 and *Morals and Legislation*, pp. 273–4.
[39] *Fragment*, p. 416.   [40] *Ibid.*, p. 417.
[41] The following exegesis is based on *Morals and Legislation*, pp. 188–9.

styled "public offences," in the latter, "semi-public offences." These comprised the second and fourth of the main classes of offences. These classes were then divided and sub-divided, each division again being determined by the operation of the particular mischief the law sought to control. Finally, Bentham further analyzed the first class of offences (private offences) into particular "genera" – the stage at which his system began to coincide with the names of offences "already current among the people."[42] This analysis would then serve as a model for the other main classes.

Bentham himself was eager to identify the particular triumphs embodied in this labored catalogue of offences. In the first place, he had eliminated the technical nomenclature adopted by Blackstone. As promised in *A Fragment on Government*, such technical terms as "misprisions" and "praemunires" had been "banished at once to the region of *quiddities* and *substantial forms*."[43] Moreover, he had fully accounted for those conventional terms which were retained. Thus Bentham claimed to have presented the first satisfactory analysis of the traditional distinction between "private" and "public offences," and the first systematic explanation of "self-regarding offences."[44] In this sense, he had constructed a truly natural – meaning fully comprehensible – system of offences. Beyond this, Bentham also claimed to have constructed a fully comprehensive system of offences. Whatever the "necessary" limits of this particular version of the division of offences, what had been catalogued was still "the logical whole, constituted by the sum total of possible offences."[45]

This success in covering the "sum total of possible offences" derived from Bentham's method of division – the "method of *bipartition*" which proceeded by "dividing each superior branch into two, and but two, immediately subordinate ones; beginning with the logical whole, dividing that into two parts, then each of those parts into two others; and so on."[46] The "logical whole" in question was the sum total of acts turned into "offences" as "the good of the community" demanded. By starting with this logical whole and by proceeding by bipartition, Bentham ensured that the Division of Offences was exhaustive.

This in fact proved a rather demanding methodology, and in several places Bentham simply abandoned it. Such lapses were always explained in terms of the "tyranny of language." It was the shortcomings in

---

[42] *Ibid.*, p. 222.
[43] *Fragment*, p. 418, and see *Morals and Legislation*, p. 207n on trusts.
[44] *Morals and Legislation*, p. 270.
[45] *Ibid.*, p. 271, and see p. 274 (paragraph 59).   [46] *Ibid.*, p. 187n.

existing vocabulary, rather than any conceptual defects, that rendered the symmetry of bipartition on occasion impracticable. The most obvious example of this was the fifth main class of offences, the "*multiform* or *heterogeneous offences*" comprising offences "by *falsehood*" or "against *trust*."[47] This class Bentham admitted to constitute "a blemish in the present system,"[48] and in dividing the class he was forced "to deviate in some degree from the rigid rules of the exhaustive method."[49] Nonetheless, by the completion of the analysis, Bentham was confident that he had restored the symmetry of the classificatory scheme by demonstrating the essentially linguistic nature of the apparent anomaly. Although this class exhibited "at first view an irregularity," this was "presently corrected, when the analysis returns back, as it does after a step or two, into the path from which the tyranny of language had forced it a while to deviate."[50]

In *An Introduction to the Principles of Morals and Legislation*, Bentham did not in fact dwell on the manner in which he had conquered the "logical whole" of legal offences. The explanation of bipartition, for example, was relegated to a footnote. This doubtless reflected the purpose of the work as addressed to legal "matter" and not legal "form."[51] *An Introduction to the Principles of Morals and Legislation* chiefly explained how according to the principle of utility the legislator could legitimately use the great engine of punishment to ensure public happiness. Accordingly, Bentham was more interested in the way in which his system of classification informed the legislator as to which sorts of penalties were appropriate to each class and sub-class of offences, an emphasis which made perfect sense given the work's original purpose of introducing "a plan of a penal code."[52] However, in 1789, Bentham decided that it would have been better for "the analytic discussion relative to the classification of offences" to be "transferred to a separate treatise, in which the system of legislation is considered solely in respect of its form."[53] This recommendation reflected the new insights which followed Bentham's examination of "what a law is," and the larger purposes the Division of Offences was to serve in the light of *Of Laws in General*.

---

[47] *Ibid.*, pp. 190–1.   [48] *Ibid.*, p. 190n.   [49] *Ibid.*, p. 196n.

[50] *Ibid.*, pp. 270–1. By the time he had decided to publish the work in 1789, Bentham believed he could dispense with the anomalous class altogether, see p. 191n. For other comments on the linguistic problems in creating the Division of Offences, see pp. 188–9n, 271–2.

[51] See *Laws in General*, pp. 233–4.

[52] See *Morals and Legislation*, pp. 274–80 on the "Characters of the five classes."

[53] *Ibid.*, p. 4.

THE COMPLETE BODY OF LAW

Bentham began *Of Laws in General* with a definition:

> A law may be defined as an assemblage of signs declarative of a volition conceived or adopted by the *sovereign* in a state, concerning the conduct to be observed in a certain *case* by a certain person or class of persons, who in the case in question are or are supposed to be subject to his power.[54]

The first part of the "volition" a sovereign or legislator "declared" in a law comprised its *"directive"* part.[55] In the simplest and most common form, the directive part specified some "object" (a type of human action) which the legislator sought to control. Thus, the directive part served "to make known to you what the inclination of the legislator is." Added to this was a further declaration which made "known to you what motive the legislator has furnished you with for complying with that inclination," and which was styled "the *sanctional* or *incitative*" part of the law. Usually the motive furnished by the legislator was "of the nature of punishment" for disobedience, in which case the sanctional part of the law was styled *"comminative."*

The *"directive"* and *"sanctional"* parts taken together composed "the notion of an object which might in a certain sense admit of the appellation of a law." But at this stage the sanctional part represented merely a *"prediction"* – "as an expression of will, it is impotent." Giving the legislative will potency concerned the "force" of the law, and required the legislator to issue a second law commanding "some person to verify the prediction that accompanied the first." The second, *"subsidiary"* law addressed all the agents involved in the execution of the law, and together with the other subsidiary laws composed the rules of "procedure." These subsidiary laws would, in turn, contain distinct directive and sanctional parts, and their own set of subsidiary laws giving "force" to the legislative will as it concerned execution and procedure. The subsidiary laws would also contain large numbers of *"exemptive"* provisions specifying those circumstances in which the subsidiary laws were not to be enforced. These exemptive

---

[54] *Laws in General*, p. 1. Only those sections of *Of Laws in General* directly relevant to the idea of a complete law are treated here. I am indebted to the earlier discussion of this theme by M. H. James in "Bentham on the Individuation of Laws," *Northern Ireland Legal Quarterly*, XXIV (1973), 357–82. For a more general account of the work, see H. L. A. Hart's articles, "Bentham's *Of Laws in General*" and "Legal Powers," in *Essays on Bentham* (Oxford, 1982), pp. 105–26, 194–219.

[55] The following exegesis is based on *Laws in General*, pp. 134–9.

provisions served the "preservation of innocence," while the subsidiary laws they qualified aimed at the "punishment of guilt."

Bentham's concern was to stress that the "principal" and "subsidiary" law regarding a particular action the legislator sought to control represented two distinct laws, rather than parts of a single analytic whole.[56] Nevertheless, "the union between a principal law and the subsidiary law" was "so close" that "one proposition is frequently enough to hold them both." The principal law, for example, frequently sufficed to announce both mandates, its sanctional part as addressed to the whole community serving as the directive part of the subsidiary law as addressed to the individuals involved in the procedure for execution. Conversely, all the laws could be formulated as subsidiary laws with the principal law merely implied. Thus a law declaring murder to be a punishable offence could be expressed: "Let the judge cause every man that commits murder to be put to death," without the direct command, "let no man on pain of death, commit murder."[57]

The distinction between principal and subsidiary laws centered on the manner in which the legal system operated as a whole. Implied within any individual legislative "act of volition" was a motive provided for obedience, and a further separate command giving "force" to the previous declaration. The two commands had to be isolated analytically, even though they related to the same action the legislator sought to control, and even though their verbal formulation might disguise their separate identities. Having established the distinction, Bentham then turned to the question of how any such command might be recognized as "complete."

Bentham introduced the analysis of the "idea of a complete law" by identifying two qualities, "*integrality*" and "*unity*" which "laid together" established the "*individuality*" of a law. "To fix the individuality of a law" was "to ascertain what a portion of legislative matter must amount to in order on the one hand not to contain less, on the other hand not to contain more than one whole law."[58]

Using the example of the simplest type of law ("a law which consists solely of a directive part"), Bentham first considered the ways in which a law might fail to achieve the first quality of "integrality or completeness." These were "in point of expression, in point of connection, and in point of design." By the first two criteria Bentham distinguished a complete law from a mass of scattered legislative matter. A law lacked "integrality" in point of "expression" when it

---

[56] See *ibid.*, pp. 143–4 and *Morals and Legislation*, p. 303.
[57] *Laws in General*, pp.143–4.
[58] *Ibid.*, p. 156. The following exegesis is based on *Laws in General*, pp. 156–62.

had not been provided with an "imperative provision." This standard served to contrast the idea of a complete law with the system of "qualificative" and "expository" clauses most laws would contain. Such clauses, whatever their likely length, could never in themselves constitute individual laws until they received an "imperative stamp." A law lacked "integrality" in point of "connection" when the legislator failed to indicate how the "great multitude of provisions" contained in most laws linked up to form a single whole. Such connection could be attained either by the method of "juxtaposition," whereby the legislator simply listed all the provisions of a law "in the same instrument without interruption," or by the method of "reference." In the latter case, the legislator directed "the reader from the place at which the chain of provisions is broken off to the place where it is resumed again." This was the only "practicable" technique for securing "connection" given the multitude of provisions found in a complete body of law. Hence, the code would require the same sort of systematic apparatus for indexing and cross-reference as that which Bentham outlined in the Digest project.

The third criterion, "integrality in point of design," was perhaps the most crucial. The design of the law referred to whether the legislator had employed the correct terms to identify the "mischief" the law sought to control. Failure here occurred when the legislator expressed himself too broadly (incompleteness "in point of *discrimination*") or too narrowly (incompleteness "in point of *amplitude*"). The latter, incompleteness in point of amplitude, resulted either when the mischief itself had been identified too narrowly ("original amplitude") or when an excessive number of qualifying provisions had been tacked on to the original command ("residuary amplitude").

Bentham illustrated such incompleteness in point of design by using the example of a Bolognese law which commanded that, "Whoso draweth blood in the streets shall be severely punished," an act which contained "every fault in point of extent of which a law is susceptible." The law was defective in point of "original amplitude" since "drawing blood" was only one of many ways in which "a mischief the same in substance may be produced." It was defective in point of "discrimination" since it failed to distinguish the mischief of bodily assault from an act of self-defense or the case of a surgeon letting blood to save a life. It was defective in point of "residuary amplitude" since the same mischief might occur in a variety of places while the law only took notice of offences occurring in the "streets."

Both Bentham's choice and his treatment of this example are of some interest beyond their illustrative value. Pufendorf had utilized the

Bolognese law in his natural jurisprudence, and it was adopted by Blackstone as an uncontroversial example of how laws had to be interpreted according to their "reason and spirit." Thus, in the case of a surgeon who had let the blood of a man fallen ill in the street, Blackstone maintained that the judge properly departed from the letter of the law and exempted the surgeon from punishment.[59] Blackstone's point, of course, was that all laws because of their generality would inevitably lead to such cases, and such judicial interpretation was needed to solve an otherwise intractable jurisprudential problem. Bentham, in his account of completeness in point of design, sought to translate this allegedly inevitable problem in law into a purely linguistic or technological matter regarding the identification of "mischiefs." Blackstone's judge, on this analysis, had not been "interpreting" the law at all. Rather, he was attempting to complete the law which the legislator himself had failed to complete in point of design.[60]

The second quality treated in the "idea of a complete law" was the "ground" of "unity." A law obtained "unity" when it contained no more legislative matter than one complete but entire law: "Let a certain quantity of discourse be recognized as constituting one complete law, if anything more be added it makes a law and something more."[61] Whereas the criterion of "integrity" ensured that a body of legislative matter comprised at least one individual law, the criterion of "unity" ensured that body of legislative matter contained not more than one individual law. A law's unity was determined by "the class of acts which it takes for its object." The "object" of the law was the "offence" the legislator sought to prevent, and therefore, the unity of the law derived from "the unity of the offence":

> That system of provisions is one law which marks out one offence: that system of provisions is more than one law which does more than mark out one offence.[62]

Although the unity of a law was identifiable, it was not "naturally determinable." This followed from the fact that "classes of offences like any other classes of acts may be distinguished from one another *ad infinitum*."[63] Accordingly, laws which took their unity from the unity of an offence could likewise be distinguished "*ad infinitum*." To adopt Bentham's example, a law establishing the exportation of corn to be an offence could be divided into separate laws barring the exportation of

[59] See 1 *Comm* 61; and see *Comment*, pp. 110–12.
[60] See *Laws in General*, pp. 162–4, where Bentham continues with a discussion of judicial interpretation.
[61] *Ibid.*, pp. 165–6.   [62] *Ibid.*, p. 170.   [63] *Ibid.*, pp. 170, 171.

wheat and barley. Again, a law against the exportation of barley could be divided into two laws against such exportation "by daytime" and "by night." As the process of dividing actions, and hence creating laws, was logically limitless, the degree of legal division in any particular code had to be determined by other criteria, which for Bentham were set by the requirements of a utilitarian system of punishment. Classes of offences were to be distinguished to the extent that each "mischief" received the appropriate penalty.[64] The legislator, for example, would distinguish the offence of theft committed to avoid starvation from the offence of theft committed for gain, since each of these types of theft required different amounts and perhaps qualities of punishment.

By the same process Bentham also accounted for the historical evolution of a legal system. Through time classes of offences came to be sub-divided in response to the awareness that certain offences required more or less serious attention than others of the same class. What had originally been formulated as a single law against homicide, for example, would come to be divided into such separate offences as premeditated homicide or homicide under provocation, and the original single offence thus would become a genus containing several species.[65] Bentham further stressed that this process was in part a function of language. Offences came to be distinguished as there were terms available in "each particular language." The English, for instance, could differentiate "theft" from "robbery," whereas the French would have to invent a term, such as "*vol avec force*," to make the same distinction.[66] One implication of this, explicit in *An Introduction to the Principles of Morals and Legislation*, was that a systematic and complete catalogue of offences required an extensive program of word-invention, and the capacity to produce such systematic terminology further meant that the law could be freed finally from the "tyranny of language."

Laws, like offences, could be created "*ad infinitum.*" But Bentham emphasized that this potential "infinity" of laws did not destroy the possibility of producing individually complete laws or a complete code of laws. In this way, the standard of "unity" contrasted with that of "integrality":

Here we see the difference between the unity of a law and its integrality: a law which was originally one may be divided in this manner into two laws, and yet both of them may be complete.[67]

---

[64] *Ibid.*, pp. 170–1.   [65] *Ibid.*, pp. 172–4.
[66] *Ibid.*, p. 174, and see *Morals and Legislation*, p. 289.
[67] *Laws in General*, p. 171.

In other words, the fact that an original law had been divided into two separate laws did not mean that the original law or the remaining laws were not "complete." Each law was still complete, provided each law marked out one offence completely "in point of expression, in point of connection, and in point of design."

This insight, the distinction between the law's integrality and its unity, assumed central importance when Bentham went on to specify the character of a "complete" code of laws. Such a code was "complete" in the first place in that it was entirely composed of individual "complete" laws. As each component of the code was identifiable as a single logical unit, the code had a determinate character. As Bentham presented it, one could literally count the number of laws in a complete code:

> The principle of unity in a law being hereby given, it follows that a complete code being given, the number of laws there are in it...is likewise given. Not the general purport only but the precise number: they might be counted, were it to answer any purpose.

The number of laws in the complete code would of course vary, "owing to the continual occasion there will ever be for new laws." Nevertheless, the fact that the code contained only complete laws meant that at any "one period the number is determinable."[68]

The code was "complete" in another, more ambitious sense. It was exhaustive. Each member of the code constituted "a single but entire law," and these individual laws comprised a comprehensive system of legislation. As Bentham unambiguously maintained in a concluding passage, "in a map of law executed upon such a plan there are no *terrae incognitae*, no blank spaces: nothing is at least omitted, nothing unprovided for."[69] Indeed, not only was it possible to achieve such legislative comprehensiveness, Bentham further claimed that he had already shown how this could be done in some detail. It was in this context, that his "natural" Division of Offences came to serve new and enhanced purposes.

The line of argument supporting this claim originated in another question which emerged at the conclusion of *An Introduction to the Principles of Morals and Legislation*, the distinction "between the *civil* branch of jurisprudence and the *penal*." The solution arrived at in *Of Laws in General* was that the distinction was "typographical" and not

---

[68] *Ibid.*, p. 172.   [69] *Ibid.*, p. 246.

"logical."[70] The analysis of a complete law demonstrated that "every law" contained "one part which is of a penal, and at the same time another part which is of a civil nature," and that there was "no such thing" as any "entire law which is penal only and not civil, nor as one which is civil only and not penal."[71] The notion that every law had a penal part rested ultimately on the most fundamental aspect of Benthamic jurisprudence. The system of legal rules properly functioned to produce public happiness by preventing mischievous acts. This was achieved by designating certain acts to be "offences," and by specifying and applying penalties to prevent their commission. Accordingly, the notion of punishment and the creation of offences was basic to the idea of law:

> Every law turns an act into an offence: and one law creates but one offence: so many offences, so many laws: for every law there is an offence: for every offence there is a law.[72]

But although the essence of law was the creation of offences, each individual law would invariably contain a vast amount of expository and qualificative matter required to establish its completeness "in point of design." Such expository and qualificative matter, moreover, would be common to many individual laws creating particular types of offences, as well as to those "subsidiary laws" through which the legislator gave "force" to his "principal" enactments. The need to contract this vast, repetitious mass of legislative matter "for the convenience of discourse" led to the separation of these complete individual laws into their civil and penal parts. The "imperative or comminative" provisions of a law were divorced from its "qualificative and expositive matter." The former material "laid the foundation of a *penal* code," the latter "of what would be called a *civil* code."[73] Given the correlation of laws and offences, the civil code lacked any logical independence, it was "but the *complement* of the penal." The penal law, "which holds an act up to view in the character of an offence,"

---

[70] *Ibid.*, p. 197. See also p. 144: "It should be remembered once for all, that there is no judging of the logical division of a law from the grammatical divisions of the discourse in which it happens to be contained."

[71] *Ibid.*, p. 196, and see the summary of this analysis at *Morals and Legislation*, pp. 301–6.

[72] *Ibid.*, p. 233. For other sections of *Laws in General* where Bentham emphasized the coercive nature of law, and treated the identity between creating offences and specifying punishments, and between creating offences and making laws, see pp. 32–3 ("ends" of law), 41ff ("objects" of law), and especially 54, 176 and 179. For an earlier version of the argument, see *Comment*, p. 88: "The affair of its having *prescribed a duty*, and *created* an *offence* is only the language we use in speaking of what the Law has done."

[73] *Laws in General*, pp. 197–8.

for that reason "claims the head in the order of intellection and enunciation."[74]

Since all laws as logical units created offences, it followed that a complete catalogue of offences contained in outline a complete system of laws. As Bentham put it, "a complete analysis of all the offences...includes a complete account of everything that can be done in the way of law."[75] Accordingly, what was required to specify a complete body of laws was a complete system of legal offences. Such a "complete analysis of all the offences" was precisely what Bentham believed he had achieved in the Division of Offences in *An Introduction to the Principles of Morals and Legislation*. That analysis was complete because Bentham had dissected by bifurcation "the logical whole, constituted by the sum total of possible offences." But while this catalogue was originally designed for the plan of a substantive penal code only, Bentham could now claim that it served as an outline for a complete code of laws. The Division of Offences and *Of Laws in General* taken together furnished "a complete and pretty detailed plan of a complete body of the laws...[for] by this parcelling out what relates to the several offences, the whole law is parcelled out."[76] Thus the corollary to the original claim that the Division of Offences was exhaustive was the later claim that *Of Laws in General* presented a plan of legislation in which "nothing is at least omitted." And thus what had first been conceived as a systematic alternative to Blackstone's "technical arrangement" became a blueprint for the *Pannomion*:

> To class *offences*...is therefore to class *laws*: to exhibit a complete catalogue of all the offences created by law, including the whole mass of expository matter...would be to exhibit a complete collection of the laws in force: in a word, a complete body of law; a *pannomion*, if so it might be termed.[77]

In maintaining that the envisaged legislative system would "exhibit a complete collection of all the laws in force," Bentham registered a more ambitious claim than might initially appear. At the outset of *Of Laws in General*, he had not restricted his definition of law to the immediate legislative edicts of the sovereign.[78] Included within the notion of law were also those "acts of volition" which the sovereign endorsed "in the way of adoption," and these included virtually every permitted

---

[74] *Ibid.*, p. 234.   [75] *Ibid.*, p. 252.   [76] *Ibid.*, pp. 233–4.
[77] *Morals and Legislation*, p. 305.
[78] *Laws in General*, p. 3: "The latitude here given to the import of the word *law* is it must be confessed rather greater than what seems to be given to it in common."

social practice in a political community. Thus, Bentham was careful not to restrict such "adopted laws" to the mandates issued by "power holders" in the exercise of public government. Rather, "every mandate" – "trivial or important" – which was "not illegal" constituted "in one sense or the other the mandate of the sovereign." In the same way that the orders "of the general" or "of the judge" embodied the sovereign's adopted mandates, so did "the mandates of the master, the father, the husband, [and] the guardian." Indeed, "not a cook is bid to dress a dinner, a nurse to feed a child, an usher to whip a school boy, an executioner to hang a thief, an officer to drive the enemy from a post, but it is by [the sovereign's] orders."[79]

By virtue of this analysis, Bentham indicated how a manifold range of permitted social customs could be located within a comprehensive system of legislative prohibitions. However, by including all these practices, "trivial or important," within the definition of the law, he profoundly increased the difficulty of characterizing the nature of a complete code. For while it appears perfectly feasible to catalogue all the commands immediately issued by the sovereign (the task of the traditional programs for statute consolidation or of Bentham's own Digest project), it is much less clear how the commands the sovereign "adopted" might be identified in a complete code, one in which all the laws could be counted. Bentham explored the difficulty in terms of the law of property, admittedly perhaps the most demanding example he could have confronted. According to his definition, the law of property contained all the private agreements for the use and transfer of property which the legislator permitted. "To be complete," Bentham observed, the body of laws "must be understood as including *inter alia* the whole body of conveyances," and therefore in order to specify "a complete body of the laws taken at any given period," it was equally necessary to specify "a complete collection of the several conveyances which within the dominion of the state are in force at the instant of that period."[80]

Given this requirement, it was "not possible" ever "to draw...out at length" all the existing law "relative to property."[81] But this impossibility, as in the case of the possible infinitude of offences, did not destroy the completeness of the code nor the individuality of the law of property. This followed from the criterion of "unity" which characterized a complete law. As all the legal matter regarding property

---

[79] Ibid., pp. 22–3. For a valuable elucidation of Bentham's position here, see J. H. Burns, "Scottish Philosophy and the Science of Legislation," *Royal Society of Edinburgh Occasional Papers*, No. 3 (1985), 11–29, especially pp. 19–21.
[80] *Laws in General*, pp. 179–80.   [81] *Ibid.*, p. 178.

related to a single offence (termed "*wrongful occupation of property*"[82]), all this legal matter comprised a single law:

> Such as the offence is such is the law: therefore if the offence is *one*, the law considered in a certain point of view, must be *one* also.[83]

Thus, from one point of view (the adopted conveyances) the law of property was "infinite," while from another point of view (the offence of wrongful occupation) the law of property was identifiable as a single complete law. All that was required was a verbal mechanism for presenting this single law so that it could be seen to contain this "infinite multitude of [adopted] laws." Bentham here again translated the jurisprudential problem into a matter of linguistic technique. The legislator could indicate effectively which mandates regarding property he had "adopted" by "translating" this law "out of the imperative into the assertive form."[84] The single law concerning "wrongful occupation" would be formulated not as a command, but as an "exposition of a few such words as proprietary, proprietary subject, proprietary rights, proprietor or right-holder, title, form of conveyance and the like," and it was only on the occasion of any "particular conveyance" coming "into controversy" that this law would have to be retranslated "into a command."[85]

Through this account, Bentham sustained the logic of legal completeness in the face of the "infinite multitude" of legal private agreements observed in any community. He further indicated that the complete code was "complete" in another, altogether more radical sense. All the private practices allowed by the sovereign could be located, and be seen to be located, within this structure of legislative provisions. Having delineated the nature of a complete body of law, Bentham's next task was to explain why this conception of legal completeness alone provided the proper structure for successful law-making.

---

[82] *Ibid.*, p. 176 and *Morals and Legislation*, pp. 226–32.
[83] *Laws in General*, p. 181.   [84] *Ibid.*, pp. 178–9.
[85] *Ibid.*, p. 180.

Conclusion: The province of legislation determined

Bentham concluded *Of Laws in General* with a brief survey of the "uses" of the work, in which he pointed to the more practical implications for law-making of the preceding analysis of "what *a law* is."[1] In particular he made plain that what he had now identified as a "complete body of laws" constructed "according to a method of division grounded on natural and universal principles,"[2] could alone satisfy the requirements for a utilitarian system of legislation. Much of the argument turned on the interdependence Bentham established between an individual complete law and complete body of laws. In *An Introduction to the Principles of Morals and Legislation* he maintained that "the notion of a complete law must first be fixed before the legislator can in any case know what it is he has to do, or when his work is done."[3] He now insisted that "before any such specimen" of an individual complete law could "be found," "a perfect plan of legislation must first have been produced."[4] Moreover, any individual law, "how complete soever in itself," was "never completely adapted to its purpose...until it be completely put together." And this was again dependent on "the idea of such a body" of complete laws having "been formed."[5] No particular piece of legislative policy could achieve its purpose unless it was formulated as a complete law, and this, in turn, required its being a part of a complete system of laws.

Bentham further claimed that the analysis of a complete law provided the proper means for comprehending the nature of the legal system as a whole and for evaluating the merits of its parts. In the first place (to return to the problem with which the work began), by identifying "what *a law* is," Bentham demonstrated the artificiality of the distinction between civil and penal law.[6] Until this was done, and

---

[1] *Morals and Legislation*, p. 282, where this version of the question is given.
[2] *Laws in General*, p. 232.
[3] *Morals and Legislation*, p. 282.
[4] *Laws in General*, p. 183.   [5] *Ibid.*, p. 159.
[6] See above, chapter 13 at nn70–74.

until the imperative character of law was placed at the center of jurisprudence, it was impossible to recognize the logic of any system of legal rules. As Bentham put it, "till then, it remains in darkness."[7] The same analysis also furnished a mechanism for assessing "the propriety" of the law "in point of matter." This was achieved by removing the individual laws from their typographical arrangement in the civil and penal codes, and examining them in terms of their analytic parts. The "vigour" of the law was then exposed by its "imperative clauses," its "mildness" by the "qualificative" provisions. The estimate of its "wisdom" and "utility" was swiftly secured by comparing the "happy proportionality and correspondency between the two."[8]

Only a complete system of laws could be amended or altered successfully, since only in such "a perfect plan of legislation" could the "effects and influence" of each enactment "with certainty and precision be traced on and coloured by reference throughout the whole body of the laws." In contrast, in an incomplete system of legislation the individual laws could never "be distinguished from one another," and therefore "when a new statute is applied" it remained "next to impossible to follow it through and discern the limits of its influence." In such an incomplete system, any new legislative provision was unavoidably "like water poured into the sea."[9]

The complete system of laws, moreover, provided for the first time the required structure for the proper functioning of the judiciary. Unless the code was complete, no individual law could be complete, and if the laws were incomplete, it fell upon the judge to complete the legislator's will through the "obscure, voluminous and unsteady form of customary jurisprudence."[10] By enabling the legislator to complete his will by himself, the "regular plan" furnished in *Of Laws in General* offered "a powerful palliative" and in time "a complete and effectual remedy" to this source of common law. Indeed, "such a degree of comprehension and steadiness" might be achieved by the legislator, "as to render the allowance of liberal or discretionary interpretation on the part of the judge no longer necessary."[11]

In each of these claims, Bentham was clearly invoking objectives he had first placed on the legislative agenda in the early 1770s. The same concern to rid English law of its "obscurity, uncertainty and confusion" which informed the critique of common law and characterized the Digest project, likewise gave practical purpose to the analytic discussion of *Of Laws in General*. In this sense, Bentham's writings of the early

---

[7] *Laws in General*, p. 234, and see p. 232.   [8] *Ibid.*, pp. 236–8.
[9] *Ibid.*, p. 236.   [10] *Ibid.*, p. 241.
[11] *Ibid.*, p. 240. See also pp. 242–5 for further "uses" of the work.

1780s can be read as a more systematic and rigorous treatment of the same set of legal problems. From another standpoint, however, the material can be viewed as Bentham's final departure from the conventions of English legal theory.

The first decisive step in this direction was of course the initial critique of common law jurisprudence, and the radical proposal for the transformation of the common law into statute. But it appears that what Bentham envisaged for his common law Digest, as in the case of the statute Digest, largely conformed to the traditional Baconian model of a consolidated statute book. By the completion of *Of Laws in General*, it was clear to Bentham that this solution in itself could never be sufficient. Simply reducing and ordering the contents of the legal system, regardless of any attendant changes in the substance of the law, could never meet the full requirements for correct legal form. What was needed was the construction of a body of law complete in all its branches, since otherwise no particular legislative provision could attain the necessary completeness or secure its intended purpose. Unless the legislator aimed at the *Pannomion*, he could never fully know "what he is to do, or when his work is done."

Probably the clearest indication of the change in Bentham's legislative ambitions lies in his treatment of "digestion" in the context of the "uses" of *Of Laws in General*. Bentham retained the notion of transforming common law through a legislative Digest, but the Digest project lost its identity as an autonomous legislative program. As the goal which had emerged for Bentham was now the creation of a complete body of laws according to "a perfect plan of legislation," digestion and statute consolidation could be presented merely as the *de facto* result of securing this objective:

> Conceive a complete code to be established *uno flatu*. If in any point it be re-enactive of the old law, it will *pro tanto* be a digest of such old law: if the old law were in the statutory form, of the statute law: if in the customary form, of the customary law.[12]

Both Digests were thus relegated to by-products of Bentham's new legislative system. Nonetheless, the fact that this program did incorporate the notion of statute consolidation meant that there remained an important point of coincidence between Bentham's *Pannomion* and the more conventional schemes for statute consolidation. But it is crucial to recognize, especially in the light of later legal developments and the alleged impact of Benthamic ideas on them, that

---

[12] *Ibid.*, pp. 235–6. See also Bentham's letter of 1782 to Lord Ashburton, *ibid.*, p. 310.

although Bentham's legislative system still contained a program for statute consolidation, it was no longer constituted by it.[13] In his insistence that the work of the legislator had to proceed in terms of "a perfect plan of legislation," Bentham had come to endorse just that sort of radical project for legislative revision and creation which virtually all the proponents of statute consolidation carefully eschewed in their own proposals.

Another revealing indication of the alteration in Bentham's perspective is found in his heightened aspirations for the notoriety of the law. As his own understanding of the legal system now centered on the idea of a complete and methodical body of laws, Bentham came to believe that the subject as well needed to be able to view the legal system as a coherent, logical whole. On the basis of the synoptic Division of Offences in *An Introduction to the Principles of Morals and Legislation*, which had "parcelled out" the "whole law," Bentham now envisaged the possibility of presenting the whole of the law in communicable form.[14] Accordingly, the earlier project for promulgating "personal codes" was relegated, like the Digest project, to a secondary position. Such codes would still be profitably produced, and the legislative structure in *Of Laws in General* alone furnished the proper framework for their production. Nevertheless, a far more formidable ambition for legislative composition and promulgation had emerged: each individual could master the entire code. The "parts or contents" of the legal system would become "an object of arithmetic" and its "lineaments and limits," an "object of mensuration." And "the whole code" would be accommodated within "one book."[15] "In a system thus constructed upon this plan," Bentham lavishly concluded, "a man need but open the book in order to inform himself what the aspect borne by the law bears to every imaginable act that can come within the possible sphere of human agency."[16]

In the process of arriving at this new commitment to a complete system of legislative codification, Bentham had assembled an arsenal of jurisprudential analysis with which to confront English legal conventions, particularly that part of legal orthodoxy which insisted upon the inherent limitation of the legislative capacity. By turning to these features of *Of Laws in General*, it is possible to characterize Bentham's

---

[13] As Bentham himself stressed in his correspondence of 1828, "Mr. Peel is for consolidation in contradistinction to codification: I for codification in contradistinction to consolidation," *Bentham Memoirs, Bowring*, X, 595.

[14] See above, chapter 13 at n76.

[15] *Laws in General*, pp. 234–5, and see p. 310.

[16] *Ibid.*, p. 246.

position more sharply, as well as to review briefly the principal issues which this study has been concerned to recover.

In the first place, Bentham was now equipped with a simple formula through which to explain all previous failures in the art of legislation. Legislative success depended on legal completeness. Yet, it was only possible to perceive this as the goal for legislation following the construction of an exhaustive and methodical system of legal classification, and the capacity to produce such a system of arrangement, in turn, depended on the prior advance of legal learning and legal practice generally. As Bentham explained in *An Introduction to the Principles of Morals and Legislation*, "*truth* and *order* go on hand in hand. It is only in proportion as the former is discovered, that the latter can be improved." Hence, the construction of a "natural arrangement" for law was necessarily one of the last stages in the development of a legislative science. Nonetheless, until that "certain order" had been secured, "truth can be but imperfectly announced."[17] On the basis of this account, it was no longer necessary to treat the defects of the law wholly as the result of legislative "indolence" or "inattention," or even in terms of the obstructive influence of the legal profession. Rather, such defects could be seen as the inevitable consequence of the delayed advance of the science of legal form.[18] Since the required "certain order" had only now been identified, this further meant that the next stage in the growth of legislative science had to be one of vigorous invention. As Bentham emphasized in 1789, "he who...wants an example of a complete body of law to refer to, must begin with making one."[19]

By virtue of the same analysis, Bentham had acquired a much richer understanding of the English legal system with which to counter the Blackstonean assessment of English law. As before, Bentham insisted that common law could never exist as an authentic system of legal rules. His previous writings, however, had left unclear how this positivist claim met Blackstone's argument, which not only enjoyed wide acceptance but seemed vindicated by recent legal history, that any careful reading of English law would reveal the substantive superiority of common law over statute. The essence of Bentham's response remained the same in that he still pointed to the legislator's failures as the cause of that kind of judicial activism which Blackstone thought so

---

[17] *Morals and Legislation*, p. 273n, and see p. 299n.

[18] Bentham also stressed that the analysis of legal form and identification of a complete body of laws required a "*logic of the will*" which had been ignored by philosophers since the time of Aristotle; see *Morals and Legislation*, pp. 8, 299n, and the discussion in *Laws in General*, pp. 93–132 ("Aspects of a Law").

[19] *Morals and Legislation*, p. 8, and see *Laws in General*, p. 159.

worthy of praise. But after *Of Laws in General* he could explain this phenomenon with greater precision and insight. English statute and common law had to be taken together as a single body of incomplete legal rules, in which common law functioned as an inevitable judicial attempt in particular cases to complete the legislator's will.[20] By identifying the cure, complete law, Bentham had achieved a sharper perception of the disease, common law. By the same token, he had finally overcome Blackstone as he had overcome his conventional categories of analysis. The correct understanding of the English legal experience was not to be found in the established dichotomy between common law and statute. Instead, the contrast lay between the complete body of law and the incomplete system of statute with its unavoidable appendage, common law.

The Blackstonean position, though, had not relied solely on a simple, empirical appeal to the actual condition of English law. It was further grounded on a set of assumptions and doctrines which alleged the inherent incapacity of human legislators to create satisfactory systems of comprehensive legal rules. Here too Bentham had developed the necessary analytic tools to combat these doctrines.

Probably the most pervasive of such doctrines derived from the basic premise of equity in law. As explained in *A Treatise of Equity*, since "the rules of the municipal law are finite, and the subject of it infinite," cases would invariably arise "which cannot be determined" by the laws. Since human laws were necessarily defective in this way, "equity" which embodied "the whole of natural justice" had to be acknowledged as "more excellent than any human institution."[21] Bentham readily conceded part of this doctrine. He accepted that new cases would emerge which would lead the legislator to alter his enactments, and further recognized that the need for many such alterations was likely to come to the notice of the judge before the legislator himself. But he was careful to treat the inevitability of such legal change in such a way that it did not become a claim against the legislative capacity itself. In a complete system of laws such difficult cases would be exceptional. They could therefore be brought to the attention of the legislator directly, and any alteration in the law effected "in the concise and perspicuous form of statute law." On this basis, "the simplicity of the legislative plan would be preserved from violation" – the legislator "might need a censor," but would remain "his own and sole interpreter."[22]

[20] *Laws in General*, pp. 239–40.
[21] *Treatise of Equity*, I, 9; and see the discussion above, chapter 3 at nn6–12.
[22] *Laws in General*, pp. 241, 232–3.

Further and more critically, in his distinction between the "completeness" and "unity" of an individual law, Bentham explicitly denied the broader claims of equity jurisprudence.[23] Human laws were of course finite and their subject-matter, human offences, potentially infinite. But this potential infinity of legal matter did not impugn the completeness of the law. It merely signified that offences, like all human actions, could be distinguished *ad infinitum*. Notwithstanding this, the code was still complete just as the Division of Offences was exhaustive. By beginning with "the logical whole, constituted by the sum total of possible offences," and by analyzing this whole according to "the rigid rules of the exhaustive method," Bentham ensured the production of a system of legal rules in which "nothing is at least omitted, nothing unprovided for."[24] The type of completeness achieved in this respect did not mean that the legislator was relieved from having to make any further alterations in his enactments. It was likely that altered circumstances would lead the legislator to introduce further distinctions in his catalogue of offences, and by this process to identify mischievous acts at a level of particularity previously ignored. Nonetheless, as Bentham later stressed, the fact that the legislator could never anticipate each particular variety of social mischief in no way compromised the logical completeness of this plan of legislation:

> I acknowledge that it is not possible to foresee [offences] individually, but they may be foreseen in their species... a person may be assured that every species of offence are comprised in the tables which this work includes, although he may not be assured that every possible individual offence has been foreseen.[25]

Similar claims against the capacity of legislators figured in the cautious strictures of the proponents of statute consolidation and in the arguments deployed by Kames, Mansfield and many common lawyers in support of judicially orchestrated legal change. According to Hale, "the reformation of any law were very easy," if it was simply a matter of applying "a plaister" to a particular "sore." But "the great business of a reformer" was to ensure that "his remedy" did not introduce "some other considerable inconvenience" or remove "some other considerable convenience" which the unreformed law "brought with

---

[23] See the discussion above, chapter 13 at nn62–7.
[24] See the discussion above, chapter 13 at nn46–53 and nn75–7.
[25] *General View of a Complete Code of Law*, in *Bowring* III, 205. The "tables" Bentham refers to correspond to the Division of Offences in *Morals and Legislation*. The relation between the *General View* and *Laws in General* is described below, at nn52–3 and nn62–3.

it."[26] Given such dangers, legal improvers immediately observed the inherent advantages of proceeding with legal change through the practice of the courts. As Sir Francis Buller explained to the Court of King's Bench, statute law operated "like a powerful tyrant that knows no bounds" and "mows down all before it." But the common law acted with a "lenient hand," which "roots out that which is bad and leaves that which is good."[27] The legislator, in Kames's more detailed formulation, generally acted "with a view to particular cases," but produced a rule which then obtained "in general upon all similar cases." Since man was "but short sighted with regard to consequences," the frequent result of such law-making was that "in remedying one evil, a greater is produced." In contrast, the judiciary crept "along with wary steps," and only upon the "induction of many cases" fashioned "with safety" a general rule. The general rules of common law as a result naturally attained a level of excellence unavailable to legislation.[28]

Bentham had already argued for the non-existence of such rules of common law. But again, he was now equipped with a further set of arguments with which to dismantle the very foundations of the established case for the wisdom of the common law. The Benthamic legislator was specifically *not* acting with, as Kames put it, "a view to particular cases." Instead, he was supplied with a structure which enabled him "to take a view of the whole field" that lay before him.[29] In this system of comprehensive legislation, "the vast and hitherto shapeless expanse of jurisprudence" had for the first time been "collected and condensed into a compact sphere which the eye at a moment's warning can traverse in all imaginable directions."[30] Moreover, among the special merits of this achievement was to supply a methodical framework which gave "room for making alterations" in the laws "without inconvenience." Only in a legal system "constructed upon a regular and measured plan" could the impact of every legal provision, "whether it was an entire law, a provision expositive, limitative or exceptive," be identified "with certainty and precision...throughout the whole body of the laws."[31] Lastly, once the goal for the legal system was identified in legal completeness, it became apparent that the judiciary, whatever the volume of cases adduced, could never generate that comprehensive system of legal rules which

[26] Hale, *Amendment of Laws*, pp. 262–3, discussed above, chapter 9 at n62.
[27] *Roe v Galliers* (1787), 2 Term Rpts 139, (where Buller attributes the phrase to Wilmost, C.J.).
[28] Kames, *Dictionary of Decisions*, p. iii, discussed above, chapter 8 at n6.
[29] UC xxvii. 165, cited above, chapter 13 at n30.
[30] *Laws in General*, p. 246, and see p. 232 (point 2).   [31] *Ibid.*, p. 236.

alone ensured the realization of legal policy. In the light of his new standard, Bentham was able to turn the judicial argument for sophisticated and carefully tempered legal rules against the judiciary itself. Thus he emphasized the *"unaccommodatingness"* of common law rules, which admitted of "no temperaments, no compromises, no compositions: none of these qualifications which a legislator would see the necessity of applying."[32] In sum, the most damning feature of judge-made law was that it could never be complete.[33]

Contemporary doctrine posed a further basic challenge to the legislator. This concerned the commonplace piece of social wisdom which pointed to the inevitably limited impact of the law upon the ultimate well-being of any political community.[34] As Samuel Johnson remarked in response to one of the most socially interventionist specimens of eighteenth-century legislation, "A country is in a bad state, which is governed only by law because a thousand things occur for which the laws cannot provide."[35] Hence, according to Edmund Burke, it became "one of the finest problems in legislation" to determine "what the state ought to take upon itself to direct by the public wisdom, and what it ought to leave...to individual discretion."[36] When interpreted as a point about legislative policy and the proper extent of the penal sanction, there was much in these sentiments with which Bentham was likely to concur, particularly in the period before his conversion to radical politics. "There are cases in which the legislator ought not (in a direct way at least, and by means of punishment applied immediately to particular *individual* acts) to attempt to direct the several other members of the community," he explained in *An Introduction to the Principles of Morals and Legislation*. And thus among the necessary tasks of Benthamic legislative science was "to give an idea of the cases in which ethics ought, and in which legislation ought not (in a direct manner at least) to interfere."[37]

At the same time, however, the formal elements of Bentham's theory of legislation served to repudiate the more conservative implications of the conventional wisdom that, as Burke bluntly put it in 1770, "the laws reach but a very little way."[38] In his definition of law and his

---

[32] *Ibid.*, p. 194n.
[33] See *ibid.*, pp. 184–95, "No customary law complete."
[34] See, for example, the discussion of Kames on patriotism above, chapter 8 at n14.
[35] Johnson's comment on the act abolishing hereditary jurisdictions in Scotland, cited in James Boswell, *Journal of a Tour to the Hebrides with Samuel Johnson* (1785), ed. R. W. Chapman (Oxford, 1970), p. 274.
[36] Burke, *Thought and Details on Scarcity* (1795), in *Works*, V, 166.
[37] *Morals and Legislation*, p. 285.
[38] Burke, *Thoughts on the Cause of the Present Discontents* (1770), in *Works*, I, 470.

account of the sovereign's "adopted" mandates in *Of Laws in General*, Bentham indicated that this attitude to legal rules was essentially unfounded.[39] All social practices, "trivial or important," operated within the recognizable framework of the legislator's will. Any command allowed in the community was a command the legislator sanctioned by way of adoption, and all such commands, given the proper linguistic formula, could be identified precisely within a complete body of laws. The whole of the community's social system, no less than the whole of its legal system, was to be located analytically within the province of legislation. Even in those areas of social life where the legislator did not immediately intervene, his will obtained. The only true limitation on the capacity of the legislator that remained was the calculation of felicity, guided by the unique moral principle which "neither requires nor admits of any other regulator than itself."[40]

The ideal of a complete body of laws which emerged in *Of Laws in General*, and which remained the central concept in Bentham's system of legislative science, thus contained a final response to the conventions of English theory. What has been emphasized here is the extent to which the evolution and character of this conception of legislation can be viewed as a response to that legal theory, in part as addressed to the figure of Sir William Blackstone, and in part as addressed to the legal problems he had placed to the fore in the *Commentaries*. In the course of identifying the *Pannomion* as the legislative goal, however, Bentham departed decisively from that legal theory. Bentham himself, of course, was always eager to emphasize these departures from orthodoxy. His first major venture in legal theory, the 1776 *A Fragment on Government*, was also, as he later claimed, "the very first publication" to invite liberation "from the trammels of authority and ancestor-wisdom on the field of law."[41] Unfortunately, his own explanation of his novelty, especially in the form of his elderly autobiographical pronouncements, seriously distorted the character of the legal tradition in which he was schooled, and thereafter greatly confounded the scholarly assessment of the legal orthodoxy he strove to supplant.[42]

Nowhere was this distortion more pronounced or more effective than in Bentham's efforts to account for his innovations by presenting his youthful self as an isolated reforming spirit in a legal setting of

[39] See the discussion above, chapter 13 at n79.
[40] *Morals and Legislation*, p. 33.
[41] *Fragment*, p. 424n.
[42] For this scholarly assessment, see the discussion above, Introduction at nn24–7.

entrenched complacency, insularity and obsequiousness.[43] Yet, as we have seen, by 1776 the failures of parliamentary legislation and the problems this situation created for future legal development were established and pervasive themes in English legal thought. Bentham's early strictures against parliamentary "incapacity and inattention" and his elaborate litany of legislative abuses confirmed and did not depart from this contemporary consensus.[44] Nor were the various responses to the challenges posed by eighteenth-century parliamentary law-making in any sense greatly distinguished by their complacency or uncritical conservatism, even in those instances when the challenge was met by a familiar rehearsal of the wisdom of the common law. Bentham's legislative science had its many rivals in the more pragmatic and institutionally balanced approaches to legal improvement developed by his contemporaries. It was only the adoption of the controversial Benthamic premise that legal modernization in England had to operate exclusively through parliamentary statute which transformed these complex alternative strategies into "an antipathy to reformation."[45]

Even Bentham's notorious utilitarian convictions may have been a less isolating element in his legal program than he preferred to suggest.[46] As the case of Kames's equity jurisprudence best reveals, he was not alone in identifying utility as the key principle of the modern legal improver. And as the case of Blackstone's adoption of Beccaria's penal doctrines cogently indicates, neither was Bentham alone in rushing to embrace the newly fathered "censorial jurisprudence" of the continental reformers.[47] Bentham's version of utilitarianism, like his favored canon of Enlightenment authorities, was scarcely representative, and there remained profound differences in outlook and approach among the eighteenth-century moralists and jurists who alike invoked "the principle of utility."[48] Yet, as Bentham's contemporaries easily recognized, "the fashion of scrutinizing public measures according to

[43] For a characteristic instance, see the "Preface intended for the Second edition of *A Fragment on Government*" (1823), *Fragment*, pp. 502–45.

[44] *Comment*, p. 160, cited above, chapter 12 at n17.

[45] See *ibid.*, p. 394, where the "antipathy to reformation" is indicated as the "grand and fundamental" blemish of Blackstone's *Commentaries*.

[46] *Ibid.*, pp. 515–17. Bentham's first critics readily distinguished the radical features of his utilitarian ethics from the (seemingly) less heterodox character of his utilitarian legal doctrines. For an important early example, see [Francis Jeffrey], "Bentham, *Principes de législation, par Dumont*," *Edinburgh Review*, IV (1804), 572–92.

[47] See *Fragment*, p. 403n, for Bentham's praise of Beccaria as "the father of *Censorial Jurisprudence*".

[48] For two valuable recent commentaries on these issues, see J. H. Burns, "Jeremy Bentham: From Radical Enlightenment to Philosophic Radicalism," *The Bentham Newsletter*, VIII (1984) 4–14, and Haakonssen, *The Science of a Legislator*, pp. 40–1.

the standard of their utility" was a characteristic feature of the recent
"progress of science relative to law and government." Through the
course of the century, as John Millar reported, the practice had indeed
"become very universal."[49]

What this study of Bentham's relations to English legal conventions
suggests is that the distinctiveness of his position owed less to his
utilitarianism or to his commitment to legal change, and rather more to
his singular preoccupation with the logic of legal form. Having thus
followed Bentham's progress to the *Pannomion*, the major part of the
subsequent history of Bentham's science of legislation lies beyond the
concerns of this study.[50] Something remains to be said, however, of his
activities prior to his 1789 decision finally to publish what he had come
to perceive as inadequate: *An Introduction to the Principles of Morals and
Legislation*.[51] The immediate task which lay before him was to rework
the material in *An Introduction* and *Of Laws in General* for the purposes
of a direct and expanded account of a complete system of legislation.
As we have seen, Bentham believed these works to contain, implicitly
at least, such an account. As he explained in a letter of 1784, "the task
of invention has for some time been accomplished, and all that remains
is to put in order ideas ready formed."[52]

Bentham embarked upon this ordering of ideas sometime about
1783, in a work provisionally titled, *Projet d'un corps complet de droit*. Its
first part, the *Projet forme*, was drawn from the Division of Offences
and *Of Laws in General*, and described the structure and nature of a
complete body of law. The second part, the *Projet matière*, treated the
substantive content of the legislative system.[53] That Bentham drafted
the work in French, in the hopes of securing a wider European
audience for his production, neatly epitomizes the general theme
considered here: the extent to which Bentham's jurisprudence had by
the mid-1780s outgrown the assumptions and tenets of contemporary
legal speculation in England. Even at the outset of his career in
jurisprudence, Bentham had not thought to limit himself to an English
setting.[54] Then, as later, he frequently and eagerly entertained the
ambition of serving as a legislator to a foreign sovereign. But the
decision to present his legislative science in the language of the

---

[49] Millar, *Historical View of English Government*, IV, 305.
[50] I have tried to assess some features of this story in "From Bentham to Benthamism,"
199–224.
[51] See *Morals and Legislation*, pp. 3–4, for a summary of the work's shortcomings.
[52] *Corr.* III, 293.
[53] The *Projet forme* appears to be a successor to the "*Corpus Juris*" project described by Bentham
in a 1782 letter to Lord Ashburton, reprinted in *Laws in General*, p. 308. For a description of
the *Projet* mss., see J. H. Burns, "The Bentham Project," in J. D. Baird (ed.), *Editing Texts
of the Romantic Period* (Toronto, 1972), pp. 79–80.
[54] See the discussion above, chapter 11 at n3.

Continental philosophy, like his 1785 voyage to Russia, shows how Bentham was now distancing himself from the narrower and more immediate preoccupations of English legal writers and law reformers, such as those, for example, which had figured so prominently in his own Digest program.

This departure from England was not intended to be permanent, nor did it mean that Bentham had abandoned his interest in practical legal improvement at home. While in Russia Bentham penned the *Defence of Usury*, which he published in London in 1787 and which he soon described as a practical application of the principles of "natural arrangement" first sketched in *A Fragment on Government*.[55] In February, 1788, he returned to London armed with his "simple idea in Architecture," the "Inspection-house" design, whose implementation in the form of the Panopticon prison was to occupy so much of his energy and resources for the next twenty years.[56] At the same time, Bentham had apparently not lost sight of the unfulfilled task "to put in order ideas ready formed." He reported in the 1789 Preface to *An Introduction to the Principles of Morals and Legislation*, that his "present designs" consisted of the publication of a massive ten-part exposition of the "principles of legislation," intended "to prepare the way for the body of law itself exhibited *in terminis*." Included within this program was the examination of the principles of penal and civil law, as well as the "plan of a body of law, complete in all its branches, considered in respect of its *form*; in other words, in respect of its method and terminology." In addition, the *Pannomion* now contained topics less central to the analytic discussion in *Of Laws in General*, such as the principles of legislation in matters of "*constitutional* law," "*political tactics*," "*finance*" and "*political economy*."[57] In the process of unveiling the outlines of this projected legislative system, Bentham also acknowledged the scale and arduousness of the labor he had set himself. When he confronted the irksome question, "Are enterprises like these achievable?," Bentham modestly and rather uncharacteristically responded, "He knows not."[58]

In doctrinal terms, it is clear that Bentham never wavered in his confidence that such enterprises were indeed achievable, that it was possible and necessary to construct and execute comprehensive and methodical systems of positive legal management which would display "the dictates of utility in every line."[59] At a more personal level,

---

[55] See *Morals and Legislation*, pp. 4–5.
[56] *Corr.* III, 502–3. For a brief summary of these episodes, see 'From Bentham to Benthamism,' 205–10.
[57] *Morals and Legislation*, pp. 5–6.   [58] *Ibid.*, p. 9.
[59] *Ibid.*, p. 7.

though, it is equally clear that Bentham himself was most unlikely ever
to exhibit such a system. Even at this early stage, Bentham's intellectual
efforts were marked by what J. H. Burns has described as "a
fundamental paradox" in his career – "the lifelong ambition to create
a systematic body of doctrine and the persistent failure to make real
progress towards such a system."[60] Bentham, in his eighties, would
still be struggling to complete the four main branches of the system of
legislation which had taken shape over forty years before.[61]

Bentham's desperate difficulty in putting "in order ideas ready
formed" is evinced in most of the material examined here: the
unfinished critique of Blackstone, the abandoned Digest project, the
unpublished analysis of "what *a law* is." But the general problem, as
well as the manner of its eventual resolution for Bentham, is perhaps
most cogently displayed in the fate of his first attempt to present the
Pannomion, the *Projet d'un corps complet de droit*. Despite an optimistic
report in 1783 that the *Projet* was nearly finished,[62] Bentham never
succeeded in concluding the work, although he had completed virtually
the whole of the first part concerning the structure and method of a
complete system of law. The *Projet forme*, however, did not reach
publication until it was taken in hand by Etienne Dumont. Dumont
produced a truncated version of the text in his 1802 *Traités*, which later
appeared in English translation in the Bowring edition as *A General
View of a Complete Code of Law*.[63] Notwithstanding the real merits of
Dumont's editorship, the essay at best represented a thin and even
pathetic return on Bentham's original investment. The complete system
of legislation which embodied Bentham's most important legal
doctrines, and which he insisted provided the sole framework for
successful law-making, was left without a full or systematic presentation. Already before the publication of *An Introduction to the Principles
of Morals and Legislation*, the style of Bentham's "genius for legislation"
had become apparent. As his friend, George Wilson, shrewdly observed
in 1787:

> Your history, since I have known you, has been to be always running
> from a good scheme to a better. In the meantime, life passes away and
> nothing is completed.[64]

---

[60] Burns, "Bentham Project," p. 76, and see also "From Bentham to Benthamism," pp.
200–2.

[61] See J. H. Burns, "Dreams and Destinations: Jeremy Bentham in 1828," *Bentham Newsletter*,
I, (1978), 22.   [62] *Corr*. III, 151 and n.

[63] Jeremy Bentham, *Traités de Législation civile et pénale…, publiés en François par Ét. Dumont, de
Génève*, 3 vols (Paris, 1802), III, 195–434 and *Bowring* III, 155–210. Elie Halévy provides an
account of Dumont's handling of these materials in *La Formation du Radicalisme Philosophique*,
I, Appendix 1.   [64] *Corr*. III, 526.

BIBLIOGRAPHY

Primary sources

Bacon, Francis, *The Works of Francis Bacon*, ed. James Spedding, Robert Leslie Ellis, Douglas Denon Heath, 14 vols. (London, 1857–74).

Ballow, H. [?], *A Treatise of Equity [1737], with the additions of Marginal References and Notes*, by John Fonblanque, 2 vols. (London, 1793–4).

Bankton, Andrew McDouall, Lord, *An Institute of the Laws of Scotland in Civil Rights: with Observations upon the Agreement or Diversity between them and the Laws of England*, 3 vols. (Edinburgh, 1751–53).

Barrington, Daines, *Observations on the More Ancient Statutes ... with an Appendix being a proposal for new modelling the Statutes* (1766), 3rd edn (London, 1769).

Bayley, John, *A Short Treatise on the Law of Bills of Exchange, Cash Bills and Promissory Notes* (London, 1789).

Beccaria, Cesare, *An Essay on Crimes and Punishments, translated from the Italian* (1767), 3rd edn (London, 1770).

Bell, George Joseph, *Commentaries on the Laws of Scotland and the Principles of Mercantile Jurisprudence* (1804), 2nd edn (Edinburgh, 1810).

Bentham, Jeremy, *A Comment on the Commentaries and A Fragment on Government* (1776), ed. J. H. Burns and H. L. A. Hart (London, 1977).

An Introduction to the Principles of Morals and Legislation (1789), ed. J. H. Burns and H. L. A. Hart (London, 1970).

Traités de Législation civile et pénale ..., publiés en François par Ét. Dumont, de Génève, 3 vols. (Paris, 1802).

The Works of Jeremy Bentham, published under the supervision of his Executor, John Bowring, 11 vols. (Edinburgh, 1838–43).

The Correspondence of Jeremy Bentham, volume I: 1752–76 and volume II: 1777–80, ed. Timothy L. S. Sprigge (London, 1968); volume III: 1781–88, ed. Ian R. Christie (London, 1971).

The Limits of Jurisprudence Defined, ed. Charles Warren Everett (New York, 1945).

Of Laws in General, ed. H. L. A. Hart (London, 1970).

Bever, Thomas, *A Discourse on the Study of Jurisprudence and the Civil Law* (Oxford, 1766).

Blackstone, William, *An Analysis of the Laws of England* (London, 1756).

"Blackstone's Letter ... Whilst a Student at the Middle Temple," *Harvard Law Review*, XXXII (1918–19), 975–6.

Law Tracts in Two Volumes (Oxford, 1762).

Commentaries on the Laws of England (1765–69), ed. Edward Christian, 4 vols. (London, 1803).

Commentaries on the Laws of England, ed. Joseph Chitty, 4 vols. (London, 1826).

Blackstone's Commentaries on the Laws of England, ed. William Hammond, 4 vols. (San Francisco, 1890); [variorum edition of the first eight editions of the *Commentaries*].

Commentaries on the Laws of England: A Facsimile of the first edition of 1765–1769; vol 1, intro. Stanley N. Katz; vol 2, intro. A. W. B. Simpson; vol 3, intro. John H. Langbein; vol 4, intro. Thomas A. Green (Chicago, 1979).

The Sovereignty of the Law. Selections from Blackstone's Commentaries on the Laws of England, ed. Gareth Jones, (London, 1973).

A Reply to Dr Priestley's Remarks on the Fourth Volume of the Commentaries on the Laws of England (1769), rpt. in *An Interesting Appendix to Sir William Blackstone's Commentaries on the Laws of England* (Philadelphia, 1773), pp. 35–47.

Boswell, James, *Journal of a Tour to the Hebrides with Samuel Johnson* (1785), ed. R. W. Chapman (Oxford, 1970).

Private Papers of James Boswell from Malahide Castle, prepared for the press by Geoffrey Scott, 18 vols. (private printing, Mount Vernon, N.Y., 1928–34).

Boswell's London Journal 1762–1763, ed. Frederick A. Pottle (London, 1950).

Boswell in Holland 1763–1764, ed. Frederick A. Pottle (London, 1952).

Boswell for the Defence 1769–1774, ed. William K. Wimsatt and Frederick A. Pottle (London, 1960).

Boswell, Laird of Auchinleck 1778–1782, ed. Joseph W. Reed and Frederick A. Pottle (New York, 1977).

Boswell, James, ed., *The Decision of the Court of Session, Upon the Question of Literary Property*, (Edinburgh, 1774).

Brougham, Henry Lord, *Speeches of Henry Lord Brougham...with Historical Introductions*, 4 vols. (Edinburgh, 1838).

Burke, Edmund, *The Works of the Right Honorable Edmund Burke* (1865–67), 8th edn., 12 vols. (Boston, 1884).

Burn, Richard, *The Justice of the Peace and Parish Officer* (1754), 9th edn, 3 vols. (London, 1764).

The History of the Poor Laws, with Observations (London, 1764).

Observations on the Bill...for the Better Relief and Employment of the Poor (London, 1776).

Butler, Charles, *The Reminiscences of Charles Butler, Esq. of Lincoln's Inn* (London, 1822).

Campbell, John Lord, *The Lives of the Chief Justices of England* (1849) 2 vols. (Boston, 1850).

The Lives of the Lord Chancellors and Keepers of the Great Seal, 8 vols. (London, 1845–69).

Cary, John, *An Essay on the State of England, in Relation to its Trade* (Bristol, 1695).

Chambers, Robert, *A Course of Lectures on the English Law* (1767–73), ed. Thomas M. Curley, 2 vols. (Madison, Wis., 1986).

Child, Josiah, *A New Discourse of Trade* (London, 1693).

Chitty, Joseph, *A Treatise on the Laws of Bills of Exchange, Checks on Bankers, Promissory Notes, Bankers Cash Notes and Bank Notes* (London, 1799).

Cobbett, William, *Parliamentary History of England*, 36 vols. (London, 1806–20).

Coke, Edward, *The First Part of the Institutes of the Laws of England, or, a Commentary upon Littleton* (1628), 13th edn by Francis Hargrave and Charles Butler, 2 vols. (London, 1775–88).

Dalrymple, John, *An Essay towards a General History of Feudal Property in Great Britain* (1757), 2nd edn (London, 1758).

DeLolme, Jean Louis, *The Constitution of England, or an Account of the English Government* (1771), (London, 1775).

A Discourse upon the Exposition and Understanding of Statutes, ed. Samuel E. Thorne, (San Marino, Cal., 1942).

Eden, William, *Principles of Penal Law* (1771), 2nd edn, (London, 1771).

Evans, William David, *A General View of the Decisions of Lord Mansfield*, 2 vols. (Liverpool, 1810).

"The Action for Money Had and Received," in *Essays on the Action for Money Had and Received, on the Law of Insurances, and on the Law of Bills of Exchange and Promissory Notes* (Liverpool, 1802 [?]), pp. 1–122.

Fearne, Charles, *An Essay on the Learning of Contingent Remainders and Executory Devises* (1772), 3rd edn (London, 1776).

Copies of Opinions ascribed in Eminent Council, on the Will which was the Subject of the Case of Perrin v Blake ... Addressed to the Right Honourable William, Earl of Mansfield (London, 1780).

Fielding, Henry, *An Enquiry into the Late Increase of Robbers, with some Proposals for Remedying this Growing Evil* (1751), in *The Complete Works of Henry Fielding*, ed. William Ernest Henley, 16 vols. (London, 1903), XIII, 5–129.

Foster, Michael, *A Report of some Proceedings on the Commission of Oyer and Terminer ... to which are Added Discourses Upon a Few Branches of the Crown Law* (London, 1762).

Francis, Richard, *Maxims of Equity, collected from and proved by Cases* (London, 1727).

Furneaux, Philip, *Letters to the Hon. Mr Justice Blackstone, concerning his Exposition of the Act of Toleration ... in his Celebrated Commentaries on the Laws of England*, 2nd edn (London, 1771).

A General Index to the 12–17th Volumes of the Journals of the House of Commons (1778), compiled by Nathaniel Forster and reprinted by the Order of the House of Commons (House of Commons, 1803).

Gibbon, Edward, *Edward Gibbon's Autobiography* (1827), ed. M. M. Reese (London, 1971).

Gilbert, Jeffrey, *The History and Practice of the High Court of Chancery* (London, 1758).

Gilbert, Thomas, *Plan for the better Relief and Employment of the Poor* (London, 1781).

Observations on the Bills ... relative to Houses of Correction (London, 1782).

Grotius, Hugo, *The Rights of War and Peace (1625) ... wherein are explained, The Law of Nature and Nations ... translated in English, to which are added all the large notes of M. Barbeyrac* (London, 1738).

Hale, Matthew, Preface to *Un Abridgment des plusieurs Cases et Resolutions del Common Ley...per Henry Rolle* (London, 1668).
    The History of the Common Law of England (1713), ed. Charles M. Gray (Chicago, 1971).
    Considerations touching the Amendment or Alteration of Laws, in Francis Hargrave (ed.), *A Collection of Tracts, Relative to the Law of England* (London, 1787), pp. 249–89.
Hamilton, Alexander, James Madison, and John Jay, *The Federalist Papers* (1787–8), ed. Clinton Rossiter (New York, 1961).
Hargrave, Francis, ed., *Collectanea Juridica, Consisting of Tracts Relative to the Law and Constitution of England*, 2 vols. (London, 1787).
    A Collection of Tracts, Relative to the Law of England (London, 1787).
Harris, James, *Hermes, or a Philosophical Enquiry concerning Universal Grammar* (London, 1751).
Hastell, John, *Precedents of Proceedings in the House of Commons*, 4 vols. (London, 1776–96).
Holliday, John, *The Life of William late Earl of Mansfield* (London, 1797).
House of Commons Sessional Papers of the Eighteenth Century [facsimile edn], ed. Sheila Lambert, 147 vols. (Wilmington, Del., 1975–76).
Hume, David, *Letters of David Hume*, ed. J. Y. T. Greig, 2 vols. (Oxford, 1932).
Huntingford, John, *The State of the Statute Laws Considered* (London, 1796).
Jefferson, Thomas, *The Writings of Thomas Jefferson*, ed. Paul Leister Ford, 10 vols. (New York, 1892–99).
[Jeffrey, Francis], "Bentham, *Principes de legislation, par Dumont*," *Edinburgh Review*, IV (1804), 572–92.
Johnson, Samuel, *The Rambler* (1750–52), ed. W. J. Bate and Albrecht B. Strauss, 3 vols. (New Haven, 1969).
Jones, William, *An Essay on the Law of Bailments* (London, 1781).
The Letters of Junius, ed. C. W. Everett (London, 1927).
Kames, Henry Home, Lord, *Remarkable Decisions of the Court of Session, from 1716 to 1728* (Edinburgh, 1728).
    The Decisions of the Court of Session, from its First Institution to the present Time. Abridged and digested under proper Heads, in Form of a Dictionary (1741), 2 vols. (Edinburgh, 1797).
    Essays on Several Subjects concerning British Antiquities, composed anno 1745 (1747), 3rd edn (Edinburgh, 1763).
    Essays on the Principles of Morality and Natural Religion (Edinburgh, 1751).
    Historical Law Tracts, 2 vols. (Edinburgh, 1758).
    Principles of Equity (1760), 2nd edn, corrected and enlarged (Edinburgh, 1767).
    Elucidations respecting the Common and Statute Law of Scotland (Edinburgh, 1777).
    Select Decisions of the Court of Session, from 1752 to 1768 (1780), 2nd edn (Edinburgh, 1799).
    Loose Hints on Education, chiefly concerning the Culture of the Heart (Edinburgh, 1781).
    Sketches of the History of Man (1774), 4th edn, considerably enlarged by the Last Additions and Corrections of the Author, 4 vols. (Edinburgh, 1788).

The Liverpool Tractate, an eighteenth-century manual on the procedure of the House of Commons, ed. Catherine Strateman [Sims] (New York, 1937).

Mackintosh, James, *A Discourse on the Study of the Law of Nature and Nations* (1799), in *Miscellaneous Works of... James Mackintosh*, 3 vols. (London, 1846), I, 339–87.

Madan, Martin, *Thoughts on Executive Justice, with respect to our Criminal Laws* (London, 1785).

Meredith, William, *Letter to Dr Blackstone by the Author of the Question Stated, to which is prefixed, Dr. Blackstone's Letter to Sir William Meredith* (London, 1770).

Millar, John (Professor at Glasgow), *An Historical View of English Government* (1803), 4 vols. (London, 1812).

Millar, John (advocate), *Elements of the Law relating to Insurance* (Edinburgh, 1787).

Miller, Philip, *The Gardener's Dictionary*, 2 vols. (London, 1731–9).

Mitford, John (Lord Redesdale), *A Treatise on the Pleadings in suits in the Court of Chancery by English Bill* (1780), 5th edn (London, 1847).

Montesquieu, Charles Louis de Secondat, Baron, *The Spirit of the Laws* (1748), trans. Thomas Nugent and intro. Franz Neumann (New York, 1949).

North, Roger, *A Discourse on the Laws, now first printed... by a Member of the Inner Temple* (London, 1824).

Paley, William, *The Principles of Moral and Political Philosophy* (London, 1785).

Park, James Allan, *A System of the Law of Marine Insurances* (London, 1787).

Parkes, Joseph, *A History of the Court of Chancery* (London, 1828).

Postlethwayt, Malachy, *The Universal Dictionary of Trade and Commerce, translated from the French of the Celebrated Monsieur Savary, with Large Additions and Improvements*, 2 vols. (London, 1751–5).

Pothier, Robert Joseph, *A Treatise on the Law of Obligations or Contracts* (1761), trans., intro. and notes William David Evans, 2 vols. (London, 1806).

Powell, John Joseph, *Essay upon the Law of Contracts and Agreements*, 2 vols. (London, 1790).

Ram, James, *The Science of Legal Judgment* (London, 1834).

Ramsey, John (of Ochtertyre), *Scotland and Scotsmen in the Eighteenth Century*, ed. Alexander Allardyce, 2 vols. (Edinburgh, 1888).

The Letters of John Ramsay of Ochtertyre, ed. Barbara L. H. Horn (Edinburgh, 1966).

Rayner, John, *Observations of the Statutes relating to the Stamp Duties* (London, 1786).

Romilly, Samuel, *Observations of a Late Publication, intitled, Thoughts on Executive Justice* (London, 1786).

"Papers relative to Codification... by Jeremy Bentham," *Edinburgh Review*, XXIX (1818), pp. 217–37.

Memoirs of the Life of Sir Samuel Romilly, written by himself, with a selection of his Correspondence (1840), 2nd edn, 3 vols. (London, 1840).

Ruffhead, Owen, *The Statutes of the Realm, from Magna Carta to the end of the Last Parliament, 1761*, 8 vols. (London, 1769).

Sedgwick, James, *Remarks Critical and Miscellaneous on the Commentaries of Sir William Blackstone* (London, 1800).

Sheridan, Charles, *Observations on the Doctrine laid down by Sir William Blackstone, Respecting the extent of the Power of the British Parliament* (London, 1779).

Smellie, William, *Literary and Characteristical Lives of John Gregory, Henry Home, David Hume and Adam Smith* (Edinburgh, 1800).

Smith, Adam, *The Theory of Moral Sentiments* (1759), ed. D. D. Raphael and A. L. Macfie (Oxford, 1976).

  An Inquiry into the Nature and Causes of the Wealth of Nations (1776), ed. R. H. Campbell, A. S. Skinner, and W. B. Todd, 2 vols. (Oxford, 1976).

  Lectures on Jurisprudence, ed. R. L. Meek, D. D. Raphael, and P. G. Stein (Oxford, 1978).

Stair, James Dalrymple, Viscount, *The Institutions of the Law of Scotland*, (1693), ed. D. M. Walker (Edinburgh, 1981).

A Complete Collection of State Trials, compiled by T. B. Howell, 21 vols. (London, 1816).

Stewart, Dugald, *Account of the Life and Writings of Adam Smith, LL.D.* (1793), rpt. in Adam Smith, *Essays on Philosophical Subjects*, ed. W. P. D. Wightman and J. C. Bryce (Oxford, 1980).

Stuart, Andrew, *Letters to the Right Honorable Lord Mansfield* (Dublin, 1773).

Sullivan, Francis Stroughton, *An Historical Treatise on the Feudal Law, and the Constitution and Laws of England* (London, 1772).

Tytler, Alexander Fraser (Lord Woodhouselee), *Memoirs of the Life and Writings of the Honourable Henry Home of Kames ... Containing Sketches of the Progress of Literature and General Improvement in Scotland during the greater part of the Eighteenth Century*, 2 vols. (Edinburgh, 1807).

Wood, Thomas, *An Institute of the Laws of England, or The Laws of England in their Natural Order, according to Common Use* (1720), 4th edn corrected (Dublin, 1724).

  Some Thoughts Concerning the Study of the Laws of England in the Two Universities (1708), rpt. in Wood, *Institute of the Laws of England*.

Wooddeson, Richard, *Elements of Jurisprudence* (London, 1783).

  A Systematical View of the Laws of England, 3 vols. (London, 1792–3).

Wynne, Edward, *Eunomus: Or, Dialogues concerning the Law and Constitution of England*, 4 vols. (London, 1774).

Yorke, Philip (Lord Hardwicke), *A Discourse of the Judicial Authority Belonging to the Office of Master of Rolls in the High Court of Chancery* (London, 1727).

Yorke, Philip C., *The Life and Correspondence of Philip Yorke, Earl of Hardwicke*, 3 vols. (Cambridge, 1913).

Zouch, Henry, *Observations upon a Bill ... to punish by Imprisonment and hard Labour* (London, 1779).

  Hints respecting the Public Police (London, 1786).

Secondary works

Allen, C. K., *Law in the Making*, 5th edn (London, 1951).

Anderson, B. L., "Provincial Aspects of the Financial Revolution of the Eighteenth Century," *Business History*, XI (1969), 11–22.

"Money and the Structure of Credit," *Business History*, XII (1970), 85–101.

Appleby, Joyce, "Republicanism in Old and New Contexts," *William and Mary Quarterly*, XLIII (1986), 20–34.

Ashton, T. S., *An Economic History of England: The Eighteenth Century* (London, 1955).

Atiyah, P. S., *The Rise and Fall of Freedom of Contract* (Oxford, 1979).

"Common Law and Statute Law," *Modern Law Review*, XLVII (1985), 1–28.

Baker, J. H., "New Light on *Slade's Case*," *Cambridge Law Journal*, XXIX (1971), 51–67, 213–36.

"Criminal Courts and Procedure at Common Law 1550–1800," in J. S. Cockburn (ed.), *Crime in England 1550–1800* (London, 1977), pp. 15–48.

"Review of A. W. B. Simpson, *A History of the Common Law of Contract. Volume 1: The Rise of the Action of Assumpsit* and S. J. Stoljar, *A History of Contract at Common Law*," *American Journal of Legal History*, XXI (1977), 335–41.

"From Sanctity of Contract to Reasonable Expectation?," *Current Legal Problems* (1979), 17–39.

An Introduction to English Legal History, 2nd edn (London, 1979).

"The Law Merchant and the Common Law before 1700," *Cambridge Law Journal*, XXXVIII (1979), 295–322.

"Origins of the 'Doctrine' of Consideration, 1535–1585," in M. S. Arnold, T. A. Green, S. A. Scully and S. D. White, eds., *On the Laws and Customs of England: Essays in Honor of S. E. Thorne* (Chapel Hill, 1981), pp. 336–58.

"The Refinement of English Criminal Jurisprudence, 1500–1848," in Louis A. Knafla, ed., *Crime and Criminal Justice in Europe and Canada* (Waterloo, Ontario, 1981), pp. 17–42.

"English Law and the Renaissance," *Cambridge Law Journal*, XLIV (1985), 46–61.

Banning, Lance, "Jefferson Ideology Revisited: Liberal and Classical Ideas in the New American Republic," *William and Mary Quarterly*, XLIII (1986), 3–19.

Barker, Ernest, *Traditions of Civility* (Cambridge, 1948).

Essays on Government, 2nd edn (Oxford, 1951).

Barton, J. L., "The Enforcement of Hard Bargains," *Law Quarterly Review* CIII (1987), 118–47.

Beattie, J. M., "Crime and the Courts in Surrey 1736–53," in J. S. Cockburn, ed., *Crime in England 1550–1800* (London, 1977), pp. 155–86.

Crime and the Courts in England 1600–1800 (Princeton, 1986).

Boorstin, Daniel J., *The Mysterious Science of Law (An Essay on Blackstone's 'Commentaries')* (Cambridge, Mass., 1941).

Brewer, John, *Party Ideology and Popular Politics at the Accession of George III* (Cambridge, 1976).

Brewer, John and John Styles, eds., *An Ungovernable People. The English and their law in the seventeenth and eighteenth centuries* (London, 1980).

Browning, Reed, *Political and Constitutional Ideas of the Court Whigs* (Baton Rouge, 1982).

Bryce, James, *Studies in History and Jurisprudence*, 2 vols. (Oxford, 1901).

Burns, J. H., *The Fabric of Felicity: The Legislator and the Human Condition* [Inaugural Lecture, University College London] (London, 1967).

"The Bentham Project," in J. D. Baird, ed., *Editing Texts of the Romantic Period* (Toronto, 1972), pp. 73–87.

"Dreams and Destinations: Jeremy Bentham in 1828," *Bentham Newsletter*, I (1978), 21–30.

"Jeremy Bentham: From Radical Enlightenment to Philosophic Radicalism," *Bentham Newsletter*, VIII (1984), 4–14.

"Scottish Philosophy and the science of legislation," *Royal Society of Edinburgh Occasional Papers*, no. 3 (1985), 11–29.

Burns, Robert P., "Blackstone's Theory of the 'Absolute' Rights of Property," *University of Cincinnati Law Review*, LIV (1985), 67–86.

Burrow, J. W., *Evolution and Society* (Cambridge, 1966).

Cairns, John W., "Institutional Writings in Scotland Reconsidered," *Journal of Legal History*, IV (1983), 76–117.

"Blackstone, An English Institutist: Legal Literature and the Rise of the Nation State," *Oxford Journal of Legal Studies*, IV (1984), 318–60.

"Blackstone, the Ancient Constitution and the Feudal Law," *Historical Journal*, XXVIII (1985), 711–17.

Campbell, R. H. and Andrew S. Skinner, eds., *The Origins and Nature of the Scottish Enlightenment* (Edinburgh, 1982).

Carter, Jennifer, "The Revolution and the Constitution," in Geoffrey Holmes (ed.), *Britain after the Glorious Revolution* (London, 1969), pp. 39–58.

Cockburn, J. S., ed., *Crime in England 1550–1800* (London, 1977).

Colley, Linda, "Eighteenth-Century English Radicalism before Wilkes," *Transactions of the Royal Historical Society*, 5th series, XXXI (1981), 1–19.

In Defiance of Oligarchy: The Tory Party, 1714–60 (Cambridge, 1982).

Collini, Stefan, Donald Winch and John Burrow, *That Noble Science of Politics: A Study of Nineteenth-Century Intellectual History* (Cambridge, 1983).

Coquillette, Daniel R., "Legal Ideology and Incorporation II: Sir Thomas Ridley, Charles Molloy and the Literary Battle for the Law Merchant, 1607–1676," *Boston University Law Review*, LXI (1981), 315–71.

Cotterell, Mary, "Interregnum Law Reform: the Hale Commission of 1652," *English Historical Review*, CXXXIII (1968), 689–704.

Croft, Clyde Elliott, "Philip Yorke, First Earl of Hardwicke – An Assessment of his Legal Career," unpublished Ph.D. thesis, Cambridge University, 1982.

Dicey, A. V., *Lectures on the Relation between Law and Public Opinion in the Nineteenth Century* (London, 1905).
"Blackstone's *Commentaries,*" *Cambridge Law Journal,* IV (1932), 286–307.
Introduction to the Study of the Law of the Constitution, 9th edn (London, 1939).
Dickinson, H. T., *Liberty and Property. Political Ideology in Eighteenth-Century Britain* (London, 1977).
Dickson, P. G. M., *The Financial Revolution in England: A study in the development of public credit, 1688–1756* (London, 1967).
Dinwiddy, J. R., "Bentham's Transition to Political Radicalism," *Journal of the History of Ideas,* XXXVI (1975), 683–700.
"Bentham on Private Ethics and the Principle of Utility," *Revue Internationale de Philosophie,* CXLI (1982), 278–300.
Doolittle, I. G., "Sir William Blackstone and his *Commentaries on the Laws of England* (1765–69): A Biographical Approach," *Oxford Journal of Legal Studies,* III (1983), 99–112.
Dunn, John, "The Politics of Locke in England and America in the Eighteenth Century," in J. W. Yolton, ed., *John Locke: Problems and Perspectives* (Cambridge, 1969), pp. 45–80.
Dworkin, Ronald, *Taking Rights Seriously* (London, 1977).
Fifoot, C. H. S., *Lord Mansfield* (Oxford, 1936).
Finnis, John N., "Blackstone's Theoretical Intentions," *Natural Law Forum,* XII (1967), 163–83.
Fletcher, F. T. H., *Montesquieu and English Politics, 1750–1800* (London, 1939).
Forbes, Duncan, "Scientific Whiggism – Adam Smith and John Millar," *Cambridge Journal,* VII (1954), 643–70.
Hume's Philosophical Politics (Cambridge, 1975).
Gay, Peter, *The Enlightenment: An Interpretation,* 2 vols. (London, 1967–70).
Green, Thomas Andrew, *Verdict According to Conscience. Perspectives on the English Criminal Trial 1200–1800* (Chicago, 1985).
Gutteridge, H. C., "Does English Law Recognize a Doctrine of Unjustified Enrichment?," *Cambridge Law Journal,* V. (1934), 223–29.
Haakonssen, Knud, *The Science of a Legislator: The Natural Jurisprudence of David Hume and Adam Smith* (Cambridge, 1981).
"Hugo Grotius and the History of Political Thought," *Political Theory,* XIII (1985), 239–65.
"John Millar and the Science of a Legislator," *Juridical Review,* XXX (1985), 41–68.
Halévy, Elie, *La Formation du Radicalisme Philosophique,* 3 vols. (Paris, 1901–4).
Hanbury, H. G., "The Recovery of Money," *Law Quarterly Review,* XL (1924), 31–42.
The Vinerian Chair and Legal Education (Oxford, 1958).
Harrison, Ross, *Bentham* (London, 1983).
Hart, H. L. A., "Blackstone's Use of the Law of Nature," *Butterworths South African Law Review* (1956), 169–74.
Essays on Bentham (Oxford, 1982).

Hay, Douglas *et al.*, *Albion's Fatal Tree: Crime and Society in Eighteenth-Century England* (London, 1975).

Helmholz, R. H., "Assumpsit and *Fedei Laesio*," *Law Quarterly Review*, XCI (1975), 406–32.

Heward, Edmund, *Lord Mansfield* (Chichester, 1979).

Holden, J. Milnes, *The History of Negotiable Instruments in English Law* (London, 1955).

Holdsworth, William, *A History of English Law*, 16 vols. (London, 1922–66).

  "Blackstone's Treatment of Equity," *Harvard Law Review*, XLIII (1929), 1–32.

  "Gibbon, Blackstone and Bentham," *Law Quarterly Review*, LII (1936), 46–59.

Holmes, Geoffrey, *Augustan England. Professions, State and Society, 1680–1730* (London, 1982).

Hont, Istvan and Michael Ignatieff, eds., *Wealth and Virtue. The Shaping of Political Economy in the Scottish Enlightenment* (Cambridge, 1983).

Horwitz, Henry, *Policy and Politics in the Reign of William III* (Manchester, 1977).

Horwitz, Morton J., *The Transformation of American Law 1780–1860* (Cambridge, Mass., 1977).

Hume, L. J., *Bentham and Bureaucracy* (Cambridge, 1981).

Ibbetson, David, "Assumpsit and Debt in the Sixteenth Century: the Origins of the Indebitatus Count," *Cambridge Law Journal*, XVI (1982), 142–61.

  "Contract Law: *Slade's Case* in Context," *Oxford Journal of Legal Studies*, IV (1984), 295–317.

Innes, Joanna and John Styles, "The Bloody Code in Context: Eighteenth-Century Criminal Legislation Reconsidered. A Report of Work in Progress" (unpublished paper, December, 1984).

  "The Crime Wave: Recent Writing on Crime and Criminal Justice in Eighteenth Century England," *Journal of British Studies*, XXV (1986), 380–435.

An Introductory Survey of the Sources and Literature of Scots Law, Stair Society Publications, I (Edinburgh, 1936).

Jackson, R. M., *The History of Quasi-Contract in English Law* [in H. D. Hazeltine (general editor), *Cambridge Studies in English Legal History*] (Cambridge, 1936).

James, M. H., "Bentham on the Individuation of Laws," *Northern Ireland Legal Quarterly*, XXIV (1973), 357–82.

Jezierski, John V., "Parliament or People: James Wilson and Blackstone on the Nature and Location of Sovereignty," *Journal of the History of Ideas*, XXXII (1971), 95–106.

Kennedy, Duncan, "The Structure of Blackstone's *Commentaries*," *Buffalo Law Review*, V (1979) 209–382.

King, Peter, "Decision-Makers and Decision-Making in the English Criminal Law, 1750–1800," *Historical Journal*, XXVII (1984), 25–58.

Knafla, Louis A., "Conscience in the English Common Law Tradition," *University of Toronto Law Journal*, XXVI (1976), 1–16.

Kocher, Paul H., "Francis Bacon on the Science of Jurisprudence," *Journal of the History of Ideas*, XVIII (1957), 3–26.

Kramnick, Isaac, "Religion and Radicalism: English Political Theory in the Age of Revolution," *Political Theory*, V (1977), 505–34.

"Republican Revisionism Revisited," *American Historical Review*, LXXXVII (1982), 629–66.

Lambert, Sheila, *Bills and Acts: Legislative Procedure in Eighteenth-Century England* (Cambridge, 1971).

Landau, Norma, *The Justices of the Peace, 1679–1760* (Berkeley, 1984).

Langbein, John H., "The Criminal Trial before the Lawyers," *University of Chicago Law Review*, XLV (1978), 263–316.

"*Albion's* Fatal Flaws," *Past and Present*, XCVII (1983), 96–120.

"Shaping the Eighteenth-Century Criminal Trial: A View from the Ryder Sources," *University of Chicago Law Review*, L (1983), 1–136.

Lehmann, William C., *Henry Home, Lord Kames, and the Scottish Enlightenment* (The Hague, 1971).

Lieberman, David, "From Bentham to Benthamism," *Historical Journal* XXVIII (1985), 199–224.

Lobban, Michael, "Blackstone and the Science of Law," *Historical Journal*, XXX (1987), 311–35.

Long, Douglas G., *Bentham on Liberty. Jeremy Bentham's idea of liberty in relation to his utilitarianism* (Toronto, 1977).

Lucas, Paul, "Blackstone and the Reform of the Legal Profession," *English Historical Review*, LXXVII (1962), 456–89.

"*Ex parte* Sir William Blackstone, 'Plagiarist'; A Note on Blackstone and Natural Law," *American Journal of Legal History*, VII (1963), 142–58.

Lücke, H. K., "*Slade's Case* and the Origin of the Common Counts," *Law Quarterly Review*, LXXXI (1965), 422–45, 539–61, and LXXXII (1966), 81–96.

Luig, Klaus, "The Institutes of National Law in the Seventeenth and Eighteenth Centuries," *Juridical Review*, XVII (1972), 193–226.

MacCormick, Neil, "Law and Enlightenment," in R. H. Campbell and Andrew S. Skinner, eds., *The Origins and Nature of the Scottish Enlightenment* (Edinburgh, 1982), pp. 150–66.

Maine, Henry, *Ancient Law. Its Connection with the Early History of Society and its Relation to Modern Ideas* (1861), rpt. of the Beacon Paperback edition, intro. Raymond Firth (Gloucester, Mass., 1970).

Maitland, F. W., *Equity: A Course of Lectures*, ed. A. H. Chaytor and M. J. Whittaker, (Cambridge, 1932).

Selected Historical Essays, ed. Helen M. Cam (Cambridge, 1957).

Maitland, F. W., ed., *Bracton's Note Book*, 3 vols. (London, 1887).

Meek, Ronald L., *Social Science and the Ignoble Savage*, (Cambridge, 1976).

Milsom, S. F. C., 'Reason in the Development of the Common Law," *Law Quarterly Review*, LXXXI (1965), 496–517.

"Law and Fact in Legal Development," *University of Toronto Law Journal*, XVII (1967), 1–19.

Historical Foundations of the Common Law, (London, 1969).

"The Nature of Blackstone's Achievement," *Oxford Journal of Legal Studies*, I (1981), 1–12.

"The Past and the Future of Judge-Made Law," *Monash University Law Review*, VIII (1981), 5–18.

Namier, L. B., *The Structure of Politics at the Accession of George III*, 2 vols. (London, 1929).

Namier, L. B. and John Brooke, *The History of Parliament. The House of Commons 1754–1790*, 3 vols. (History of Parliament Trust, H.M.S.O., 1964).

Oldham, James C., "The Origins of the Special Jury," *University of Chicago Law Review*, L (1983), 137–221.

"Eighteenth-century Judges' Notes: How They Explain, Correct and Enhance the Reports," *American Journal of Legal History*, XXXI (1987), 9–42.

Pares, Richard, *King George III and the Politicians* (Oxford, 1953).

Phillipson, Nicholas T., "Culture and Society in the Eighteenth-Century Province: The Case of Edinburgh and the Scottish Enlightenment," in Lawrence Stone, ed., *The University in Society*, 2 vols. (Princeton, 1974), II, 407–48.

"Lawyers, Landowners and the Civic Leadership of Post-Union Scotland," *Juridical Review*, XXII (1976), 97–120.

"The Scottish Enlightenment," in Roy Porter and Mikuláš Teich, eds., *The Enlightenment in National Context* (Cambridge, 1981), pp. 19–40.

Pocock, J. G. A., *The Ancient Constitution and the Feudal Law* (Cambridge, 1957).

Politics, Language and Time. Essays on Political Thought and History (London, 1972).

The Machiavellian Moment: Florentine Political Thought and the Atlantic Republican Tradition, (Princeton, 1975).

"The Machiavellian Moment Revisited: A Study in History and Ideology," *Journal of Modern History* (1981) LIII, 49–72.

Virtue, Commerce, and History. Essays on Political Thought and History, Chiefly in the Eighteenth Century (Cambridge, 1985).

Pocock, J. G. A. and Richard Ashcraft, *John Locke: Papers read at the Clark Library Seminar* (Los Angeles, 1980).

Pocock, J. G. A., ed., *Three British Revolutions: 1641, 1688, 1776* (Princeton, 1980).

Pollock, Frederick, "A Plea for Historical Interpretation," *Law Quarterly Review*, XXXIX (1923), 163–69.

Porter, Roy, *English Society in the Eighteenth Century* (Harmondsworth, 1982).

Posner, Richard A., "Blackstone and Bentham," *Journal of Law and Economics*, XIX (1976), 569–606.

Postema, Gerald J., "The Expositor, the Censor, and the Common Law," *Canadian Journal of Philosophy*, IX (1979), 643–70.

Bentham and the Common Law Tradition (Oxford, 1986).

Pound, Roscoe, "Common Law and Legislation," *Harvard Law Review*, XXI (1908), 383–407.

Prest, Wilfrid, "The Dialectical Origins of Finch's *Law*," *Cambridge Law Journal*, XXXVI (1977), 326–52.

Prichard, M. J., "Nonsuit: A Premature Obituary," *Cambridge Law Journal*, XVIII (1960), 88–96.

Radzinowicz, Leon, *A History of English Criminal Law and its Administration from 1750*, 5 vols. (London, 1948–86).

Robinson, O. F., T. D. Fergus, and W. M. Gordon, *An Introduction to European Legal History* (Abingdon, Oxon., 1985).

Ross, Ian Simpson, *Lord Kames and the Scotland of his Day* (Oxford, 1972).

Sedgwick, Romney, ed., *The History of Parliament. The House of Commons 1715–54*, (H.M.S.O., 1970).

Shalhope, Robert E., "Toward a Republican Synthesis: The Emergence of an Understanding of Republicanism in American Historiography," *William and Mary Quarterly*, XXIX (1972), 49–80.

"Republicanism and Early American Historiography," *William and Mary Quarterly*, XXXIX (1982), 334–56.

Shapiro, Barbara J., "Law and Science in Seventeenth-Century England," *Stanford Law Review*, XXI (1969), 727–66.

"Codification of the Laws in Seventeenth-Century England," *Wisconsin Law Review* (1974), 428–65.

"Law Reform in Seventeenth-Century England," *American Journal of Legal History*, XIX (1975), 280–312.

"Sir Francis Bacon and the Mid-Seventeenth Century Movement for Law Reform," *American Journal of Legal History*, XXIV (1980), 331–62.

Sharpe, J. A., 'The history of crime in late medieval and early modern England: a review of the field," *Social History*, VII (1982), 187–203.

Simpson, A. W. B., *An Introduction to the History of Land Law* (Oxford, 1962).

"The Common Law and Legal Theory," in A. W. B. Simpson, ed., *Oxford Essays in Jurisprudence*, 2nd series (Oxford, 1973).

A History of the Common Law of Contract; Volume 1: *The Rise of the Action of Assumpsit* (Oxford, 1975).

"Innovation in Nineteenth Century Contract Law," *Law Quarterly Review*, XCI (1975), 247–78.

"The Horwitz Thesis and the History of Contracts," *University of Chicago Law Review*, XLVI (1979), 533–601.

"The Rise and Fall of the Legal Treatise: Legal Principles and the Forms of Legal Literature," *University of Chicago Law Review*, XLVIII (1981), 632–79.

Smith, T. B., *The Doctrines of Judicial Precedent in Scots Law* (Edinburgh, 1952).

Scotland, The Development of its Law and Constitution [volume 2 of *The British Commonwealth: The Development of its Laws and Constitution*, general editor George W. Keeton], (London, 1962).

Stein, Peter, "The General Notions of Contract and Property in Eighteenth-Century Scottish Thought," *Juridical Review*, VIII (1963), 1–13.

"Law and Society in Eighteenth-Century Scottish Thought," in N. T.

Phillipson and Rosalind Mitchison, ed., *Scotland in the Age of Improvements* (Edinburgh, 1970).

Legal Evolution. The Story of an Idea (Cambridge, 1980).

Steintrager, James, *Bentham* (London, 1977).

Stephen, Leslie, *History of English Thought in the Eighteenth Century* (1876), 2 vols. (London, 1962).

The English Utilitarians, 3 vols. (London, 1900).

Stoljar, S. J., *A History of Contract at Common Law* (Canberra, 1975).

Story, Joseph, *Commentaries on the Law of Bills of Exchange, Foreign and Inland* (Boston, Mass., 1843).

Stourzh, Gerald, *Alexander Hamilton and the Idea of Republican Government* (Stanford, Ca., 1970).

Styles, John, "Criminal Records," *Historical Journal*, XX (1967), 977–81.

"Embezzlement, industry and the law in England, 1500–1800," in Maxime Berg, Pat Hudson and Michael Sonenscher, eds., *Manufacture in Town and Country before the Factory* (Cambridge, 1983), pp. 173–210.

"Sir John Fielding and the Problem of Criminal Investigation in Eighteenth-Century England," *Transactions of the Royal Historical Society*, 5th series, XXXIII (1983), 127–49.

Sutherland, Lucy, "William Blackstone and the Legal Chairs at Oxford," in René Wellek and Alvaro Ribeiro, eds., *Evidence in Literary Scholarship: Essays in Memory of James Marshall Osborn* (Oxford, 1979), pp. 229–40.

Sutherland, L. S. and L. G. Mitchell, eds., *The History of the University of Oxford: The Eighteenth Century* (Oxford, 1986).

Sutherland, L. Stuart, "The Law Merchant in England in the Seventeenth and Eighteenth Centuries," *Transactions of the Royal Historical Society*, 4th series, XVII (1934), 149–76.

Thomas, P. D. G., *The House of Commons in the Eighteenth Century* (Oxford, 1971).

Thompson, E. P., "The Moral Economy of the English Crowd in the Eighteenth Century," *Past and Present*, L (1971), 76–136.

"Patrician Society, Plebeian Culture," *Journal of Social History*, VII (1974), 382–405.

Whigs and Hunters. The Origin of the Black Act (London, 1975).

"Eighteenth-century English Society: class struggle without class?" *Social History*, III (1978), 133–65.

Tuck, Richard, *Natural Rights Theories. Their origin and development* (Cambridge, 1979).

Tully, James, *A Discourse on Property. John Locke and his Adversaries* (Cambridge, 1980).

Venturi, Franco, *Italy and the Enlightenment*, ed. Stuart Woolf (New York, 1972).

Walker, David M., "Equity in Scots Law," *Juridical Review*, LXVI (1954), 103–47.

The Scottish Jurists (Edinburgh, 1985).

Walker, David M., ed., *Stair Tercentenary Studies* (Edinburgh, 1981).

Waterman, Julian S., "Thomas Jefferson and Blackstone's *Commentaries*," *Illinois Law Review*, XXVII (1933), 629–59.

Williams, Orlo Cyprian, *The Historical Development of Private Bill Procedure and Standing Orders in the House of Commons*, 2 vols. (H.M.S.O., 1948–49).

The Clerical Organization of the House of Commons 1661–1850 (Oxford, 1954).

Willman, Robert, "Blackstone and the 'Theoretical Perfection' of English Law in the Reign of Charles II," *Historical Journal*, XXVI (1983), 39–70.

Winch, Donald, *Adam Smith's Politics. An essay in historiographic revision* (Cambridge, 1978).

"Science and the Legislator: Adam Smith and After," *Economic Journal*, CXIII (1983), 501–20.

Young, David, "Let Us Content Ourselves with Praising the Work While Drawing a Veil Over its Principles: Eighteenth-Century Reactions to Beccaria's *Crimes and Punishments*," *Justice Quarterly* I, (1984), 155–69.

"Property and Punishment in the Eighteenth Century: Beccaria and his Critics," *American Journal of Jurisprudence*, XXXI (1986), 121–35.

INDEX

CPSIA information can be obtained at www.ICGtesting.com
Printed in the USA
LVOW120211240312

274540LV00001B/41/A